DIVIDED ARSENAL

World War II indisputably led to the reform of federal racial policies. Daniel Kryder, in *Divided Arsenal*, asks why that reform turned out to be limited in scope. To do so, he examines the wartime roles of blacks in the Army, in factories, and in agriculture. Kryder finds that central governments have two main goals during war – the full mobilization of wartime production and its own survival in office. Limited racial reform, then, represented a means to serve the central government's larger concerns and was not an end in itself. Nevertheless, Kryder argues, these modified reforms, by both stanching and stimulating insurgency and thus contributing to the ongoing struggle between advocates and statesmen, shaped both the scale and scope of the future American state and the subsequent civil rights movement.

Divided Arsenal presents a fascinating account of wartime racial relations and policymaking in three vital segments of the national mobilization for war. In doing so, it analyzes the accelerated black migration to northern cities, the racial climate on southern farms, the reverse migration created when northern black recruits were sent to southern military bases, patterns of racial violence in the Army – including the uprising in 1943 at Camp Stewart, Georgia – and the creation and casework of the Fair Employment Practices Committee. Professor Kryder concludes that while the war produced a wide range of ameliorative and repressive federal race policies, particular outcomes depended on what best served the government's broader goals of winning the war and staying in power.

Daniel Kryder is Associate Professor of Political Science at the Massachusetts Institute of Technology.

DIVIDED ARSENAL

Race and the American State During World War II

DANIEL KRYDER

Massachusetts Institute of Technology

CAMBRIDGE
UNIVERSITY PRESS

PUBLISHED BY THE PRESS SYNDICATE OF THE UNIVERSITY OF CAMBRIDGE
The Pitt Building, Trumpington Street, Cambridge, United Kingdom

CAMBRIDGE UNIVERSITY PRESS
The Edinburgh Building, Cambridge CB2 2RU, UK
40 West 20th Street, New York, NY 10011-4211, USA
10 Stamford Road, Oakleigh, Melbourne 3166, Australia
Ruiz de Alarcón 13, 28014 Madrid, Spain
Dock House, The Waterfront, Cape Town 8001, South Africa

http://www.cambridge.org

First published 2000
First paperback edition 2001
Reprinted 2000

Printed in the United States of America

Typeset in Sabon

A catalog record for this book is available from the British Library

Library of Congress Cataloging in Publication data is available

ISBN 0 521 59338 7 hardback
ISBN 0 521 00458 6 paperback

To my mother and father,
Mary Jeanne and J. Earl Kryder,
with love and appreciation

Contents

Contents

Preface and Acknowledgments

The casualties and victors of war include states as well as armies. Enduring states like the American one win major wars in part by rallying the full productive potential of their populations and by controlling disruptions within their ranks. Shrewd rebels, on the other hand, know that wars can fatally weaken authorities and their institutions. Because of this, analysts of politics since ancient times have studied the effects of war on strategies for resisting, gaining, or exercising political power. Working within this tradition, I have here two objectives, one each for the historian and the social scientist: first, to describe the causes and effects of race management policies in America during World War II, and second, through these policy studies, to develop a set of general claims about the methods used by central authorities to regulate social friction in nominally democratic nations at war. I hope to demonstrate that the connection between these two endeavors is found in the strategic motivations of American statesmen, who in their planning and direction of this particular mobilization followed enduring rules of Western warmaking.

War has a curious bipolar character in studies of the political prospects of American social groups. On the one hand, social histories of war are replete with descriptions of the new economic and political opportunities encountered by racial and ethnic minorities and women. War crises redeploy workers with new skills to new locales and launch important episodes of industrial and manufacturing development. In the process, wars set authorities off-balance and undermine social norms. Wars can, it seems, help to liberate oppressed groups, even if in an indirect and piecemeal fashion. On the other hand, there is a darker, authoritarian side of war resulting from heightened economic regulation and social regimentation. In grave crises, central authorities ration foodstuffs and fuel, set prices and wages, tax commerce and incomes, and police and conscript citizens in an effort to organize and deploy a maximum level of destructive force.

Wars produce similar contradictions in historical studies of American race relations. The two world wars caused the employment and enfranchisement of hundreds of thousands of black Americans who seized new opportunities to escape the rural South and the most repressive forms of white supremacy. But this race vanguard also faced new obstacles to individual achievement and interracial amity. In what appears to be a pattern, racial crowd violence in this century has coincided with wars and their immediate aftermath. Overall, wars have produced both ameliorative and repressive federal race policies, including the heightened surveillance of African American organizations.

To try to make sense of this ambivalent but seemingly recurrent historical record, and in particular to explain central authorities' roles in these episodes, I turned to two theoretical perspectives on wars' effects on race politics. An ideational model rooted in Gunnar Myrdal's pathbreaking *An American Dilemma* (1944) argues that the progressive reform of race practices and policies results from individuals' attempts to reconcile their racist behaviors with democratic war-fighting ideals. This claim is addressed on both substantive and theoretical grounds in Chapter 1. While the nation's core ideals seem to have positively influenced Cold War–era political developments, somewhat less empirical attention has been focused on the causes and nature of World War II–era policies. White psyches, the evidence suggests, were not necessarily driven by war to abandon racist assumptions and ideologies. More importantly, the ideational model does include a robust conceptualization of executive power and interest.

The central theoretical goal of this work is, therefore, to assemble a model of the political and organizational determinants of wartime policy responses to imminent or actual social insurgencies. This concern stems in part from what I see to be the disproportionate attention social scientists have dedicated to social movements, as opposed to authorities, in such struggles. The approach employed here, built upon the work of scholars of European statecraft, explains executive policies as products of shifting challenges to national security and to the ruling party. I introduce a simple sequence whereby officials seek to adjust the social friction that follows from a large-scale mobilization. More specifically, I argue that within this sequence one can explain most of the variation in the timing and the quality of policies aimed at a disruptive group by the ebb and flow of two factors: elections and threats to national security.

The approach echoes David Mayhew's *Congress: The Electoral Connection* (1974), in which the political scientist decided to "conjure up a vision" of members of Congress as single-minded seekers of reelection and then studied the behavior that presumably followed from this assumption. In a similar fashion, I propose a simple, abstract, two-pronged assumption about the overriding goals of wartime statesmen, and then posit that characteristic policy responses follow from these imperatives. Like Stephen Krasner in *Defending the National Interest* (1978), I attempt to demonstrate empirically, through policy-making case studies, that American decision makers consistently sought these same identifiable goals.

Three cases of racial manpower policies – those governing black factory workers, farm laborers, and army troops – focus attention on the independent effect of the varying political and economic opportunities available to African American labor in different "sectors" of the war mobilization. To be sure, the opportunities for protest in each case helped to determine the particular nature of racially motivated claims on statesmen. Army policies constrained opportunities to such an extent that they helped cause collective and militant black resistance, for example, while a new prosperity in farm families prompted southern white landowners to complain of blacks' withdrawal from field work. Despite such contextual differences in claim-making, subsequent race adjustment policies in each of the three spheres were broadly determined by state officials seeking production efficiency and political gains in response to war-fighting exigencies and the campaign timetable. In addition to analyzing these policies and their political context, this book documents the methods by which executives accomplish overriding goals – that is, war prosecution and regime maintenance – by sacrificing very salient but secondary goals, in this instance, a centralized and permanent program of social reform.

These three workforce policy cases are empirically important, combining to account for more than four out of five black workers in 1944. The agricultural sector was the single largest employer of African Americans at the time. In addition, despite the political importance usually attached to organized labor in this period, the number of black army inductees surpassed by more than fifty percent the number who joined unions during the war. These two cases are compared to the more familiar story of factory workers, who had access to the precocial Fair Employment Practices Committee. The findings are consistent with recent research on the evolution of New Deal liberalism, which finds that this war forced the Democratic party coalition to confront divisive race and labor policy questions. The research presented here, however, focuses entirely on presidential rather than congressional attempts to manage race friction in these spheres. Throughout I have tried to re-create administrators' views of the political-economic context so as to better grasp their strategic motivations and calculations. Toward this end, the book, in effect, peers over the shoulders of the statesmen managing this war.

The analysis confronts a puzzle implied by recent work in American political development. Historically oriented political scientists have argued for some time that political institutions exert independent and formative effects on political outcomes, in part through state officials' pursuit of interests separate from the needs of particular parties and social groups. This state-centered literature also argues that war temporarily empowers the state through that degree of centralization of authority thought necessary for national survival. If these claims were true, it would seem likely that this World War would powerfully and permanently alter those public policies linking social groups and governing institutions. But the enduring effects of this war on race policies and institutions are somewhat difficult to discern. Why and where did the monster Leviathan hide? This research demonstrates that statesmen believe that war-fighting is at times best served by the insulation of the executive, that is, the purposeful avoidance of the construction of permanent institutional vehicles for the expression of societal interests and appeals. Most historical-institutional work favors studies of the genesis and evolution – or more often in the American case, the failure – of permanent national bureaucracies administering programs of social provision, employment assistance, or market regulation. But in both peace and war, temporary agencies with constrained powers ease intergroup conflicts and cushion threatened interests when more substantial or permanent solutions are beyond the reach of institution-builders. The statesmen examined here hoped that relatively minor adjustments would defuse claims for permanent change. They were not always correct in this regard. But these temporary enabling reforms, in both stanching and stimulating insurgency, clearly shaped the scale and scope of the American state, although in ways that are neither obvious nor easily measured.

Several caveats are in order. There is here only a trace of Eleanor Roosevelt's work on race-related projects during the war, due to the fact that this analysis focuses largely on the formal administration of federal manpower programs. Fortunately, the reader can turn to Doris Kearns Goodwin's fine *No Ordinary Time* (1994) to correct this lacuna. Second, the book's preoccupation with statecraft means that it fails to systematically address the important question of precisely how and why various social forces organized and mobilized for both planned or spontaneous activity. The forms of social mobilization in this period vary widely; a satisfactory answer to this question would require a sustained and complex analysis of its own. Instead, in line with the view of contemporary statesmen, new forms of racial insurgency that directly involved war-related participants, sites, arguments, or authorities are simply judged to be prima facie evidence of the causal effect of war on group formation and action. Doug McAdam's *Political Process and the Development of Black Insurgency* (1982) remains an acute summary of the factors that can facilitate social movement emergence, and the present analysis is at least compatible with his model.

Finally, I should like to make it clear that this book was not intended to be an indictment of the American effort in the Second World War, nor of the race adjustment policies described herein, nor of central state intervention in race relations more generally. On the first point, the majority of Americans of all races clearly believed, as I do, that the war was a just enterprise. This was unquestionably one source of the strength of the nation's effort. On the second, related point, the motivations of White House race officials in the thirties and forties have received somewhat less scrutiny than those of extremely liberal or reactionary politicians. The book tries to explain how the war crisis, and federal administrators' efficiency and electoral concerns that followed from it, created attitudes toward reform that were not simply reducible to white racism or white egalitarianism. One should, I would argue, expect wartime statesmen to behave in the ways described here. The study is thus intended to edify citizens of democracies who often are asked by executives to assent to exceptional acts of discretionary power during wars and foreign policy crises, often without the minimally sufficient information necessary for an informed choice. At the same time, I agree with the many Americans of the time who believed that the FDR administration did more to correct racial injustice than any other post–Civil War presidency. On the final point, this book should not be misread to condemn federal intervention in race relations. For one thing, it demonstrates why it is difficult to imagine how basic civil rights could have reached southern blacks in any other way. As for the period under investigation, the book intends to better catalog the causes and consequences – and both the benefits and costs – of the central state's unusually tight embrace of African Americans. Our political imaginations might well benefit from revisiting a not-too-distant moment when advocates wrestled with statesmen so ferociously that both contributed to a moment of explosive innovation and experimentation in race mobilization tactics and policymaking practices. The net result brought the nation ever so slightly closer to her founding egalitarian ideals.

Portions of this research have been published previously in article format: "Race Policy, Race Violence, and Race Reform in the U.S. Army During World War II," *Studies in American Political Development*, vol. 10, no. 1, Spring, 1996; and "The American State and the Management of Race Conflict in the Workplace and in the Army, 1941–1945," *Polity*, Summer, 1994.

I am indebted above all to the gifted advisement of Richard Bensel, under whose careful and kind direction this study was undertaken and completed. I am also very grateful to Ira Katznelson, who taught me the period and its players, and whose support and critique animated and sharpened this work. I also sincerely thank Charles Tilly, who performed an essential role as this study's *provocateur*, and whose distinctive imprint on this study is unmistakable. I am proud that the book is an amalgam of their research agendas and analytic methods. They bear no responsibility for my errors or misjudgments.

I also offer thanks to Maria Torre, Matthew Turner, William Potter, and Joshua Trauner for their excellent research assistance. Too numerous for individual mention, I regret to say, are the many contributors and commentators I have encountered over the last few years. Gerald Gill and Desmond King, to give two examples, contributed generously to the project at important junctures. I am very grateful to Alex Holzman of Cambridge University Press for his steady but enthusiastic support of this project. I greatly appreciate the very timely financial support I received from the Franklin D. Roosevelt Library Institute and later from the Harry S. Truman Library Institute. The research staff at each presidential library was extremely helpful. My sincere gratitude goes to Aaron Friedberg of the Research Program in International Security at Princeton's Center of International Studies for the opportunity to undertake manuscript revisions during a fellowship year. I single out Dean Philip Khoury to accept my thanks for the institutional support provided to me by various wings of MIT. I also am very grateful to my colleagues in the Political Science Department there. A list of those who have been helpful to me and to this project would simply be too lengthy, but Stephen Van Evera has been a particularly responsible critic. I also extend my warm thanks to Jeff Kryder, Charles Stein, and Lisa Kearns for repeatedly and happily bucking me up. Finally, I extend my deepest appreciation to Anne Raffin. From the beginning to the end of this work, she has counseled and cheered me, thoughtfully and patiently. I thank her with my whole heart.

Note on Sources and Usage

When a footnote contains substantive material from sources other than the one originally referenced in the note, I have followed the practice of arranging the references in the order of the referenced material. That is, the first reference listed refers to claims or quotations in the body of the text, the second reference to the first substantive claim or quotation in the note, and so on. The full citation to each book or article title is provided by the first such citation in each chapter, as are full references for archival materials. The terms "Negro" and "Colored" are used only in quotations of primary materials; wartime writers did not always capitalize the words, and their original form is retained.

1

A Divided Arsenal: The Problem and Its Setting

You should understand, therefore, that there are two ways of fighting: by law and by force. The first way is natural to men, and the second to beasts. But as the first way often proves inadequate one must needs have recourse to the second. So a prince must understand how to make a nice use of the beast and the man . . . he cannot survive otherwise.

Niccolò Machiavelli, *The Prince*, Ch. 18

War is a conflict between societies as well as armies. Joseph Stalin, who owed his nation's survival to the awesome resilience of the Soviet people, according to legend once toasted Franklin Roosevelt with the remark that "Detroit was winning the war." Every account of the Allied victory in World War II assigns a weighty role to American materiel supplies, which we now know arrived in the field largely unchecked by delays caused by social unrest. But mobilization officials realized that the American "arsenal of democracy" was divided in two interrelated ways: between industrialized and agrarian sections, and between black and white manpower.

The famous metaphor dates from a Fireside Chat of December 29, 1940. Liberated from electoral concerns after months of careful campaigning, which ultimately required an explicit pledge that the nation would not go to war, Franklin Roosevelt now spoke more freely as the nation's commander-in-chief. The end of the election season had shifted attention firmly toward foreign affairs and the address contained his most forceful statement on the unfolding war to date. There could be, he announced, no peace between America's government and the Fascist masters of the Axis nations – "a gang of outlaws" who sought to enslave the human race. But the prospects for stopping the Nazis anytime soon seemed grim. A month earlier, the German Air Force had hammered Coventry to the effect of over one thousand casualties, and scores of English towns braced themselves for the arrival of the deadly saturation bombing technique. Still worse, Britain, her dollar credits exhausted, could not afford to purchase the additional American supplies necessary to her survival. The president therefore used the radio address to charge the nation with a new and grave responsibility: The United States "must be the great arsenal of democracy" for the effort to contain the unrelenting expansionism of the fascist "warmakers." At the urging of Harry Hopkins, Roosevelt also reassured Allied audiences with a surprising disclosure, namely that "the latest and the best of information" indicated that the enemy could not win the war. This announcement, which captured the headlines the next day, rested on nothing more than his personal conviction that Lend-Lease would release the nation's considerable industrial might and make an Allied victory inevitable.

Despite Roosevelt's heartfelt optimism, this was by no means a foregone conclusion. Statesmen sensed and subsequent events confirmed that the conflict would be a war of production, in which national power ultimately depended on the mass support of governing regimes. The Allies, for example, shifted their strategic air offensive to target production facilities only after two years of indiscriminate bombing of cities had failed to damage the morale of, or subvert the Nazi's control of, the German people. To take another critical example, Hitler's siege on Stalingrad stalled because of the vast reserves of soldiers that the Soviet state managed to draw from the nation's interior. Churchill remarked in 1940 that Hitler's best chance for victory was a break in the national unity of England. In fact, on the night of the "arsenal" address, London endured one of the most intensive bombing raids of the war; the Germans and Japanese often created major disturbances such as this to diminish the effect of FDR's speeches on allied morale.[1] In the United States, class, ethnic, and race friction quickly emerged as the most potent obstacle to an efficient mobilization by causing numerous, if minor, delays in the Army and in civilian life. Hitler, for one, believed that the Americans would eventually fracture their government on the tensions and hatreds created by isolationists and the country's myriad ethnic groups and races. *Life* magazine posed the problem starkly for the production capital of the war: "Detroit can either blow up Hitler or it can blow up the U.S."

The causes of the racial friction seemed apparent to contemporaries. By 1945, one million African Americans had joined the armed forces and another million had moved from the southern countryside into cities

---

1. Robert E. Sherwood, *Roosevelt and Hopkins: An Intimate History*, New York, Harper & Brothers, 1948, pp. 225–8.

across the nation. Coincidentally, the number working in agriculture and in domestic service dropped dramatically.[2] In four years, there had been more occupational diversification for this group than had occurred in all the years since the Civil War.[3] The vast social change contributed to widespread unrest. The Social Science Institute at Fisk University counted 242 racial confrontations in forty-seven cities in 1943 alone, many involving soldiers, and major race disturbances struck New York, Los Angeles, Beaumont, Detroit, and Mobile.[4] The trends alarmed contemporary observers in Congress, the Army, the FBI, and the War Production Board. Rep. Vito Marcantonio (D, NY) warned the White House that "anti-Negro outbreaks have been stimulated precisely in those areas which are keys to successful war production and in and about military training areas."[5] As this book makes clear, such conflict was eventually brought under control. In June 1944 the massive Allied invasion of Western Europe proceeded essentially as planned. By the fall, an assistant to Franklin Roosevelt congratulated the administration for having escaped "the dangerous summer season" without a single major racial disturbance.[6] When FDR won his third reelection a month later, the war had entered its end-game and no serious social divisions at home checked the triumphant advance of American forces abroad.

This book describes and analyzes the methods used by President Franklin Roosevelt and his wartime assistants to unleash the nation's

2. The entire black population numbered 9.26 million in 1940. Harold G. Vatter, *The U.S. Economy in World War II*, New York, Columbia University Press, 1985, p. 127; U.S. Bureau of the Census, *Sixteenth Census of the United States: 1940*, Population, vol. III, The Labor Force, USGPO, 1943, pp. 41–2.

3. Robert Weaver, *Negro Labor: A National Problem*, New York, Harcourt Brace and Company, 1946, p. 74.

4. "Review of the Month," *Monthly Summary of Events and Trends in Race Relations*, no. 2, 1944; Stanley Sandler, "Homefront Battlefront: Military Racial Disturbances in the Zone of the Interior, 1941–1945," presented to the 1991 American Historical Association Conference, Chicago, Illinois, December 27–30, 1991, np.

5. Vito Marcantonio to FDR, June 16, 1943, 93, Colored Matters, Franklin D. Roosevelt Library [hereafter FDRL]. This book builds on several influential analyses of race in the wartime period, in particular Richard Dalfiume, "The 'Forgotten Years' of the Negro Revolution," *Journal of American History*, vol. 55, January 1968; Harvard Sitkoff, "Racial Militancy and Interracial Violence in the Second World War," *Journal of American History*, vol. 58, December 1971; Harvard Sitkoff, "American Blacks in World War II: Rethinking the Militancy-Watershed Hypothesis," in James Titus, ed., *The Home Front and War in the Twentieth Century*, Washington, D.C., USGPO, 1984. For a contemporaneous overview, see Charles S. Johnson, *To Stem This Tide: A Survey of Racial Tension Areas in the United States*, Boston, The Pilgrim Press, 1943.

6. Memorandum, Jonathan Daniels to FDR, September 28, 1944, OF 4245, OPM, CO-FEP, FDRL.

military power by managing race conflict in three sectors of the national political economy: industry, agriculture, and the Army.[7] The case histories, for all of their differences, share a self-righting policy-making sequence by which the war mobilization intensified social conflict, which in turn compelled central authorities to invent new programs and policies of control and amelioration. Two factors explain the timing and the quality of the central state's policy responses to the friction plaguing these manpower spheres: a reelection imperative, which explains the clustering of ameliorative policies and symbolic gestures during presidential campaigns; and an efficiency imperative, which explains the predominance of social-control and race "adjustment" policies during the peaks of war-fighting or unrest. In sum, the Roosevelt administration implemented policies that may have appeared progressive, but other purposes – the full mobilization of industrial production and the maintenance of the party coalition – outweighed in importance the principle and the goal of egalitarian social reform.

Wars, Presidents, and Reform in American History

African Americans once believed in the liberating potential of war – through the concurrent centralization of political and coercive power in the hands of the president. While urging blacks to join his March on Washington Movement in 1941, A. Philip Randolph exhorted FDR to emulate the courage of Abraham Lincoln who, faced with a grave wartime emergency, preserved American democracy by proclaiming the slaves free.[8] The Union war effort had not only destroyed slavery; Lincoln's commanders also experimented with the redistribution of wealth in the conquered South. The warmakers and their political allies in the victorious North even attempted to regulate access to political power in the region to the freedmen's advantage. The social impact of the Civil War was such that a black leader predicted – in a sentiment repeated

7. Here Army and War Department will be used interchangeably to connote the organization through which the central state conducted nonnaval military operations; the Navy retained a separate cabinet office at the time. The Army is simply the uniformed personnel pursuing this project, while the War Department "could be termed the connecting link between the President and the Army." The book's comparative interest in manpower policy will in effect focus the analysis on ground forces training facilities and eschew a study of Army Air Force policies, which produced a singular record on race for a number of reasons particular to that branch. John D. Millett, "The War Department in World War II," *American Political Science Review*, vol. 40, no. 5, 1946, p. 865.
8. "CALL Colored Americans to Washington, D.C. for Jobs and Equal Participation in National Defense, July 1," Boston *Guardian*, June 7, 1941.

from time to time throughout the first half of this century – that American involvement in the Great War would lead to a "second emancipation" of his people.[9] Considering Southern whites' choke hold on the Democratic party and Congress alike, and the glacial pace of constitutional and legal change, there were at the time few political alternatives so promising as an executive at war.

Relative to the importance once attached to war, however, there has been relatively little analysis of its effects on racial beliefs, practices, and policies since Gunnar Myrdal's *An American Dilemma* (1944). Drafting and revising the manuscript between 1941 and 1943, Myrdal and his stellar collaborators could hardly avoid documenting contemporary race debates.[10] The book – his "war work" as he put it – displayed a confident optimism that human nature would combine with the new social science to bring racial policy and everyday practices into line with core American values through a virtuous process of "cumulative causation," in which gains in one sphere of social or political relations would spur progress in other areas.[11] Myrdal's final chapter, "America Again at the Crossroads" explicitly explored the choices posed by yet another war for "liberty and equality." American blacks were again wondering what the conflict would mean for them, precisely because war had historically served a progressive, liberating function:

> The three great wars of this country have been fought for the ideals of liberty and equality to which the nation was pledged. As a consequence of all of them, the American Negro made great strides toward freedom and opportunity. The Revolutionary War started a development which ultimately ended slavery in all Northern states, made new import of slaves illegal and nearly accomplished abolition even in the South – though there the tide soon turned in a reaction toward fortification of the plantation system and of Negro slavery. The Civil War gave the Negro Emancipation and Reconstruction in the South – though it was soon followed by Restoration of white supremacy. The First World War provided the Negro his first real opportunity as a worker in Northern industry, started the Great

9. Quoted in Lawrence W. Levine, "Marcus Garvey and the Politics of Revitalization," in John Hope Franklin and August Meier, eds., *Black Leaders of the Twentieth Century*, Urbana, University of Illinois Press, 1982, p. 112.

10. Gunnar Myrdal, *An American Dilemma: The Negro Problem and Modern Democracy*, with the assistance of Richard Sterner and Arnold Rose, New York, Harper & Brothers Publishers, 1944, pp. x–xvii.

11. Walter A. Jackson, *Gunnar Myrdal and America's Conscience: Social Engineering and Racial Liberalism, 1938–1987*, Chapel Hill, University of North Carolina Press, 1990, p. 163; see also Chapters 4–6; David W. Southern, *Gunnar Myrdal and Black-White Relations: The Use and Abuse of An American Dilemma, 1944–1969*, Baton Rouge, Louisiana State University Press, 1994.

Migration out of the South, and began the "New Negro" movement –
though the end of the War saw numerous race riots and the beginning of a
serious decline in employment opportunities. After the advances on all three
occasions there were reactions, but not as much ground was lost as had
been won. Even taking the subsequent reactions into account, each of the
three great wars in the history of America helped the Negro take a permanent step forward.[12]

Of all the historical events reviewed in *An American Dilemma*, war
served as the most powerful single mechanism by which what Myrdal
termed the "American Creed" and the "American Dilemma" came to be
understood by the black and white masses.[13]

In this view, after the Civil War's promise was wasted by an ineffectual reconstruction and the abandonment of freedmen by the Republican
Party, plans for conventional political struggle within formal institutions
were replaced by an emphasis on individual moral and economic development, championed by Booker T. Washington and his associates. Myrdal claimed that World War I – most, importantly, its ideological implications – dealt this philosophy a mortal blow among more militant
blacks.[14] The draft of whites, the end of immigration, and the war boom
prompted northern firms to hire blacks. Myrdal considered the subsequent migration and urbanization of African Americans to be a powerful
ameliorative force, for it contradicted the "peaceful and innocent" accommodation of rural blacks.[15] Although the War Department segregated black soldiers in training and assignments, the psychic and economic impact of military service also was substantial. Roughly 400,000
blacks were drafted and around 200,000 traveled to France.[16] But Myr-

12. Myrdal, *An American Dilemma*, p. 997.
13. The idea that the racial caste system contradicted core American ideals was already
    prominent in public discourse at the time, given the obvious incongruity between
    Allied war aims and domestic policies. As an official in the March on Washington
    Movement put it in 1941, "Everyone was talking about democracy, even in the dark
    South, but their actions belied their words." The Pittsburgh *Courier's* Double V
    Campaign, signifying victory over "enemies" at home and abroad, reflected in essence
    the same contradiction. Letter, John Eardlie to FDR, August 16, 1942, OF 4245-G,
    OPM, COFEP, War Manpower Board, FDRL; Raleigh *News & Observer*, April 7,
    1941; Patrick S. Washburn, *A Question of Sedition: The Federal Government's Inves-
    tigation of the Black Press During World War II*, New York, Oxford University Press,
    1986; Lee Finkle, *Forum for Protest: The Black Press During World War II*, Ruther-
    ford, NJ, Fairleigh Dickinson University Press, 1975; Rayford Logan, ed., *What the
    Negro Wants*, Chapel Hill, University of North Carolina Press, 1944.
14. Levine, "Marcus Garvey," p. 112.
15. Myrdal, *An American Dilemma*, pp. 200, 295, 745.
16. He acknowledged that the nation to which they returned was frighteningly hostile.

dal primarily was interested in the impact of such developments on popular thought, particularly among whites, who more often discussed the "American way of life" and acknowledged a lack of democracy in politics. The foment raised the hopes of blacks and drew their attention to "their anomalous position" in the so-called democracy.[17]

Like the First World War, World War II aggravated the Dilemma through organizational, socioeconomic, and ideological processes.[18] Myrdal was relatively vague in explaining a new vitality in race advancement organizations.

> He has seen his strategic position strengthened not only because of the desperate scarcity of labor but also because of a revitalization of the democratic Creed . . . He cannot allow his grievances to be postponed until after the War, for he knows that the War is his chance.[19]

The war also favored race organizations by requiring a further "concentration of responsibility" in economic and public affairs through national unions and federal administration.[20] Most importantly, black leaders recognized the improved constellation of political, economic, and ideational opportunities.

Myrdal may well have hoped that the socioeconomic effects of the Second World War would resemble those of the First World War through migration and occupational diversification. Unfortunately, up

Ten of the seventy blacks lynched in 1919 were soldiers; more were killed and injured in the twenty-five race riots of the same year. Myrdal, *An American Dilemma*, p. 745.

17. Myrdal, *An American Dilemma*, pp. 193, 563, 745. James Weldon Johnson likewise wrote of the cynicism and "spirit of defiance born of desperation" that marked the end of the First World War. Quoted in Eugene Levy, "James Weldon Johnson and the Development of the NAACP," in Franklin and Meier, eds., *Black Leaders*, p. 89.

18. Oddly, Myrdal's reading of the interwar period paints it as more productive than – and generally unaffected by – the two world wars. The period reenforced progressive trends by providing blacks with full legal equality in the North, while the South was increasingly unstable, pressured from a rising legal culture within the region as well as principled attacks – on the poll tax, for example – from without. Although the occupational status of blacks was deteriorating, the increasingly liberal nature of national politics promised to improve their economic prospects. The white man was "in a dilemma," having not yet altered his behavior to reflect his loss of confidence in the theory that had structured his racial worldview. The slow decline in racist ideology Myrdal called "the most important of all social trends in the field of interracial relations." The eventual elimination of racist caste theory was well advanced and irreversible by this point, for it was sustained by the American Creed. Myrdal, *An American Dilemma*, pp. 999, 1001–2, 1003–4, 1010.

19. Myrdal, *An American Dilemma*, pp. 409, 852.

20. Myrdal, *An American Dilemma*, p. 1010.

to the time the concluding chapter was written – August 1942 – there were few new factory jobs available to blacks, and consequently very little of the migration that marked the Great War. In fact, despite Myrdal's general claim that war would improve political and economic opportunities for minorities, the facts of the ongoing mobilization looked very grim in his reporting. The need for new labor was primarily in skilled occupations dominated by whites, and since firms and the federal government had largely accommodated themselves to unions, there were fewer opportunities to attain employment as replacements for organized workers. Other factors suppressing black employment included the small portion of defense spending located in the South and the large Depression-fed reserve pool of white labor available for most defense jobs. The Fair Employment Practices Committee (FEPC), despite representing "the most definite break in the tradition of federal unconcernedness" toward bias in employment, was at the time "moribund" and therefore represented only "something of a promise for the future."[21]

His analysis of the armed forces was equally discouraging. The majority of the Army's training facilities were located in the South, firing the resentment of both races toward the policy. Even late in the war, the service of African Americans, most often in labor battalions, was in percentage terms much lower than their proportion of the civilian population, as was the case in manufacturing as well (see Appendix 1.3). The Navy had stopped employing them except as messmen or menial laborers. The war had actually interrupted a process of increasing interracial cooperation and fellowship in the South in the thirties, he reported. Many observers were predicting race riots for the immediate future, and Myrdal himself believed there would be a reaction against any wartime gains.[22]

How could this dire situation lead to any optimism at all? Myrdal sensed that as the war continued, trends would rapidly improve. Black Americans were better educated and, backed by a more robust press and stronger organizations, much better prepared to stake their claims. The Depression and the war had broken the tradition of noninterference by government in employment, and Myrdal believed this would favor the prospects of blacks, because he apparently believed liberal forces to be ascendant in national politics. By promoting the unionization of the workforce and the regulation and planning of the economy, war would break down economic discrimination, particularly in the North. With

21. Myrdal, *An American Dilemma*, pp. 409–10, 416.
22. Myrdal, *An American Dilemma*, pp. 419–20, 1014.

demobilization, the threat of mass unemployment would require large-scale federal intervention, and no presidential administration would allow unemployment to affect blacks disproportionately. Federal agencies, in order to secure public support, would present fair employment policies as essential to national economic development. Other forms of bias would then decline "according to the law of cumulative causation" to which Myrdal frequently referred. As for an eventual reaction, Myrdal argued that a ratchetlike protective mechanism would limit losses as it had in the past.[23]

These organizational and political-economic developments were, however, incidental to Myrdal's primary focus on ideology. In line with his overriding claim that the "Negro problem has its existence in the American's mind" and hence that significant developments in race relations stem from "changes in people's beliefs and valuations," Myrdal was interested in material trends only in so far as they influenced the ideology of Americans, particularly whites. In the midst of an ideological war – the Allies fought to resuscitate democracy in continents dominated by totalitarian, racist regimes – blacks calling for democracy at home could "with new reason, point to the inconsistency between American ideals and practices." The war was thus accelerating the demise of caste theory by forcing a "deeper split" in the "moral personality" of the white southerner. In addition, the nation had a new responsibility to prove to the world that it could integrate its races as it assumed a global leadership role; American power and stability now depended on the support and goodwill of other nations. Myrdal counseled action, for the peace would bring new and complicated social and economic problems whose governance required "political decision and public regulation" informed by social engineering and social scientific, causal theories. In sum, as African Americans became more assimilated and better educated, their continued exclusion from various spheres of society made them increasingly impatient; "the international upheavals connected with the two World Wars and the world depression brought these developments to a crisis."[24]

A schematic representation of Myrdal's theory underscores the centrality of the white belief/behavior contradiction to his explanation of political change (see Figure 1.1). The empirical record, however, does

---

23. Myrdal, *An American Dilemma*, pp. 423–4, 426, 1005–6, 1011.
24. Most declarations of rights derived from American manifestos such as Wilson's Fourteen Points and FDR's Four Freedoms, and many observers expected the creation of an international legal apparatus for appeal by oppressed minority groups. Myrdal, *An American Dilemma*, pp. 426, 998, 1004, 1008–9, 1019–23.

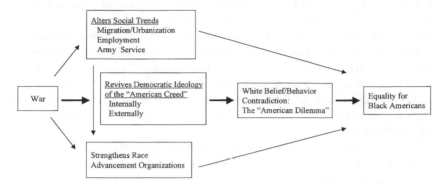

Figure 1.1. *An American Dilemma*: Myrdal's model of the effects of war upon racial attitudes and black liberation.

not confirm Myrdal's central prediction, for historians have generally not ascribed great importance to war in general, or World War II in particular, in explanations of the eventual achievement of statutory racial equality. The nation's experience prompts the question: Why did the collision of egalitarian ideals and racist practices in the United States between 1941 and 1945 not fulfill Myrdal's expectations and produce significant and lasting changes in the ideologies and laws governing race relations?

Broadly speaking, Myrdal underestimated the chameleonlike adaptability of racist attitudes to shared ideals and to changes in the political economy. Even today, wholly American if archaic racist beliefs remain embedded within various veins of our overarching national creeds, and the legacies of racial disadvantage continue to influence Americans' experiences with schools and labor markets, for example.[25] More specifically, Americans were less familiar with the aims of the war and their relationship to democratic ideals than Myrdal believed. Innovative mass advertising techniques, self-interest, and a concern for one's comrades-in-arms, no less than ideology, explained Americans' support for the war, in both civilian and military settings.[26] In addition, Myrdal may not have appreciated the extent to which racist attitudes could not only

25. Rogers M. Smith, "Beyond Tocqueville, Myrdal, and Hartz: The Multiple Traditions in America," *American Political Science Review* 87, September 1993; Gary Gerstle, "Race and the Myth of the Liberal Consensus," *The Journal of American History*, September 1995.
26. See Paul Fussell, *Wartime: Understanding and Behavior During World War II*, New York, Oxford University Press, 1989. Critical reexaminations of wartime ideology and practice include John Dower, *War Without Mercy: Race and Power in the Pacific War*, New York, Pantheon Books, 1986; Richard Polenberg, "The Good War? A

weather but exploit the disruption of war. The First World War mobilization, it was reported, actually transformed a great many indifferent whites into racists by sending northern soldiers into the South – converting many of them to local sentiments and practices – and racist southerners to the North "to spread their infamous spawn of race prejudice wherever they go."[27] A similar effect obtained in the Second World War.[28] The Army, some argued, had done more to develop race consciousness by segregating its forces in communities where it had not been standard practice than had "the Bund or the Ku Klux Klan."[29] The widespread collective race violence in the immediate aftermath of World War I, and during World War II as well, indicates that retrograde racial attitudes were not only resistant to wartime ideals, but at times emboldened or aggravated by them. In sum, while democratic war aims undermined many Americans' views of racially biased attitudes and practices, white attitudes in the aggregate apparently did not swing decidedly to favor equal rights for minorities due to the combined effects of two world wars.[30]

Reappraisal of How World War II Affected American Society," *The Virginia Magazine of History and Biography*, vol. 100, no. 3, July, 1992; John Morton Blum, *Liberty, Justice, Order*, New York, W. W. Norton & Company, 1993, ch. 10; Michael C. C. Adams, *The Best War Ever: America and World War II*, Baltimore, The Johns Hopkins University Press, 1994; Desmond King, *Separate and Unequal: Black Americans and the US Federal Government*, New York, Oxford University Press, 1995.

27. "Southern Americanism," Pittsburgh *Courier*, November 23, 1940.

28. In response to a petition that was based in part on the "democratic war" argument, an assistant secretary of war wrote: "Frankly, I do not think that the basic issues of this war are involved in the question of whether Colored troops serve in segregated units or in mixed units and I doubt whether you can convince the people of the United States that the basic issues of freedom are involved in such a question . . ." John McCloy, quoted in Ulysses Lee, *The Employment of Negro Troops*, U.S. Army in World War II, Special Studies, Office of the Chief of Military History, U.S. Army, Washington, D.C., 1966, pp. 158–60.

29. Historian David Brion Davis, then an Army security policeman, wrote from his station in Stuttgart, Germany in early 1946 that segregation "causes misunderstanding and swings the larger, undecided group toward intolerance." "New Edifice Situated in Arlington, Va.," Chicago *Defender*, October 18, 1941; Julius Adams, "Southerners Invade the North While Northerners 'Stay Put,' " New York *Amsterdam News*, March 25, 1944; David Brion Davis, "World War II and Memory," *The Journal of American History*, vol. 77, no. 2, September 1990, p. 586.

30. Wartime political discourse may have emphasized universalistic and inclusive principles, and public opinion data seems to indicate a modest shift toward support for integration. Among white soldiers, the factor that over time correlated most strongly with positive attitudes toward Army integration was experience with integrated divisions or companies. Sherie Mershon and Steven Schlossman, *Foxholes and Color Lines: Desegregating the Armed Forces*, Baltimore, The Johns Hopkins University Press, 1998, pp. 105–14, 142–3, 177.

The State and Social Conflict: Lessons from the Long View

The publication of Myrdal's book – which performed a priceless service in amassing an overwhelming evidentiary record of a racial caste system that was both wholly American and un-American – may have had as much influence on political attitudes and practices as did the belief-behavior contradiction it meant to reveal. But his desire to illuminate the single and apparently extraordinary American case entailed the cost of inattention to the experiences of European nations where wars have continually caused social unrest and, as a consequence, political and institutional reform. "Preparation for war, paying for it, and mending its damage" have after all been the primary concern of European states for over five hundred years. As the scale of warmaking grew to encompass larger armies, more expensive weaponry, and costlier supplies, rulers increased their national budgets, debts, and taxes in turn.[31] Extracting resources for war has in modern times required the state to produce and allocate goods itself. Through this first "command" stage of the warmaking cycle – the assignment of manpower and capital – central authorities directly shape subsequent economic development and social group formation.[32] In this case, American planners invented a sharply sectional mobilization, particularly as it affected race relations (see Maps 1.1 and 1.2). Preexisting economic capacity drew the largest war supply contracts to northern and coastal cities where production officials could readily induce private firms to convert factories, retrain workers, and produce war materiel. The relative underdevelopment of the southern economy, combined with abundant and inexpensive land and a warmer climate, led military officials to funnel soldiers rather than contracts into the region. Approximately three-quarters of black training facilities were

---

31. The need for mass production of war materiel grew rapidly in the twentieth century. The total daily supply of a French army corps was 120 tons at the beginning of World War I; by the war's end, a single division required two hundred tons per day. Hans Spier, "Class Structure and Total War" (1939), in *Social Order and the Risks of War*, Cambridge, Massachusetts, MIT Press, 1952, p. 255.
32. For the fullest application of this logic to American political development, see Richard Franklin Bensel, *Yankee Leviathan: The Origins of Central State Authority in America, 1859–1877*, New York, Cambridge University Press, 1990. See also Gregory Hooks, "The Rise of the Pentagon and U.S. State Building: The Defense Program as Industrial Policy," *American Journal of Sociology*, vol. 96, no. 2, September, 1990, p. 398. Synthetic treatments of American society during World War II include Richard Polenberg, *War and Society*, Philadelphia, J. B. Lippincott Co., 1972; John Morton Blum, *V Was for Victory*, New York, Harcourt Brace Jovanovich, 1976. For an efficient overview of economic developments during the war, see Vatter, *The U.S. Economy in World War II*.

Map 1.1. Army camps housing sizable numbers of black troops, 1941–45. Source: Ulysses Lee, *U.S. Army in World War II, Special Studies: The Employment of Negro Troops*, Washington, D.C., USGPO, 1966; "Stations, Camps, Posts Where Colored Troops are Located," Pittsburgh *Courier*, June 14, 1941. Cities listed in Appendix 1.1.

Map 1.2. Urban areas receiving in excess of $700 million in war supply contracts, 1940–5. Source: U.S. Bureau of the Census, *County Data Book*, Washington, D.C., USGPO, 1947, pp. 13–55. Cities listed in Appendix 1.2.

placed in the rural South, where race relations were influenced far more
by instruments of coercion than of capital. This is an exemplary case of
state "efforts to channel resources and manpower into war" having the
effect of molding "the state apparatus in way that complements and
exploits the strengths and organizing structures of economic activity."[33]

But as national armies have incorporated additional manpower, they
have made themselves more dependent on mass support and thus more
vulnerable to new demands and popular resistance.[34] There are always
those who refuse to work, or insist on new benefits or terms for their
services. Warmakers typically curtail civil liberties and strike deals with
group leaders. Rulers have likewise always struggled to discipline sullen
and belligerent soldiers, prone to mutiny for pay or for the elimination
of cruel punishments. Through all of this, the manpower and resource
needs of states at war compel rulers to innovate as they repress and
bargain with social groups, or adjudicate their disagreements, so as to
gain their compliance or cooperation.[35] In this second, self-righting stage
of warmaking, there is a renegotiation of the trade-off between a state's
demands – that is, a citizenry's "obligations" – and social groups' and individuals' legitimate claims, or "rights."[36] Here again the United States is
no exception to the rule that sustained wars recast state institutions and
political relationships between citizens, social groups, and authorities.[37]

33. Bensel, *Yankee Leviathan*, pp. 96–7.
34. Relatively successful, war-induced, general insurgencies are less common than failed
    resistance activities of particular groups, but include the uprising of the Parisian
    communards at the close of the Franco-Prussian War of 1871, systemic rebellion in
    Russia in 1905 and 1917, and the movement for national independence in Ireland
    during World War I. Charles Tilly, *Coercion, Capital, and European States, AD 990–
    1990*, Cambridge, Massachusetts, Basil Blackwell, 1990, p. 74; W. J. Hale, *War and
    Society in Renaissance Europe, 1450–1620*, New York, St. Martin's Press, 1985; Perry
    Anderson, *Lineages of the Absolutist State*, London, NLB, 1974; Stanislav Andreski,
    Military Organization and Society, London, Routledge, 1954.
35. Tilly, *Coercion, Capital, and European States*, pp. 96–103; Hale, *War and Society*,
    pp. 166–72.
36. Over the long term, European national authorities adapted their political institutions
    to their economies. Robust urban economies generated a surplus that state agents and
    warmakers commandeered with relative ease; tax systems were thus less coercive in
    these settings than in polities where vast lands and sluggish commerce required exten-
    sive centralized bureaucracies to extract equivalent sums. Tilly, *Coercion, Capital, and
    European States*, p. 100; Edward Shorter and Charles Tilly, *Strikes in France, 1830–
    1968*, New York, Cambridge University Press, 1974; Leopold H. Haimson and
    Charles Tilly, eds., *Strikes, Wars, and Revolutions in an International Perspective*,
    New York, Cambridge University Press, 1989.
37. Efforts to ratify this century's two constitutional revisions enlarging the franchise, the
    Nineteenth Amendment granting women the right to vote (1920), and the Twenty-
    sixth Amendment lowering the voting age to eighteen (1971), gained momentum from
    World War I and the Vietnam War, respectively.

In this view, the war's immediate effect was political-economic rather than ideological, with the auxiliary effects of empowering civic organizations and state institutions, and accelerating and intensifying their bargaining relationships. Civic leaders realized that a total war increased the leverage of race advancement organizations. Most fundamentally, this resulted from activists' appreciation of the foregoing logic of warmaking: a severe national security threat necessitated new terms for incorporating leaders and for utilizing masses. It was hoped that the terms would include ameliorating reforms. By the summer of 1943, *The Crisis* called the "long war" argument "the question currently debated wherever colored Americans gather and talk."[38] As Horace Cayton described it early in the mobilization: "The graver the outside danger to the safety of this country, the more abundant the gains will likely be."[39] To the question of what will aid the southern black, one journalist answered,

> Personally, I believe a long war is the cure-all. Porters and Pullman workers with whom I talked agreed . . . The casualties of a long war will hit at their doorsteps and maybe they'll learn . . . [40]

Leaders like A. Philip Randolph realized that even circumscribed roles in a war economy grant insurgents a modest degree of power, since planned or spontaneous disruptions of production threatened to undermine the efficiency of the mobilization. In addition, the mobilization tightened labor markets and eventually generated new incomes for blacks that helped produce record-setting membership gains for organizations, enabling them to mount more effective recruiting and protest campaigns.[41] Finally, race organizations sensed that war undermined the power of local authorities, as quick and unilateral central state intervention, such as FEPC investigations of a firm's hiring policy, violated the New Deal's careful demarcation of central and local powers. Whether to enforce federal law or defend local custom was a question

---

38. "The 'hope' here, as we see it, is a war threat so terrible that they will be glad to have engineers and combat pilots regardless of complexion." Benjamin Quarles, "Will a Long War Aid the Negro?," *The Crisis*, September 1943, p. 268; George S. Schuyler, "A Long War Will Aid the Negro," *The Crisis*, November 1943; "Plane Factory Qualifications Don't Mean a Thing When You Are Colored," Philadelphia *Plain Dealer*, September 6, 1940.

39. Ironically, the American state itself created the perception that the security threat was grave. Horace Cayton, "Negro Morale," *Opportunity*, December 1941, p. 375.

40. "Yes, Leave the South, Now!," Baltimore *Afro-American*, February 26, 1944.

41. Between 1916 and 1920, James Weldon Johnson increased the membership of the National Association for the Advancement of Colored People (NAACP) tenfold to ninety thousand. The Association broke membership records again in World War II. Levy, "James Weldon Johnson," p. 89.

that was pragmatically but inconsistently answered. For all of these reasons, race advancement organizations were empowered by world war. What of the central state?

State and Party Imperatives in Wartime

Whether authorities performed roles as advocates or antagonists of these newly empowered organizations, racial struggle during World War II occurred in the context of a vast extension of relatively centralized state regulatory and police power.[42] Directing this enhanced power was a complicated strategic game for the American executive, which combines what are in most Western political systems the separate duties of chief of state and head of government. This fundamental combination of labor creates for the wartime president two distinct political imperatives: The chief of state most effectively projects national power through an optimally efficient mobilization, while the head of government must protect the political power of his ruling coalition by mounting successful campaigns and elections.[43] Somewhat paradoxically, electoral survival and congressional strength require the president to champion the particular needs of coalition members and social groups, while war-fighting often is best served by the insulation of the Commander-in-Chief from these same political projects. Each goal, however, necessitates social peace.

The party chief is a role familiar to observers of peacetime politics. As for the chief of state, this analysis adopts a simple and widely shared definition of the central state as national administrative capacity, or

42. World War II caused the greatest centralization of American political and economic control in history. This differs from the context surrounding civil rights protest in the 1950s, when social institutions indigenous to the black community and thus insulated from white control struggled mightily to draw central authorities into the Deep South. Vatter, *The U.S. Economy in World War II*, New York, Columbia University Press, 1985, p. 87; Doug McAdam, *Political Process and the Development of Black Insurgency, 1930–1970*, Chicago, University of Chicago Press, 1982.

43. Among the war's combatants, the American constitutional system was unique in mandating national elections at two-year intervals. They have never been suspended or delayed on account of war. The analysis resembles Wildavsky's and Greenstein's "Two Presidencies" theses in distinguishing between these two roles. The former's conclusions regarding the president's superior strength in foreign policy, however, are inductively drawn from congressional roll call votes and are specific, he claims, to the Cold War period. The latter's analysis focuses on Eisenhower's "self-conscious use of political strategies that enabled him to carry out both presidential roles without allowing one to undermine the other." Fred I. Greenstein, *The Hidden-Hand Presidency: Eisenhower as Leader*, Baltimore, Johns Hopkins University Press, 1994, p. 5; Aaron Wildavsky, "The Two Presidencies," *Trans-Action*, vol. 4, no. 2, 1966.

those institutions and officials that legitimately regulate, command, and coerce individuals and groups throughout a national territory, at times to project national power abroad.[44] Somewhat more restrictive is the theoretical expectation, adopted here, that state officials pursue broad interests of the national community rather than the particular interests of discrete classes or groups.[45] Within the constellation of federal institutions, the constitution grants the executive branch these responsibilities of the statesman as well as a relatively advantageous institutional design through which to pursue them. Combining an ill-defined but clearly national range of responsibilities – which have come to include intelligence-gathering – with a moderate degree of insulation and a high degree of enforcement power, it is predisposed toward determining and acting on broad national interests. The president's assistants, the executive agencies, and the bureaucracy are more fully insulated from societal influences, and thus are even better positioned for the task.[46] Thus this is where one should expect to find statesmen striving to attain national security abroad and at home.[47]

44. See, for example, John A. Hall and G. John Ikenberry, *The State*, Milton Keynes, Open University Press, 1989, pp. 1–2; Stephen Skowronek, *Building a New American State: The Expansion of National Administrative Capacities, 1877–1920*, New York, Cambridge University Press, 1982.

45. Stephen Krasner, *Defending the National Interest*, Princeton, Princeton University Press, 1978.

46. The Preamble to the Constitution indicates that the federal system was intended to "insure domestic Tranquility." This can be considered one of the executive's "inherent" powers. Its full powers, unlike those of Congress, were not specifically enumerated; Article II's vesting clause refers only to "the executive power." The Supreme Court has generally confirmed the view that the Constitution does not clearly limit the president's actions in pursuit of social order or the nation's international standing and sovereignty. In *U.S.* versus *Curtis-Wright Export Corporation* (1936), eight of the nine old men of the Supreme Court, so intent on restricting presidential power in the early New Deal, distinguished between the internal and external powers of government in noting that the former, drawn at the founding from preexisting states, were specified in the Constitution. The latter powers arose from the colonies upon their independence and "in their collective and corporate capacity as the United States of America." The executive, they found, naturally contains a "plenary and exclusive" power to act in international relations, for it is best suited to gather and hold confidential information and act swiftly upon it. The Constitution's specific grants of power in foreign affairs, such as the congressional power to declare war are, in this expansive but generally accepted view of presidential power, considered exceptional. Arthur M. Schlesinger, Jr., *The Imperial Presidency*, Boston, Houghton Mifflin Company, 1973, pp. 100–3.

47. Two criteria indicate an institution designed to favor statesmen: centralization, the placement of authority at the central state level rather than the subordinate levels of government; and insulation, the shielding of policy making from democratic processes and from particular societal interests. The permeability of Congress to particular local concerns make it an unlikely vehicle for planning in the national interest in any case. The judiciary offers superior insulation from societal pressures, but essentially no

But limited democracies such as the United States in 1941 suffer from disadvantages during war scares and mobilizations. Democracies tend not to be bellicose nations, and thus their mobilizations tend to be rushed and chaotic responses; even those reacting to explicit external threats are typically poorly prepared for war.[48] At the same time, democracies must attend in some way to a variety of organized groups' preferences and claims, which may violate efficiency considerations. Finally, caste groups in such cases are due to their exclusion from the routine operation of commerce and society often spatially or occupationally concentrated, or both, and pose a variety of potential problems for the mobilization. Thus, the Commander-in-Chief is plagued to some extent by the party competition that he has in his other capacity helped to arrange. Despite these disadvantages, skillful statesmen can overcome such complex challenges because their own strategic arsenal bristles with political weaponry, some well-worn, some newly minted.

For this president, the difficulty of assembling a ruling party was so great that a good deal of FDR's legend rests on his mastery of the task. Here it will suffice to note that Roosevelt had succeeded throughout the thirties in submerging issues such as race that would have split northern reformers from their conservative southern colleagues.[49] To southern congressmen, the expansion of central state authority posed a potentially serious threat to their highly exploitative, racially biased regional economy. In northern cities, however, blacks comprised an emergent faction of the local Democratic party, and by the late thirties these voters and their allies demanded that the administration pursue civil rights reforms. This bipolar Democratic party coalition affected the mobilization by

coercive power with which to enforce its rulings. Bensel, *Yankee Leviathan*, pp. 106–13.

48. General George C. Marshall alluded to this problem on the morning after the attack on Pearl Harbor, December 8, 1941: "But the most interesting aspect of the moment is that as a Democracy, we have suffered assault; violent attack without notice and without declaration, in the manner of those nations who operate on a basis of force . . . my problem as Chief of Staff has been to organize in the shortest possible time a body of troops, and to find whatever way to do that most expeditiously." Remarks, General George Marshall to Conference of Negro Newspaper Editors, December 8, 1941, Segregation/Discrimination: Armed Services, 104–1, 104–2, Conference of Negro Newspaper Representatives, Papers of William Hastie, Harvard Law School Library, Cambridge, Massachusetts.

49. V. O. Key, *Southern Politics in State and Nation*, New York, Alfred A. Knopf, 1949, p. 359; Richard F. Bensel, *Sectionalism and Political Development, 1880–1980*, Madison, University of Wisconsin Press, 1984; Ira Katznelson, Kim Geiger, and Daniel Kryder, "Limiting Liberalism: The Southern Veto in Congress, 1933–1950," *Political Science Quarterly* 108, no. 2, Summer, 1993.

causing White House officials to respond in contradictory ways to the conflicting pressures of southern white segregationists, on the one hand, and blacks and their allies on the other. Thus party imperatives constrained experimentation in the fields examined here. But the war crisis enabled FDR to move policy beyond these coalitional constraints, at least temporarily. For one thing, the war occasioned the replacement of many politically motivated officials with war administrators with new goals. In addition, while FDR continued his New Deal practice of attempting to suppress race politics, new war imperatives and institutions enabled him to implement new policies through executive fiat.[50]

Distinguishing State-Building from Party-Building Initiatives

Given the qualities of this national case, a number of observable implications regarding the timing, motivations, and quality of social policy follow from this model of wartime statesmanship (see Table 1.1). The overarching claim that wartime statecraft altered policy is a conclusion that can be drawn first through a comparison of wartime race policy with preexisting social policies implemented in the absence of the security threat, and, second, through a comparison of the timing, quality, and goals of policy innovation across the three sectors examined here. Each case therefore attends briefly to New Deal patterns of policymaking and finds that inherited practices were incompatible with new tasks. Regarding *timing*, elections should shape executive policy through the cyclical and proactive pursuit of voters – particularly ideological moderates and swing voters – for roughly six months during the campaign season every four years. Election victory relieves this pressure, and the executive should revert to insulating policies and practices, which will in turn gradually give way to another round of credit-claiming and position-taking some three years later.[51] Mid-term elections will cause much more modest intervention by the executive than presidential elections.

50. Since this analysis treats the central state's relations with one largely disfranchised social group, it is more narrowly focused than explanations of the war's effects on comprehensive social policy development, or those attending to the constraining effects of mass societal pressures and attitudes on a nation's foreign policy. For works of these types, see Edwin Amenta and Theda Skocpol, "Redefining the New Deal: World War II and the Development of Social Provision in the United States," in Margaret Weir, Ann Shola Orloff, and Theda Skocpol, *The Politics of Social Policy in the United States*, Princeton, Princeton University Press, 1988; Thomas J. Christensen, *Useful Adversaries: Grand Strategy, Domestic Mobilization, and Sino-American Conflict, 1947–1958*, Princeton, Princeton University Press, 1996.
51. For a full and foundational treatment of such electoral-oriented actions and their institutional implications in Congress, see David Mayhew, *Congress: The Electoral*

Table 1.1. *The President's Systemic Roles and Corresponding Imperatives.*

Systemic Role	Imperative	Immediate Goal	Trigger	Policy Pattern
Chief of State	national security	order, efficiency	unpredictable disorder, foreign attack	sequence
Leader of Party	political permanence	(re)election	scheduled opposition campaign	cycle

Policy responses to national security and social order concerns should on the other hand result from a reactive, sequential process. Military attacks or declarations of war signal the executive to launch a rapid mobilization, which can cause new forms of social friction. Sudden and full mobilizations necessarily conform to the economic contours of a nation; capital moves into cities capable of rapid industrial expansion and military installations emerge where an agreeable climate combines with cheap land. The first effects are thus exaggerations of preexisting political-economic patterns. This and the subsequent development of new economic capacity in new areas combine to destabilize social norms and relations. The national interest in an efficient mobilization compels central authorities such as the president to ameliorate the causes of the friction and repress open challenges to social order.[52] Thus a sequence of two stages – command and adjustment – characterize central state-society relations in total mobilizations.

Regarding the *quality* of state and party building policies, throughout the mobilization process the chief of state seeks to shed constraints on policy, through centralized and insulated administrative authority. The electoral cycle of party-building activity on the other hand causes the head of government to emerge from his isolation to embrace potential voters. While state and party concerns both animate a president's ac-

---

Connection, New Haven, Yale University Press, 1974; Edward Tufte, *Political Control of the Economy*, Princeton, Princeton University Press, 1980.

52. For analyses of different forms of social and state control of racial instability and unrest, see Ira Katznelson, *Black Men, White Cities: Race, Politics, and Migration in the United States, 1900–30, and Britain, 1948–68*, Chicago, University of Chicago Press, 1973, pp. 62–85; McAdam, *Political Process*, pp. 26–7.

tions, it is possible to gauge the salience of both imperatives in a given executive act, because each is best served by particular policy tools: an orderly mobilization by surveillance, repression, conflict-adjustment mechanisms and substantive concessions; reelection primarily by symbolic gestures and substantive concessions. Furthermore, a party chief's reelection plans typically involve incorporating elites into a national machinelike party structure. The statesman's plans for increasing mobilization efficiency, since it is at root a problem of economic organization, primarily focus on the optimal utilization of masses of manpower. When a national election is imminent, the problem of political survival rises in importance, and the executive branch extends very public but often symbolic concessions to secure a targeted vote.[53] Otherwise, however, political considerations remain secondary to the supreme goal of warmaking. The polity's tradition of suspending partisan attacks on foreign policies during war reenforces this pattern.

In addition to the timing and quality of policy reform, there is also substantial evidence of the distinct state- and party-building attitudes, motivations, and *goals* of executive officials. Statesmen clearly and self-consciously pursue insulation of the executive in the absence of a campaign, primarily so as to limit the expenditure of executive resources on resolving conflicts between societal groups or between groups and the state. In each case examined below, officials assessed the effects of what were initially very hasty state- and party-building efforts on party strength and on the insulation and centralization of the state. Adjustments of policies followed to better serve these interests, for gestures originally aimed at party-building subsequently hindered the mobilization. For example, a black official, William Hastie, appointed to the War Department for political reasons, thereafter pursued social justice goals that were disruptive to warmaking efficiency in the eyes of statesmen; he was quickly driven from office.

---

53. In practice, party and state imperatives do not function in complete isolation. The party chief cannot escape his international obligations, nor can the statesman afford to flatly ignore the preferences of his constituents. Depending on the relative gravity and the timing of various threats, decisions in one sphere can service the needs of the other. Through 1944, for example, FDR tried to ensure that no foreign policy interfered with his reelection campaign. This interdependence also can influence external conditions if opponents choose to exploit it. Hitler and Stalin were, in fact, "the first foreign statesmen who wanted to include the American electoral timetable in their calculations." Robert Dallek, *Franklin D. Roosevelt and American Foreign Policy*, New York, Oxford University Press, 1989, p. 481; John Luckacs, *The Hitler of History*, New York, Knopf, 1997, p. 155.

The policy histories that follow are organized to evaluate the proposition that the wartime president consistently pursued comprehensive national goals and partisan electoral goals in these ways. In this case, the New Deal coalition's bipolar mix of white segregationist and interracial reform constituencies threatened to disrupt both the internal political and external security goals of the Democratic Party and the central state, respectively. Statesmen in the self-righting and stealthy wartime American state offset the instability it caused by inventing new methods with which to monitor, regulate, buy off, and repress these groups. The Roosevelt White House ultimately gained control over the nascent black insurgency, to the benefit of both the nation's war project and the president's prospects for reelection.

Overview

This exploration of the impact of war mobilization on social conflict and state formation is organized as a series of focused comparisons of spheres of manpower management. The two years prior to the American declaration of war serve as a policy baseline that framed subsequent debates. Partisan imperatives clearly shaped the founding of war manpower policy (see Chapter 2), for black Americans' disillusionment with New Deal practices in the context of the war scare caused the reform of race adjustment policies in industry and the army during the presidential campaign of 1940. Notwithstanding the rising disorder involving soldiers, the Army's first race adjustment mechanism – a reversion to complaint-fielding techniques of the past – also was born as a campaign gesture. Reflecting a growing sense of illegitimacy surrounding the efforts of the so-called Black Cabinet, the African American appointee charged with opening defense employment to minorities, Robert Weaver, proved unable to effect change rapidly enough for more militant race leaders and their followers. A. Philip Randolph's planned march on the capital thus explicitly offered an alternative route to power. The introduction of social order concerns (see Chapter 3) includes an overview of changing patterns of conflict between soldiers and police that followed from the induction of large numbers of black recruits. It was Randolph's good fortune that capital city police appeared to be ineffectual at the time of his march threat, in part due to defense-related in-migration. Thus the analysis emphasizes the role of the social order imperative in both Roosevelt's response to the march as well as the orientation of the White House toward the Army and the early FEPC. This interest of statesmen, it is argued, helped set the stage for an extended struggle over the agency's procedures and power.

A subsequent analysis of the Committee ascribes its reorganization as well as its complaint casework to the ebb and flow of both party and central state goals (see Chapter 4). The black wartime migration that began in late 1942 was peculiar in beginning later that the white migration, and in concentrating African American workers in certain cities, war sectors, and firms to a greater degree than European Americans. This spatial concentration of black factory labor was well served by the warmakers' pragmatic, discretionary, and decentralized policies. An analysis of FEPC complaints indicates that central state presence influenced both rates of complaints and rates of adjustments; enforcement efforts were generally more prompt in war-vital war sectors and cities.

Two subsequent chapters address changing patterns of friction in army camps, and the executive's response to them, through the analysis of racial confrontations involving American soldiers (see Chapter 5). These events occurred in the South at rates that corresponded to the concentration of black troop training facilities there. Soldiers often resisted police enforcing segregation at frontiers of black-white contact, such as buses and post exchanges. In part due to the Army's prior capacity for exacting violence, and in part due to the political predominance of white segregationists in the region, race policy in this sphere was initially repressive. As the quality of confrontations changed over time, War Department officials, including Black Cabinet members, reexamined the effects of segregation on military efficiency and party success. Significant innovation resulted, including the development of programs of recreation, indoctrination, policing, surveillance, and a modest relaxation of segregation. A close study of a representative case of a racially motivated incident at Camp Stewart, Georgia, draws out these patterns of cause and effect in greater detail (see Chapter 6).

The policy record in the third manpower sphere, agriculture, resulted from the privileged position of southern whites in the Democratic party. The mobilization drew substantial numbers of African American workers out of this sector, in turn greatly improving the market leverage of those that remained (see Chapter 7). Because of the complaints of white landowners, the central state ceded authority over this sphere to local authorities. At the same time, due to the ability of the southern black leadership to accommodate itself to southern whites, the White House considered the possibility of promoting this black leadership – as an alternative to "northern militants" – by solidifying its position among its clientele through an expanded Agricultural Extension Service (AES) program. The analysis turns to consider the work of White House officials charged with tracking and analyzing patterns of unrest and consolidating the administration's racial monitoring capacity. Finally, attention returns to the politics and policies generated by the 1944 presidential election, which further shifted the state's orientation from reaction to prevention based on intelligence-gathering and moderate amelioration (see Chapter 7).

The sectionally organized mobilization opened new opportunities for African Americans and improved their organizations' leverage over authorities. But the White House believed that political necessity and efficiency concerns limited the possible responses of an otherwise strengthened state. For both of these reasons, statesmen sought temporary and decentralized administrative forms to defuse the race crisis – thereby enabling the war effort and insulating the executive from potentially debilitating intraparty conflict. The central state policies that resulted were more complex and specialized, but the new techniques and capacity served to maintain rather than to undermine segregation. While the Roosevelt regime invented policies of race management that appear "progressive" on the surface, overarching imperatives associated with the full mobilization of industrial production, as well as political considerations that underpinned the Roosevelt coalition, clearly outweighed goals of inter-racial reform. A summary of this argument and a consideration of the implications and effects of these policies comprise a concluding chapter.

2

The Executive and Political Imperatives: Presidential Campaigns and Race Management Policies on the Eve of War

If you could have a Northern ship and a Southern ship it would be different. But you can't *do* that.

FDR, September 27, 1940.[1]

In ways that anticipated wartime patterns, the race policy struggle of the preparedness period veered from electoral to social order concerns. Thus, the general direction of subsequent reforms in employment and the Army were first charted in the presidential campaign of 1940, which seemed more promising to black Americans than those of the recent past. Intensifying a process already underway, both parties courted them with an unprecedented openness and aggressiveness outside the South. In addition, threats to American isolationism had begun to place political competition in the context of rearmament, economic expansion, and the gradual centralization of power in the executive as commander-in-chief. As the parties' bids for votes escalated, the Roosevelt administration, in a classic use of the Black Cabinet, promoted and appointed several African American officials to key advisory roles in industrial employment and the armed forces.

While these campaign gestures of 1940 set the stage for subsequent policy struggles, the president and his strategists were unaware that many African Americans viewed such appointments as a retrograde method for co-opting elites and for drawing masses into the governing coalition. The White House and the party, on the other hand, found the work of New Deal – and World War I – race appointees satisfactory. In similar ways and for similar reasons, these early manpower initiatives in the Army and in factories were unsuccessful, and launched two parallel

---

1. R. J. C. Butow, "The FDR Tapes: Secret Recordings Made in the Oval Office of the President in the Autumn of 1940," *American Heritage*, vol. 33, no. 2, February/March, 1982, p. 24, emphasis in original.

internal conflicts over race policy. The chapter ends with an examination of an important precondition to the wide appeal of Randolph's idea: the militants' impatience and frustration with this Black Cabinet system of race advisement and adjustment.

For the period covered by this study, policy was essentially the result of statesmen's attempts to retain public office and maximize the manpower and economic product of an uneasy collaboration with race organizations and individuals pursuing new rights and privileges. In the aftermath of the 1940 elections, new Army and employment policies favored, as one would expect, those groups representing predominant Democratic party racial interests in the South and the North, respectively. White oligarchs of the southern states had already staked out their role as the stern hosts to segregated Army training facilities. In fact, the rapid politicization of military affairs stemmed from the widely held belief that southern whites actually dominated the administration of the nation's armed forces, a half-truth reinforced by the location of the majority of training facilities and camps in the South.

Employment policies favored, if mainly in their potential, blacks in Northern cities. By the late thirties, race advancement organizations' complaints regarding employment discrimination were met with three types of sympathetic responses: proportionality, individual complaint adjustment, and a community utilization approach. Faced with new demands for a fair share of the jobs created by the defense expansion, FDR reverted to past form by assigning Robert Weaver to the Office of Production Management. In addition, organizations like the NAACP and the Urban League had by the summer of 1941 developed a robust but largely ineffective private system to combat racist employment policies. This chapter describes three aspects of the race management system that were activated by the election of 1940: the Black Cabinet system of party-building and grievance adjustment; the efforts of these political appointees to open the defense economy to black participation through three overlapping types of employment strategies; and the gradual breaking-down of the Black Cabinet system in the face of more militant claims for more tangible reforms.

The Black Cabinet, Impending War, and the Election of 1940

The New Deal Democratic Party coalition included two principal partners. One, the southern white plantation elite, consistently resisted race reform, and the second, northern industrial and manufacturing workers, was ambivalent about the prospect of interracial equality. In addition to these large groups, whose representatives in effect wielded veto power over policy proposals challenging their prerogatives, the coalition also included poorer farmers and smaller, overlapping urban groups sympathetic to egalitarian reforms: ethnic minorities, many of whom were second-generation Americans; religious minorities, especially Jews and Catholics; and finally, the northern urban poor. Northern blacks, drawn to the cities by the Great War mobilization, industrialization, and reformist rhetoric and relief programs, joined this coalition in increasing numbers in the thirties. While all these groups supported certain forms of central state intervention, the stability of the New Deal compact rested largely on the mutual accommodation of the two principal regionally based partners and their representatives in national institutions.[2]

During Roosevelt's first two terms, black federal appointees, or the Black Cabinet, attempted to incorporate African American elites and voters into the coalition in several ways: by providing information on and analysis of the problems of black Americans; by combating discrimination in the administration of government assistance; by fielding complaints from black constituents; by increasing the number of black federal employees; and by serving as public policy spokesmen for the administration. Despite their qualifications – FDR's advisers were described as a "new type" of professional, rather than political, appointee – most of the Cabinet members held strictly advisory positions. Influencing policy depended on the openness of their supervisors, the relative centralization of their agency's policy making and implementation, and the amount of community pressure that the Cabinet member managed to bring to bear on the department. Toward that latter end, black officials often leaked insider information to allies in the press, then pointed to the concern that this news engendered to demand additional concessions from their white employers.[3] One student of the Cabinet claimed that the "ideal" black leader was one who could "appear to Negroes as absolutely uncompromising and to whites as reasonable."[4]

---

2. In addition to employing conflict-diffusing devices such as seniority norms, the committee system, and grants of authority to the executive branch bureaucracy, New Dealers invented a "cooperative federalism" that allowed "national policies to vary widely in response to differences in regional politics." Local state authorities formulated policy, while the federal government funded and administered the system through discretionary executive agencies. New Deal agencies dealing with manpower, such as the National Youth Administration, fit this model well. Richard Bensel, *Sectionalism and American Political Development, 1880–1980*, Madison, University of Wisconsin Press, 1984, pp. 149, 403.
3. Nancy J. Weiss, *Farewell to the Party of Lincoln: Black Politics in the Age of FDR*, Princeton, Princeton University Press, 1983, pp. 139, 148–9.
4. John B. Kirby, *Black Americans in the Roosevelt Era: Liberalism and Race*, Knoxville,

The cabineteer at the Federal Emergency Relief Administration (FERA) operated what he termed an "adjustment bureau" that responded to complainants with advice, policy clarifications, or personal intervention.[5] The National Youth Administration (NYA) and the Interior Department also had separate black departments with their own small staffs. At the NYA, Mary McLeod Bethune tried to guarantee the equal – albeit separate – participation of blacks in youth training programs and in the administration of the agency. She presided over a staff of seven in the Division of Negro Affairs, and her assistants were expected to help implement and report on the director's program, and serve as liaisons between the division and state and local NYA bureaus. Bethune's own goals for the division included building a "fact-finding and public relations agency" that would create a national Negro NYA advisory committee composed of blacks, compile and distribute information on black organizations, and maintain positive relations with local NYA officers. The division's role was "the adaptation of the program to the needs of Negro people and the interpreting of the program to them."[6] The Black Cabinet was the primary means by which the Roosevelt administration recruited and incorporated northern black leaders and voters into the New Deal coalition.

Tangible results were expected of this arrangement, as over time, the symbolic value inherent to the appointments dissipated. In 1939 Bethune wrote to NYA Director Aubrey Williams that it was "very necessary that something very outstanding be done for my people to assure them of the gains" of the New Deal. She suggested appointing blacks to judgeships, to various New Deal agencies, and as a "special assistant" to the Secretary of War. The administration's opponents in the upcoming election, she pointed out, "see clearly the inadequacies in the numerous federal departments."[7] Faithful New Dealers and, more important, African Americans themselves, noted the exclusion of blacks from jobs in federal agencies supervised by such heralded reformers as the "liberal Dr. Archibald MacLeish" at the Library of Congress and Henry Wallace

University of Tennessee Press, 1980, pp. 106–10; Motz, "Black Cabinet," p. 74, quoted in Kirby, p. 110.

5. Weiss, *Farewell to the Party of Lincoln*, pp. 149–50; David Brinkley, *Washington Goes to War*, New York, Alfred A. Knopf, 1988, p. 79.

6 B. Joyce Ross, "Mary McLeod Bethune and the National Youth Administration: A Case Study of Power Relationships in the Black Cabinet of Franklin D. Roosevelt," in *Black Leaders of the Twentieth Century*, John Hope Franklin and August Meier, eds., Urbana, University of Illinois Press, 1982, pp. 198, 208, 209; "Henry A. Hunt and Black Agricultural Leadership in the New South," *Journal of Negro History*, p. 475.

7. Letter, Mary McLeod Bethune to Aubrey Williams, October 17, 1941, correspondence – B, papers of Robert C. Weaver, Schomberg Center for Research in Black Culture, New York Public Library.

at the Agriculture Department.[8] The race press reported the rejection of black workers after they had received letters of certification from the Social Security Administration and the Federal Housing Authority, among others.[9] Permanent as opposed to emergency agencies offered the fewest opportunities; the Departments of Agriculture, War, and Navy had the worst reputations.[10] America's armed forces were widely believed to be dominated by southern officials and ideology, and Roy Wilkins called the War Department the "toughest" in government.[11] In May 1940, the Committee on Negro Americans in the Defense Industries published a letter sent to the co-chairmen of the National Defense Board, demanding equal defense training and employment opportunities for blacks. Two months later, at the outset of the presidential campaign season of 1940, the renamed National Defense Advisory Commission appointed Robert C. Weaver to direct the Labor Division's efforts to bring blacks into the mobilization.

In the spring of 1940 the Pittsburgh *Courier* sponsored the creation of the Committee on National Defense to push for an increase in black personnel in all branches of the armed services.[12] Even after the Selective Service Act was amended in August to prohibit racial discrimination in the selection of trainees, the National Negro Congress opposed passage of the legislation because it would "increase the influence of the anti-Negro Army forces in determining the course of our government."[13] The *Courier* urged readers to vote for the Republican Wendell Willkie, since those who did otherwise would "put the South in the saddle. The South runs our Congress, our Army and our Navy, and there is not very much left of our country after that."[14] The possibility of American involvement

8. Kansas City *Call*, "Jobs Scarce at Library of Congress," July 26, 1940; Baltimore *Afro-American*, "Wallace is Lily-White No. 1 in U.S.," August 24, 1940.

9. At this stage, complaints in these cases were filed with the local NAACP in the hope that they would be publicized, and the organization obliged by reporting them to newspapers. "Procedure Shows Race Applicants Given Run-Around," Pittsburgh *Courier*, August 2, 1941.

10. Weiss, *Farewell to the Party of Lincoln*, p. 115.

11. Roy Wilkins, "Watchtower," *Amsterdam News*, November 2, 1940.

12. Neil A. Wynn, *The Afro-American and the Second World War*, New York, Holmes & Meier Publishers, 1975, p. 22; on the role of the black press in this period, see Lee Finkle, *Forum for Protest: The Black Press during World War II*, Rutherford, NJ, Fairleigh Dickinson University Press, 1975; Patrick S. Washburn, *A Question of Sedition: The Federal Government's Investigation of the Black Press During World War II*, New York, Oxford University Press, 1986.

13. "Cites Danger to Negro if Army is Given Rule," Washington *Tribune*, August 24, 1940; Harvard Sitkoff, *A New Deal for Blacks: The Emergence of Civil Rights as a National Issue*, New York, Oxford University Press, 1978, pp. 392–3.

14. In the twenties, the *Courier* and its publisher, Robert Vann, gained prominence and circulation by reporting on issues of wide appeal; beginning in 1938, the paper detailed

in the ongoing war, and the ascendance of the Army in the nation's civic life, had placed War Department troop policies at the center of the campaign for black votes in 1940. At the time, three basic beliefs framed the Army's utilization of nonwhites. First, blacks should be segregated into separate units because the system had proven satisfactory, because the issue involved social questions that the Army could not address alone, and because severe social disruption would result from integration. Second, black soldiers were not suited to modern warfare because of racial characteristics, primarily inferior intelligence. Finally, black officers should not be utilized, because experience had proven a lack of leadership character and because of the inherent distrust of blacks for black direction. These assumptions combined to limit the participation of black soldiers to separate, largely service-oriented units led by white officers.[15]

The Army entered the war with a four-year-old mobilization policy that set the share of nonwhite soldiers at 9 to 10 percent, "approximately in proportion to total manpower available," and directed that the ratio of black combat troops to service troops match that of whites. Neither policy survived in practice. The 1940 Protective Mobilization Plan produced an Army that was 5.8 percent black, with disproportionate assignment of nonwhites to service units such as the Quartermaster Corps.[16] Northern Democrats attempted to amend the Defense Act and the Selective Service and Training Act in 1940 to prohibit segregation and discrimination in the selection and assignment of trainees, but both bills passed with fairness clauses so mild that War Department practices were not significantly altered.[17] At the end of 1941, while every fourth man in the Corps of Engineers was black, the proportion was less than one in fifty in the Air Corps, Medical Department, and Signal Corps. In addition, the Army passed over black selectees in filling color quotas. Although the Selective Service Act of 1942 again required the War Department to absorb blacks in proportion to their population in the country, delayed construction of segregated facilities and a shortage of training cadres precluded this.[18] Since the Army was segregated, poorly

the exclusion of African Americans from the Army. "Southern Americanism," Pittsburgh *Courier*, November 23, 1940; Washburn, *A Question of Sedition*, p. 34.

15. Ulysses Lee, *The Employment of Negro Troops*, U.S. Army in World War II, Special Studies, Office of the Chief of Military History, U.S. Army, Washington, D.C., 1966, pp. 39–50.

16. Ibid., p. 42.

17. "Cites Danger to Negro if Army is Given Rule," Washington *Tribune*, August 24, 1940; Sitkoff, *A New Deal for Blacks*, pp. 392–3; Mershon and Schlossman, *Foxholes and Color Lines*, p. 44.

18. Some congressmen from Louisiana and South Carolina called for the construction of additional camps and hospitals for black draftees, and the rapid replacement of those rejected. Memorandum, Jonathan Daniels to FDR, June 26, 1943, OF 4245, OPM,

educated black soldiers could not be widely scattered among other recruits, as was the practice with whites. Disqualifying most of these
selectees contributed to a race maldistribution problem that continued
in numerous forms for the duration of the war.[19]

At their 1940 convention, Republicans adopted a strong civil rights
plank that pledged support for a federal antilynching law, guaranteed
voting rights, and promised to end discrimination in the armed forces
and in federal employment. To spread the word, the head of the Negro
Division of the GOP campaign outlined an appeal to black voters acknowledging their "peculiar problems," such as unemployment, discrimination, and civil rights. He promised to use the majority of its funds for
door-to-door neighborhood canvassing rather than for a speaking campaign and to feature black speakers on party-sponsored radio programs
and sound trucks.[20] The two largest black newspapers, the Pittsburgh
Courier and the Baltimore *Afro-American*, endorsed Willkie.[21] Black
newspaper readers could not help being aware of their potential power.
A fall 1940 Gallup survey showed that the election would most likely be
decided in closely contested states like New York, Pennsylvania, Illinois,
Ohio, and New Jersey. The tighter the race, analysts agreed, the more
likely that the black vote would be the decisive factor.[22]

As the election neared, White House officials showed little interest in
racial issues and hesitated to break from traditional approaches to segregating the races in the Army. On September 27, 1940, FDR met with
Secretary of the Navy Frank Knox and Assistant Secretary of the Army
Robert Patterson in order to discuss the issue with the NAACP's Walter
White, the Sleeping Car Porters Union's A. Philip Randolph, and Bethune and T. Arnold Hill of the NYA.[23] The black leaders presented a
memorandum that called for the designation of Air Corps training facilities for blacks, the use of black reserve officers for active service, and,
most important, the immediate integration of the Army. While this program was not remotely possible, Roosevelt promised that blacks would

Committee on Fair Employment Practices, Philadelphia, FDRL; Clarence S. Johnson,
To Stem This Tide: A Survey of Racial Tension in the Unites States, Boston, The
Pilgrim Press, 1943, p. 83.

19. Lee, *The Employment of Negro Troops*, pp. 111–12, 125.
20. Sidney R. Redmond, head of the St. Louis NAACP, was the GOP official. "Republicans Plan Special Campaign to Win Negro Vote," Memphis *Times*, September 23,
1940.
21. Sitkoff, A *New Deal for Blacks*, pp. 303–4.
22. "Republicans Plan Special Campaign to Win Negro Vote," Memphis *Times*, September 23, 1940; "Negroes Hold Deciding Vote," New York *Age*, October 12, 1940.
23. Wynn, *The Afro-American and the Second World War*, p. 23; "Memorandum as
suggested basis of conference, White House, September 27, 1940," Correspondence –
W, Weaver papers.

be utilized proportionally in the combat services, in contrast to War Department practice during "the World War." FDR argued that this was "*something*," since white and black units might then find themselves deployed in adjacent battlefield areas. "The thing is," he said,

> we've got to work into this. Now, suppose you have a Negro regiment . . . *here*, and right over here on my right in line, would be a white regiment . . . Now what happens after a while, in case of war? Those people get shifted from one to the other. The thing gets sort of backed into . . . gradually working in the field together, you may back into it . . . [24]

Before concluding the conference by promising to consult with other government officials and then contact the black leaders, the president agreed to the suggestion that the War and Navy Departments each appoint someone to administer matters related to black manpower.[25] Secretary of War Henry Stimson later refused to concede anything of substance to the petitioners, whom he privately accused of the "deliberate use of the war emergency to stir unrest and force new policies" upon the nation.[26] The next day, however, an editorial in the Pittsburgh *Courier* noted the pessimism that engulfed black Americans as they prepared for a level of discrimination in the Army that would, they believed, at least equal historical patterns. The newspaper called for the immediate appointment of a black Assistant Secretary of War to serve as a "clearinghouse," as had been the case during the last war. His office could respond to complaints

> registered by Negro soldiers and civilian groups, and his voice in councils of government would do much to improve the administration of the Army where Negroes are concerned, as did that of Dr. Emmett J. Scott during the last war to make the world safe for democracy.[27]

24. These comments were recorded on a hidden "continuous film recording machine" operating at Roosevelt's request between August and November, 1940. R. J. C. Butow, "The FDR Tapes: Secret Recordings Made in the Oval Office of the President in the Autumn of 1940," *American Heritage*, vol. 33, no. 2, February/March, 1982, p. 24; ellipses and italics in published transcript.

25. "Conference at the White House, September 27, 1940," enclosed in letter, Walter White to Robert Weaver, October 7, 1940, Correspondence – W, Weaver papers.

26. Elsewhere, Stimson noted the "tremendous drive" by blacks to exploit the final days of the campaign so as to force the military to implement reforms "not in the interest of sound national defense." Sitkoff, *A New Deal for Blacks*, pp. 306–7; Phillip McGuire, *He, Too, Spoke for Democracy: Judge Hastie, World War II, and the Black Soldier*, Westport, CT, Greenwood Press, 1988, pp. 9–10.

27. Scott, an assistant to Booker T. Washington at the Tuskegee Institute, served as special assistant to the secretary of war during the Great War. In 1940, he joined the staff of the Republican National Committee to direct publicity in the black press. "Wanted: A Negro Assistant Secretary of War," Pittsburgh *Courier*, September 28, 1940; Weiss, *Farewell to the Party of Lincoln*, pp. 268–9.

The paper called on black citizens to flood the capital with letters calling for another such appointment, noting that the presidential campaign provided an unusual opportunity to lobby for the position.[28]

On October 9, the White House released a statement on racial policy drafted following the September meeting; it ostensibly aimed to inform nonwhites of various opportunities to serve, but it did so in misleading ways. The claim that "negroes are being given aviation training" in fact referred to privately run courses. The statement also restricted black chaplains and physicians to separate units and excluded blacks from officer rank in the regular Army. The most glaring misjudgement was a plain announcement that the War Department would retain its Jim Crow policy and not "intermingle" the races in one regiment.[29] The statement did not produce the desired effect. Roy Wilkins of the NAACP reported that African Americans resented the "stupid bulletin on Army-Navy jim crow."[30] To make matters worse, with the election only weeks away, presidential press secretary Steven Early assaulted a black policeman in New York City while breaking through a security cordon to catch the presidential train. FDR's staff scrambled to correct the damage. Through complicated machinations, a Democratic party official arranged for the police department to issue a prearranged statement in the name of the black officer.[31] NAACP chief Walter White's telephone "rang night and day" with calls from the President's friends asking what else could be done to repair the breach. Pressed for more detailed information by black leaders, the Army released a new list of approved or planned black units.[32]

On October 10, FDR met with Knox to survey the damage. After first

28. "Wanted: A Negro Assistant Secretary of War," Pittsburgh *Courier*, September 28, 1940.
29. C. B. Allen, Charleston, *News & Observer*, October 30, 1940. In addition, the press release was so badly worded that it implied that the segregation policy actually resulted from the White House conference with black leaders. The text of the release is reproduced in Lee, *The Employment of Negro Troops*, pp. 76–7.
30. Roy Wilkins, "Watchtower," *Amsterdam News*, November 2, 1940; McGuire, *He, Too, Spoke for Democracy*, pp. 8–9.
31. The official, Oscar Ewing, thought the handling of the incident helped account for Roosevelt's success in black districts in the 1940 election. It was due to such symbolic gestures that "inarticulate" black Harlemites "knew deep in their heart that Roosevelt was pitching on their team." Oscar Ewing, Oral History Interview, pp. 120–7, Harry S. Truman Library [hereafter HSTL], Independence, MO. On the 16th, the War Department declared that black aviation units would be formed in the Army Air Corps. On parallel policy developments in the Air Corps, Navy, and Marines throughout the war period, see Sherie Mershon and Steven Schlossman, *Foxholes and Color Lines: Desegregating the U.S. Armed Forces*, Baltimore, Johns Hopkins University Press, 1998.
32. Roy Wilkins, "Watchtower," *Amsterdam News*, November 2, 1940; Sitkoff, *A New Deal for Blacks*, p. 308.

proposing that the Navy consider placing black bands on white ships, Roosevelt suggested that the Army and Navy each employ a black spokesman, recalling his tenure as an Assistant Secretary of the Navy during the Great War:

> In the Navy Department in the old days I had a boy who volunteered by the name of *Pryor*. . . . He used to be my colored messenger . . . Well, Pryor, *now*, is one of the best fellows we've got in the office and he handles all my . . . cases from the Department of Justice. . . . He summarizes the whole thing . . . a great boy. . . . He was just a clerk in the Navy Department and I used *him*. People went to him with any kind of question. Can we do *this*? Can we do *that*? Can we get another opening *there*? And he was of very, very great service. I think you can do that in the Army and the Navy . . . get somebody colored [who will act as] the clearinghouse.[33]

Two weeks before the election, with polls showing the Republican Willkie cutting into FDR's lead, the president assigned William Hastie, dean of Howard University Law School, to the Secretary of War as his "Civilian Aide on Negro Affairs" and promoted Col. Benjamin O. Davis, Sr., the Army's ranking black officer, to brigadier general.[34] The electoral considerations that motivated these appointments attracted wide commentary. White Army officers belittled Davis's promotion as "an out-and-out political move" to gain black votes in New York and Illinois, and Stimson privately disapproved of the appointments.[35] The initiative was especially significant to African Americans, because the units that would make up the general's new 4th Cavalry Brigade had for ten years served as so-called dog-robbers for white officers, emptying garbage, shining boots, and cleaning the officers' homes.[36] The appointment

33. These comments also were recorded. The official mentioned may be Frederick D. Pryor, secretarial clerk to General Edwin Watson, FDR's military aide. R. J. C. Butow, "The FDR Tapes," p. 24; ellipses, italics, and bracketed note in published transcript.

34. Lee, *The Employment of Negro Troops*, pp. 78–9. At the same time, Campbell C. Johnson was appointed assistant to the director of Civil Service. Roosevelt also named a black assistant to the Director of Selective Service, and he wrote a letter to the black committee members clearing them of the charge of endorsing segregation. Sitkoff, *A New Deal for Blacks*, p. 309.

35. Davis was sixty-three and, according to law, would retire at the end of the following year. Generally, such promotions occurred at least four years before scheduled retirement. White officers pointed out that if he were to command a brigade in the Second Cavalry Division as planned, the policy of segregating officer command lines would be violated, as the brigade was directed by white officers. Marvin E. Fletcher, *America's First Black General: Benjamin O. Davis, Sr., 1880–1970*, Lawrence, KS, University Press of Kansas, 1989, p. 85; Allen, Charleston *News & Observer*, October 30, 1940; "Republicans Say Davis' Elevation 'Political Trick'," Pittsburgh *Courier*, November 2, 1940.

36. The term referred to soldiers performing servant duties. " 'Dog Robber' Days Over for 9th, 10th Cavalries," Kansas City *Call*, February 1941.

served its political purpose. Two days before the election, for example, Roy Wilkins used his newspaper column to proclaim the president's efforts "heroic." Black activists had openly and successfully exploited the temporary leverage generated by the upcoming election. "Of course it was hammered out under pressure," Wilkins wrote. "All concessions in government are the result of pressure."[37]

The Civilian Aide to the Secretary of War in Theory and in Practice

The appointments exemplified the complaint-driven race management system that reigned in the White House in 1940, and that dated, in its particulars, from 1917. Evidence of Roosevelt's conception of "just" mechanisms to manage black soldier grievances is found in a letter of approval FDR sent to the organizer of the Conference on the Participation of the Negro in National Defense, which convened in November 1940 at Hampton Institute, Virginia. FDR asked the college's president to permit him to study the findings of the conference.[38] "A great soldier" of the First World War, he offered,

> Major General Hugh L. Scott, said that the best way to hold the Negro's loyalty was "to see that he had no wrongs to brood over." General Scott believed in fortifying precept with example. He selected a young Negro lieutenant, promoted him to his staff with instructions to spend his time among various organizations of colored men to investigate possible sources of grievances. When this officer unearthed a complaint which he could see was unfounded, his duty was to handle it by himself; when he found what appeared to him to be a legitimate grievance his orders were to report it to General Scott, who saw to it that the wrong was immediately righted. I can assure you that in our present defense effort we shall profit by General Scott's high conception of justice.[39]

37. Roy Wilkins, "Watchtower," *Amsterdam News*, November 2, 1940; Sitkoff, *A New Deal for Blacks*, p. 309.
38. Indeed, Roosevelt had found in Hampton's white director, Malcolm MacLean, a race moderate with a liberal but realistic vision of black advancement. While the defense committee of the conference concluded that the Navy and Marine Corps were "the most undemocratic and un-American aspect of our government," MacLean's recommendations for the full utilization of blacks in the defense effort were less aggressive. He chose to emphasize the black citizen's six responsibilities, which included physical fitness and "patience for the long-term pull." In early 1942 Roosevelt would select MacLean to become the second chairman of the FEPC. Hastie and Walter White supported the appointment. "Conference Findings Section Raps U.S. Military Services," Newport *News Press*, November 27, 1940; Merl E. Reed, *Seedtime for the Civil Rights Movement: The President's Committee on Fair Employment Practice, 1941–1946*, Baton Rouge, Louisiana State University Press, 1991, pp. 48–9.
39. FDR's letter grafted this passage nearly verbatim from Scott's published memoirs; this

Secretary Stimson, another Great War veteran, likewise distinguished between three categories of black complaints: remediable, trivial, and impossible.[40] Stimson's appointment letter to Hastie reflected this orientation. While expressing the hope that the new assistant would aid in drafting and reforming the Army's black manpower policies, he charged Hastie with investigating "complaints" about the treatment of black soldiers and the department's civilian workers, and suggested that Hastie visit camps and stations to observe and report on black participation in national defense.[41] The White House certainly did not share Wilkins's view that the appointments gave African Americans "a channel through which we can fight."[42] Hastie was concerned about official expectations for, as one War Department official noted, he did not want to be "merely a repository for all Negro complaints."[43] He viewed Emmett Scott as an "adjuster" and considered declining the appointment rather than assume a similar appeasing role.[44]

The major reforms of this period – the appointments in particular – stemmed from political imperatives related to the 1940 election. A year later, the race management philosophy of War Department officials had changed very little. Hastie's office was only one of several charged with evaluating black soldier complaints; the adjutant general's office and inspector general's office likewise fielded them. The complaint-adjusting function was repeatedly cited, for example, during a War Department conference with black journalists on December 8, 1941, the day after the Japanese attack on Pearl Harbor.[45]

"soldier" was chief of staff from 1914–17. The text is on p. 619 of Hugh Lenox Scott, *Some Memories of a Soldier*, New York, The Century Company, 1928; "Roosevelt to Study Results of Hampton Defense Conference," Pittsburgh *Courier*, November 23, 1940.

40. Stimson was secretary of war under Taft (1911–13), served in the war as a colonel in a field artillery regiment, and was secretary of state under Hoover (1929–33). Henry L. Stimson and McGeorge Bundy, *On Active Service in Peace and War*, New York, Harper and Brothers, 1947, p. 463.
41. Lee, *The Employment of Negro Troops*, p. 80.
42. Roy Wilkins, "Watchtower," *Amsterdam News*, November 2, 1940.
43. Memorandum, Huntington Thom to Assistant Secretary of War, October 21, 1940, "Problems of Racial Character," papers of John Ohly, HSTL.
44. McGuire, *He, Too, Spoke for Democracy*, pp. 10–12.
45. The event resembled a 1918 War Department conference with black leaders, most of whom were editors of newspapers; the meetings were thought to have promoted the black public's dedication to the war effort. Washburn, *A Question of Sedition*, pp. 15–16; Wynn, *The Afro-American and the Second World War*, p. 23; Lee, *The Employment of Negro Troops*, pp. 142–3; "Plans for Negro Division at Fort Huachuca Revealed," Atlanta *Daily World*, December 10, 1941.

At this early stage of the mobilization, indifferent War Department officials relied on a retrograde but minimally effective race management technique dating from the Great War: the fielding of "legitimate grievances" mainly by high-profile Black Cabinet appointees. While the administration looked back to the Great War, most northern blacks looked forward to new pressure tactics and strategies, for they viewed the earlier period with bitterness, as their dedication to the nation had not been rewarded. Federal policies had indeed successfully managed their claims. A *Courier* editorial, titled "We Remember 1919," announced that the race was "no longer blindfolded" to "the injustices and hypocrisies" of the nation.[46] Among militant northern race leaders, the notion that segregation could be "righted" by the investigation of individual complaints was badly outdated. By 1941, the Black Cabinet was drawing criticism not only from the press but also from mainline civic leaders.[47]

Over the course of the war, two additional forces within the Army assailed this method of monitoring and adjusting black soldier dissatisfaction. In the camps, spontaneous violence and organized protest rendered obsolete this method of complaint adjustment. And from his position within the wartime Black Cabinet, William Hastie simply refused to limit his work to the adjuster's role, instead attacking segregation directly. An officer in the adjutant general's office noted that Hastie "makes no bones about it that 'the time for minorities to make their gains is the time of national emergency.' "[48] Recognized as an unusually militant cabineteer and a new type of uncompromising leader, Hastie consulted continually with the press and with leaders of national organizations. In addition to unrelenting calls for grand reforms such as desegregation, Hastie also pursued lesser initiatives, including pressuring the department to place recruiting advertisements in black-owned media, to increase the number of black medical personnel in the Army, and to reform the surgeon general's policy by which blood plasma was segregated by the Red Cross.[49] His eventual achievements in gaining blacks equal treatment in the armed forces appear to have resulted as much from providing policy information and strategic insight and advice to civilian leaders as from pressing for bureaucratic change from within.[50] In effect, the state had incorporated a leader of an insurgent

46. Quoted in Washburn, *A Question of Sedition*, p. 101.
47. Kirby, *Black Americans in the Roosevelt Era*.
48. Lee, *The Employment of Negro Troops*, p. 145.
49. Phillip McGuire, "Judge Hastie, World War II, and Army Racism," *Journal of Negro History*, October, 1977, pp. 353–5, 359.
50. In late 1940, for example, Hastie explained to White and Randolph that their petitions to the president would focus attention on his work. "If such inquiries are made, I will

movement into the administration of defense preparedness. The misjudgement stemmed from the retrograde response of FDR, a "veteran" of the First World War, who turned to traditional methods when challenged by an election within an unexpected defense crisis. The forward-thinking Hastie proved to be much too independent, for his primary allegiance remained with the NAACP. Subsequent chapters will consider Hastie's fate.

Robert Weaver and the Negro Employment and Training Branch

Compared to the military, reforms in the employment sphere, while still grounded in Black Cabinet techniques, favored black workers slightly more so, by seeking to alter longstanding patterns of exclusion and discrimination within a mobilization that posed unprecedented difficulties for black job applicants. War production had never before demanded such a high percentage of skilled and semiskilled workers, and the Depression had forced the elimination of most training programs; those that survived trained mostly white workers. In addition, employment would be concentrated in precisely those fields from which blacks had been traditionally barred: welding, electrical, machine, and sheet metal work. As a result, as the white unemployment rate declined sharply, from eighteen to thirteen percent between April and October 1940, the nonwhite rate remained unchanged at twenty-two percent.[51]

When the National Defense Advisory Commission (NDAC) appointed Robert C. Weaver to direct the Labor Division's efforts to bring blacks into the mobilization, few black administrators were more closely associated with or more knowledgeable about the New Deal. Weaver was the vice chair of the Federal Council of Negro Advisers – the Black Cabinet's professional association – and had served in advisory roles at the Department of the Interior and the United States Housing Authority.[52] The NDAC was replaced by the Office of Production Management

undoubtedly be asked what the situation is with reference to particular matters." McGuire, "Judge Hastie," p. 353.

51. Robert Weaver, *Negro Labor: A National Problem*, New York, Harcourt, Brace and Company, 1946, p. 19.

52. At the time, members of the council included: Emmer Martin Lancaster, Joseph Houschins of the Department of Commerce; Judge William Hastie, Truman Gibson of War; Constance E. H. Daniel, Jerome Robinson and Giles Hubert of Agriculture; William H. Houston, Louis Mehlinger, Louis Lautier of Justice; Howard D. Woodson of Treasury; Dr. William J. Thompkins, recorder of deeds; Ralph E. Mizells, post office; Cornelius King, Farm Credit Administration; Major Campbell C. Johnson, Selective

in 1941, and its co-director, Sidney Hillman, subsequently created branches of Negro Employment and Training, under Weaver, and Minority Groups – intended to address concerns related to racial minority groups other than blacks – to be lead by liberal southerner Will Alexander. Working with other units of OPM, these branches were charged with removing barriers to minority worker participation in national defense training and employment. Although the NDAC in 1940 instructed defense contractors not to discriminate against workers because of age, sex, race, or color, and Hillman had again requested the full utilization of all workers in April, his instructions were widely ignored by both employers and federal manpower officials.[53] Between January and March 1941, for example, the U.S. Employment Service (USES) placed thirteen blacks – out of a total of 8,769 workers – in selected essential occupations in aircraft production. Blacks accounted for 5 of the 1,066 placements in electrical equipment manufacturing; 245 out of 35,000 workers in foundry, forging, machine shop, and metal processing work. In shipbuilding, which accounted for a large percentage of black skilled employment in the First World War, nonwhites accounted for 1.7 percent of the 1,500 essential placements, and for less than five percent of the 30,000 placements in iron and steel. Overall, from October 1940, to March 1941, the USES placed over 150,000 men in twenty defense sectors; four percent were black. In a September 1941, Bureau of Employment Security survey, employers indicated that over half of the openings expected in selected war industries over the next six months would explicitly bar black applicants.[54]

Weaver's Negro Employment and Training Branch (NETB) battled

Service; Robert C. Weaver, Frances H. Williams, Robert R. Taylor, Theodore R. Poston, Defense; William Trent, Public Works; Frank S. Horne, Charles Johnson, Henry Lee Moon, Edward Lovett, Charles S. Duke, Housing Authority; Alfred E. Smith, Dutton R. Ferguson, WPA; Lawrence Oxley, Dr. Charles E. Franklin, Ira DeReid, Roy Ellis, Social Security Board; Dr. Ambrose Caliver, Department of Education; Joseph H. B. Evans, T. Arnold Hill, Pauline Redmond, Ora B. Stokes, Nel Hunter, and Feginald Johnson, Mary Bethune, NYA; Benita Lewis, Children's Bureau; and Edgar G. Brown, CCC. "Members of Federal Council of Negro Government Advisers Listed," Atlanta *Daily World*, May 4, 1941.

53. This was also the heyday of the Vocational Educational National Defense Training Program (VEND) administered by the U.S. Office of Education. In 1940, Congress placed a nondiscrimination clause in defense training legislation, and the Commissioner of Education instructed state and local boards of education to facilitate the training of blacks, but discrimination riddled this program as well. Louis Kesselman, *The Social Politics of FEPC: A Study in Reform Pressure Movements*, Chapel Hill, University of North Carolina Press, 1948, p. 10; "Minorities in Defense," October 15, 1941, printed materials, 1923–53, Weaver papers.

54. Weaver, *Negro Labor*, pp. 20, 27.

employment discrimination "on a plant- or industry-wide basis," engaging in extended negotiations with firms and their personnel managers over hiring policies and practices.[55] More broadly, he pitched his appeals to city elites' long-term interests: The failure to utilize locally available, unemployed black labor would draw many thousands of white migrants to areas unable to bear them and their families permanently, creating an array of costly social problems such as acute housing shortages and vice. Since most wartime jobs were unlikely to survive the armistice and the subsequent defense economy contraction, he argued, these cities would find their populations permanently bloated by the unemployed, requiring costly expenditures on police, education, and health programs. At the same time, blacks not absorbed by defense industries would continue to constitute a chronic relief problem. Thus, he argued, southern communities would benefit materially from the decision to substitute training for migration. Weaver believed it imperative to make this argument "a part of community thinking" so that southern white attitudes toward minority employment "depart from the realm of sentiment into the consideration of the economic and social factors involved."[56] This "community utilization" strategy carried little of the moral force of later FEPC techniques pursuing the principle of fairness through the adjustment of individual complaints.

When he turned from whole cities to sectors, Weaver focused much of his work on defense construction projects, both because blacks had long served as skilled workers in this sector and because it already provided southern blacks with the most opportunities in the preparedness period.[57] As early as December 1940, Weaver announced modest gains in worker placements in the construction industry, and by March 1941, more than 2,500 blacks were employed on Army construction projects in the South.[58] Several factors in addition to the policies of the NDAC

55. With a staff of fifteen in Washington and ten in the regions, Weaver was to develop programs, supervise staff, "and interpret results to the Negro and general public." Weaver also "devised means of getting consideration of the problems of minority groups' employment in the consciousness and, ultimately, in the operations" of coordinating and contracting agencies. Reed, *Seedtime*, p. 24; letter, Robert C. Weaver to Sara Southall, May 17, 1948, Correspondence – S, Weaver papers.
56. Letter, Robert C. Weaver to Will W. Alexander, January 15, 1941, correspondence – A; for a similar view from the field, see teletype message, Cy Record to Robert C. Weaver, September 16, 1942, Correspondence – Ro, Weaver papers.
57. Weaver, *Negro Labor*, p. 4.
58. "40 Carpenters at Camp Meade," Atlanta *Daily World*, December 13, 1940; "See Racial Employment Policies Changing by Non-Discrimination Policy Adopted by Labor Unions," New York *Age*, December 21, 1940; "Weaver Reveals Hiring of Negro Union Workers," Washington *Tribune*, December 14, 1940; Weaver, *Negro Labor*, pp. 28–30.

help account for the relatively heavy use of black labor on these cantonment construction projects. In the first place, there was a relatively deep supply of black carpenters with skills suited to the building of wooden tent cabins and barracks. Some observers ascribed this to the longstanding emphasis on trade and industrial training in the South.[59] But many southern black carpenters, such as those working on Fort Jackson, South Carolina, had first participated in federally sponsored projects and in union activity during the construction of public housing projects during the Depression. In Louisville, and at Camp Gordon, in Chamblee, Georgia, the affiliation of black carpenters with the local AFL began during the construction of public housing during the thirties, and their work in construction led in turn to an increase in black union participation.[60] As early as 1934, while working for the Housing Division of the Public Works Administration (PWA), Weaver attempted to ensure the equitable employment of black labor through the incorporation of nondiscriminatory clauses in construction contracts. Later, when Weaver moved to the U.S. Housing Authority, he administered a system that required local authorities to insert in all construction contracts a nondiscriminatory employment provision; housing units were subsequently occupied on a quota system as well. Thus, the sector was distinguished by a brief but important precedent of nondiscrimination in federally sponsored construction. In 1941, the Federal Works administrator directed the payment of a set proportion of the value of monthly defense housing construction payrolls to black workers. The proportion was to be drawn from the most recent occupational census showing a community's number of black and white construction workers; the hiring of this proportion of nonwhite workers would thereafter be considered evidence of nondiscrimination.[61] This proportional workforce strategy was, however, a viable option only in a very small number of sectors.

Weaver and the mobilization agencies occasionally joined forces with the National Urban League or the NAACP to focus attention on

---

59. "N. C. Boom Town Called Uncle Sam's Powder Keg," Baltimore *African-American*, February 8, 1941.
60. Clarence R. Johnson, "Negro Labor in Public Housing," *The Crisis*, February 1941, p. 44; Weaver, *Negro Labor*, pp. 28–30.
61. Again, this order may be traced to the work of Weaver in the PWA and to the policies of the U.S. Housing Authority in the late 1930s. In the twenty-three months ending in October 1940, 13.5 percent of all wages paid to labor in the construction of USHA-aided projects went to blacks. Paul D. Moreno, *From Direct Action to Affirmative Action: Fair Employment Law and Policy in America, 1933–1972*, Baton Rouge, Louisiana State University Press, 1997, p. 58; "Negroes Must Receive Share," New York *Amsterdam News*, March 29, 1941; Johnson, "Negro Labor in Public Housing," p. 61.

discrimination in the industry. In early 1941, the Atlanta Urban League complained that Camp Gordon was not hiring qualified black carpenters. The next day the chapter's executive secretary and an assistant joined a NDAC consultant in a visit to the camp, where officials claimed that local white unions had not referred any black workers and agreed to hire forty black carpenters and fifteen painters.[62] Similarly, the executive secretary of the Kansas City Urban League announced in August that Weaver's NETB had succeeded in removing local trade union bans on black membership. Several hundred black construction workers were thereafter employed on defense projects, including black carpenters and hod carriers employed in the construction of the North American Aviation factory and the Lake City Ammunition plant.[63] But Weaver's emphasis on defense construction, due to the regional concentration of Army training facilities, focused much of his work on the South. Eleven out of the thirteen construction projects Weaver listed in 1941 as employing black workers were located in census South states.[64]

In addition to the community utilization and census quota systems, fielding and adjusting such collective and individual complaints remained a principal duty of the Black Cabinet, and it was the primary means for adjusting grievances in the Army as well. Building upon years of similar petitioning, organizations such as the NAACP and the Urban League had invented and refined, through countless appeals, a local, informal complaint procedure well before the establishment of the FEPC.[65] The central state was growing increasingly receptive to such

62. "Atlanta Urban League Gets Defense Jobs for Negroes at Camp Gordon," Oklahoma City *Black Dispatch*, March 8, 1941.

63. For their part, Urban League officials researched the local black labor pool, interviewed employers, and held conferences of city officials and employers, among other tactics. "Lower Defense Jobs Bars in Kansas City, Missouri, Area; Negroes Get Jobs," Oklahoma City *Black Dispatch*, August 9, 1941; Thomas A. Webster, "Employers, Unions, and Negro Workers," *Opportunity*, October 1941, pp. 295–7.

64. They were Forts Jackson and Croft, South Carolina; Camp Robinson, Arkansas; Forts Wheeler, Gordon, and Benning, Georgia; Fort Forest, Tennessee; Fort Knox, Kentucky; Fort Blanding, Florida; Fort Bragg, North Carolina; U.S. Army Hospital and U.S. Naval Base Airport, Louisiana; Fort Riley, Kansas; Fort Monroe; Virginia. Weaver also trumpeted gains made in northern industrial cities. In the fall of 1941, he listed sixteen defense industry plants employing blacks, of which eleven were located in New York, New Jersey, and Ohio. Weaver, *Negro Labor*, pp. 28–31; "Dr. Robert Weaver of OPM Lists Firms Which are Opening Their Doors," Kansas City *Call*, October 17, 1941.

65. If an Urban League official was remotely accurate in claiming that the organization and its affiliates had, by around this time, placed 150,000 black workers into previously segregated plants, their efforts would have dwarfed those of the FEPC, whose records document the direct adjustment of less than five thousand cases. Jesse Thomas

appeals. For example, the Durham NAACP complained in January 1940 to the head of the Fair Labor Standards Administration, that southern textile owners were firing black workers and replacing them with whites, rather than pay the former the minimum of 32.5 cents per hour as required by the law.[66] When Weaver helped to secure work for forty black union carpenters at Camp Meade, Maryland, it was in response to a complaint filed with Commissioner Hillman by a black AFL official – who also happened to be the executive secretary of the Baltimore Urban League.[67] A full year before the creation of the FEPC, some federal agencies had created procedures for processing such complaints. When, in June 1940, a black Census Bureau employee claimed that he had been denied promotion because of his race, a United Federal Workers local appealed his case to the complainant's division chief, to Commerce Department personnel officials, and finally to Secretary Harry Hopkins. In this instance, the department agreed to place the grievance before an outside arbiter, T. Arnold Hill, a black staff assistant at the NYA and formerly the Director of Industrial Relations for the National Urban League (NUL). Although Hill returned a decision against the worker, union local officials claimed the arbitration was a significant achievement "establishing the right of the employee to obtain an impartial hearing of grievances, which cannot be settled within the department."[68]

These employment complaints and investigations typically involved an unsatisfying series of ad hoc appeals and protracted negotiations. When the Little Rock Urban League discovered that no black carpenters were being employed to construct Camp Robinson, their local executive secretary contacted both the organization's national office and its St. Louis branch, where the headquarters of the construction company was located. As a result of League pressure, the company agreed to employ black workers, and the Arkansas State Employment Service agreed to

Moore, *A Search for Equality: The National Urban League, 1910–1961*, University Park, Pennsylvania State University Press, 1981, p. 93, quoting Granger, *End of an Era*, p. 98.

66. "Wage Board Urged to Probe Mill Owner Who Fired Workers," Chicago *Bee*, January 7, 1940.

67. "40 Carpenters at Camp Meade," Atlanta *Daily World*, December 13, 1940; "See Racial Employment Policies Changing by Non-Discrimination Policy Adopted by Labor Unions," New York *Age*, December 21, 1940; "Weaver Reveals Hiring of Negro Union Workers," Washington *Tribune*, December 14, 1940.

68. The union, Local 23, was a CIO affiliate. Hill directed the League's Department of Industrial Relations when it was created in 1925. "Census Worker Loses D.C. Color Bar Case," Baltimore *Afro-American*, June 29, 1940; Moore, *A Search for Equality*, pp. 66–7.

refer qualified black carpenters to job calls at the camp. When five black stewards working for the Army Engineers were dismissed after complaining of unfair work conditions, they carried their case to their union, the National Maritime Union of America, which in turn asked for the assistance of the NUL in pressuring the federal government for an investigation of the dismissals. The executive secretary of the League contacted the Department of Justice Civil Liberties Unit and the LaFollette Civil Liberties Committee. Concurrently and nationwide, local affiliates of the League petitioned their Congressmen to seek an unbiased review of the case. When the chief of Army engineers finally investigated the complaint and held a hearing, he found that the stewards' discharge was indeed unfair and ordered their reinstatement.[69] Activists often responded to defeats by publicizing biased practices and agitating for reform in newspapers, basing their demands on the right of all citizens to participate in federally sponsored employment. In a typical encounter, a job seeking delegation led by National Negro Congress members met with the personnel manager of R. Hoe and Company, a defense machine production firm in Harlem. Told that the firm did not hire black workers, the delegation issued a statement arguing that since the company contracted with the federal government, it was "under a moral obligation to practice a democratic employment policy."[70] Such claims seem to have had little effect on whites, but the episodes provided reform organizations with a powerful general tool for recruitment and mobilization, because the same race organizations that brokered arrangements with firms also often served as employment services, interviewing candidates and thus controlling access to the new jobs. When the St. Louis Urban League reached an agreement with the U.S. Cartridge Company to offer some forty executive positions and an entire assembly line to blacks in a new plant, the League's announcement to the press read like a job advertisement; "especially wanted" were men with mechanical or teaching backgrounds and experienced machinists.[71] Another effort jointly

69. "Race Workers Hired on Jobs in Arkansas," Norfolk *Journal and Guide*, January 11, 1941; "U.S. Workers Reinstated After Urban League Protest," Norfolk *Journal and Guide*, July 20, 1940.

70. " 'We Don't Hire Negroes,' Firm Tells Delegation," New York *Daily Worker*, December 5, 1940.

71. When the city's Urban League learned that the Chamber of Commerce was studying local production patterns for defense purposes, the League submitted a list of fifteen hundred names of black workers capable of working in defense industries. "Negroes Will Man One Unit," Kansas City *Call*, August 8, 1941; Arnold B. Walker, "St. Louis' Employers, Unions and Negro Workers," *Opportunity*, November, 1941, p. 337.

waged by the Cleveland NAACP and the Cleveland Urban League succeeded in gaining thirteen black women jobs as elevator operators in the Ohio Bell Telephone Building. In this instance, the company chose the workers after interviewing two hundred females recommended by the three organizations.[72]

Despite occasional successes, these appeals produced two outcomes that were detrimental to the mobilization: a protracted and often unsatisfying series of interviews between claimants, company officials, and central state agents and, most often, additional organized protest activity. In an account widely publicized in February 1941, Charles A. Collier, industrial secretary of the New York Urban League, described the lengthy negotiations that accompanied his attempts to alter the discriminatory hiring practices of three New York City area aircraft manufacturers. He began by writing to the president of the Brewster Aeronautical Corporation and conferring with the company's personnel department regarding the availability of trained black airplane mechanics. The personnel director admitted that the firm did not employ blacks because white workers would object, and when Collier asked him to receive applications from two black mechanics, the candidates were interviewed, and their applications filed. After a month, Collier returned to discuss the matter again with the personnel director and found that he had been transferred to another department. Another executive told him that company executives were still considering the question. After this second visit, Collier formed an interracial committee to secure employment for blacks in aircraft production, including representatives of the Catholic Interracial Council, the committee for Employment Opportunities for Negroes, the National Conference of Christians and Jews, and the New York Urban League. Dissatisfied with the results of the negotiations with Brewster, the committee then contacted Senator Robert F. Wagner (D, NY) who in turn discussed the case with William Knudsen, Director of the Office of Production Management. Knudsen's January reply was sympathetic but noncommittal, and reminded the committee "that there is no legal means by which we can require private concerns to employ any particular type of help."[73]

---

72. In Columbus, Ohio, the Urban League maintained a "revolving fund" from which trainees could borrow $10 for tool purchases; the loan was repaid when the trainee found work. "Ohio 'Phone Co. Employs Race Girls," Chicago *Defender*, August 2, 1941; "Dr. Robert Weaver of OPM Lists First Which are Opening Their Doors," Kansas City *Call*, October 17, 1941.

73. Of the twenty-four hundred persons employed at the second firm investigated, the Republic Aviation Corporation in Farmingdale, Collier reported that one person – a chauffeur – was black. An official explained that managers feared worker resis-

To black activists experienced with these efforts, the later creation of the FEPC promised to augment and in many cases replace this private activity with a federal agency that would legitimate their claims and pursue them and in an expert, standardized, and enforceable fashion. Race leaders sought to perfect and federalize what they knew to be an imperfect system. It was in large part due to the failings of this hodge-podge of complaint-adjustment mechanisms, and of the Black Cabinet that presided over it, that A. Philip Randolph organized his March on Washington Movement.

The War Economy and Growing Criticism of the Black Cabinet

Excluded groups pursue new tactics of claim-making when inherited methods appear obsolete, or unsuited to a new political-economic context that national crises can introduce. Such was the case as discrimination persisted through 1940 and early 1941 in all areas of defense employment – unions, businesses, training-within-industry programs, and state employment services – while the Roosevelt administration refused to take any concrete action to aid minority employment. The segregationist bottleneck in Congress held fast, and Roosevelt explained his reluctance to act in familiar terms: "the South would rise up in protest."[74] Job gains in semiskilled work such as carpentry contrasted sharply with the resistance African Americans faced in technologically advanced aircraft plants, and complaints poured into the White House and cabinet offices. In May 1940 the NAACP asked President Roosevelt to issue an executive order prohibiting employment discrimination in airplane and armament plants or to ask Congress to do the same before it considered his defense program.[75] The president ignored the petition, and while it was apparent to all concerned that racial discrimination could restrain a total defense mobilization, reformers lacked the political leverage or party support to effect the reforms they sought.

tance to integration would interfere with efficient defense production. During subsequent visits, firm officials discussed matters with the committee, but would not agree to plan a gradual integration of black mechanics at the plant. The third company investigated did not respond to the League's calls and letters. "3 Factories Refuse Jobs to Race Men," Norfolk *Journal and Guide*, February 15, 1941; "Airplane Factories Want Skilled Help; Won't Hire Negroes." Pittsburgh *Courier*, February 15, 1941.

74. Louis Ruchames, *Race, Jobs & Politics: The Story of the FEPC*, New York, Columbia University Press, 1953, p. 15.

75. This may be the earliest reference to this executive order. "F.D.R. Asked to Stop Discrimination in Plane Factories," Baltimore *Afro-American*, May 25, 1940.

At times the struggle appeared hopeless. The Eastside Chamber of Commerce of Los Angeles publicized a contract between the state's relief administration and the NYA, in which the latter pledged to certify for aircraft mechanical training only white, second generation American youths.[76] The Seattle Urban League's executive secretary called for blacks to unite against these "damnable exclusion tactics," but there was no consensus on the strategies to be pursued.[77] When the president of a steel works in Kansas City advised Urban League investigators that the company would maintain its whites-only employment policy, the League contacted a member of the NDAC who replied, "I know nothing else you or I could do."[78]

The orthodox route to gain officials' consideration was through black federal administrators. By the spring of 1941, the Federal Council of Negro Advisers had grown to forty-one members, and the group – of which Bethune was chair – met monthly to discuss their methods and goals. These leaders, administrators, and educators were spending a good portion of their time promoting the emergency program by explaining federal policy to their constituents. For example, an African American representative of the Office of War Information (OWI) explained the various functions of his agency to a conference of black educators in December 1942:

> There is a vital job to be done in interpreting to our people the enormous implications of this struggle for us as Americans and as members of a racial minority . . . Confidence must be developed in the progressively liberating functions which this war can serve and is serving in desirably affecting the political and economic status of the Negro and people of color the world over, as well as little men everywhere.[79]

Despite its growth and its considerable accomplishments in gaining fairer policy making and implementation, however, the Black Cabinet had begun to falter under the stress of the mobilization. Many civic leaders believed that its party and allegiance-building accomplishments had outpaced its achievements in substantive policy reform.

As early as February 1941, Dr. Rayford W. Logan, chairman of the

76. Lawrence F. Lamar, "Training is Opened to Negroes," Atlanta *Daily World*, October 16, 1940.
77. "Employment for Negroes Impossible at Boeing; Conditions Unchanged," Seattle *Northwest Enterprise*, November 6, 1940.
78. "Kansas City Industry Has Big Contract But Will Not Hire Negroes," Kansas *City Call*, October 11, 1941.
79. "OWI Functions Explained to Race Educators," Pittsburgh *Courier*, December 19, 1942.

Courier's Committee on National Defense, surprised fifteen hundred blacks attending Philadelphia's first mass meeting on defense issues with a ringing critique of three prominent defense administrators. Conceding that he had endorsed the appointments of his personal friends – Hastie, Weaver, and Campbell Johnson of Selective Service – Logan announced that "they are just being used as 'barriers' against 'pressure groups' like this committee." Many other leaders shared the opinion, he said, that "we are getting a grand 'run-around' in Washington."[80] NAACP members, too, were impatient as they gathered for a June meeting. The temper of the association's branches explained the delegates' "sharp questions" of Hastie, Weaver, and Ira A. DeReid of the USES, particularly about employment in national defense industries.[81] Lucius C. Harper, columnist for the Chicago *Defender*, called local Black Cabinets a collective "millstone around the neck of the race." While claiming to control and deliver the black vote, dishonest city-level cabineteers enriched themselves in the process of distributing very scant patronage to their followers; the members of the national Black Cabinet merely aggrandized themselves on a larger scale. Powerless and poor judges of black interests, they served to secure the black vote in key swing states such as Illinois, Michigan, Ohio, and Indiana.

> These "Black Cabinet" members who usually occupy "posts of importance" are nothing more than professional letter-writers whose duty it is to satisfy Negro complaints by mail, and keep protesting delegations, or discourage them, from storming the various governmental departments and the White House with just grievances.

Harper called for the immediate dissolution of all "bought-and-paid-for" cabineteers and the reinvention of a national black leadership.[82] W. E. B. DuBois later dedicated his newspaper column to an analysis of the two types of black officials in Washington. One sort was the "upper clerk" who apologized for his department's lack of sympathy; the other pursued cooperation from his agency, and in its absence, simply resigned. "It is, of course, this second type of official alone who is useful and valuable. The other is nothing."[83]

---

80. Partisan differences within the black leadership helped account for this critique. John A. Saunders, "3 Defense Aides Used to Check Pressure Groups," Pittsburgh *Courier*, February 22, 1941.
81. "Sharp Protest, Militant Action Listed for Body," Atlanta *Daily World*, June 17, 1941.
82. Lucius C. Harper, "Dustin' Off the News," Chicago *Defender*, October 11, 1941.
83. He thought William Hastie exemplified the valuable type. Quoted in Phillip McGuire, "Judge Hastie, World War II, and Army Racism," *Journal of Negro History*, October 1977, p. 358.

Such leaders criticized the work of the Black Cabinet in mobilization matters in particular. Black officials in the Office of Production Management (OPM) had disappointed the race leadership in New Orleans to such an extent that locals considered Weaver's NETB "a mere buffer between the powers-that-be in Washington and the Negro people." Weaver's representatives had confined themselves, in very brief visits, to meeting with white labor and business representatives. This approach, it was argued, would not reveal the discriminatory practices and attitudes that barred minorities from jobs. Others claimed that Dr. Will Alexander, the minority groups' representative, failed to deliver on a promise to authorize the training of several hundred blacks in shipbuilding skills, having instead arranged for the training of a mere forty bricklayers and welders. The industrial secretary of the New Orleans Urban League wrote that the training recommendation seemed to be an effort "on the part of someone up the line to pacify Negroes," rather than an honest attempt to fully integrate them into the mobilization.[84] Black editorialist Charlie Cherokee believed that Weaver had repeatedly made the mistake of "making grand optimistic announcements," even when a large plant had hired only a few black workers. The official, and the Cabinet system more broadly, was losing the public's confidence.[85]

These professionals attempted to adapt their public relations tactics to the changed public attitudes. By 1939, the Cabinet system had grown so entrenched that Weaver wrote a generic "job sheet," or position description, for "a Special Assistant, Consultant or Racial Adviser in a Federal Agency," with blank sections to accommodate the name of the appropriate authorizing agency and other distinguishing facts.[86] Fifteen months later, however, Weaver, in recommending candidates for appointments to the War Department and the Selective Service Administration, suggested calling the positions "administrative assistants"; *administration* was now to be emphasized over advisement. Blacks, he explained, felt that the titles of "special assistants or advisers" implied "a minimum of responsibility," and any official so designated "starts out with a handicap."[87] The professional titles of blacks in federal agencies

---

84. A local school official used this low OPM recommendation to justify restricting its welding courses to whites. "Dixie Leaders Brand Negro OPM Setup as Mere Buffers," New York *Amsterdam News*, November 25, 1941.
85. Reed, *Seedtime*, p. 32.
86. Letter, Robert C. Weaver to T. Arnold Hill, July 26, 1939, Correspondence – H, Weaver papers.
87. "Administrative Assistant" was his own title at the time, in the Division of Labor Supply. Memorandum, Robert C. Weaver to Mr. Reeves, October 14, 1940, Correspondence – R, Weaver papers; see for example Pauline Redmond Coggs, "Race Relations Advisors – Quislings or Messiahs?," *Opportunity*, July 1943, pp. 112–14.

at the beginning of the war confirms the centrality of these increasingly discredited advisory and "educative, interpretive" roles.[88] Of fourteen black administrators in the Department of Agriculture, three were Agricultural Adjustment Administration field representatives, and three were assistants to white division directors. The U.S. Housing Authority also employed fourteen, of whom eight were advisers; five of these were race relations advisers. The OPM employed eleven, including Weaver, a "public relations counselor," and six field assistants. The Social Security Board's ten black professionals included a consultant-in-charge for minority groups, three employment specialists, and three "special representatives."[89]

Walter White's reaction to such appointments also reflected his concern that blacks in federal departments effect substantive change rather than serve symbolic roles. In September, when FDR suggested to black leaders that the War and Navy Departments employ a black administrator – eventually, William Hastie – White warned that the president meant "someone in an advisory capacity rather than one with authority," such as an assistant secretary of war.[90] The problem even plagued Weaver's own promotion in April, 1941, when he became "Chief" of the NETB. White wrote to tell him that his new position was inferior even to Hastie's, since he had been placed in charge of "a Jim Crow division in OPM." He also wrote to Hillman insisting that Weaver be considered a bona fide administrator with responsibility for forming and executing bureau policies.[91]

Members of the Black Cabinet in turn modified their work to exploit the growing discontent. In 1941 a black advisor told a group of race leaders that whenever the *Courier* or *Defender*

> gives me hell in an editorial or Walter White writes me a stinging letter, I take it in to my chief and tell him that I won't be any use to the agency unless I can produce or if Negroes think I'm an Uncle Tom.

Only then could the advisor gain concessions that had been pursued for weeks.[92]

88. Weiss, *Farewell to the Party of Lincoln*, p. 154.
89. "Who's Who in U.S. Government Offices," Baltimore *Afro-American*, November 29, 1941.
90. Hastie's position at War was called "Civilian Aide to the Secretary." "Conference at the White House, September 27, 1940," enclosed in letter, Walter White to Robert Weaver, October 7, 1940, Correspondence – W, Weaver papers.
91. Letter, Sidney Hillman to Walter White, July 3, 1941; letter, Walter White to Robert Weaver, July 26, 1941, Correspondence – W, Weaver papers.
92. Kirby, p. 148, quoted from Lawrence, "Negro Organization in Crisis," pp. 217–18; see also Motz, "Black Cabinet," pp. 56–62.

A week after Pearl Harbor, black sociologist and journalist Horace R. Cayton felt compelled to defend the besieged Cabinet members, arguing that their roles were impossible to perform. One of them had told him recently that they were not "called in until there is a mess and then told to straighten it out." Very rarely consulted on matters of policy, or appraised of important reforms, they were instructed to "interpret the new policy to the Negro public," which gave the impression that they were in some way responsible for their agency's actions. Cayton again called for the integration of the advisers into the policy-making process.[93]

All these criticisms resulted from the Cabinet members' inability to secure a reasonable share of the rapidly expanding defense economy for their clientele. Black leaders thus searched for more effective means by which to press their case. Even venerable race advancement organizations such as the NAACP were subject to criticism. In keeping with its past practice, for example, the NAACP designated January 26, 1941 "National Defense Day," and held protest meetings in twenty-three states. The organization petitioned Knudsen to call on the General Motors Corporation, his former employer, to end discriminatory practices. Knudsen simply refused.[94] Black Americans were, according to the *Courier*'s George S. Schuyler, "getting fed up on these frauds" of private conferences and petitions. The columnist called instead for a group that had "worked out some technique of fighting other than sending letters and telegrams of protest."[95]

Conclusion

It was ironically the relative success of the Black Cabinet system during the New Deal that rendered the White House ill-prepared for black America's discontent in 1940 and 1941. The effort to gain votes in the presidential election of 1940 through high-profile appointments exemplified the political technique by which the administration gained political support both in the short term, in appreciation for the gesture itself, and it was thought, in the longer term, through the efforts of cabineteers to incorporate black voters into the governing coalition by publicizing the administration's efforts and by adjusting their clients' complaints. This

---

93. Cayton noted several exceptions; Robert Taylor of Defense Housing participated in policy formation, and Judge Hastie and Mary Bethune were distinguished by their willingness to criticize their agency's policies. Horace R. Cayton, "Black Cabinet," Pittsburgh *Courier*, December 13, 1941.
94. Moore, *A Search for Equality*, pp. 90–91.
95. Pittsburgh *Courier*, November 30, 1940, as quoted in Garfinkel, *When Negroes March*, p. 38.

complaint-adjustment process seemed to best capture the president's ideal system of race management, and dominated the practice of federal race management in the immediate prewar period in the armed forces as well as in employment matters.

During the preparedness period, state officials wielded or contributed to three overlapping and still experimental techniques for promoting black employment within and outside of federal agencies. In defense housing construction, officials retained a version of the quota system reserving jobs in proportion to the local African American workforce. Extending this approach to other economic spheres, where whites defended their prerogative to claim all desirable jobs, appears to have never been seriously considered. Second, through a complaint-adjustment approach, central authorities evaluated the claims of black workers and applicants on a case-by-case basis through a variety of practices in different agencies; usually, race advancement organizations contributed personnel and resources to these appeals and petitions. Finally, Robert Weaver pursued a community utilization approach in which claims of equity and fairness were replaced by appeals to white political and commercial elites' interests in economic, social, and fiscal stability. Eventually, Weaver's strategy would be subordinated to a strengthened complaint-adjustment approach, standardized and sanctioned by the state in the form of the FEPC. Thus, the executive order creating the FEPC in effect appropriated and legitimized the complaint-adjustment practices invented and refined by black workers and organizational leaders in this prewar period.

This attempt to solidify black voters' identification with the Democratic party in 1940 only partially succeeded, for the particular reason that one of the appointees, Hastie, pursued goals seen to be disruptive, and for the general reason that the Cabinet system itself was coming under the attack of African American militants. The real need, in the eyes of the many who chose to confront segregation and mistreatment directly, was for substantive policy change rather than symbolic gestures. In addition, more and more blacks began to resist what they viewed as racist persecution and punishment at the hands of civilian and military police. This militancy helps explain why the administration created the FEPC. The analysis now turns to consider the fragile national security and social order context within which statesmen bargained with A. Philip Randolph and his allies in the spring and summer of 1941.

3

The Executive and National Security Imperatives: Unrest and Early Struggles over Racial Manpower Policies

Long-range planning, in my judgement, is of the utmost importance. In such planning, consideration of the color and race problem is of first-line significance. But there is a danger of such long-range planning becoming projects of wide influence in escape from the realities of war. I am not convinced that we can be realists about the war and planners for the future at this critical time.

FDR, March 16, 1942[1]

A study of the American state's racial manpower policies during World War II must explain the extraordinary Executive Order 8802 of 1941. For many observers then and scholars since, the order creating the Fair Employment Practices Committee was something wholly new and unique. But the document was in reality an appropriate if unprecedented product of the prewar American political scene, in that it drew on well-established norms of complaint adjustment. While adjusting individual complaints had long been FDR's preferred method for handling black grievances, the particular form of the concession was an important break in the tradition of federal authorities' deference to and practice of racial discrimination. Given this, it is important to know what caused the concession to be granted. To put it another way, since state officials had previously concluded that granting the claim was unprofitable from either a political party or mobilization-efficiency perspective, what remains puzzling is less the form of the concession, but its cause. The question involves the relationship between the timing of an innovative movement tactic and the consequences of state officials' continued refusal to respond to it in turn. The following analysis attempts to determine whether the White House argument that violence would result from the

1. Letter, FDR to Edwin Embree, President, Julius Rosenwald Fund, March 16, 1942, Official File (OF) 93, Colored Matters, FDRL.

March on Washington, should it be held, was motivated by concern for violence or was instead part of a bluffing strategy. If there was reason to believe violence would result from the march, was this merely a product of Washington's oft-cited southern culture, or was the city particularly unstable at the time?[2]

In fact, two factors made the demonstration particularly worrisome to White House officials. First, a racially charged "crime wave" that most observers charged to fragmented and incapable police forces dogged the capital city in the spring and summer of 1941, stoking racial tension to the degree that a march could plausibly spark a riotous debacle, particularly if authorities were ill-prepared to contain it. Second, the march date of July 1 fell, as it turned out, at a critical moment in the nation's unfolding engagement with the war. Roosevelt did not take a strong lead during the spring 1941 crisis, when Hitler's forces prevailed in Egypt, Yugoslavia, and Greece. The president knew his navy was too thin to effectively patrol both the Atlantic and the South Pacific, and he thought the American public was unprepared for war. By early June, however, FDR had apparently concluded that the nation would join the fighting; he was simply waiting for someone else to "fire the first shot."[3] The looming Nazi invasion of the Soviet Union heightened the sense of unease and anticipation in the capital. Randolph's strategic and tactical sense thus fortuitously coincided with a peculiar conjunction of "neighborhood" and global events to produce the executive order. The instability in Washington was not uncommon nationwide, as the new forms of collective race violence that emerged in 1941 often involved black soldiers.

The FEPC's roots in proposed collective action, which in effect men-

2. Despite a wide consensus surrounding the import of this policy, less attention has been paid to its precise causes. Generally, accounts of the episode assert that the march would have been a public/international embarrassment; that it would have disrupted the Democratic party coalition; or that FDR acted to avoid violence. No one has addressed the veracity of the latter claim, which was clearly an important part of the White House bargaining position. Merl E. Reed, *Seedtime for the Civil Rights Movement: The President's Committee on Fair Employment Practice, 1941–1946,* Baton Rouge, Louisiana State University Press, 1991, p. 23; Doug McAdam, *Political Process and the Development of Black Insurgency, 1930–1970,* Chicago, University of Chicago Press, 1982, p. 84; Benjamin Quarles, "A. Philip Randolph: Labor Leader at Large," John Hope Franklin and August Meier, eds., *Black Leaders of the Twentieth Century,* Chicago, University of Illinois Press, 1982, p. 156.

3. Of that June, Robert Dallek has written that if FDR "were to avoid painful wartime divisions, the nation would have to enter the fighting with a minimum of doubt and dissent, and the way to achieve this was . . . through developments abroad which aroused the country to fight." Robert Dallek, *Franklin D. Roosevelt and American Foreign Policy, 1932–1945,* New York, Oxford University Press, 1979, p. 267.

aced the president, soon came to haunt it, for it caused the seekers of social justice on the committee to work at cross-purposes from other White House race officials. While these latter statesmen hoped the concession would work to minimize militant claims and tactics, the FEPC aimed to fulfill the egalitarian promise of the vague and brief executive order. Because the concession was extended hastily and begrudgingly, however, the committee members found themselves competing with Robert Weaver's parallel effort underway at the War Manpower Commission (WMC), and struggling to overcome White House officials who were no more sympathetic to the initiative and the ideals it represented than they were prior to the march. For two full years, the FEPC fought these obstacles to legitimacy in the executive and eventually overcame them, but were allowed to do so only after the nation had emerged from the darkest period of the war.

The opening analysis of White House negotiations with Randolph attends to both the international and local events that compelled FDR to attempt to stop the demonstration. In keeping with this book's focus on the relationship between formal, institutional politics and unorthodox collective action, the chapter also describes the new forms of race violence that emerged in the preparedness period (1940–1941), because the violence conditioned the administration's response to the planned march. The possibility of disorder in the nation's capital and unrest involving soldiers caused state officials to hastily implement substantially new policies of repression and amelioration in the Army and in factories, respectively. The chapter concludes with a description of attempts by state officials in the White House and WMC to attempt to exploit or alter the committee's practices for their own political and mobilization purposes.

Innovation in Claim-Making: Randolph and the MOWM

It was in the context of the perceived failure of the New Deal Black Cabinet system of complaint adjustment that A. Philip Randolph dropped an unusual suggestion based on an analysis consonant with the criticism.[4] Most simply, he believed that small committees of elites were

4. The idea seems to date from the aftermath of the 1940 election, either from Randolph's February 1941 conference with black leaders, which included Walter White and Mary Bethune, or from Randolph's press release of January 15, 1941, denouncing Stephen Early's explanation of the government's Army segregation policy. Meier and Rudwick have demonstrated that the strategy was the culmination of extensive Depression-era direct action launched by local organizations against discriminatory businesses and school systems in cities nationwide; the tactic stems from Randolph's radical Marxist

necessary for the development of a reform program, but that intellectuals and leaders lacked the power to secure its enactment. Echoing Schuyler and other activists and journalists, Randolph argued that

> the regular, normal and respectable method of conferences and petitions, while proper and ought to be continued as conditions may warrant, certainly don't work.

The power to change law, he claimed, lay instead with black people. "Power is the active principle . . . of the masses united for a definite purpose." Randolph suggested that ten thousand blacks march on Washington, D.C., with a simple platform: national defense jobs and placement as soldiers and officers in all branches of the armed forces. Citing southern control of the armed forces, both at the highest levels of policy formation as well as at subordinate, implementation stages, Randolph urged the placement of blacks throughout the executive administration, not only to plan policies, but to "police these policies."[5] Robert Weaver himself later admitted that this plan "for more drastic action" was developed because routine methods had produced only "small results."[6]

Randolph's plan, while resonating with urban black America to a greater extent than the more sedate strategies of the Urban League and the NAACP, initially attracted only modest enthusiasm in the black press and almost no attention in the white press.[7] While the mainline race advancement organizations were inexperienced with and ill-suited to such a project, support for the movement apparently increased steadily, lashed on by its leader's fiery rhetoric. "Nothing has arisen in the life of the Negro since Emancipation," Randolph claimed, "which has gripped

and trade unionist background. While direct action was a common technique in the thirties, it was most often aimed at municipal authorities or white businesses. This promised to be African America's first large-scale demonstration aimed at federal officials. Louis Kesselman, *The Social Politics of FEPC: A Study in Reform Pressure Movements*, Chapel Hill, University of North Carolina Press, 1948, p. 13; Moore, *A Search for Equality*, p. 92; August Meier and Elliott Rudwick, "The Origins of Nonviolent Direct Action in Afro-American Protest: A Note on Historical Discontinuities," in *Along the Color Line: Explorations in the Black Experience*, Chicago, University of Illinois Press, 1976, pp. 345–7.
5. A. Philip Randolph, "Labor Leader Says Group to Parade in Washington for National Defense Jobs," Kansas City *Call*, January 31, 1941.
6. Weaver, *Negro Labor*, p. 134.
7. The *Defender*, for example, claimed that assembling ten thousand blacks to demonstrate for justice in employment "would be the miracle of the century." The Urban League's *Opportunity* and the NAACP's *Crisis* did not mention the march until their July issues. Considerable support arrived from these organizations, however, both in staff and financial aid. Moore, *A Search for Equality*, p. 111; Chicago *Defender*, February 8, 1941; Garfinkel, *When Negroes March*, p. 40.

the hearts" of blacks as much as their exclusion from the preparations for national defense.[8] Grievances continued to arrive at the White House from a variety of other sources as well. The black Peninsula Trade and Labor Union, for example, petitioned the president directly to demand jobs and request an investigation into local employment practices. Despite a Fort Eustis, Virginia, construction project that required more than three thousand carpenters, the Newport News employment office rejected all black applicants.[9]

By way of a response, administration sources were claiming by March 1941 that the NDAC was planning to appoint several additional blacks to work on placement and training problems.[10] On April 11, OPM co-director Sidney Hillman sent a letter to all defense contractors urging them to end exclusionary hiring practices. Soon thereafter, Hillman established the Minority Groups Branch in the Labor Division of the OPM.[11] The results were not encouraging. Whereas in October 1940, 5.4 percent of state employment service placements in twenty defense sectors were nonwhite, by April 1941 the percentage had actually fallen to 2.5 percent.[12] On April 16, Mark Ethridge, the future chairman of the FEPC, wrote to FDR to accept an appointment to the Manpower Commission. In an aside that presaged his strategic thinking on stanching additional movement activism, he wrote that he thought his appointment would help calm the ongoing agitation.[13] Randolph, however, continued to fill the black newspapers with lengthy analyses of the causes and goals of his movement, which he hoped would emulate the success of women and veteran marchers in winning the ballot and the bonus, respectively. This mobilization, he reminded his readers, was different from that of the First World War, when northern factories, mines, and mills actively

8. Garfinkel, *When Negroes March*, p. 42; letter, A. Philip Randolph to William S. Knudsen, June 3, 1941, OF 391, FDRL.
9. Walter White complained to FDR for failing to include a black on the eleven member labor mediation board; one of the choices was the president of a clerks union that barred membership on racial and religious grounds. "Race Barred from Federal Jobs," Chicago *Defender*, February 15, 1941; "Failure to Name Negro on New Labor Board Draws Fire," Houston *Negro Labor News*, March 29, 1941.
10. "Race May Get More Defense Positions," Pittsburgh *Courier*, March 8, 1941.
11. William Knudsen did not sign the letter. Garfinkel, *When Negroes March*, pp. 55–6.
12. The Committee on National Defense and the National Negro Council were among the organizations joining ongoing protest actions aimed primarily at the Office of Production Management. Gunnar Myrdal, *An American Dilemma*, New York, Harper & Row, Inc., 1944, p. 409.
13. Letter, Mark Ethridge to the president, April 16, 1941, papers of Mark Ethridge, Southern Historical Collection, Wilson Library, The University of North Carolina at Chapel Hill.

sought black workers to replace unavailable immigrant labor. At this early stage, unemployed workers of both races were competing directly for work.[14]

At the same time, developments abroad began to close in on the nation. As FDR watched helplessly, Hitler invaded Denmark and Norway on April 9 and overran the Low Countries on May 10, 1941. Following French and British appeals for assistance, the president asked Congress for over a billion dollars to build up the nation's military might; within two months the appropriations had surpassed $3 billion. On May 20, educator Channing Tobias, Walter White, Lester Granger, and Mary Bethune met with Hillman, who informed them that no executive order could be expected from the president.[15] Randolph was unrelenting. "In this period of power politics, nothing counts but pressure, more pressure, and still more pressure . . ."[16] In late May, FDR warned the nation of the dangers of discord at a time of fascist expansion:

> Today's threat to our national security is not a matter of military weapons alone . . . there is an added technique for weakening a nation at its very roots. . . . The method is simple. It is first, a dissemination of discord. A group – not too large – a group that may be sectional or racial or political – is encouraged to exploit its prejudices through false slogans and emotional appeals. The aim of those who deliberately egg on these groups is to create confusion of counsel, public indecision, political paralysis and eventually, a state of panic. Sound national policies come to be viewed with a new and unreasoning skepticism . . . As a result of these techniques, armament programs may be dangerously delayed. Singleness of national purpose may be undermined . . . *The unity of the state can be so sapped that its strength is destroyed.* All this is no idle dream. It has happened time after time, in nation after nation, during the last two years.[17]

As White House officials began more serious negotiations with the movement, few except Randolph ventured to predict the attendance with any

14. This was a common theme among generally pessimistic black leaders in the immediate prewar period. Weaver reminded black communities that they should not "expect to profit" from the ongoing defense program as they had in the First World War. Competition was more intense, and new technologies of war production required skilled rather than unskilled labor. "Let the Negro Masses Speak," New York *Amsterdam News*, April 12, 1941; "Negro Won't Get Jobs as Before," Atlanta *Daily World*, February 16, 1941; "Negro's Future With Labor Class, Dr. Mordecai Johnson Tells Grads," Atlanta *Daily World*, May 30, 1941.
15. Moore, *A Search for Equality*, p. 90.
16. A. Philip Randolph, "The Black Worker," May, 1941, p. 4, quoted in Garfinkel, *When Negroes March*, p. 56.
17. Quoted in Robert Dallek, *Franklin D. Roosevelt and American Foreign Policy, 1932– 1945*, New York, Oxford University Press, 1979, pp. 225–6, emphasis added.

confidence.[18] He continued to exhort black Americans to believe that their mass power, mobilized and coordinated, could force the president to issue an executive order.[19]

Most Americans were preoccupied with the intensifying naval war in the Atlantic Ocean. In a May 27 radio address, the president declared an unlimited national emergency, which gave his administration broader powers to respond to the crisis. Shortly thereafter, Randolph wrote to Knudsen to invite him to address the marchers from the Lincoln Memorial; the letter circulated rapidly among presidential assistants Stephen Early, Wayne Coy, and Marvin McIntyre, who shared the minimal race-related duties of the White House.[20] Armed with instructions from Roosevelt to stop the march, each scrambled to activate administration loyalists who had better credentials with the race leadership, such as Eleanor Roosevelt and William Hastie.[21] They also enlisted the help of Fiorello LaGuardia, whose "great influence with the New York negroes," Early thought, "might be able to convince them that there is a better means of presenting their case on its merits." On June 7, however, Mrs. Roosevelt, Aubrey Williams, and LaGuardia failed to convince Randolph and White to cancel the demonstration; on the same day, Randolph received a telegram from Secretary of the Navy Knox asking him to visit the capital for a discussion of his "project." The president instructed McIntyre to tell a black office-seeker that he was "much upset" at the prospect of the march, and that the best contribution the petitioner could make to the nation would be to "stop the march." A few days later, Coy suggested that the administration extend its support to Senate Resolution 75, which would have provided for a congressional investigation of discrimination in national defense employment. Coy thought that assurance of the resolution's passage might alone prevent the march.[22] The Senate's failure to act on the resolution led the

18. Garfinkel, *When Negroes March*, pp. 58–60.
19. "CALL Colored Americans to Washington, D.C. for Jobs and Equal Participation in National Defense, July 1," Boston *Guardian*, June 7, 1941.
20. Jonathan Daniels later recalled that these advisors were "almost reactionary" on the issue of race. "There wasn't much color *un*conscious; they were all conscious of color . . ." Letter, A. Philip Randolph to William S. Knudsen, June 3, 1941, OF 391, FDRL; Daniels quoted in Nancy Weiss, *Farewell to the Party of Lincoln*, pp. 251–2.
21. Doris Kearns Goodwin, *No Ordinary Time: Franklin and Eleanor Roosevelt: The Home Front in World War II*, New York, Simon & Schuster, 1994, p. 250; Harvard Sitkoff, *A New Deal for Blacks: The Emergence of Civil Rights as a National Issue*, New York, Oxford University Press, 1978, p. 317.
22. Letter, Stephen Early to Wayne Coy, June 6, 1941, OF 391, FDRL; Garfinkel, *When Negroes March*, p. 60; Memorandum, FDR to McIntyre, June 7, 1941, OF 93, Colored Matters; memorandum, Wayne Coy to Steve Early, June 12, 1941, OF 391, FDRL.

leadership to believe that the march was the only means available for presenting their claims to the nation.[23]

Mark Ethridge would later recall that by early June the pressure had grown "enormously"; the president told McIntyre that he could "imagine nothing that will stir up race hatred and slow up progress more than a march of that kind."[24] On the 12th, Coy reported that LaGuardia was "at work in an effort to prevent the march."[25] Ethridge later remembered thinking that the march would have had two "disastrous" effects. It would have given aid and consolation to the Axis powers and, whether by design or not, the marchers had planned the event at time when "the whole town was up in arms" over several recent rape cases. The police and the military, he recalled, took measures to prepare for any large number of blacks,

> but the inevitable result from the Negro standpoint would have been that you would have had a race riot of great proportions in the national capital and the disastrous consequence of that you can figure for yourselves.[26]

At the time of Randolph's call, the city was grappling with a "crime wave" perpetrated, according to the police, by black men. In the first three months of 1941, the Department of Justice ranked Washington, D.C., third among cities nationwide in murders and aggravated assaults, second in auto thefts, and first in robberies, burglaries, and grand larcenies. *Newsweek* called the city the "Murder Capital of the U.S."[27] By midsummer, seventeen rapes had been reported to the D.C. police; there were numerous other attempted rapes – most often of laundry attendants, apparently because they worked alone in their shops – and two widely reported rape-murders that remained unsolved.[28] On June 15, for example, a young War Department employee disappeared while grocery shopping and was discovered raped and strangled to death the following day. As weeks passed and the crime remained unsolved, the murder, according to the Washington *Post*, "transcended in interest any crime" of the previous ten years. The president commented on it at a press

23. Letter, Walter White to FDR, June 20, 1941, Correspondence – W, Weaver papers.
24. Mark Ethridge, "The Race Problem in the War," address to Harvard War Institute, undated, Ethridge papers, p. 5; memorandum, FDR to McIntyre, June 7, 1941, OF 93, FDRL.
25. Memorandum, Wayne Coy to Steve Early, June 12, 1941, OF 391, FDRL.
26. Mark Ethridge, "The Race Problem in the War," Ethridge papers, p. 5.
27. "Congressional Inquiry Spotlights Weaknesses in Washington Police Force," Washington *Post*, July 13, 1941; David Brinkley, *Washington Goes to War*, New York, Alfred A. Knopf, 1988, p. 76.
28. "U.S. Official's Daughter, 15, Attacked Here," Washington *Post*, August 7, 1941.

conference on the 17th, and the First Lady issued a warning to the young women of the city on the same day.[29] Throughout June the dailies reported sexual assaults at what were alarming rates.[30] District Commissioners announced an investigation of an apparently undermanned and undersupplied District Police Department, and a congressman from Louisiana demanded a congressional investigation of the ineffectual department and the "crime wave" that had left the city very much on edge.[31] The prospect of confronting tens of thousands of militant black marchers in this racial atmosphere was at the time a "most frightening" prospect to federal officials, according to Weaver.[32]

On the 15th, the administration publicized the president's memorandum to the co-directors of the Office of Production Management, but blacks were not impressed by the carefully worded document that stated that the president "shall expect" the OPM "to facilitate full utilization of our productive manpower," that labor "must be prepared to welcome . . . fellow workers of all racial and nationality groups," and that "industry must take the initiative in opening the doors of employment to all."[33] Instead of sapping the movement of strength, such incomplete concessions increased the confidence of the organizers. According to one march planner, the president's statement indicated that the movement's "technique" was a "proper one." As estimates of the march grew to fifty

29. "Super-Police Squad Hunts Sex Slayer of D.C. Girl," "Murder Leads Mrs. Roosevelt to Warn Girls," "Legislators Seek Investigation of Police, FBI Intervention," Washington *Post*, June 18, 1941.

30. Several prominent women called for the organization of an all-female pistol club. "Gunman Rapes Clerk After Robbery of Store," Washington *Post*, June 25, 1941; "Women Seek Pistol Practice to Guard Against Sex Fiends," Washington *Post*, June 27, 1941.

31. Two senators even introduced bills to give the FBI jurisdiction over certain felonies in the capital. The problems were not due to a lack of personnel alone; the size of the city's police force, per capita, matched many other cities with much better records. The situation was distinguished by the presence of four independent police agencies – Park, White House, Capitol, and Metropolitan – which bred confusion and irresponsibility. In addition, the city's vagrancy law, the principal means by which police cleared cities of "transient undesirables" in the thirties, was relatively lax. "Assign FBI to D.C. Crime, McKellar Asks," Washington *Post*, June 29, 1941; "Congressional Inquiry Spotlights Weaknesses in Washington Police Force," Washington *Post*, July 13, 1941; "Crime Picture," Washington *Post*, July 18, 1941.

32. The new arrivals would also join a large body of local blacks; Washington was one of four larger cities – and the one located farthest north – in which blacks formed a third or more of the population. Weaver, *Negro Labor*, p. 134; U.S. Bureau of the Census, *County Data Book*, USGPO, 1947.

33. Garfinkel, *When Negroes March*, p. 60; Ruchames, *Race, Jobs, and Politics*, pp. 18, 19; Kesselman, *Social Politics*, p. 14; "President Assails Racial Job Barrier," New York *Times*, June 16, 1941.

thousand, the march organization made the threat even more tangible by publicizing plans for the mass meeting. A silent procession of all-black state brigades would follow Constitution Avenue from the Capitol past the White House and the War Department to the Lincoln Memorial. In another reminder that such a large army of marchers would require assistance in maintaining order, the movement assigned groups of Great War veterans, high school cadets, and Boy Scouts to organize and lead brigades of three to five divisions each.[34]

The target date of July 1 grew closer, and Coy wrote the president that the recent flurry of minor concessions – including a conciliatory letter to Walter White to be released on the 24th, the date of the NAACP's conference – had "done a good deal to eliminate the urgency" behind the protest. In a mid-June memo to Roosevelt, he returned to Early's suggestion that pressure be brought to bear on the Senate Committee on Education and Labor to report – or at least hold hearings on – S.R. 75. Calling it "the only other thing which they can hope to gain," Coy believed that this action would dissipate the momentum behind the march.[35] On the same day, Randolph sent to Eleanor Roosevelt a memorandum of six proposals for the President's urgent consideration.[36]

That White House officials feared violence is indicated by Eleanor Roosevelt's repeating just such a warning to Randolph twice in the space of three days, just prior to his meeting with the president on the 18th. She may have been particularly concerned with Randolph's matter-of-fact remark that the marchers would enter hotels and restaurants to order meals.[37] LaGuardia told Randolph that the local police force included many southern whites, and that serious violence was likely.[38]

34. "Arthur Mitchell Brands Randolph 'Most Dangerous,' " Houston *Negro Labor News*, June 28, 1941.
35. "Memorandum, Wayne Coy to FDR, June 16, 1941, OF 391, FDRL.
36. The six proposals included four executive orders that would: forbid contracting with any entity refusing employment to any person on grounds of race, creed, or color; abolish race, creed, or color discrimination and segregation in all federal government departments; abolish discrimination in defense vocational and training courses; abolish discrimination in all branches of the armed services. In addition, the committee proposed that the president request Congress to legally forbid the extension of National Labor Relations Act protection to unions that deny membership to blacks, and that the president instruct the USES to supply workers regardless of race, creed, or color. Letter, A. Philip Randolph to Eleanor Roosevelt, June 16, 1941, OF 391, FDRL.
37. It is unlikely that she used such warnings as a tactic of intimidation, as may have been the case with other officials, for Mrs. Roosevelt was clearly worried. "I feel very strongly that your group is making a very grave mistake . . ." wrote the president's wife, an unquestioned champion of civil rights. Goodwin, *No Ordinary Time*, p. 250.
38. As recently as 1937, the Washington, D.C., Court of Appeals had enjoined the peaceful picketing of a business by job-seeking blacks. One opinion cited the public interest

When FDR and several defense administrators met with the black leaders, he personally urged them to cancel the March.[39] He told those assembled that he would not address the demonstrators in part because he thought that Americans would resent such a march – or indeed one by Irish or Jewish protesters – as an attempt to "coerce the Government and make it do certain things." But FDR also was concerned about the possibility for violence. Black participants reported that the president told movement leaders that the march was "a grave mistake," not only unlikely to accomplish their goals, "but on the contrary may create serious trouble." When Walter White confirmed Randolph's estimate of one hundred thousand marchers, FDR reportedly called the plan "bad and unintelligent," claimed not to have heard about Senate Resolution 75, and told the gathering that he could not offer anything unless the march was canceled.[40]

At the same time, the president said that he wanted discrimination ended, and that he would place his office behind efforts to secure defense jobs for blacks. Again citing the complaint-adjustment mechanism that he had recently extended to the Army in the persons of Hastie and Davis, FDR said that he thought the main problem was that blacks "had nowhere to go to present their grievances and complaints when they were victims of discrimination by defense industries." Following his half-hour discussion with the delegation, the president instructed his officials to meet immediately with Randolph and White to draft a plan for the president's consideration. Hillman claimed that considerations of national defense must precede reform, and argued that existing agencies were capable of supervising fair employment. Knudsen agreed, but both

in preventing the violence that would likely result from any racially motivated picket. Only in 1938 did the Supreme Court rule in the same case – *New Negro Alliance* – that such pickets were labor disputes protected from injunctions by the Norris-La Guardia Act. David Brinkley, *Washington Goes to War*, p. 82; Paul D. Moreno, *From Direct Action to Affirmative Action: Fair Employment Law and Policy in America, 1933–1972*, Baton Rouge, Louisiana State University Press, 1997, pp. 43–54.

39. Present at the conference were the president, Stimson, Knox, Knudsen, and Hillman, LaGuardia, NYA Director Aubrey Williams, the coordinator of the Social Security Board, Anna Rosenberg, Randolph, White, Frank R. Crosswaith, chairman of the Negro Labor Committee, and Layle Lane, vice president of the American Federation of Teachers. Knox argued with Randolph over whether black and white sailors should be assigned to the same ships. "Roosevelt Won't Address Marchers to Washington," New York *Amsterdam News*, June 28, 1941; "Race Leaders Stand Pat on Job Demands, Chicago *Defender*, June 28, 1941; Sitkoff, *A New Deal for Blacks*, pp. 320–2; Goodwin, *No Ordinary Time*, p. 251.

40. The bad faith in which the early gestures were offered may have lent Randolph the impression that the warnings of violence were mere bluffs. Letter, Walter White to FDR, June 20, 1941, Correspondence – W, Weaver papers.

men volunteered their cooperation in improving the situation. Upon adjourning, the group planned to meet again within the next two weeks to consider the president's proposal that "a special board be set up to receive and act upon complaints of racial discrimination in the defense program."[41] On the 19th, LaGuardia submitted the committee's recommendations to the president. They proposed an executive order that would provide for the inclusion of a statement of nondiscriminatory policy in all defense contracts and thus notify government departments and unions of their obligation to end discrimination. LaGuardia also recommended the creation of a "Grievance Committee" to receive complaints.[42]

On the 21st the Washington *Post* reported two holdups at pistol point, a housebreaking, a robbery, and two assaults, evidence that the "crime wave rolls on," while a Louisiana senator speculated that the police department was unable to staunch the crime "because of the unusual conditions existing in our Nation, which have caused a great influx of people into the District and environs from elsewhere." The Chairman of the House District Committee suggested that the Arlington Cantonment's military police battalion be trained in civilian police problems and deployed to the city. The defense emergency was causing the city to grow "more swiftly than civil authorities have been able to expand the Police Department to proportions adequate for the public safety."[43] For his part, J. Edgar Hoover advised the Solicitor General and the Attorney General that the Communist Party might attempt to convert the march into a demonstration of its own.[44]

The following day, June 22, Germany launched its well-rumored attack on the Soviet Union; slightly over a week remained before the scheduled march. The international situation appeared increasingly grave, and as the Nazis pushed eastward, Secretary of War Stimson, reflecting on Roosevelt's cautious leadership, wondered in his journal whether America had "lost her way" and questioned whether the nation

41. "Roosevelt Won't Address Marchers to Washington," New York *Amsterdam News*, June 28, 1941; "Race Leaders Stand Pat on Job Demands, Chicago *Defender*, June 28, 1941; Sitkoff, *A New Deal for Blacks*, pp. 320–2; Goodwin, *No Ordinary Time*, p. 251.

42. Memorandum, F. H. LaGuardia to the president, June 19, 1941, President's COFEP, papers of John H. Ohly, Harry S. Truman Library, Independence, MO.

43. Most of those suspected of and arrested for these crimes were black. "D.C. Crime Wave Rolls On, With Six Felonies in One Day," "Herring Determined to Bring FBI Into the Strieff Slaying," "Randolph Asks Military Police Help for D.C.," Washington *Post*, June 21, 1941.

44. Memorandum, John Edgar Hoover to the Solicitor General, June 20, 1941, FEPC Collection, Southern Labor Archives, Georgia State University.

could master the crisis.[45] With only days remaining, the *Post* editorialized – without reference to the march – that the city's lawlessness resembled that of a nineteenth-century frontier town.

> A condition not altogether removed from downright anarchy prevails in the capital of a Nation which has embarked on the mission of restoring international order and justice to an anarchic world.[46]

On the 24th, as public estimates of attendance surpassed one hundred thousand, the LaGuardia committee offered the marchers a draft executive order for comment and revision. That day, the undersecretaries of War and Navy notified the president that they did not favor the order, primarily because it would interfere with contracting for munitions.[47] Their counsel was rejected; when the march leadership found that the document did not mention discrimination in government employment, an acceptable clause was quickly added and Randolph canceled the protest.[48]

The following day, Roosevelt issued Executive Order 8802, prohibiting discrimination in federal government and defense industry employment and establishing a Committee on Fair Employment Practice (FEPC) to "receive and investigate" complaints of discrimination. The committee soon planned a series of public hearings in major cities, hoping to gauge various regions' employment situations, publicize the Executive Order, and correct actual cases of discrimination through negotiation and public suasion.[49] The president would appoint a chairman and four part-time volunteer officials, who would be lodged within the Office of Production Management. The order instructed all federal agencies and departments dealing with defense training and vocational programs to administer their work without discrimination, for the committee lacked a field staff. Furthermore, all defense contracts negotiated by federal purchasing agencies were to include a "provision obligating the

45. Henry L. Stimson and McGeorge Bundy, *On Active Service in Peace and War*, New York, Harper and Brothers, 1947, p. 371.
46. "Anarchic Washington," Washington *Post*, June 26, 1941.
47. Memorandum, Robert Patterson and James Forrestal to the president, June 24, 1941, OF 93, FDRL.
48. "Simply stated, the march was postponed because its main objective, namely the issuance of an executive order banning discrimination in national defense, was secured in conference with the President." Fearing that the agreement had been reached rather late in the game, the administration requested that Randolph inform blacks of the "postponement" of the march on a national radio network. "A. Philip Randolph Explains Inside Facts Behind 'March' on Washington in New York City," Houston *Negro Labor News*, August 16, 1941; Garfinkel, *When Negroes March*, p. 61.
49. Kesselman, *Social Politics*, pp. 15–24.

contractor not to discriminate against any worker because of race, creed, color, or national origin."

When White House officials determined that the march tactic and the capital setting was a potentially volatile combination, they indirectly acknowledged the effects of the defense mobilization on each factor. The demands themselves were not new, but the tactics caught statesmen off-guard because the war mobilization had so quickly rendered Black Cabinet methods obsolete. The consequences of continuing to refuse to meet Randolph's demands were unclear – because the novelty of the effort made predictions of participation uncertain – but potentially grave, for reasons of social order and international instability. Local authorities were apparently unable to maintain social order in daily life, much less professionally manage confrontations between the marchers and their opponents. The success of the March threat was thus a product of the incompatibility of inherited race management techniques within the new war mobilization context. These founding circumstances would have substantial consequences for the administrative development of the FEPC.

Defense Preparedness and Racial Violence

While attracting widespread praise from African Americans, the creation of the FEPC neither assuaged the militants nor interrupted a sense of looming racial crisis in the nation's capital. The House of Representatives approved legislation in August to provide a hundred additional policemen for the city after Rep. John Rankin (D, MS) predicted "the greatest race riots this country has ever seen unless we give police protection to the white people of the District."[50] Throughout the summer, crime and rumors disabled the capital.[51] Just prior to Labor Day, the police learned that blacks were planning a demonstration to follow the city's holiday parade. Marchers planned to invade restaurants and businesses along Pennsylvania Avenue on Labor Day and "create scenes" if they were not given service. Soon every hotel lobby in the city was manned by plainclothes officers, "fully armed and expecting trouble"; white suburban employers dismissed their black domestic workers early to avoid any related demonstrations. Although these rumors and the

50. "Capitol Fears Race Riots," Knoxville *Journal*, August 16, 1941.
51. In July, in one of the fastest prosecutions on record, a district court jury condemned to death a twenty-one-year-old black resident thirty-five days after he allegedly raped and robbed a laundry shop attendant. "Civic Groups Offer to Help Combat Crime," Washington *Post*, July 11, 1941; "D.C. Woman's Attacker is Condemned to Death," Washington *Post*, July 30, 1941.

reactions to them revealed how nervous white residents were at this time, no incidents occurred.[52]

The troubles in Washington reflected a nationwide sense of racial instability that stemmed from the preparedness effort. In the late thirties, urban crime and racial crowd violence were generally products of poor, segregated neighborhoods crowded with new migrants.[53] The retirement of thousands of acres of crop land under the auspices of the Agricultural Adjustment Administration drove thousands of sharecroppers and their families into nearby cities and onto relief rolls, particularly in the South.[54] The "contested area" race violence of the era often tested the limited capacity of police forces, as battles between white police and black crowds attempting to liberate a criminal suspect were as common as fights between civilians over recreation areas.[55] While these familiar forms endured in many American cities – including New York City, which also suffered a well-publicized black "crime wave" in the summer and fall – soldiers assumed a new prominence in the incidents. Of nineteen cases of collective racial violence drawn from black newspapers in

52. "Negroes Going on Rampage Rumors Throws D.C. White Folk into Race Scare," Oklahoma City *Black Dispatch*, September 20, 1941.
53. Morris Janowitz, "Patterns of Collective Racial Violence," in Hugh Davis Graham and Ted Robert Gurr, eds., *Violence in America: Historical and Comparative Perspectives*, New York, Signet Books, 1969; Herbert Shapiro, *White Violence and Black Response: From Reconstruction to Montgomery*, Amherst, University of Massachusetts Press, 1988.
54. In 1940, the Memphis police commissioner complained that the city had too few jobs for its black laborers, and suggested that recent migrants would be better off if they returned to farming. White elites offered to pay to transport those willing to resettle on farms. "Memphis Police Start Campaign to End Danger of Race Riots," Nashville *Globe & Independent*, December 16, 1940; "Memphis Fears Race Trouble, Reds Are Blamed," Oklahoma City *Black Dispatch*, December 21, 1940; "Not Enough Jobs, So Memphis Terror Tries to Drive Out Negroes," Birmingham *Southern News Almanac*, December 26, 1940; Roger Biles, "The Persistence of the Past: Memphis and the Great Depression," *The Journal of Southern History*, vol. LII, no. 2, May 1986, pp. 198–200.
55. For example, in Charlotte, a group of blacks freed a criminal suspect from police custody and then attacked two white officers with rocks and bottles. In early July, whites leaving a church picnic in South Philadelphia battled with black residents for nearly an hour; five were seriously injured. On August 9, five knifings resulted from sporadic fighting at a Santa Monica amusement area; a month later, a similar racial fight wounded four. "Negro Riot Against Police Looks Ominous," Charlotte *News*, June 24, 1940; "Riot Near As Police Fire on Youths," Philadelphia *Tribune*, July 18, 1940; "White, Colored Fight; 5 Jailed," Philadelphia *Tribune*, July 11, 1940; "4 Whites, 1 Negro Injured," New York *Age*, August 9, 1940; "Negroes Win Exaggerated 'Riot'; Police Blasted by Public Opinion and Radio," Oklahoma City *Black Dispatch*, September 7, 1940.

1941, seventeen involved soldiers.[56] One can hardly overstate the open hostility that greeted these men, particularly in the South. Some cities and towns such as Windy Hill, South Carolina, and Ruston, Louisiana, curtailed interracial friction by simply declaring whole sections off-limits to blacks.[57] The towns surrounding Fort Huachuca, Arizona, banned black servicemen altogether.[58] After the black 94th Engineer Battalion set up camp near Gurdon, Arkansas, on August 9, local police ordered their officers to keep the soldiers out of town. About 250 soldiers then encountered a highway blockade manned by approximately one hundred white civilians, highway patrolmen, and military policemen. Later that week, a crowd of whites attacked the camp and threatened to burn it if the battalion did not leave the area. Many of the soldiers fled the camp, and the Army, altogether.[59] Attention immediately focused on military and civilian police systems in the South; while at least twenty-seven southern and border cities employed black civilian policemen in 1941, none of these were located in the five Deep South states of Louisiana, Mississippi, Alabama, Georgia, and South Carolina.[60]

56. April produced several incidents. Soldiers found the body of a black private hanging, his hands tied behind him, in the woods of Fort Benning, Georgia. An Army investigation failed to explain the death to the satisfaction of most blacks. "Southern Youth Congress Issues Stirring Protest," Nashville *Globe and Independent*, April 25, 1941.

On the 20th, brawling broke out between black soldiers from Fort Jackson, South Carolina, and local white boys. A large group of white soldiers marched on the black camp, but were intercepted and turned back by military authorities. "Probe Pushed into Fort Riot," Columbia [South Carolina] *Record*, April 22, 1941; "Race Soldiers, White CCC Boys Clash in S.C.," Atlanta *Daily World*, April 29, 1941.

On April 5, when two black privates became disorderly while riding a bus from Columbus to Fort Benning, Georgia, the driver stopped just inside the entrance to the camp. While being arrested, one soldier rushed the MP and was shot and killed instantly. "Unruly Soldier Killed by MP at Ft. Benning," Baltimore *Afro-American*, April 5, 1941.

Finally, a Raleigh policeman beat a black private with a blackjack so badly that he thought it necessary to take the GI to the hospital. In the city's first such case, a black civic association successfully petitioned the police commissioner to suspend the officer. "Of National Importance," Raleigh *News & Observer*, April 7, 1941; "Raleigh Cop Suspended for Attack on Soldier," Baltimore *Afro-American*, April 19, 1941.

57. Two black soldiers from Fort Custer, walking in Ruston, exchanged words with a white civilian who ordered them off the street. The white man returned with a city policeman and two MPs to beat the GIs, who were told "to let that be a lesson to them." "Negro Soldiers Not Allowed in Windy Hill, S.C," Atlanta *Daily World*, August 7, 1941; "Hold Four for Army Flogging at Ruston, La.," Chicago *Defender*, October 4, 1941; "2 White M.P.'s Demoted, Fined for Beating Soldier," Chicago *Defender*, November 15, 1941.

58. Lee, *The Employment of Negro Troops*, pp. 309–14.

59. "NAACP Hears of Trouble," St. Louis *Argus*, August 22, 1941; "War Officials 'Through With' Gurdon Incident," Kansas City *Call*, December 5, 1941.

60. Most of these forces employed separate black police units to patrol minority neighbor-

Events repeatedly confirmed the long-standing claim of black activists like Hastie that white police were as likely to cause as to quell disturbances. When Houston police attempted to chase black soldiers from the streets, the unit's provost marshal told the officers that the soldiers were disturbing no one. "Your presence and treatment of these boys only serves to incite them," he told them, who then quit the scene.[61] A *Courier* reporter visiting thirteen Army camps found not only that all the MPs he encountered were white, but that in the camp towns of Columbus, Georgia, and Alexandria, Louisiana, white MPs "strut and eagle-eye through the Negro district with their arms cocked to strike someone. Their attitude is challenging and repulsive." The reporter called for fully trained and equipped black military policemen to increase both the respect of white MPs for black citizens and the respect of black Americans for the police.[62]

In another pattern that would hold during the war, ten of the nineteen confrontations of 1941 occurred in the late summer months of August and September. These were likely to center on recreation and public facilities, including bars.[63] In Tampa, in August, a crowd gathered when a white MP attempted to arrest two black soldiers. A third soldier intervened and drew a knife. After a brief struggle, the MP shot this soldier. A fourth GI leaped on and seized another MP; shot, he ran through the crowd until he collapsed. The MPs then held their guns on the crowd as they removed their injured prisoners.[64] Tampa produced a brutal public beating of a black soldier in September; seven MPs drew their guns to help civilian police drive a crowd away.[65] Violence also

hoods. Of the twenty-seven cities deploying such units, seventeen were located in Florida, Oklahoma, and Texas. The cities were Laurel and Wilmington, Delaware; Charleston and Wheeling, West Virginia; Lexington and Louisville, Kentucky; Knoxville and Memphis, Tennessee; Jacksonville, Miami, Sarasota, Fort Myers, Tampa, and Daytona Beach, Florida; Baltimore, Maryland; Charlotte, North Carolina; Muskogee, Oklahoma City, Okmulgee, and Tulsa, Oklahoma; Austin, Beaumont, Galveston, Houston, San Antonio, Fort Worth, and Corpus Christi, Texas. "Walter Cheevers Says: Atlanta Needs Negro Police," Atlanta *Daily World*, September 21, 1941.

61. "Blocks Effort to Chase Men," New York *Amsterdam News*, August 30, 1941; "Race Rioting Spreads After Dance in Town," Chicago *Defender*, September 20, 1941.
62. "Brutal White MP's Stir Trouble in Army Camp," Pittsburgh *Courier*, June 14, 1941.
63. These included a North Philadelphia disturbance at a swimming pool where the races swam separately at hour and one-half intervals. Fifty police cars and several hundred patrolmen brought order to the area after more than twenty whites were injured. "Relations Strained Over a Week," Norfolk *Journal and Guide,* July 2, 1941; "Ducking a Boy in Pool Starts a Race Riot," New York *Telegram*, July 2, 1941.
64. "Two Soldiers Protest MP's 'Nigger' Shot," Chicago *Defender*, July 26, 1941.
65. The next month, Little Rock's black business district produced a street battle that injured two black soldiers and seven other persons; one hundred soldiers were involved. "Soldiers Flogged by Military Police," Norfolk *Journal and Guide*, September

plagued buses and depots, and black soldiers assigned to manual labor or other service duties – typically undertrained and resentful – were very active in these early disturbances.[66]

In short, the War Department posted black troops to areas where custom, law, and the police combined to severely constrain their rights and actions. Most camp towns or cities had so restricted the black business and recreation district that it either abutted or surrounded the local vice district. One contemporary analysis concluded that there were "far too many Negro soldiers stationed in extremely sensitive southern areas, usually near small communities with an insufficient Negro civil population to absorb the Negro soldiers on pass."[67] Compounding the likelihood of violence, the military enterprise itself taught as much aggression as it did discipline. Hastie pointed out that it was difficult to train a "duel personality" to produce a "fighting man" toward the enemy and a "craven" who accepted inhuman treatment at home.[68]

Fayetteville, North Carolina, August 5, 1941

As a general rule, mistreatment inherent to the initial mobilization caused various forms of black soldier resistance, which in turn led to a repressive response on the part of authorities. A representative case of this mistreatment-resistance-repression dynamic is found in Fayetteville, North Carolina, in 1941, which according to an official history was "a serious portent of future difficulties" for the Army.[69] Ten months prior to Pearl Harbor, the Baltimore *Afro-American* had already nicknamed Fayetteville, North Carolina, "Uncle Sam's Powder Keg." Less than ten miles from the city lay Fort Bragg, the nation's largest Army camp, and visitors sensed a "seething undercurrent" of racial animosity coursing through the area. In two months the town's population had grown from twenty thousand to thirty-five thousand and the narrow road that con-

13, 1941; "3 Shot as Soldiers Riot in Little Rock," Baltimore *Afro-American*, October 11, 1941.

66. Of the seventeen incidents in 1941 that involved soldiers, ten involved members of identified units. Of these, seven involved members of service, engineer, or quartermaster battalions. This reflected the overrepresentation of black soldiers in support-service or overhead units, which accounted for roughly 50 percent of all blacks in the Army in December 1942. The rate for whites was 21.6 percent. Lee, *Employment of Negro Troops*, p. 134; Mershon and Schlossman, *Foxholes and Color Lines*, pp. 53–6.

67. Memorandum, Army Service Forces to Colonel Roamer, October 7, 1944, OF 4245, War Department Material Concerning Minority, October–December, 1944, FDRL.

68. Quoted in Richard M. Dalfiume, *Desegregation of the U.S. Armed Forces; Fighting on Two Fronts, 1939–1953*, Columbia, University of Missouri Press, 1969, p. 46.

69. Lee, *The Employment of Negro Troops*, p. 351.

nected the camp to the town was often packed with crowded cars and segregated buses, sometimes day and night. The thousands of black artillery trainees visited the downtown area each week, drinking and milling about in crowded streets. Because very few establishments welcomed their business, there was little else for them to do.[70] Local merchants usually doubled prices for soldiers, and even the white soldiers changed into civilian clothing to visit the town. According to one, it was "the only way to feel easy at all."[71]

August 4, 1941, was payday for the 34th Coast Artillery Brigade, and its black GIs relaxed and celebrated in Fayetteville the next day and night. Regulations required soldiers to vacate the streets by 1:00 A.M., and as the last "Negro" bus pulled into the railroad station stop at midnight, there was a commotion on board. When soldiers inside the bus began pushing and fighting, apparently arguing about fares, four white military policemen boarded the bus and swung their nightsticks while attempting to arrest the troublemakers. In the midst of this, black Pvt. Ned Turman seized one MP's .45 caliber pistol and opened fire. "I'm gonna break up you MP's beating us colored soldiers," he is said to have shouted. One shot killed an MP and two others were wounded. As the crowd surrounding the bus scrambled to find cover, more white MPs made their way onto the vehicle. In the ensuing gun battle, Turman was shot dead, and seven black soldiers were wounded.

After initial press reports, information about the incident was hard to come by. Military authorities canceled all leave for the four thousand black soldiers at the camp and transferred them to another reservation nine miles away. The commander of the fort announced that the military police would not discuss the incident, pending an investigation by General Davis and three other officers who promptly visited the camp for that purpose. City police also refused to supply additional information to reporters.[72] Results of the War Department's study were released in November, in the form of a letter from Secretary of War Henry Stimson to the NAACP. Despite press reports that white military policemen "ran wild" following the gunfight, cursing and beating black soldiers, Stimson

---

70. "N.C. Boom Town Called Uncle Sam's Powder Keg," Baltimore *African-American*, February 8, 1941.
71. "Race, White Trainees Given Cold Shoulder," Chicago *Defender*, June 21, 1941.
72. Roi Ottley, *'New World A-Coming': Inside Black America*, New York, Arno Press, 1969, p. 312; "Probe Slaying of 2 Soldiers in Bus Battle," Chicago *Tribune*, August 7, 1941; "9 Hurt in Gun Battle," Philadelphia *Tribune*, August 7, 1941; "Ft. Bragg Bus Dispute Ends with Two Dead," Atlanta *Daily World*, August 7, 1941; "4,000 Negro Soldiers Moved to Prevent Racial Clashes," Hopeville [Georgia] *Statesman*, August 19, 1941; Lee, *The Employment of Negro Troops*, p. 351.

explained that the detainment and listing of all witnesses was a necessity misunderstood by the soldiers. The secretary warned blacks against believing newspaper accounts describing the incident in sharply racial terms. The investigating officers, he reported, found that "in no respect" did the incident or its aftermath

> acquire any semblance of a conflict of racial sentiments; and that the occurrence did not arise from, or cause any, tendency toward racial discrimination.[73]

Not everyone agreed. The killings, according to *The Crisis*, were the direct result of the Army's policy of segregating black soldiers and assigning "ignorant, prejudiced, white southern" GIs to military police units. While a court martial ultimately exonerated the MPs of any wrongdoing, at least one black newspaper praised Pvt. Ned Turman's actions as "heroic."[74]

When the fort's public relations bureau began weekly national broadcasts of a radio show that usually included an entertainment act from one of the black units, the Chicago *Bee* called it propaganda aimed at convincing listeners that the camp's black soldiers were having "a wonderful time." But certain conditions had actually worsened. Black troop buses ran only half as often as they had before the shoot-out, and officers instructed mess sergeants to lock up their meat cleavers and butcher knives.[75] Black troops on leave now began dressing in civilian clothes to avoid the constant "dogging" of white military policemen. When the soldiers were paid on September 5, exactly one month after the gunfight, all but two of the larger black units were off post on maneuvers, and Fayetteville was calm.[76]

The War Department pursued more substantial innovations in its policing and recreational programs. When an Army general addressed several hundred black soldiers at the September 20 dedication of the capital's recreation camp for black troops, he noted that high morale required the fair and equal treatment of all troops. The Army, he said, was correcting the conditions responsible for recent events "which have tended to disrupt our progress." With facilities for five hundred men, a

73. "Same Gun Used, War Dept. Says," Norfolk *Journal and Guide*, November 22, 1941.
74. "The Army Must Act," *The Crisis*, September 1941, p. 279; "US Removes Fort Bragg Commander," Baltimore *Afro-American*, October 11, 1941.
75. Army morale officers also began to plan dances for black soldiers at Fayetteville State Teachers College. "Fort Bragg Launches Propaganda Program to Show All is Well," Chicago *Bee*, September 1, 1941; Lee, *The Employment of Negro Troops*, p. 351.
76. "Fort Bragg," Chicago *Bee*, September 1, 1941; "Bragg's First Pay Day After Tragedy, Peace," Kansas City *Call*, September 19, 1941.

softball diamond, a golf course, and recreation tents, the new camp, the camp commander said, resembled "a deluxe hotel." Other such facilities were under construction in Lincoln Park, Chicago; at the Tuskegee Institute; and in Raleigh, North Carolina, less than fifty miles from Fort Bragg. A month later, thirty-one black troop recreation centers were being built; all but three were located in the South and West.[77]

William Hastie also addressed the assembled soldiers, and denied that military investigations were devices for deceiving the public about the mistreatment of blacks. The entire "Fort Bragg controversy," he declared, had been thoroughly and fairly studied, leading to a number of corrective measures, including the assignment to the camp of a provost marshal expert in military policing, increased officer supervision of MPs while in civilian communities, and the establishment of a separate military police headquarters in Fayetteville. Officials also planned a unified Corps of Military Police, including black and white permanent personnel who were systematically and identically trained, equipped, and supervised.[78] Commenting on Hastie's speech, the New York *Age* noted that the policing reforms failed to reassure most black Americans for whom "the only real solution of the problem is a square deal to Negroes" serving in the military or working in civilian branches of government. Fort Bragg also received a new post commander who quickly summoned his entire military police corps to the post theater where he cautioned them against the abuse of their authority, and announced plans to establish a school for them. The War Department, he told the men, planned to professionalize military policing through battalions comprised of select enlisted men and carefully trained officers.[79]

The incident typified the early forms of military race conflict: it occurred in the South, off post, and involved the policing of a brawl. The military police, outnumbered, typically mishandled a minor incident and then overreacted to subsequent challenges. Officers usually further segregated black soldiers following such fights, either by removing them to other facilities, or by restricting them to quarters. Civil and military authorities normally refused to offer detailed information on the incident

---

77. "Army Opens Its Newest Recreation Camp for Negro Soldiers at Anacostia Flats," Washington *Post*, September 21, 1941; "Army Men Not Getting Fair Part of Centers," Baltimore *Afro-American*, November 1, 1941.

78. A provost marshal heads a unit of military police. Hastie's speech also included a great deal of criticism of War Department policy. "Army Opens Its Newest," Washington *Post*, September 21, 1941; Lee, *The Employment of Negro Troops*, p. 357; McGuire, *He, Too, Spoke for Democracy*, pp. 59–60.

79. "Easing Inter-Racial Friction at Army Training Camps," New York *Age*, October 4, 1941.

pending a thorough review, although the black press tried to fill this breach. Usually, the camp provost marshal officially interpreted events for public consumption; in this case, the conflict was significant enough to require the combined intervention of Stimson, Hastie, and Davis. Official accounts often described the events as unrelated to racial concerns, and the army usually deployed conventional public relations efforts with minor ameliorating reforms. The primary response of Army officials at this stage, however, was to seek to perfect their policing apparatus.

Divergent Goals for Racial Manpower Policy: Statesmen and FEPC Staff

Racial unrest had rapidly developed to systemic levels not seen in the United States since the last war. This social disorder framed the early years of the first incarnation of the FEPC, which to make matters worse, began its work with little more than the enabling charter that was the curt executive order. Given the overriding focus on preventing the demonstration and the relatively brief period for officials to analyze fair employment goals and the proper means to meet them, little thought went into the design of the policy mechanism itself. An attorney who helped draft and revise the order recalled asking Wayne Coy what the document should say. "All I know," Coy replied, "is the President says you gotta stop Randolph from marching."[80] The committee, composed of a chairman and four members appointed by the president, would work in the Office of Production Management. Because of a lack of publicity, lack of interest on the part of the major unions, and a budget limited to $80,000 for the first year, the FEPC was initially quite weak. On July 18, Roosevelt issued Executive Order 8823, which increased the committee's membership to six.[81] The FEPC then planned a series of public hearings in major cities, hoping to gauge various regions' employment situations, and through negotiation and public suasion, correct actual cases of discrimination. Los Angeles was the site of the first hearing in October 1941; others in Chicago, New York, and Birmingham followed within eight months. The hearings followed a set proce-

---

80. Joseph L. Rauh, Jr., quoted in Studs Terkel, *"The Good War:" An Oral History of World War Two*, New York, Ballantine Books, p. 335.
81. FDR appointed Mark Ethridge, the publisher of the Louisville *Courier-Journal* as chairman of the committee. The volunteer members included David Sarnoff, industrialist and President of RCA; Earl Dickerson, African American and First International Vice President of the Brotherhood of Sleeping Car Porters; Milton P. Webster, African American and Chicago City Councilman; and, William Green and Philip Murray, leaders of the AFL and CIO, respectively. Reed, *Seedtime*, pp. 22–3.

dure: the chairman opened the meeting with a statement explaining the committee's mandate. Prominent citizens followed with testimony on local employment practices, and representatives of labor and management answered questions on hiring and training patterns. Finally, the committee issued a series of general directives or directives to employers against whom complaints had been lodged.[82]

Through successive hearings, specific criteria emerged by which examiners could attempt to demonstrate employer and union discrimination. For example, the Los Angeles hearings led to a set of directives to defense industries recommending, among other things: the elimination from work applications of questions involving race or religion; the employment of minorities "in all phases" of work; the notification of the committee when employees refused to work with minorities; the public announcement by private firms of halts in discriminatory practices; and action by union officials to end discriminatory practices. Following the Chicago meeting, the committee supplemented its general directives with specific recommendations to individual corporations.

The committee initially utilized the staffs of Weaver's and Alexander's branches of the OPM Labor Division for investigations and employer contact. When finding no immediate resolution, these branches could certify a case to the president's committee, which would investigate it and recommend to federal agencies measures aimed at solving the case. In addition, the committee attempted to deal with discrimination in federal government employment, police the enforcement of nondiscriminatory clauses in defense contracts through contracting agencies, coordinate committee programs with those of state and local employment agencies, and maintain contact with minority organizations.[83]

If, as argued, the state's interest in an efficient and stable mobilization animated the creation of the committee, symptoms of this purpose should appear in its early administrative history. In fact, the first two years of its work were marked by substantial differences of opinion among its members, as administrators favoring mobilization concerns struggled to subdue those volunteer members pursuing social justice. In part because it was a concern for social order that forced Roosevelt to bargain with black leaders in 1941, the FEPC did not immediately resolve the struggle between the central state and the militant black

82. Ruchames, *Race, Jobs, and Politics,* p. 25; Reed, *Seedtime,* p. 69.
83. Early in 1942, when the War Production Board replaced the OPM, it absorbed Hillman's Labor Division, but as labor shortages worsened, FDR created the War Manpower Commission in April and named Paul V. McNutt its chairman. Reed, *Seedtime,* pp. 29, 53; "Minorities in Defense," October 15, 1941, Printed Materials, 1923–1953, Weaver papers; Weaver, *Negro Labor,* pp. 135–6.

leadership. White House officials hoped that the creation of the committee would pacify the northern militants, but like the concessions preceding the order, it had the opposite effect. The FEPC's first chairman,
Mark Ethridge, believed that "the agitators" had promoted the march
so zealously that they were compelled to portray its cancellation as the
result of a great concession. Hence activists unrealistically hailed the
executive order as "a sort of second Emancipation Proclamation." Ethridge himself found the order "plain enough." The committee was to
make recommendations to government departments and to the president
for carrying out the order. It was to receive complaints and then
refer them to and investigate them through the appropriate department.
Its own staff – an executive secretary, an assistant, and a handful of
"troubleshooters" – were to wait until the OPM had attempted to adjust
a situation before acting. "It is obvious that Negroes have been led to
believe a good deal more than the truth by their own leaders," he wrote
at the time.[84]

After a year's work, considerable confusion remained as to the exact
form and purpose of the committee. One member criticized the agency
for having failed to articulate its functions and scope of authority, and
called for a new executive order granting it wide latitude and power.
The second chairman, Malcolm MacLean, disagreed, arguing that the
committee was "a policy-forming, deliberative, judicial body," parallel
to a federal court.[85] The first two chairmen of the FEPC did agree that
the committee should pursue the overlapping goals of fairer employment
practices and the insulation of the president from this brand of social
conflict. The mark of success was, they thought, identical on both fronts:
a reduction in complaints. Because of the heightened expectations the
executive order inspired, Mark Ethridge considered the committee a
valuable forum for strategic and symbolic gestures that might actually
weaken black militants. When the volunteer committee members asked
the president to issue a memorandum directing all federal agencies to
end discriminatory hiring practices, this was quickly done. Ethridge sug-

84. These leaders would have preferred "somebody like Winston Churchill" to be appointed executive secretary. Ethridge later recalled that "the thing was overplayed and
overestimated by the Negroes, the Negro press particularly," which received the order
as if it were a new Magna Carta or Ten Commandments. "The Negroes were given
the idea that automatically, by the issuance of an executive order, all of their problems
would be cured and all of them would go to work, forty acres and a mule." Letter,
Mark Ethridge to Stephen Early, August 20, 1941, OF 93, FDRL; Mark Ethridge,
"The Race Problem in the War," p. 14, Ethridge papers; Reed, *Seedtime*, p. 33.

85. Reed, *Seedtime*, p. 58.

gested that it would be a "brilliant and dramatic stroke" if the president would sign the letter in the presence of the committee and release copies thereafter. "I think it would do more to show action than anything else."[86] If the state's primary concern for an orderly mobilization partly explains the executive order, it also justified the progressive if incremental reform of employment practices, according to Ethridge. "Certainly," he noted after six months of work,

> we have accomplished what the President wanted: we paralyzed any idea of a march on Washington and we have worked honestly for a better measure of justice for the Negroes. They have more jobs in government and industry than they ever had; they have less cause for complaint than they ever had, and they know it . . . [OPM Chief Sidney] Hillman tells me that his complaints have been greatly reduced; I know that those we get from the White House are occasional, rather than a flood.[87]

The committee's second chairman also attempted to insulate the president from blacks' claims. To the petition of a group of black religious leaders, Malcolm MacLean of Hampton Institute proposed responding "carefully so that it would take the heat off the president and at the same time not give undue encouragement." As for the work of the committee, MacLean wrote:

> In fact, as I see it, the job of me and the Committee is to keep the heat off the "Boss" and at the same time to make as steady progress in practical ways as we can.[88]

At this early juncture, agency heads acting on White House instructions viewed the committee, in part, as a tool to reduce, deflect, and absorb discontent.[89]

Along these same strategic lines, Ethridge tried to limit the publicity given to the complaint-adjustment aspect of the committee, since he

86. Letter, Mark Ethridge to Stephen Early, August 20, 1941, OF 93, FDRL.
87. Letter, Mark Ethridge to Stephen Early, December 23, 1941, OF 4245, OPM, Committee on Fair Employment Practice, FDRL.
88. "I need . . . to get instructions from you," he also wrote. Letter, Malcolm S. MacLean to Marvin H. McIntyre, February 24, 1942, OF 93, FDRL. On MacLean and his political advice to the president, see also Reed, *Seedtime*, pp. 48–51.
89. This cautiousness applied to angry whites as well. When a police chief informed the president that agitators and federal agencies had undermined white supremacy in the South and had made Alabama's blacks "impudent, unruly, arrogant, law breaking, violent and insolent," Executive Secretary Lawrence Cramer drafted a letter of response, but FDR's aides rejected it. There appears to have been no reply. Letter, Eugene "Bull" Connor to FDR, August 7, 1942, OF 4245, FDRL.

believed that publicizing information related to discrimination stimulated additional unrest.[90] The feeling was common in the administration. The under secretaries of War and Navy, for example, feared that such a complaint board might arouse as much as allay racial prejudices.[91] The Civil Rights Section in the Justice Department worried that the FEPC gave "widespread new publicity to economic, political and social injustices" by highlighting previously obscured forms of discrimination. In doing so, it further provoked the critics of the administration.[92] As with race reform debates in the thirties, White House "avoidance was the rule," and extreme caution characterized officials in other departments as well.[93] But these white directors learned that they could not easily control the committee, and its black volunteer members in particular, who were competing directly with the WMC and Robert Weaver's attempts to improve employment opportunities through other means.

Divergent Approaches to Racial Manpower Policy: The NETB and FEPC Staff

In contrast to the volunteer race membership of the FEPC, officials at the War Manpower Commission believed that the overt politicization of employment policy was unlikely to produce lasting gains for black Americans. But the more accommodating approach of the WMC suffered from obvious drawbacks of its own to most African Americans, for it appeared to be unprincipled and indirect, and it seemed to fail to deliver jobs.

The differences in strategy separating the FEPC from the WMC are

90. Letter, Mark Ethridge to Stephen Early, December 23, 1941, OF 4245, FDRL; Reed, *Seedtime*, p. 33.
91. Memorandum, Robert Patterson and James Forrestal to the President, June 24, 1941, OF 93, FDRL.
92. The Undersecretary of War advised FDR against releasing a summary of FEPC hearings on discrimination in defense training, since it might further alienate local officials who administered the program, particularly in the South. He recommended that the Office of Education secure local compliance through "private persuasion" or through its control of funds. Justice Department memo quoted in Reed, *Seedtime*, pp. 99, 185; memorandum, Robert P. Patterson, Undersecretary of War, to FDR, July 14, 1942, OF 4245, FDRL.
93. In considering whether to pursue sedition charges against the militant black press, for example, Justice Department officials, calculating the effects of declaring African American newspapers unmailable, concluded that it "could only result in aggravating further unrest . . ." Weiss, *Farewell to the Party of Lincoln*, p. 249; memorandum, Coral Sadler to D. W. Barco, October 29, 1942, quoted in Washburn, *A Question of Sedition*, p. 140.

most clearly revealed by contrasting examples of the discrete community utilization work of Alexander and Weaver in the Labor Division from the public, complaint-adjustment orientation of the FEPC. The approaches differed in three important ways. First, in his negotiations with unions and employers, Weaver stressed local white elites' self-interest in providing for black training and employment in order to avoid housing, policing, and servicing large numbers of white migrants. FEPC activists based their claims on the national nondiscriminatory policy enunciated in the executive orders and, by extension, on the principle of fairness they enunciated. Second, in practice the Labor Division's staff met primarily with white employers, personnel managers, and federal and union officials. The committee, on the other hand, built its casework through sympathetic interviews of minority workers, applicants, and organizations. Finally, with reference to publicity, Weaver's NETB most often announced positive news of agreements reached and black workers employed. In addition, its parent organization, the WMC, broadly publicized the goal of full manpower utilization – including minority workers – through radio, feature articles, and booklets.[94] The early FEPC, on the other hand, despite the moderating influence of its white directors, publicized noncompliance with national policy. Because the FEPC confronted contractors with charges of discrimination and reviewed their employment practices in public hearings, "politically sensitive administration leaders preferred the quiet ways of the Labor Division to the FEPC's public activity."[95] Weaver's accomplice in the WMC, Will Alexander, thought that the executive secretary of the FEPC was "doing a very bad job" because of the latter's "publicity policy." Alexander described it as "always telling what they are going to do and not what they have done," as opposed to Weaver's policy of announcing job openings after negotiations had succeeded. The committee, Alexander thought, had not acted on the results of its hearings, but instead had "become largely a publicity agency for the doctrines of Walter White and Randolph."[96]

Weaver believed that the political origins of the committee – its close affiliation with the more militant black leadership and its birth as a stepchild of a demonstration canceled at the eleventh hour – had driven

94. This realm of public relations Weaver called "the most significant aspect of the commission's early work." Weaver, *Negro Labor*, p. 139.
95. Reed, *Seedtime*, pp. 81–2; Weaver, *Negro Labor*, p. 133.
96. Alexander thought Chairman MacLean was beholden to the two leaders because he sought their support to shore up his precarious status as president of Hampton Institute. Jonathan Daniels, *White House Witness: 1942–1945*, New York, Doubleday and Company, 1975, pp. 95–6.

its members to emphasize those activities that would garner support for it rather than develop the most promising long-term plans and programs. Internally, the committee focused on holding hearings and issuing cease-and-desist orders to the detriment of developing enforcement efforts in contracting agencies and other federal departments. Again, due to the circumstances of its creation, Weaver believed the committee was attempting to absorb all government operations related to minority employment. In part because the NETB was associated with employment gains, however limited, it appeared to interfere with the FEPC's need to gather and reward public support. In addition, the field staffs of the NETB and the Minority Branch weakened the FEPC's call for a field staff of its own. Lacking investigators, the committee had to choose between investigating fewer cases more fully or additional cases that were but nominally researched. Driven by its militant clientele, it pursued the latter strategy and distributed many cease-and-desist orders without detailed investigations. This, Weaver thought, was probably "the most serious administrative error" that the committee made, for it cost the FEPC considerable prestige in government and industry.[97]

The second major problem with FEPC operations, Weaver believed, was its overreliance on individual complaints as the basis for public hearings on firms' employment practices. Black applicants, he argued, knew that very few establishments would consider them for employment, and thus "flocked" to the gates of those plants known to employ minorities, which were often the very same large firms with which the NETB and the Minority Groups Branch had worked to open jobs to nonwhites. Since large numbers of blacks applied to these firms, the result was a large number of complaints, including some that were not valid. But very few minority workers applied to the most discriminatory firms, and thus very few complaints and a small fraction of the work of the hearings and investigations focused on these worst offenders. For example, despite Weaver's and Alexander's extensive work with management at the Lockheed-Vega Corporation in Los Angeles, which had led to a cooperative agreement to increase black employment there, the FEPC's executive secretary had responded to a single complaint of failure to employ by notifying the firm that the committee was considering holding a public hearing on discrimination there.[98] This paradoxical

---

97. Weaver, *Negro Labor*, pp. 138–9.
98. While Weaver believed that all complaints should have been investigated according to its staffing levels, he thought that the FEPC had some discretion in determining which complaints would be developed in public hearings. Daniels, *White House Witness*, pp. 95–6; letter, Robert C. Weaver to Rabbi Louis Ruchames, January 13, 1948, Correspondence – R, Weaver papers; Weaver, *Negro Labor*, pp. 134–45.

process, by which the most progressive firms attracted the most complainants, fed resentment toward the FEPC among even sympathetic
managers and officials. Weaver thought a broad, economic approach to
the "over-all aspects of minority groups' utilization" rather than a legal-
istic approach to individual complaints would have better served the
FEPC.[99] Other federal officials worried that such public hearings might
exacerbate interracial animosity in tense production areas. In late 1942,
for example, management and Army representatives feared that a
planned hearing in Detroit would aggravate race tensions there and
suggested that violations be "worked out through cooperative effort
in camera rather than in the white light of publicity."[100] The Industrial Personnel Division of the War Department likewise found that
public hearings often crystalized the opposition instead of resolving the
conflict.[101]

Considering the extremely delicate political circumstances that led to
the Executive Order, and central state officials' subsequent aversion to
publicity that might cause additional organized protest, one of the chief
problems posed by the committee to the party coalition and to the
mobilization – and a chief source of contention among manpower officials – was the confrontational tenor and publicity that characterized the
FEPC's public hearings, findings, and directives. The relatively militant
technique and tone of the directives to employers was largely the work
of the two black volunteer members of the original committee, both
southern-born men who had built their careers in the North. To a greater
degree than the other members, Milton Webster, vice president of Randolph's Brotherhood of Sleeping Car Porters and a leader in the Chicago
Republican organization, and Earl Dickerson, a Chicago Urban League
leader and Democratic alderman, insisted on attacking discrimination
openly and without compromise. Dickerson was apparently the first
member to propose public hearings and in September 1941 convinced
the committee to schedule the first three. He then helped to mold their
form and tone, often criticizing draft findings for being too weak and
instructing the staff to avoid using words such as "persuade" and "encourage." Dickerson, concerned that Executive Order 8802 had changed

99. He noted that the committee substantially improved its ability to consider the relative
accomplishments of different plants over the course of the war but never overcame
its inability to address the worst practices, which had nonetheless generated no
complaints. Weaver, *Negro Labor*, pp. 143–4.
100. Memorandum, C. T. Keppel and A. H. Raskin to the Undersecretary of War, December 24, 1942, Labor Morale, Ohly papers.
101. Memorandum, W. C. Leland to James P. Mitchell, June 28, 1943, Labor Discrimination, Racial Character, Ohly papers.

hiring patterns very little in the short term, preferred findings that clearly stated a firm's guilt and directed it to report on its changed policies. Whether or not it was his work alone, after the Birmingham hearings "tough language" came to characterize FEPC findings and directives.[102]

Conversely, two cases of Weaver's preferred method exemplify the WMC's approach to adjusting "the over-all aspects" of the minority manpower problem.[103] These investigations, conducted in southern cities in 1942, also demonstrate how the prospects for correcting discriminatory practices varied in different cities, depending on the relative mobilization and organization of the black and white segments of the city. In April, Cy Record, one of Weaver's lieutenants, summarized his work in Memphis, Tennessee. Political affairs there were governed by the centralized machine of Boss Crump, whose control reached into the "Unions, the Churches, the Social Agencies, the Fraternal Organizations, and into all other affairs of organized community life."[104] When Record attempted to force an Iron Workers local to accept a black rodman, he was referred to their international office, which explained that the candidate was unqualified for membership in the union. Record believed that if the FEPC were to pursue this particular complaint, Crump and an allied senator, Democrat Kenneth McKellar, would enter the dispute, pressuring OPM to end its attempt to adjust the case. More important, Record thought the case a good example of why "we will get nowhere" by approaching discrimination through individual complaints. First, only a small fraction of victims reported their claims to federal authorities. Since discrimination by local employers or union officials was a matter of policy, investigators would necessarily be directed to the governing international or central office, which might flatly condone the practice or pass the complaint back to the local, complicating and obscuring an otherwise simple matter. Third, even if a settlement were reached in a particular case, no precedent was set, nor was any policy necessarily changed. Finally, and perhaps most important, in attempting to address each individual case, "we cannot enlist the support and concern of the Negroes of the community on a group basis." In Memphis, for example, since the Crump machine presented particular risks for race organizing of any kind and thus made local

---

102. Dickerson later described himself as "the leader of all the agitation that went on in the committee." Terkel, *The Good War*, p. 339; Reed, *Seedtime*, pp. 34, 44–5.
103. It is unusually difficult to recreate Weaver's work since his offices' files were apparently lost or destroyed. See August Meier and Elliott Rudwick, *Black Detroit and the Rise of the UAW*, New York, Oxford University Press, 1979, p. 248, fn 38.
104. This discussion is drawn from Memorandum, Cy W. Record to Robert C. Weaver, April 11, 1942, Correspondence – R, Weaver papers.

groups reluctant to undertake action on a collective basis, Memphis residents were denied the advantages that accrue to organized groups, namely that:

> By acting as a group, they are able to muster a great deal more support behind their effort to adjust cases of discrimination. They are able too, to prevent complaints of discrimination from being treated or dismissed as the inconsequential complaints of some trouble maker.

For all these reasons, a policy of pursuing individual complaints signaled firms and unions that no serious attempt was being made to force the practices of the entire organization into permanent compliance with national policy.[105]

The NETB, by contrast, adopted a broad planning perspective on a given metropolitan labor market and its particular pattern of race relations. Before making any direct attempt to correct discriminatory practices in Memphis, Record recommended determining the probable number, type, and wages of workers the area would require over the course of the war; the policies of local firms and unions on the utilization of nonwhite workers; the number and skill level of available black workers; the nature of the local leadership and the potential for the further organization of the black population; the racial attitudes of the white machine leadership; and the willingness of the War Production Board, the FEPC, and the president to systematically combat discrimination in this area. Once all this was clear, Record suggested assigning a full-time representative to Memphis to investigate all defense-related discrimination, involve local race organizations, and refer to Washington for "the quickest possible disposition" any matters that officials could not adjust locally. In addition, he recommended assigning an FEPC official to the city to investigate defense employment practices and to call before the committee violators of national policy in that vicinity at the same time that the local investigator was attempting to adjust matters locally.

Four months later, Record reported on Charleston, South Carolina, where he found that substantial progress had been made "to establish channels locally." A local Negro Community Council had been established, apparently at his urging, which nearly reflected the breadth of the Crump machine in drawing from black "Churches, Fraternal Organizations, Educational Institutions, and one Trade Union." Though only a month old, the body had met with the local administrative council to

---

105. Ironically, this collective approach would be supplanted by a complaint-centered approach championed by the committee born of collective action threatened by Randolph.

discuss the creation of a training program for blacks and had launched a campaign to register potential trainees in the area. The organization could now base its demands for additional training courses and facilities upon this registry. The council also had gained the reinstatement of three black Navy Yard workers discharged in a labor dispute through direct negotiations with the Labor Board at the Charleston Navy Yard. The board agreed to consider other such appeals from the council in the future. The Common Laborer's Union, on the advice of Record, had likewise established direct channels for the prevention and punishment of violence against black workers. Still, despite some promises of changes to come, the Defense Training Program trained only whites, mainly for jobs at the Navy Yard. Record recommended that OPM contact the U.S. Office of Education directly, for the Yard planned to nearly double its payroll over the next eighteen months, and shortages already existed in several skilled categories. While blacks at the time represented 15.8 percent of the shipyard workers, they accounted for only 3.4 percent of the skilled workers.[106] Overall, it appeared that a combination of local organizational strength and central state intervention had achieved significant gains. In effect, Record pursued the accelerated development – and federal reinforcement – of the preexisting, informal, indigenous, and organization-based system of complaint reporting and adjustment described in Chapter 2.

WMC minority branches established comparable techniques for gaining the cooperation of unions, particularly unions that already included some nonwhite members. Again the goal was to establish and develop enduring local civic mechanisms to monitor employment practices and evaluate bias claims. Instructions suggested securing the union's general policy statement on black members and then reminding local officers of their responsibility to impress upon their members the necessity for full manpower utilization under the national nondiscriminatory policy. The plan advised reaching out to minority members of unions through the local community's "stable and articulate" black organizations. Two methods were suggested for encouraging the development of fair practices inside unions: organize an antidiscrimination committee composed of representatives of several trade unions, or establish a fair employment practices committee at a local or international union level to consider bias complaints and confer with management and federal officials on nondiscriminatory policy. Both bodies would help create an atmosphere favorable to the acceptance of black workers before their hiring and

106. Letter, Cy Record to Robert Weaver, August 7, 1942, Correspondence – R, Weaver papers.

monitor reactions after hiring. Assistance from the plant's War or Navy Department representative would help prepare the workforce for additional minority workers, and any resistance would be met firmly and promptly by union, company, and federal authorities.[107]

Robert Weaver argued that the WMC's potential effect on minority integration was demonstrated most effectively in Baltimore, where the commission implemented a voluntary job control program beginning in the summer of 1942. Commission staff developed agreements governing the referral of workers through the USES, directed programs to secure additional training facilities for blacks and, to boost their employment and acceptance, built relationships with preexisting minority organizations. In Weaver's view, this broad program, oriented toward brokering agreements among federal authorities, private firms, and indigenous organizations, established "adequate machinery" to translate WMC policy pronouncements into fact.[108] The resolution of the competition between the broad political-economic approach of the WMC and the complaint-centered, principled approach of the FEPC is a subject of the next chapter.

Conclusion

The FEPC's Birmingham hearing of June 1942 attracted widespread attention in part due to Mark Ethridge's remarks clarifying the committee's position of segregation. Apparently intending to reassure a region organized around the economic and political subjugation of blacks, he informed the audience that the FEPC had no position on segregation, since "no power in the world," including the combined forces of the Allies and Axis, could force southern whites to abandon it. But the remark that revealed more of the administration's hand was his simple observation that Executive Order 8802 was "a war order, not a social document."[109]

From the political biographer's perspective, FDR's treatment of Randolph was merely another example of the president's familiar use of tactical parries aimed at co-opting protest movements. By promoting partial reforms, Roosevelt repeatedly turned aside demands for more radical change: the Agricultural Adjustment Act and the emergency Farm Credit Act of May and June 1933 checked radical Milo Reno and his

107. War Manpower Service, WMC, "A Suggested Outline of Procedures and Techniques for Dealing with Manpower Problems in Cooperation with Union Labor," undated, Labor Discrimination (Racial Character), Ohly papers, HSTL.

108. Weaver, *Negro Labor*, p. 140.

109. Ruchames, *Race, Jobs, and Politics*, p. 25; Reed, *Seedtime*, p. 69.

Farmers' Holiday Association, just as the federal old age pension section of the Social Security Act of 1935 undercut the radical Townsendite movement.[110] Other precedents must have echoed in FDR's memory. As the Democratic presidential candidate in 1932, he had benefited a great deal from Herbert Hoover's inept and cruel handling of the Great War veterans' Bonus Expeditionary Force in 1932, which marched on Washington and – more important – stayed behind in their tents after the demonstration ended. Recall, finally, that as assistant secretary of the navy, FDR worked in Washington, D.C., during the local racial violence of 1919, which gained ferocity from a "crime wave" trumpeted by the Washington *Post*.[111]

But any other skilled statesman would have responded in a similar way in this case. Circumstances related to the war – local social order concerns and the desire to retain flexibility to respond to an impending attack – combined to raise the costs of refusing Randolph's claim and forced the president to grant a substantial and unprecedented concession. It was this extraordinary political context that also stamped the FEPC's work with a constituency-service orientation within a larger network of agencies and officials pursuing efficiency rather than social justice concerns. As we will see, the FEPC's struggle for relevancy and power against opponents in the White House and War Manpower Commission remained at the mercy of mobilization and electoral concerns until a recast FEPC finally assumed a stable position in the war administration during the violent summer of 1943.

The potential for disorder that propelled Randolph's demands was not limited to the capital city. Following a series of incidents of collective race violence that can be considered transitional, the Fayetteville event anticipated several characteristics typical of those wartime incidents analyzed in Chapter 5. Confrontations often revolved around segregated buses and recreation areas, and occurred in overcrowded camp towns. Undertrained MPs, outnumbered by soldiers, often overreacted to a minor incident and in so doing stimulated additional resistance. Officials often isolated black soldiers following fights, either by removing them to other facilities or by restricting them to quarters. Subsequent chapters

110. Elizabeth Sanders, "The President and War," April 2, 1991, unpublished manuscript, p. 2.
111. Roosevelt wrote to his wife on July 23, 1919, that the crowds and police never approached their home, although he heard occasional gunshots in the distance: "It has been a nasty episode and I only wish *quicker* action had been taken to stop it." *FDR: His Personal Letters, 1905–1928*, Elliott Roosevelt, ed., New York, Duell, Sloan, and Pearce, 1948, pp. 479–80, emphasis in original; Shapiro, *White Violence and Black Response*, p. 153.

demonstrate that, although the War Department's repertoire of responses to resistance grew more complex over the course of the war – to include public relations efforts, indoctrination, and occasional ameliorating reforms – the principal institutional responses to unrest remained policing and repression.

The mobilization thoroughly shocked preexisting political and economic norms and patterns, causing a number of salient and interrelated effects in the field of race management, including the stimulation of friction and the weakening of preexisting party mobilization techniques such as the Black Cabinet. But in order to fully explicate the methods by which the FEPC mediated the relationship between the mobilization and black workers, the analysis now turns to consider the ways that war stimulated a migration of opportunity that concentrated black industrial workers in key mobilization cities and sectors. In order to play an important role in the resulting friction and accommodation, the FEPC had to first survive challenges from opponents and rivals in the White House and WMC.

4

The Racial Politics of Industrial Employment: Central State Authority and the Adjustment of Factory Work

The causes of the riots are apparent. During the last three years the population of Detroit has increased by 485,000 people, many of whom are colored. There are no subways or elevated trains in Detroit so that the transportation situation is particularly difficult causing great over-crowding in the buses. The housing situation, particularly among the colored sections, is deplorable. The same is true of the recreation situation, which is greatly over-burdened and over-crowded. The Detroit Police Department is, in spite of the increase in population, actually 250 men short of budget allotments. Moreover, many of the present policemen are not well trained on account of the number of men who have been drafted and whose places had to be filled from the only available and often inadequate personnel. These conditions prevail generally throughout the country ... It is extremely interesting that there was no disorder *inside plants*, where colored and white men worked side by side ...

Attorney General Francis Biddle to FDR, July 15, 1943[1]

The near-total mobilization of a nation's material and human resources requires warmakers to search for new and more effective mechanisms with which to adjust potentially debilitating class, race, and ethnic conflicts, and the WMC and the FEPC were among the agencies that enabled this regime to exploit its productive potential as fully and as efficiently as it did. One of the effects of the invention of the FEPC was to reorient a large part of the preexisting, informal complaint activity toward the central state. In return for a temporary grant of legitimacy to the most reasonable of these fairness claims, the warmakers hoped the FEPC would incorporate black leaders into the governing regime and facilitate the utilization of black manpower in factories. The concession promised to weaken militancy both immediately through the march's cancellation,

1. Memorandum, Francis Biddle to Franklin Roosevelt, July 15, 1943, OF 93, Colored Matters, FDRL; emphasis in original.

and for the duration of the war by substantially standardizing the complaint process, as race advancement organizations' work shifted from making claims on authorities to making cases for authorities. The public confrontation between the movement leader and the president, however, politicized the committee's early operation and subsequent development, and as in the Army, state officials' reassessment of this manpower initiative began at once. This internal reform process reveals White House officials seeking further insulation, by stifling grievances as well as by adjusting them.

Those states that do not launch wars but merely respond to attacks, suffer, relative to aggressors, an inherent disadvantage in marshaling their human resources for war. To the degree that abnormal state-society compacts such as the FEPC are reached very quickly, they are more fragile than the products of the routine deliberations of peacetime politics. For one thing, the state's overriding concern for efficiency in the mobilization undermines their effectiveness, since societal and state actors will disagree on the reform's primary intent. In addition, the state simply may be unfamiliar with the civic group's recent development – its new members, strategies, and attitudes – since the reform is not a product of the sustained interplay of pressure groups and parties in formal institutions such as Congress. Finally, following from these factors, the policy may be disruptive simply because it is poorly or vaguely designed.

The subsequent operations of the FEPC indicate sets of state and party ends and means that were distinct from both advocates and opponents of racial equality. An internal White House debate, albeit a narrowly circumscribed one, continued through the crisis year of 1943, as state officials in effect tested and discarded two approaches to the problems of black manpower discontent and underutilization before the FEPC was reformed for the last time in May 1943 into what proved to be a useful hybrid. From Weaver's "community utilization" model, FDR and his advisors drew the keynote of labor market efficiency and the procedural tactic of favoring local negotiations. From the first FEPC, the president retained the individual complaint trigger and the investigate-and-adjust response mechanisms. As in the Army, the administration deployed some policies and appointments that aided blacks. Officials pursuing the general goal of regime survival, however – through the full mobilization of industrial production and the maintenance of the governing party coalition – defeated and in some cases personally replaced those officials seeking the more particular goals of specific groups, both egalitarian and racist.

The investigative casework of the second FEPC during the full-blown mobilization of 1943–44, the evidentiary core of this chapter, reflect several broad patterns in the utilization of black factory labor that are consistent with a state- and party-centered analysis. First, the spatial and sectional concentration of war contracts helped channel black workers, after an initial delay, toward contract-rich cities. Thus, when the FEPC opened twelve regional offices in 1943–44 to receive individual complaints, their investigative work focused on war-critical cities and sectors. The concentration of state spending for production, as well as the location of race advancement organizations such as the NAACP and the Urban League, combined to generate modestly disproportionate shares of complaints in northeastern and coastal production capitals such as New York City and San Francisco. The concentration of FEPC casework in war sectors, however, was even more focused. The FEPC's investigative and enforcement efforts focused on civilian employees in the Army, the Navy, and the aircraft and shipbuilding industries. This paradoxically reflects the salience and even the effectiveness of fair employment policies in state and state-sponsored sectors. Biased practices occurred at these sites at unexceptional rates. But because these installations required legions of new workers, and because they formally complied with the executive order, black individuals and organizations aimed their applications and campaigns at them. Relatively prompt responses to these cases encouraged additional complaints in turn. Thus grievances against war agencies, other arms of the central state, and state-sponsored sectors such as munitions, accumulated at rates out of proportion to their black workforces. The evidence, presented as a sequential argument, indicates that the FEPC's potential to enhance executive insulation and increase mobilization efficiency by relieving domestic tensions directly shaped warmakers' plans for the committee, the design and the procedures of the reformed FEPC, and the casework of the agency in 1943–44.

Pursuing Efficiency: The Assessment and Adjustment of Staffs, Agencies, and Procedures

Since neither Weaver's Negro Employment and Training Branch nor the initial FEPC provided for the incorporation of black elites and the utilization of black masses without unacceptable costs, White House officials spent nearly two years assessing and altering the practices of these competing agencies.[2] Weaver's relatively quiet diplomacy among local organ-

2. FDR often assigned the same task to multiple agencies or administrators, in effect delaying decisions until the public politics surrounding the assignment ripened; the ensuing bureaucratic competition sometimes produced more effective practices. Richard

izations may have promised to lay the foundation for long-term interracial amity, but its gradualistic approach was ill-suited to black leaders' expectations, which ran at a heightened wartime pace. The so-called confrontational tone of the first FEPC reversed these effects: It fortified the administration's standing among race leaders, but caused resistance on the part of southern white oligarchs, firm managers, and federal contracting officials.[3] While this interagency competition continued, hopes were high on the FEPC's first anniversary. The annual budget was to increase to $1 million, which would fund twelve regional offices, and FDR apparently suggested that he would direct the committee to investigate discrimination in the armed forces as well as in the workplace. Without warning, however, on July 30, 1942, Roosevelt transferred the committee to the WMC, supervised by Paul McNutt. Although several reasons animated the move, including McNutt's desire to consolidate all manpower planning, FDR transferred the FEPC "in order to control and weaken it." Its supporters saw this as an effort to placate the committee's enemies – again, federal agency heads, employers, and Southern Democratic Congressmen – by removing the FEPC from the secure perimeter of the president's Office of Emergency Management.[4] As an independent presidential agency, the committee had received funds through the relatively insulated Executive Office; under McNutt, funding would be requested as part of the larger WMC budget request from Congress, where hostile commercial and segregationist interests could sabotage the unit and its requests.

The transfer followed a meeting between FDR and the Bureau of the Budget director, Harold Smith, who worried that the committee's hearings, findings, and directives were limiting the nation's productive capacity by disturbing the state's relations with war contractors. FDR and

E. Neustadt, *Presidential Power and the Modern Presidents: The Politics of Leadership from Roosevelt to Reagan*, New York, The Free Press, 1990, pp. 131–4.

3. For a contrast of Weaver's "careful" investigations, tactful negotiations with employers, and "polite" prodding of federal officials with the strategy of the FEPC, "which sought to expose and embarrass recalcitrant" firms and unions, see August Meier and Elliott Rudwick, *Black Detroit and the Rise of the UAW*, New York, Oxford University Press, 1979, pp. 111–12.

4. The fact that McNutt was considered a possible Democratic Party presidential nominee made him appear to black leaders particularly vulnerable to the committee's opponents. Merl E. Reed, *Seedtime for the Civil Rights Movement: The President's Committee on Fair Employment Practice, 1941–1946*, Baton Rouge, Louisiana State University Press, 1991, pp. 54, 74–6; letter, John Eardlie to FDR, August 16, 1942, OF 4245, OPM, Committee on Fair Employment Practices, WMC, FDRL. The Reed volume is by a wide margin the finest history of the FEPC, and the analysis in this chapter draws heavily upon it.

Smith apparently agreed that the FEPC should respond to complaints by simply referring them and the complainant to the appropriate government office. In language reminiscent of Weaver's efficiency arguments, the president thought the transfer would enable the committee to better contribute to the "complete utilization of the available manpower of the country." Within a week, the White House released a memo that described the shift as a move to strengthen the committee, yet black leaders knew otherwise. The WMC had to approve every field office decision to charge an employer with discrimination; the WMC would supervise a single staff through its own regional directors; the WMC could veto FEPC recommendations on hearings, personnel, and field operations; and the FEPC would not act on complaints in industries already monitored by Weaver and the Labor Division of the WMC.[5]

What accounts for the primacy of war-fighting concerns at this juncture? The tensions surrounding the committee's work concerned the president. As the mobilization accelerated toward a total war effort in mid-1942, FDR hoped to encourage political parties and factions to suspend the routine practice of politics so as to conserve the nation's resources and focus them on production for war. The Allies began the year in very difficult circumstances and he feared that the country might "dissipate energies needed for the fighting."[6] The Soviets' defense against the Nazi siege on Leningrad had just begun, grimly and inauspiciously. The initial phase of the Pacific campaign was disastrous, as Japan swiftly conquered the Philippines, Malaya, and Burma, while destroying an Allied fleet in the Java Sea. Disagreements divided the major partners of the alliance on such grave issues as the timing and target of the Anglo-American invasion of Europe, and the proper means for the relief of China. The latter required many more aircraft than were available, while the former project required an armada of unbuilt ships. Still worse, forty percent of the American public simply did not understand what the war was "all about."[7]

But, at this critical point in the second half of 1942, the midterm election campaigns intensified, and race activists again played their political card. The FEPC captured a significant concession: the committee and the commission agreed in October to a qualified administrative fusion, which in effect ended McNutt's reign as arbiter of fair employ-

5. Reed, *Seedtime*, pp. 75, 79, 81–3; John Eardlie to FDR, August 16, 1942, OF 4245, FDRL.
6. Robert Dallek, *Franklin D. Roosevelt and American Foreign Policy, 1932–1945*, New York, Oxford University Press, 1979, p. 360.
7. Dallek, *FDR and American Foreign Policy*, p. 358.

ment policy. Most importantly, Weaver's NETB and Alexander's Minority Group Branch of the WMC were abolished, and their investigators were reassigned to the FEPC, now the single operating agency within the WMC on all matters related to workplace discrimination. The FEPC also regained control of the appointment of field investigators. Significantly, McNutt retained control over the scheduling of hearings. The midterm elections had driven the administration to demote Weaver and eliminate the FEPC's competitors in the field, for their relative lack of popularity among blacks made them expendable.[8] The NAACP and the FEPC had gained these "large concessions" from McNutt by threatening the resignation of certain committee members during the campaign season; McNutt resented the fact that the committee "undertook to hold him up on the basis of the Negro vote" in this episode.[9] Thus, state officials' ongoing assessment of the initiative had been interrupted by the regular election cycle prescribed by the American Constitution, and militants again managed to propel the FEPC forward through the skillful application of leverage that on this occasion was of the electoral variety.[10] Again, the potential costs of ignoring the insurgents' threat were deemed too great to ignore.

After the election, however, the salience of such politically motivated gestures and thus the leverage of the militants receded dramatically. Reasserting the primacy of production over political concerns, McNutt on January 11, 1943, followed White House instructions and indefinitely postponed hearings on discrimination in the railroad industry. The White House also delayed hearings on Washington, D.C.'s Capital Transit Company's refusal to train and hire black platform men and motormen. According to a memorandum from the Civil Rights Section of the Justice Department, the Capital Transit case was being pursued by the FEPC amid such great publicity that it threatened to become a "super Scottsboro" incident at a most inopportune time. Tensions surrounding these investigations provided the immediate motivation for McNutt to "immobilize the Committee" in this way.[11]

---

8. McNutt later reneged on his promise to transfer Weaver's field representatives; they would work instead for WMC regional directors. Meier and Rudwick, *Black Detroit*, p. 112. For an example of the continuing importance of this staff, see Reed, *Seedtime*, pp. 86–7, 97.

9. Daniels, *White House Witness*, p. 116; Reed, *Seedtime*, p. 99.

10. Personifying his own call for a suspension of politics as usual, FDR absented himself from the 1942 congressional elections. He remarked wishfully just prior to the vote that he hoped "the country will forget politics for two years." Dallek, *FDR and American Foreign Policy*, p. 361.

11. This local case had contributed to Jonathan Daniels's rise in the White House in

Specific war-fighting concerns also played a major role in the post-ponements. Late in the evening of January 9, the president secretly left for a nearly two-week long conference with Winston Churchill at Casablanca, where they discussed operations against Japan, as well as plans for a cross-channel attack in 1944 and the Mediterranean theater's relationship to that invasion. Allied victories in late 1942 in Guadalcanal and in North Africa and the Soviets' resolute defense of Leningrad contributed to the sense that the war's momentum had finally reversed. Before he left, in a White House session concerning the transit case, FDR cryptically told Earl Dickerson only that he wanted the case delayed until his return.[12] Thereafter, FDR acknowledged that the war had reached a turning point, but cautioned the nation against premature celebrations: "There is no time now for anything but fighting and working to win."[13]

At this critical stage of the war, the partial neutralization of the committee, American statesmen thought, best served warmaking ends. The reassessment period appeared indefinite; FDR would wait four months before resolving the impasse. Several committee members' resignations, including MacLean's, further weakened the FEPC. Despite mounting protests, however, McNutt held fast, for elections were a distant concern.[14]

The Reorientation of Race Manpower Policy for Factories

Unlike Allied prospects abroad, domestic social order deteriorated rapidly through the spring of 1943. There were new and more serious

November, as the FEPC announced its investigation of the company on the last day of a poll tax fight in Congress. Daniels promptly wrote to FDR that the announcement could both frighten southern segregationists and unfairly raise black expectations. Race policy, he suggested, required "more wisdom and tact." In this way, Daniels offered his advisory services, and the president immediately accepted them. Reed, *Seedtime*, p. 99; memorandum, Jonathan Daniels, Bureau of the Budget, to Franklin Roosevelt, November 24, 1942, OF 93, FDRL.

12. Dickerson's recollection, that FDR personally asked him to postpone a hearing on the Capital Transit Company just before departing for what turned out to be the Yalta Conference, was apparently flawed. The request must have occurred in early January 1943, since he recalled that the deferment was followed by the reorganization of the committee, and since Dickerson no longer served on the FEPC at the time of Yalta in February 1945. The second committee attempted to press forward with the transit case, but company officials succeeded in delaying the full hearing for three years. Studs Terkel, *"The Good War:" An Oral History of World War Two*, New York, Ballatine Books, 1984, pp. 338–9; Reed, *Seedtime*, pp. 95–8, 103.

13. Quoted in Dallek, *FDR and American Foreign Policy*, p. 373.

14. The committee nonetheless continued to hold hearings and to issue cease-and-desist orders "thick and fast," as one black columnist put it. Quoted in Reed, *Seedtime*, p. 90.

outbreaks of violence in the Army, while firms, federal officials, and unions defied the nondiscrimination order to varying degrees nationwide. Thus, this reassessment of the committee attracted an unusually broad spectrum of administration officials. A consensus nonetheless immediately emerged among White House advisors that FEPC reforms should moderate the agitation of "extremists" of all kinds through changes in procedures, staffing, and the location of the agency in the mobilization hierarchy.

Lawrence Cramer, FEPC executive secretary, reminded the White House that any further weakening of the committee would stimulate extremist protest despite appeasing the racially motivated opponents of the policy. Instead, reforms should aim at those who agreed in principle with the policy but objected to the confrontational public hearings and hostile directives issued to employers. He suggested elaborating existing agreements with contracting agencies to encourage adjustment by negotiation, and employing the public hearing method only when an agency had failed to correct a grievance. Cramer also recommended that FDR meet with congressional leaders to prevent the policy "from becoming a party issue." An emotional, public debate would be "unfortunate, both from a domestic and from an international point of view."[15]

The so-called White Cabinet unanimously supported procedural reforms for similar reasons. The Justice Department's Victor Rotnem thought the committee had worked "infinite" harm by widely publicizing "economic, political, and social injustices." White House aide MacIntyre opposed the issuance of directives, even when discrimination was established, and thought that the hearings encouraged "extremists" of all kinds. Daniels thought FEPC operations often followed the preferred course of White and Randolph, the leaders of the "more radical Negro group." While no course of action would completely halt the ongoing "agitation and friction" surrounding the FEPC, he recommended that the president restate his opposition to discrimination but insist – in a version of the classic call of statesmen that partisan politics be abandoned during wars – that no group attempt to further its interests at the expense of the allied effort. Daniels thought that the "forces of agitation" should be at most a minority on the committee, which also should include the "best type" of southern conservative. Echoing the aims of the abolished NET and Minority Groups branches, he argued that the committee should pursue a "war policy" aimed at promoting the use of all available local manpower.[16] When McNutt met with

15. Memorandum, Lawrence Cramer to Marvin McIntyre, "Subject: Reorganization," January 15, 1943, OF 4245, FDRL.
16. Reed, *Seedtime*, p. 99; memorandum for Marvin McIntyre, January 26, 1943; memo-

representatives of several civil rights organizations in January and February, discussions focused on the proper institutional location of the FEPC; whether the committee's procedures should be reoriented toward "adjustment and negotiation," with public hearings reserved for cases resisting adjustment; and whether cease-and-desist orders and directives should be issued only with the approval of contracting agencies.[17]

Senior members of the war cabinet, such as Secretary of State James Byrnes and Attorney General Francis Biddle, considered the FEPC useful as an insulating "buffer" that deflected black grievances away from the president and the White House staff. Biddle, whom the president had asked to study the situation and who had conferred with, among others, Ralph Bunche and William Hastie, concluded that the FEPC should be reorganized into a new committee of full-time members attached to the WMC and using its field staff. Drawing on Weaver's work, he thought that "negotiations and persuasion locally, through men of local standing" largely should replace public hearings.[18] According to a national party leader, the FEPC had become a powerful "symbol," and much more would be lost than gained if it were abolished. He correctly predicted that the committee would be given its own field staff and returned to the Office of Emergency Management (OEM) in the White House. Public hearings and public directives were to be options of "last resort." If at all possible, he suggested, disputes should be settled locally. "Political repercussions from such disputes," he hoped, would thus be largely eliminated.[19]

In February 1943 Roosevelt presided over a conference on the renovation of the committee and on May 27 issued Executive Order 9346.[20]

randum, Jonathan Daniels to Marvin McIntyre, January 25, 1943, General Files, January 1943–March 1944, papers of Jonathan Daniels, Southern History Collection, University of North Carolina at Chapel Hill [hereafter SHC-UNC].

17. "Draft Letter of Invitation," undated, "Committee Members," Office Files of Malcolm Ross, June 1940–June 1946 (A–Z), Selected Documents of Records of the Committee on Fair Employment Practice in the Custody of the National Archives, Microfilming Corporation of America, 1970 [hereafter SDR-COFEP]; Reed, *Seedtime*, pp. 106–7.

18. Memorandum of Francis Biddle memorandum to the president, January 29, 1943, OF 4905, War Manpower Commission, FDRL; Reed, *Seedtime*, pp. 93–4, 103, 105, 108.

19. The official echoed the NETB in suggesting that firms consult with the local chapter of the Urban League or some comparable local organization. The Aluminum Company of America, he noted, had nearly eliminated all race complaints in this way. Memorandum, Oscar R. Ewing, vice chairman of the Democratic National Committee, to FDR, March 5, 1943, "Pol. Mem., '40 '46," papers of Oscar Ewing, HSTL.

20. The delay was in part due to the search for a new chairman. For a discussion of similar organizational questions surrounding the Minority Groups branch of the WMC, see memorandum, Philleo Nash to Jonathan Daniels, April 22, 1944, Box 29, OWI Files No. 1, papers of Philleo Nash, HSTL.

The committee returned to the OEM as an independent agency, and retained the right to hold hearings and recommend corrective measures to the WMC. The White House also granted fair employment advocates much of what they desired, namely, independent status, a field staff, and the right to hold hearings and issue directives. But the new FEPC, if more capacious, was a less confrontational entity. "Adjustments" of individual complaints by regional offices would assume as much importance as cease-and-desist orders aimed at whole firms and sectors. The reorientation in operations was reinforced by the replacement of the most militant members of the committee. Earl Dickerson, the group's most powerful agenda-setter and most forceful proponent of confrontational hearings and harshly worded directives, was released; he knew it had been because he "had been so aggressive." The new chairman, Monsignor Francis Haas, chose largely white personnel from the National Labor Relations Board for his staff.[21]

As the new committee extended its regionally organized field operations, the staff also sought a more positive relationship with the press. Acknowledging that extremists had polarized and dominated the debate, Cramer urged the committee to retain a skilled public relations officer "to avoid as many complications as possible on either side."[22] The committee hired a specialist to manage the release and distribution of committee information and policy, hoping to swiftly stabilize the committee's image in the eyes of the general public, which seemed to know more about its failings than its achievements.[23] In sum, the White House reforms entailed three primary, overlapping tactics: removing the FEPC as far as possible from political debates so to insulate the executive from

21. When Msgr. Haas resigned on Oct. 1, Malcolm Ross, widely viewed as a Biddle protégé, was appointed his successor. Attention turned to administering the field office system, reaching agreement with the USES on handling discriminatory referrals, and pursuing permanent status from Congress. In September the committee held the southern railroad hearings, but the firms and unions involved subsequently ignored the FEPC's directives, and the committee certified the case to the president. FDR appointed the Stacey Committee to deal with the problem in January 1944. Terkel, "*The Good War*," p. 339; Reed, *Seedtime*, pp. 112–13, 130–1, 137.
22. Memorandum, Lawrence W. Cramer to Marvin McIntyre, January 15, 1943, OF 4245, FDRL.
23. Memorandum, St. Clair Bourne to Father Haas, August 27, 1943, Office Memoranda, October 1942–January 1945, "B," Office Files of Malcolm Ross, June 1940–June 1948, FEPC Headquarters Records; see also memorandum, Max Berking to Malcolm Ross, May 4, 1944, Office Memoranda, October 1942–January 1945, "B," Office Files of Malcolm Ross, June 1940–June 1948, FEPC Headquarters Records; see also memorandum, Theodore A. Jones to Malcolm Ross, September 5, 1944, Documents File, all in SDR-COFEP.

potentially debilitating social pressures; reforming the committee to favor adjustment over confrontation; and publicizing the positive accomplishments of the bureau instead of the unjust practices of employers.

This second FEPC, well funded and freed from WMC oversight, redoubled its ambitious national program of evaluating and adjusting individual grievances. If, after gathering information on the complaint from a variety of sources, a field investigator found an unfair practice, negotiations began with the employer or union. A satisfactory adjustment was based on "written commitments" to eliminate discriminatory practices. Take, for example, the case of an unnamed black woman who filed a complaint against the Springfield, Massachusetts Armory, claiming that her supervisor removed her from her job as a milling machine operator, "saying that it was too much money for me," and assigned a white woman to the position. The FEPC considered the Armory's account of the incident and, finding no evidence of discrimination, notified the woman and asked her if she wished the committee to take further action. She did not respond, and her case was "dismissed on merits."[24] If uncooperative, an offender faced negotiations with the committee's field director. Failing this, a hearing would produce a full case review.[25] Further noncompliance brought the threat of defense contract cancellation – an option never employed – or the suspension of U.S. Employment Service aid in securing workers. As a last resort, the case was to be referred to the president. The committee had no direct enforcement power, and the success of its directives depended largely on moral suasion and voluntary cooperation.

The members and staff of this second FEPC also adjusted the tactics championed by Dickerson and Webster, namely, that "the FEPC should publicly embarrass employers and order them to take affirmative action."[26] Consider, for example, the FEPC's response to firms' hiring practices reported by the USES. Almost all committee contact with these companies now took the form of correspondence. The first letter re-

---

24. FEPC case nos. 1-GR-60, 1-GR-57, Central Files of the FEPC, Final Disposition Reports, Region I, SDR-COFEP.
25. Public hearings, a significant dimension of the FEPC's work not examined here, continued as planned under the second committee. For close case studies of public hearings on the boilermakers' union in Portland and Los Angeles, and the effects of a threatened public hearing on aircraft and tank manufacturers in Detroit, see Reed, *Seedtime*, Ch. 9, and Meier and Rudwick, *Black Detroit*, Ch. 3. Preparations for them often prompted NTEB-style area-wide research on and analysis of racial employment patterns; firms sometimes preempted the hearings by hiring a modest number of minorities.
26. Reed, *Seedtime*, p. 34.

viewed the controlling executive order and asked the company to report its employment policy as well as issue a written notification to its employees, training institutions, and labor unions explaining that the firm intended to bring its practices into compliance with federal policy. Subsequent correspondence with the firm, according to internal instructions, required "the utmost tact." Arguments with management were to be avoided and "collateral viewpoints, for example, on social reform," were deemed particularly inappropriate. The reason for "requesting implementation of obligations" was to be described as "the clarification of a misunderstanding rather than a punitive action upon a finding of guilt." Determining the fact of discrimination, the document continued, was a time-consuming, difficult, and ultimately unnecessary addition to a request for implementation based merely on overcoming a misunderstanding. While the technique admittedly often produced mere "paper compliance," it also generated records useful for later claims against the firm and was of considerable "educational value" in clarifying the company's employment policy to all parties involved.[27]

As for the overarching goals of the FEPC, both the so-called militants and the more moderate newer members believed that the committee offered a peaceful avenue for the claims of those who otherwise might contribute to war-disrupting crowd violence and organized protest. The aggressive Earl Dickerson, acting chairman of the committee during the winter deliberations, informed FDR that in the absence of

> such a means of correcting injustices, those who have valid grievances will find it necessary through agitation, mass protest, and other direct action to seek what they properly hold to be their democratic rights.[28]

In fact, just days before Executive Order 9346 was announced in May 1943, serious crowd violence closed the grounds of the Alabama Dry Dock and Shipbuilding Company in Mobile.[29] When the new committee met for the first time in July, it reviewed the agreement forged by Chairman Haas concerning the creation of segregated shipways there. Haas publicly announced that the committee understood that it must pursue

27. Eugene Davidson, "The Processing of U.S.E.S. #510 Reports on Discriminatory Hiring Practices," July 27, 1943, "D," Office Memoranda, October 1942–January 1945, SDR-COFEP.
28. Letter, Earl B. Dickerson to the president, March 1, 1943, "Extra Copies," Office Files of Malcolm Ross, SDR-COFEP.
29. On May 25–26, crowds of whites beat black workers with pipes and clubs in an attempt to drive them from the site. Herbert Shapiro, *White Violence and Black Response: From Reconstruction to Montgomery*, Amherst, the University of Massachusetts Press, 1988, pp. 338–9.

discrimination with particular care in locations where wartime over-crowding in housing, transportation, and recreation had "bred irritation among decent people, and have afforded irresponsible persons the opportunity for shameful mob violence."[30] For his part, Daniels thought the committee performed several necessary services for the country. In addition to expanding black employment, and emphasizing the nation's determination to protect all of its people's democratic rights, "the committee has one of the most important functions in government . . . relieving domestic tensions in time of war."[31]

Another manifestation of this pacification function is provided by FEPC intervention in potential or actual strikes motivated by race. When blacks halted work at Pittsburgh's Carnegie-Illinois steel plant, an FEPC agent arrived to discuss the men's grievances, and advised them that the committee would investigate any valid complaints regarding upgrading if they returned to work. In this way, the examiner obtained enough workers to prevent the ruin of a substantial amount of coke. He then asked union officials to call a meeting with the men to explain a recent promotion agreement. When the gathering turned raucous with shouts for another shutdown, the examiner "took over." He explained the importance of their contractual obligations and, illustrating the firm's promotional sequence with a large diagram, ended further strike agitation. The rarity of racial work stoppages was in part due to the effectiveness of the FEPC, both in adjusting individual and group complaints before they could consolidate into collective unrest, and through direct interventions in nascent strike situations. Of all strikes between July 1943 and December 1944, only 1.1 percent involved racial issues.[32] Those White House officials most familiar with the renovated FEPC valued this social peacekeeping role. One can infer that the new design of the committee better suited the warmakers for in a departure from the past, there was no further assessment

---

30. Advance Release, Office of War Information, Committee on Fair Employment Practice, July 8, 1943, Summary Minutes of Meetings, SDR-COFEP.
31. Unsent memorandum, Jonathan Daniels to the president, June 26, 1943, Daniels papers, SHC-UNC.
32. The committee also may have had the unintended effect of intensifying militancy. Two strikes in Detroit in 1943, it has been claimed, stemmed from militancy "rooted in heightened expectations stemming directly from FEPC pressure." But even here, resolving the product of militancy seems to have been a more common role for the committee; ten of the twenty-six strikes in 1943–4 that prompted FEPC adjustments were located in Detroit. "FEPC Participation in Strikes," undated, in Annual Report file, Office Files of Malcolm Ross, June 1940–June 1948, FEPC Headquarters Records, SDR-COFEP; Meier and Rudwick, *Black Detroit*, p. 173; "Statement on Work Stoppages," October 1, 1944, Race Questions, SDR-COFEP.

or reform. Weaver, for one, believed that in issuing few "if any" cease-and-desist orders, and in arranging for operating agreements with other federal agencies, the work of the second committee was superior to that of the first. Its investigations and hearings, he believed, also were executed with greater care and preparation.[33]

Several conclusions may be drawn from this review of the renovation of the FEPC. Although the central state officials who founded and reorganized the FEPC were motivated by a variety of factors, including social justice goals, their constant and overriding intent was to limit those elite and mass activities that they viewed as war-disrupting. Supporters and critics alike viewed committee work as an important vehicle for relieving domestic tensions in wartime. Given that a combination of partisan and efficiency concerns led reformers to choose the individual-adjustment technique over the community utilization alternative, the FEPC's casework should to some degree mirror the distribution of complainants, and focus on cities, sites, and sectors where black workers most directly served the war mobilization. Three overlapping factors – patterns of federal contracting, the spatial concentration of black workers, and organizational assistance – in fact helped shape FEPC casework in precisely this way.

The Preconditions of Employment Complaints: Exclusion from and Discrimination within the Mobilization

At the outset of the war, the scale of the impending economic expansion was so great that many hoped it would sweep away racial discrimination altogether. Roughly seven million Americans worked in war-related production at the time of Pearl Harbor, and the Bureau of Employment Security set about adding an additional 10.5 million as quickly as possible. As the director of the bureau put it, the need for labor was so urgent that "employers will no longer be permitted to indulge their prejudices against minority groups."[34] He was wrong, of course, for blacks did not find easy entry into defense employment.

The problem was not simply that such workers lived far from factories. In the previous thirty years, the proportion of blacks living in cities had risen to nearly one-half, so that, on the eve of war, even the census South contained an African American population more heavily urbanized

33. Letter, Robert C. Weaver to Rabbi Louis Ruchames, January 13, 1948, Correspondence – R, papers of Robert Weaver, Schomberg Center for Research in Black Culture, New York Public Library; Weaver, *Negro Labor: A National Problem*, New York, Harcourt, Brace and Company, 1946, pp. 134–45.
34. Windsor Booth, "Mobilizing Our Labor," Washington *Post*, March 30, 1942.

than the native white population.[35] Thus, the expanding war economy intersected with the ongoing urbanization of the nation, in which blacks played an unexceptional role. They were no more or less likely to migrate than whites in the late thirties and during the war; their share of the migrant pool hovered around eleven percent in both periods.[36] Compared to the white migration, however, the wartime black migration began relatively late, and these workers tended to settle in cities rich in state installations such as Navy Yards and state-sponsored sectors such as aircraft production.

Three sets of factors – the legacy of the Depression, past and present discrimination, and the sectional nature of the mobilization – combined to create two stages in this wartime migration, excluding black workers from defense jobs at the outset of the war and then encouraging them to seek work in cities with large supply contracts. Until mid-1943, blacks comprised a smaller percentage of the nation's migrants than they had during the previous decade. The need for skilled workers, widespread discrimination in employment, and the concentration of contracts in the North combined to prevent the first rounds of job expansion from reaching nonwhite workers.[37]

First, the Great Depression limited the skills that minorities could offer to employers, for whites turned out many unskilled and low seniority blacks from jobs they had gained in northern industries between 1915 and 1929. In 1940 the nonwhite share of mining, manufacturing, transportation, and communication jobs, for example, was smaller than in 1910.[38] The biased preference for white workers for scarce Depression-era jobs had even dislodged blacks from traditional trade strongholds that now boomed with war-related activity, including building construction and semiskilled transportation jobs. In part because of this skills

---

35. The six cities with the most African American residents in 1940 were all north of the Potomac River, however, and New York City's black populace – roughly half a million – was the largest by a wide margin. Chicago, Philadelphia, Washington, Baltimore, and Detroit, in descending order, housed between roughly 275,000 and 150,000 blacks. Oliver C. Cox, "Population and Population Characteristics," Tuskegee Institute, *The Negro Year Book*, 1947, pp. 6–7; "Nearly Million Leave South in Past Ten Years," Atlanta *Daily World*, November 5, 1944; "40 Per Cent of Negroes Live in Cities," Kansas City *Call*, August 27, 1943.

36. "Migration," undated memorandum, West Coast Material, Office Files of Malcolm Ross, SDR-COFEP.

37. Lawrence Brooks De Graaf, *Negro Migration to Los Angeles, 1930–1950*, San Francisco, R and E Research Associates, 1974, p. 108.

38. Louis Kesselman, *The Social Politics of FEPC: A Study in Reform Pressure Movements*, Chapel Hill, University of North Carolina Press, 1948, p. 7; Tuskegee Institute, *The Negro Yearbook*, 1947, p. 350.

deficit among blacks, the Depression generally ended earlier for whites. By 1941, blacks on relief outnumbered whites by an average of two to one in proportion to their population. In larger cities like New York, Detroit, and Boston, the ratio was four to one.[39]

Through 1942, blacks' socioeconomic status had hardly changed, and the causes of black migration were the same as those inducing the Depression era's "migration of despair." Nonwhites made up an insignificant proportion of the workers arriving in Los Angeles, for example, until mid-1942.[40] In Chicago, black workers experienced no gains in defense employment through that spring, and almost no blacks were arriving from the South. But modest job growth had begun in Dixie; defense construction projects near Memphis and Birmingham had started to employ blacks in relatively large numbers, and Mobile, Norfolk-Newport News, and New Orleans began to receive large numbers of black in-migrants.[41] Thus, until mid- to late 1942, the movement of southern blacks into towns and cities occurred largely within the region, since labor shortages were not yet severe enough to make jobs widely available elsewhere.

In addition to the legacies of the past, firms' current employment policies and practices often reserved factory jobs for whites. A 1941 survey by the Social Security Board found that 51 percent of the openings anticipated in defense plants would be formally closed to nonwhite applicants. Some defense industries, particularly aircraft and ordnance, excluded black workers altogether from occupations other than janitor. Most Gulf Coast shipyards restricted black hires to unskilled and custodial jobs. Although defense needs had begun to exhaust the white male labor force by late 1941 and the rate of placements for blacks increased, the opportunities were of inferior quality. Nine out of ten blacks placed by public employment offices took service or unskilled work; the equivalent rate for whites was only five percent.[42] Unions displayed still more organized hostility toward blacks, for the conversion of factories to military production often resulted in closed shops that

---

39. In Chicago, blacks accounted for 41 percent of the city's relief rolls in mid-1942, despite accounting for 7 percent of the city's population. De Graaf, *Negro Migration*, p. 104; "Industries Using More Negro Help," New York *Times*, July 20, 1942; Herbert G. Garfinkel, *When Negroes March: The March on Washington Movement in the Organizational Politics of FEPC*, Glencoe, Illinois, 1959, pp. 19, 56–7.

40. De Graaf, *Negro Migration*, p. 102.

41. Almost immediately, the Chicago Urban League aimed its efforts at companies holding large defense contracts. "Arms Program Fails to Benefit Negro Reliefers," Chicago *Tribune*, May 18, 1942; De Graaf, *Negro Migration*, p. 111.

42. Kesselman, *The Social Politics of FEPC*, p. 7; Garfinkel, *When Negroes March*, p. 20.

removed blacks from jobs they had held through the thirties. In September 1941, blacks accounted for about one hundred of the eighty-five hundred workers in the Los Angeles shipyards; the AFL International Brotherhood of Boilermakers organized most of the yards and refused to accept blacks as full members. While securing defense contracts, the Tampa Shipbuilding Company and an AFL union established a closed shop that included an auxiliary union for the 118 blacks who were retained from the six hundred working there in 1939. Only two of those remaining held skilled jobs. Although the CIO proposed to integrate its locals and place blacks in southern ways, at this stage the resistance of white workers generally limited black employment in such yards to unskilled work.[43]

Bias affected federal job training programs as well. In December 1940 the federal government implemented a preemployment training program under the auspices of the Office of Education and the USES. Although this would become the principal means of preparing workers for defense jobs, many white officials barred blacks from the program. At the time, trainees in sixteen southern states were only 1.6 percent black, despite their accounting for more than one-fourth of the region's labor force. A year later, only 194 of the 4,640 courses in the region were open to blacks.[44] Federal authorities eventually opened more training programs to minorities, but they too followed sectional patterns for reasons of both efficiency and bias. The Office of Education's Vocational Service, for example, was operated by states and the federal government on a joint grant-in-aid basis, with most of the schooling located in larger cities with good public school and shop facilities. The four thousand schools taught new skills to workers displaced from automobile and other peacetime production, and to out-of-school youth over 17. By March 1942, only one of the twelve principal training centers lay in the South, in the High Point textile region of North Carolina.[45] Since the Office of Edu-

43. Gerald D. Nash, *The American West Transformed: The Impact of the Second World War*, Bloomington, Indiana University Press, 1985, pp. 37–55; De Graaf, *Negro Migration*, pp. 10–17, 117, 120.
44. The Social Security Board found that of the 89,529 applicants accepted for vocational training in the second half of 1940, 2,434 were black. The U.S. Office of Education reported that trainees in preemployment and refresher courses in eighteen southern and border states were only 4 percent black in January 1942. Nash, *The American West Transformed*, pp. 37–55; De Graaf, *Negro Migration*, pp. 105, 112; Tuskegee Institute, *The Negro Yearbook*, 1947, p. 350.
45. The others were New York, Buffalo, northern New Jersey, Philadelphia, Akron, Detroit, Flint, Seattle, Portland, San Francisco, and southern California. Between July 1, 1940, and January 31, 1942, the Office of Education's Vocational Service trained over

cation had no equipment or facilities of its own, instead paying half of the training costs in state-supported schools, it was effectively barred from the poorer states, and particularly the South.

The NYA was the only other federal organization feeding large numbers of workers into war industry. In 1941 the NYA trained and gave work experience to more than one million youth, usually in out-of-the-way places where there were no other opportunities for such work experience.[46] A survey in 1942 indicated that the South – with roughly 75 percent of the nation's black population – was training only 20 percent of the nation's black participants.[47] Some states restricted nonwhites to certain courses, mainly in nondefense or unskilled occupations, on the grounds that it was unrealistic to train black workers for positions unavailable to them.

Determinants of Employment Complaints: The Spatial Concentration of War Contracts

In each of these guises, discrimination coincided with another obstacle to black factory work, the sectional nature of the mobilization, for early defense contracting was concentrated in northeastern and coastal cities, far away from the bulk of the black labor force. Through February 1943, only 7 percent of the government's investment in plants and facilities was in the Deep South; in addition, approximately half the South's prime contracts went to shipyards.[48] More than two-thirds of the sixty-four war plants that employed significant numbers of black women in late 1942 were located in seven states: Pennsylvania, New York, California, Connecticut, New Jersey, Maryland, and Michigan. Conversely, two-thirds of the black labor force was located in the South, where only 13.5 percent of war contracts were placed by March 1943.[49]

two million workers for war employment. Windsor Booth, "Mobilizing Our Labor," Washington *Post*, March 30, 1942.

46. Windsor Booth, "Mobilizing Our Labor," Washington *Post*, March 30, 1942.

47. FEPC, *First Report*, in Foner and Lewis, eds., *The Black Worker*, pp. 265–72.

48. After the initial phases of conversion passed, according to the Office of War Information (OWI), warmakers attempted to spread war production facilities into areas that previously had lacked large-scale industrial activity, in part to make production less susceptible to bombing raids. "Notes on the Effects of War on the South," undated manuscript, Daniels papers, SHC-UNC, pp. 1–4; "Labor: Manpower Shortage Next?," *Time*, July 20, 1942; "City in Area of Labor Surplus," Birmingham *Age-Herald*, October 21, 1942.

49. "Remove Southern Industry Handicaps, Fortune Asks," Atlanta *Constitution*, June 26, 1943, citing July, 1943 *Fortune*; Office of War Information, Doc. NB-2368, April

While bias nationwide limited the interregional migration mainly to whites during the two-year preparedness period, the relative dearth of contracts and of industrial employment in the South ensured that the white workers that remained behind filled most defense openings through the summer of 1942.

The notion that World War II hoisted cornfield factories and spurred industrialization in the Sunbelt, while true to a degree, blurs more powerful trends, for this war's productive force originated primarily in the North, the West Coast, and above all in cities. Particularly at this early stage, warmakers contracted for goods where they could be had, and preexisting industrial and labor capacity constrained patterns of government procurement. Bernard Baruch, for example, advised FDR that the urgency of the task dictated that "work should be placed where there are workers, housing, schools, hospitals – like New York – even if the prices are higher."[50] Metropolitan counties accounted for the vast majority of war supply contracts and for roughly two-thirds of all spending for the building of industrial facilities related to the war. Contracts for the construction of military facilities, as one might expect, went largely to nonmetropolitan counties, but only by a small margin (see Table 4.1).

It is difficult to overstate the relative underdevelopment of Dixie at the time. In 1939 five northern cities – New York, Chicago, Boston, Detroit, and Philadelphia – each added more value in manufacturing to the national economy than the five Deep South states combined.[51] Because the steel, automobile, and shipbuilding industries were further concentrated in and around such cities, federal contractors spent most war money in core cities of the industrial north-central and northeast states and in coastal construction centers such as Los Angeles, San Francisco, and Baltimore. In 1940, to take one critical example, six arsenals made up the entire American munitions manufacturing industry, and all of them were located in the factory belt that stretched from the Great Lakes to Boston and Baltimore.[52] The former Confederacy contributed no cities

19, 1944, SDR-COFEP, p. 5; "WMC Faces Problem of Smashing Jimcrow Bars," New York *Daily Worker*, June 19, 1943; "Women at Work in 64 War Plants," Chicago *Defender*, October 30, 1942; "Negro Women Employed as Production Workers," Chicago *Bee*, November 8, 1942.

50. Memorandum, Bernard M. Baruch to the president, November 7, 1942, OF 4905, FDRL.

51. These states were South Carolina, Georgia, Alabama, Mississippi, and Louisiana. U.S. Bureau of the Census, *County Data Book*, Washington, D.C., USGPO, 1947, pp. 8–55.

52. By that summer, however, a renewed munitions program and new technology required new plants. The six arsenals were Frankford Arsenal, Philadelphia; Picatinny Arsenal, Dover, NJ; Rock Island Arsenal, Rock Island, IL; Springfield Armory, Springfield,

Table 4.1. *Value of War Supply Contracts and War Facilities Projects, by Type of County, 1940–1945 [in millions of dollars].*

Type of County	War Supply Contracts		War Facilities Contracts	
	Combat Equip.	Other	Industrial	Military
metropolitan	118,810	34,370	11,084	4,183
other	16,881	10,382	5,913	5,992
TOTAL	135,691	44,752	16,998	10,174
METRO % OF TOTAL	87.6	76.8	65.2	41.1

Source: U.S. Bureau of the Census, *County Data Book*, Washington, D.C., USGPO, 1947, p. 13.

to the list of twenty-five metropolitan areas gaining the largest shares of defense supply contracts over the course of the war. Of the top forty, only three – Houston, Ft. Worth, and Beaumont – were southern cities and they were all in one state (see Appendix 1.2). Texas led most regional categories, including aircraft production and shipbuilding – which together accounted for two-thirds of the region's contracts – and newly built war plants and military installations. Overall, the South was ill-equipped to profit from the nation's rearmament program, which tended to place orders in or adjacent to preexisting facilities for reasons of speed and efficiency. Before the war, the South was expanding manufacturing activity faster than the rest of the nation. Between 1939 and 1943, the region's share of total manufacturing employment actually *dropped* from 17.5 percent to 15.6 percent.[53] As one might expect, in addition to being capital-poor, the South also was labor-rich. By October 1942,

MA; Watertown Arsenal, Watertown, MA; Watervliet Arsenal, Watervliet, NY; and the Chemical Warfare Service installation at Edgewood, MD, near Baltimore. Harry C. Thomson and Linda Mayo, *The Ordnance Department: Procurement and Supply*, the U.S. Army in World War II, The Technical Services, Office of the Chief of Military History, U.S. Department of the Army, Washington, D.C., 1960, p. 363; Smith, *The Army and Economic Mobilization*, Office of the Chief of Military History, United States Army in World War II, Washington, D.C., USGPO, pp. 498–9.

53. Five states alone accounted for roughly two-thirds of the region's returns in prime contacts: Texas, Oklahoma, Tennessee, Virginia, and Georgia. "Notes on the Effects of War on the South," undated manuscript, Daniels papers, SHC-UNC, pp. 1–4.

two-thirds of the metropolitan areas with labor shortages were in sixteen northern states.[54] Conversely, approximately half the areas of labor surplus at the beginning of 1943 were in the South, where blacks accounted for between 10 and 50 percent of the population.[55]

Eventually, government planners constructed and subsidized new productive capacity in underdeveloped areas. Warmakers awarded to the southern states a substantial share of the outlays for building war plants and of total expenditures for new military facilities. While significant, such purchases paled in comparison to the vast sums spent at plants concentrated in the factory belt.[56] The mismatch between the spatial dimension of the mobilization and of racial demography, as well as a lack of skills among urban blacks and biased hiring and training practices, were thus the principle reasons for African American joblessness in this period.

Determinants of Employment Complaints: The Late Migration of Black Factory Labor

By late 1942, black workers found themselves somewhat more in demand. The National Urban League announced that forty local affiliates reported substantial gains in employment, and attributed the rise to the work of the FEPC, Weaver and his staff at the War Manpower Commission, and the efforts of private organizations.[57] A significant migration of black workers into centers of defense production had begun, bringing "the 'race problem' into the experience of hundreds of thousands of Americans who never before had any real contact with it." By early 1943, nonwhite enrollment in preemployment training courses had doubled over the previous year. Black enrollment in the Office of Education's supplementary courses – open to employed war workers – also had tripled since the war began.[58] By September minorities were widely

---

54. "Labor: Manpower Shortage Next?," *Time*, July 20, 1942; "City in Area of Labor Surplus," Birmingham *Age-Herald*, October 21, 1942.
55. New York, which boasted the largest black population of any city in the world, was also labor-rich. Weaver, *Negro Labor*, p. 26.
56. The correlation between 1939 manufacturing capacity and war contracts was particularly strong in steel and, most likely, in other sectors where facility expansion was much more efficient than wholesale facility construction, such as ordnance. James C. Cobb, "The Sunbelt South: Industrialization in Regional, National, and International Perspective," in Raymond Mohl, ed., *Searching for the Sunbelt*, Knoxville, University of Tennessee Press, 1990, pp. 30–1; Gregory Hooks, "Regional Processes in the Hegemonic Nation: The Determinants and Consequences of World War II Commercial and Military Investments," unpublished manuscript.
57. "Industries Using More Negro Help," New York *Times*, July 20, 1942.
58. Robert Weaver, *Negro Labor*, pp. ix, 88.

accepted for training and employment in many defense industries in Los Angeles, and throughout 1943 they found jobs in factory and military base construction and unskilled jobs in iron and steel and shipbuilding.[59]

Large numbers of both white and black migrants arrived in the larger cities during the spring and summer of 1943, seasons of instability, to say the least, in race relations.[60] Detroit struggled to absorb fourteen hundred migrants per week that summer, the majority of them black, as well as many hundreds of southern whites. The city's nonwhite population increased by more than a third in just a few years.[61] While Detroit's black population growth was high relative to other northern cities, more dramatic increases were reported on the West Coast, where one estimate found that the black population in ten western states had doubled between 1940 and 1943. Some seventy-five thousand blacks arrived in California between 1940 and 1943, compared with roughly 110,000 arrivals over the preceding forty years. To several well-worn northerly paths of migration, the war had added a new route: from Louisiana, Texas, Arkansas, Missouri, and Oklahoma to the Pacific Coast.[62] In 1944, the Census Bureau reported that the back population of Los Angeles had risen more than 75 percent since 1940, as the city's "Little Tokyo" neighborhood changed seemingly overnight into "Bronzeville." The *Courier* reported that black migrants were arriving there at the rate of thirty-five hundred a month.[63] The WMC reported a substantial

59. According to one survey, three-quarters of the black migration to cities between 1940 and July 1943 moved after September 1942. DeGraaf, *Negro Migration*, p. 108.
60. In addition to May's incident in Mobile, groups of white Navy personnel beat Hispanic American youths in Los Angeles over four days in June; roving crowds of both races and local police claimed thirty-four lives in June in Detroit; a black crowd action and the police response to it claimed six lives and 1,450 damaged stores in New York City in August. For the central state's response to this violence, see Chapter 7. Richard Polenberg, *War and Society: The United States, 1941–1945*, Philadelphia, J. B. Lippincott Company, pp. 126–30; Shapiro, *White Violence*, pp. 306–48.
61. "Buck is Passed in Making Provision for In-Migrants," Pittsburgh *Courier*, September 11, 1943. The total rose from 148,445 in 1940 to 211,000 in 1944. "Negroes Now 12.7% of Detroit's Population," New York *People's Voice*, September 30, 1944.
62. Three main streams of black migration had developed prior to 1930: from Georgia through the Atlantic Coast states to Pennsylvania and New York; from Mississippi and Alabama through Tennessee and Kentucky to Michigan and Ohio; and, from Louisiana through Arkansas and Missouri to Illinois and Michigan. Black migration usually took one of two forms: from southern agricultural areas to southern cities, or from southern cities and towns to northern and western industrial centers. For example, thirty-seven percent of the black migrants arriving in Mobile came from farms, whereas only fourteen percent of those who migrated to Detroit were from farms. FEPC, *First Report*, in Foner and Lewis, eds., *The Black Worker*, pp. 265–72.
63. Despite this influx, there was a critical labor shortage in the area, reflected in an unemployment rate of 1.4 percent of the labor force, roughly equal to the national average, and down from the 1940 jobless rate of about 14 percent. "A Postwar

increase in black shipbuilding employment in the area; the California Shipbuilding Corporation essentially tripled its black workforce in the second half of 1942. Still, the largest increase in black employment in the Los Angeles area was in the aircraft sector, whose firms began to hire nonwhites at all skill levels.[64]

Probably no American city experienced such a thorough and rapid transformation in its racial demography in the twentieth century as did San Francisco at this time, whose black population tripled from 19,759 in 1940 to 64,680 in 1944. While whites and blacks flooded the city, the population of other nonwhites declined sharply, due mainly to the "relocation" of Japanese American residents, who numbered 13,550 in 1940.[65] Similarly, San Diego County's black population nearly doubled in four years. Roughly 40 percent of the county's residents in 1944 had arrived in the previous four years.[66]

The scale of the movement of black workers prompted calls for federal controls. In July 1943, at the height of the war's unrest, San Francisco's mayor asked that "the Negro invasion" of the city be halted as a partial solution to the deplorable housing conditions in poorer sections of the city. The regional WMC rejected the claim on the grounds that the shipbuilding industry required the additional labor.[67] The House of Representatives' Naval Affairs Subcommittee suggested that the West Coast required strict controls on the in-migration of southern blacks to limit the movement to essential workers entering "at an orderly rate" tied to the availability of housing.[68] Black sociologist Charles S. Johnson proposed that the central state join with civic groups to settle "some portion of the Negro labor reserve" in smaller northern cities to exploit newly opened sectors and occupations.[69]

Problem," Atlanta *Daily World*, August 27, 1944; "Buck is Passed in Making Provision for In-Migrants," Pittsburgh *Courier*, September 11, 1943; "Negro Growth Almost 100 Percent," Los Angeles *Tribune*, August 14, 1944.

64. "5,200 Hired in War Jobs in One County," St. Louis *Argus*, March 26, 1943.
65. "Negroes and Whites Take Race Friction Along on Migration from the South," Chicago *Sun*, October 14, 1943; "San Francisco May Test New Migrant Solution," Chicago *Bee*, December 25, 1943; "Frisco Zoom in Negro Population Brings Race Problem to Coast City," Chicago *Defender*, January 8, 1944; "S. F. Negroes Number 64,680 Now," Los Angeles *Tribune*, July 31, 1944.
66. "Wartime Changes in Population and Family Characteristics," cited in "Census Shows Near Double San Diego Negro Population," Los Angeles *Tribune*, July 24, 1944.
67. "San Francisco Mayor Wants 'Negro Invasion' Halted," Pittsburgh *Courier*, July 3, 1943.
68. "Solons Propose New Curb on Negro Migration," Chicago *Defender*, January 8, 1944.
69. When black elites addressed this problem, they often replicated the familiar North-

Between April 1, 1940, and November 1, 1943, nearly five million Americans migrated to counties that had defense plants or military establishments.[70] In general, metropolitan areas showed rapid rates of population growth, and trends in urban counties indicated a movement away from northeastern states toward the South and West.[71] Since their migration began relatively late in the mobilization, however, the largest numbers of black migrants moved while the WMC was publicizing lists of cities with the most critical labor shortages.[72] Of the 1.5 million blacks working in defense industries in late 1944, nearly half worked in acutely labor-short areas.[73]

The modest regulatory efforts of the WMC and the USES, however, were not redistributing white and black labor efficiently and rapidly enough. The USES, serving as a national employment agency matching idle labor with job listings, was uniquely well positioned to monitor discriminatory requests for workers. When it began rejecting applications for workers from discriminatory firms, many employers simply refused to list openings with the USES, resorting instead to at-the-gate hiring. Some local offices of the service had become accustomed to favoring the specifications of employers during the Depression, when it was largely a collection of state agencies. Staff apparently worried that employers would stop using the service if it enforced the fair employment

South leadership divide. See the June 1944 *Negro Digest* debate between George S. Schuyler and Horace R. Cayton, who held that a mass South-North migration was a positive development, and Dr. F. D. Patterson of the Tuskegee Institute, who disagreed. "Resettlement of Southern Negroes Proposed," Johnson City, Tennessee *Chronicle*, July 7, 1944. See also "Migration from South Advocated by Cayton," Miami *Whip*, June 24, 1944; " 'Young Man, Go South,' " Memphis *World*, June 6, 1944.

70. More than one million of these were recruited and induced to move by the War Manpower Commission. Office of War Information, Doc. NB-2368, April 19, 1944, SDR-COFEP, p. 6.

71. By late 1943, New York state alone had lost while California had gained over a million residents since 1940. Population growth, however, did not always correlate with defense contracts: of the twenty cities that gained the largest share of war contracts, seven showed a decrease in population. Metropolitan areas such as New York, Chicago, and Boston had accumulated large reserve pools of workers in the thirties through the combined effects of the first war's expansion of factory work and the relief and public works programs of the New Deal. U.S. Bureau of the Census, *County Data Book*, Washington, D.C., USGPO, 1947, p. 2.

72. A common press release listed thirty-two cities of critical labor shortage; their repeated publication in black newspapers undoubtedly influenced many migration plans as intended. See, for example, "WMC Takes Over Hiring of Workers," Montgomery *Advertiser*, February 5, 1943.

73. War workers as a whole were less concentrated in acute labor-short areas; 38 percent labored under these conditions. Weaver, *Negro Labor*, p. 87.

policy. Other local staffs simply had no knowledge of the number and skill levels of local black workers and thus were unprepared to "sell" black workers to their clients, who imported white labor in part because they knew of no alternative. The service's director eventually agreed that it would notify employers that biased job specifications violated federal policy, and in July 1942 he agreed to supply the FEPC with the names of such employers.[74]

In another manifestation of the central state's search for efficiency, McNutt announced in early 1943 that the War Manpower Commission would assume control of the hiring of workers in labor-short areas, a step expected to freeze millions of persons in war or essential industries. Employers in such areas could hire a male worker only after a USES interview; the WMC and other approved agencies then furnished workers through USES referrals based on the importance of the firm's production to the war effort. The WMC priority referral system, in theory if not in effect, made that agency the "primary enforcer" of FDR's executive orders. Since the policy forbade hiring at the gate and did not permit the USES to refer workers to companies with biased hiring practices, companies that insisted on discriminating should have faced real difficulties securing male workers, except for certain firms producing highly critical materials. The USES, however, generally continued to service discriminatory orders for workers until September 1943, when the WMC, facing serious labor shortages, attempted to stop the practice with a policy directive that defined as discriminatory those USES referrals that were based on biased specifications.[75]

To help eliminate discrimination internal to the service, the WMC also revised a preexisting training program into a handbook entitled "The USES and the Negro Applicant" and distributed it to each of the fifteen hundred USES local offices in 1944. This was apparently the first time the federal government had distributed formal training materials aimed at the fair handling of black applicants.[76] Some additional improvement

---

74. Reed, *Seedtime*, pp. 64–5; Weaver, *Negro Labor*, pp. 145, 147.
75. Other measures prevented workers from shifting from vital to less essential work and limited the authority of employers to fire workers assigned to them through the WMC. Untitled, undated memorandum, Papers of Philleo Nash, Race Tension MI, Box 28, HSTL; Reed, *Seedtime*, p. 65; "Manpower Stabilization Plan with Hiring Controls for the Buffalo-Niagara, N.Y. Area," June 14, 1943, Labor Discrimination, papers of John Ohly, HSTL, pp. 1–3.
76. In addition, approximately twenty thousand USES receptionists, interviewers, and employer-contact personnel received two four-hour training and indoctrination sessions. "WMC Adopts Program to End Discrimination," New York *People's Voice*, February 12, 1944.

resulted from the July 1, 1944, WMC order that restricted all essential employers to acquiring workers only by USES referral or arrangement.[77] But manpower officials in the Deep South continued to display "a willful and widespread disregard" for the WMC-FEPC agreement, especially those provisions mandating equal treatment in referrals for all races. Despite the availability of black workers, and labor shortages in skilled and semiskilled jobs, the USES and employers still attempted to recruit additional whites in the South.[78]

The Spatial and Sectoral Concentration of Complaint Activity

If the fate of the first FEPC was in part determined by warmakers seeking to defuse black protest, the casework of the second FEPC was determined largely by the contours of the nation's wartime economy. The committee's task was somewhat simplified by the spatial and occupational concentration of black industrial workers. At midwar, twelve cities alone accounted for approximately 43 percent of all black factory workers: New York/Newark, Philadelphia, Baltimore, Hampton Roads, Cleveland, Detroit, Chicago, Los Angeles, San Francisco, Pittsburgh, Birmingham, and St. Louis.[79] Over the eighteen months ending on December 31, 1944, these twelve cities accounted for over 56 percent of all FEPC complaint activity. New York City alone accounted for 17.7 percent of complaints in this period (see Table 4.2).[80] Detroit, the capital of heavy war industry, produced nearly 20 percent of all cases prior to the reorganization of the FEPC in July 1943, as complaints stemmed from

77. Weaver, *Negro Labor*, p. 150.
78. Over the eighteen months beginning in July 1943, the Employment Service was the object of separate FEPC complaints in sixty-nine different cities, making it the most oft-cited government office in the casework of the FEPC. Thus, the USES suppressed complaints in the South, both by failing to report discriminatory listings, and by refusing to make nondiscriminatory referrals that placed minorities inside plants and thus facilitated later complaints concerning working conditions. A large portion of FEPC activity in the South concerned discriminatory practices on the part of government officials. Memorandum, Will Maslow to the Committee, November 10, 1944, Documents File, November 11, 1944, FEPC Headquarters Records; "Part I: Wartime Experience," Material for Final Report, Office Files of Malcolm Ross, FEPC Headquarters Records, SDR-COFEP, p. 58.
79. While these numbers are crude, the great variation in various cities' wartime patterns of racial in- and out-migration make the 1940 census an even poorer indicator of the actual distribution of black labor at midwar. Weaver, *Negro Labor*, p. 87.
80. Put another way, over half of all complaints were produced by seven cities.

the intense early concentration of defense contracting in preexisting automobile and heavy manufacturing facilities.[81] As federal investigators fanned out to discuss the fairness policy with the nation's firms and contractors, Detroit's share of complaints fell.[82]

Where black workers were employed at relatively high rates, they were generally further concentrated in certain industries, including foundry employment, and it was common for blacks in an industry to work in a few large, segregated plants. In Baltimore, more than half of the 22,478 blacks employed in reporting establishments were in shipbuilding and repair, which accounted for only 40 percent of the city's total defense employment. Three-quarters of the city's black female workers were employed in four establishments alone.[83] Black industrial and manufacturing workers in Cincinnati were likewise concentrated in two plants. The larger of the two, the Wright Aeronautical Corporation, employed more than four thousand black workers and offered the city's only significant opportunities for women and for skilled blacks.[84] In the Detroit area, 64 percent of the blacks in reporting firms were employed in aircraft manufacturing.[85] Philadelphia's three largest federal facilities – the Philadelphia Navy Yard, the Frankford Arsenal, and the Quartermaster Depot – provide another case in point. Together they employed approximately 3,168 blacks; in 1942, over half worked in the Navy Yard.[86] The Springfield Armory was far and away that city's largest

81. "Developments in the Employment of Negroes in War Industries," War Manpower Report, October 16, 1943, in Foner and Lewis, eds., *The Black Worker*, pp. 233–7.
82. Like Detroit, New York City's share declined over time; for the twelve months spanning July 1, 1943 and June 30, 1944, its share had been 20.1 percent. Fair Employment Practice Committee, *Final Report*, November, 1946, p. 114.
83. "Developments in the Employment of Negroes in War Industries," War Manpower Report, October 16, 1943, in Foner and Lewis, eds., *The Black Worker*, pp. 233–7.
84. The firm generated the city's largest number of complaints with the FEPC. Though the Cincinnati Milling Machine Company employed nearly one thousand blacks, no other company employed more than 200. "Long Tradition in Race Relations Found in Cincinnati," Chicago *Defender*, January 29, 1944.
85. The sector produced the city's largest number of complaints with the FEPC. "Developments in the Employment of Negroes in War Industries," in Foner and Lewis, eds., *The Black Worker*, pp. 235–7.
86. A very similar pattern of black employment obtained in Charleston. In Philadelphia, the Navy Yard led the city in complaints to the FEPC, producing more than twice as many as the area's next leading source, the notorious Philadelphia Transit Company. Charles Shorter, "Philadelphia's Employers, Unions, and Negro Workers," *Opportunity* 20, January, 1942, pp. 4–7; Pete Daniel, "Going Among Strangers: Southern Reactions to World War II," *Journal of American History*, vol. 77, no. 3, December, 1990, p. 901.

Table 4.2. *FEPC Complaints Concerning Race, % by*
Metropolitan Area, July 1, 1943 to December 31, 1944.

	% of Cases	Cumulative %
New York City	17.66	
Chicago	7.29	
San Francisco	6.92	
Philadelphia	5.49	
St. Louis	4.47	41.83
Detroit	4.41	
Los Angeles	4.36	
Kansas City	3.91	
Washington, D.C.	3.60	
Pittsburgh	2.21	60.32
Cincinnati	1.78	
Cleveland	1.65	
Atlanta	1.48	
New Orleans	1.39	
Houston	1.28	67.90
Baltimore	1.26	
Dallas	1.19	
Seattle	.89	
Marietta	.65	
Indianapolis	.65	72.54

Source: Analysis of casework data by author, records of the Fair Employment Practices Committee, 1941–1946 ($n = 4,608$).

employer of nonwhites; roughly one out of every five black *residents* worked there.[87]

87. By 1943, the black population of Springfield had risen to just over four thousand. Across the nation, efficiency concerns drove state sectors like armaments to create a manpower recruitment and training record similar in certain respects to the Army's. St. Louis armament firms, for example, recruited and trained thousands of workers for specialized work in ordnance manufacture but, as in the Army, the limited supply of labor forced companies to use manpower that did not satisfy minimum peacetime standards. As with battalions of raw recruits, cadres of previously trained workers and supervisors recruited new employees, established training schools, and quickly built up large workforces. To utilize unskilled employees effectively, work was simplified as much as possible and new hires trained intensively in the specific job assigned to them. Many war plants in the area adopted a hiring policy, much like the Army's national policy, that would produce a workforce mirroring the city's population ratio of 9 to

The concentrated use of blacks in larger establishments in the North and far West tended to obscure their very limited employment in smaller firms in otherwise tight labor market areas. In the Buffalo-Niagara Falls area, for example, four firms in the scientific instruments and communication equipment industries employed only twenty-six blacks out of six thousand employees. While eighty firms there engaged in important war industries, nearly half of the ninety-five hundred blacks employed in the area worked in five blast furnace, steel works, and rolling mill sites. Similar patterns held in the Akron, Dayton-Springfield, and Gary-Hammond areas. In the tighter labor market areas in Alabama, Florida, Georgia, Mississippi, and Texas, black workers were principally used as unskilled labor in shipbuilding and in government establishments.[88] Even in tight northern labor markets, there was no very significant use of *skilled* black workers in war industry. In the Detroit area, for example, the Employment Service reported in May 1943 that only 6.7 percent of blacks were in skilled classifications, compared with 20.5 percent for all employees. Even in acute labor shortage areas of the North, black worker utilization had progressed further but remained concentrated in certain occupations, firms, and industries, and the movement of blacks into skilled and semiskilled occupations remained very limited.[89] Temporary war agencies proved to be the locus of most of the advances made in skilled black employment in the federal government.[90]

The largest share of black employment in government installations, as

1, white to black. Whites supervised the black units, and War Department officials flatly denied that Executive Order 9346 required them to disregard "community customs" regarding segregation. As in the Army, the practices led to a number of racial disputes and stoppages in 1943 and 1944. Unlike Army policies, which could not be challenged directly on a camp-by-camp basis, the FEPC held hearings on various St. Louis plants in August 1944. It upheld some of the complaints and ordered two firms to abandon quota systems that underlay discriminatory hiring and firing practices. Thompson and Mayo, *Ordnance*, pp. 211–12; letter, Brig. General Edward S. Greenbaum to Malcolm Ross, May 20, 1944, Office Memoranda, Documents File, May 27, 1944, FEPC Headquarters Records, SDR-COFEP; "St. Louis Just Step Away from Dixie in Race Setup," Chicago *Bee*, January 29, 1944; "Negroes' Population Up 25%," Springfield *Union*, May 13, 1943.

88. "Developments in the Employment of Negroes in War Industries," in Foner and Lewis, eds., *The Black Worker*, pp. 235–7.
89. During the second quarter of 1943, for example, blacks accounted for 3.2 percent of all placements in skilled jobs, compared to 2.7 percent in the same quarter of 1942. Placements in semiskilled occupations were 7.6 percent in 1943 and 7.3 percent in 1942. "Developments in the Employment of Negroes in War Industries," in Foner and Lewis, eds., *The Black Worker*, pp. 233–7.
90. FEPC, *First Report*, in Foner and Lewis, eds., *The Black Worker*, pp. 265–72.

much as 70 percent, was in stevedore and other unskilled work in Army Service Forces (ASF) and Navy shore establishments.[91] By midwar in 1943, the ASF was in fact the nation's largest employer of civilian workers, and blacks comprised 13.7 percent of its 1,026,000 civilian personnel.[92] Overall, modest advances in skilled and semiskilled work for blacks, including clerical and professional positions, were offset by the entry of a million workers without prior experience, including farm laborers and women; thus the black labor force remained largely composed of unskilled and service workers.[93] The bulk of the FEPC complaints aimed at the Departments of War and Navy concerned unskilled laborers, as did most of the committee's casework.[94]

Patterns of complaint reporting to the FEPC indicate that the committee's work focused on sectors vital to the war. An enumeration using the sector categories employed in the committee casework indicates that more than one-third of all complaints regarding black workers came from five core war "sectors": aircraft construction, the Department of War, shipbuilding, the Department of the Navy, and iron and steel (see Table 4.3).[95]

While this data effectively describes the distribution of FEPC investigative resources by sector, more revealing are the shares of complaints that various sectors claimed relative to the size of each sector's black labor force. Recall that the majority of black workers had no recourse to the FEPC; 52 percent of black manpower was not prone to FEPC consideration and thus should not be considered part of the war production labor force (see Appendix 4.2). Eleven sectors, listed in Table 4.4, comprise the black war production labor force; that is, the FEPC could possibly receive complaints from these sectors if a given firm held a federal war contract. In this way, the sectoral distribution of the

91. The War Department contained three branches below the General Staff: the Army Ground Forces, the Army Air Forces, and the ASF, which governed the Army's economic mobilization activities, including procurement, supply, transport, and personnel. John D. Millett, *The Organization and Role of the Army Service Forces*, United States Army in World War II, Washington, D.C., USGPO, 1954; Smith, *The Army and Economic Mobilization*, pp. 112–15.

92. "Disclose 13.7% of Army Civil Force is Negro," Chicago *Defender*, June 26, 1943.

93. FEPC, *First Report*, in Foner and Lewis, eds., *The Black Worker*, p. 269.

94. The most cited single occupation in the casework was "laborer." Of the ten highest ranking categories produced by a provisional enumeration, five could be safely considered to be unskilled work (see Appendix 4.1).

95. The casework data in this chapter, unless otherwise noted, are drawn from author's analysis of the 4,608 cases docketed between July 1, 1943 and December 31, 1944 by FEPC regional offices (see Appendix 4.3).

Table 4.3. *FEPC Complaints, Percentage by Sector, Union, or Central State Office, July 1, 1943 to December 31, 1944.*

Sector	% of Cases	Cumulative %
Aircraft construction	9.79	
U.S. Department of War	9.05	
Shipbuilding	6.58	
U.S. Department of Navy	5.71	
Iron & steel, armor plate, cable	5.23	36.36
Railroads	4.79	
Ordnance, munitions	4.36	
Food	3.41	
AFL	3.36	
Electrical machinery	3.21	55.49
Tools, machinery, engines	3.15	
U.S. Employment Service	2.78	
Communications & optical equipment	2.63	
Miscellaneous, service, & hospitals	2.41	
Unknown	2.41	68.87
Chemicals, paint, & pharmaceutical	2.41	
Rail and motor freight	2.30	
Water freight	2.03	
Apparel	1.93	
Contract construction	1.65	79.19

Source: Analysis of casework data by author, records of the Fair Employment Practices Committee, 1941–1946 (*n* = 4,608).

roughly 3.5 million FEPC-prone black workers can be compared to the sectoral "production" of FEPC complaints by sector. The data clusters these labor force segments into FEPC overrepresented, FEPC equivalent, and FEPC underrepresented categories, as indicated. Of eleven broad sectors listed in Table 4.4, three accounted for a percentage share of complaints that was over twice their share of the black war production, or FEPC-prone labor force. Thus workers in federal war agencies, other federal government, and so on, claimed disproportionate shares of FEPC casework. To take the leading example, war agencies – that is, civilian employees of the War and Navy Departments and other executive war agencies – employed only 5.5 percent of the black war production, or FEPC-prone, labor force, but accounted for over 17 percent of FEPC cases. Adjusted for the size of each labor force, these core war

Table 4.4. *Percentage of FEPC Complaints Relative to Size of Black Labor Force, Sectors with Access to FEPC, July 1, 1943 to December 31, 1944; and Percentage of FEPC-prone Black Workers, November 1944.*

Labor Force Sector	Percentage of FEPC Complaints	Percentage of FEPC-prone Blacks	Complaints per 100,000 Workers
Overrepresented in FEPC casework			
Federal War Agencies[1]	17.3	5.5	3.84
Other Federal Government	6.0	2.8	2.56
Munitions	41.6	20.9	2.37
Aircraft	10.8	3.1	
Shipbuilding	7.5	5.2	
Other munitions	7.1	5.1	
Iron and steel	5.8	1.7	
Ordnance	5.0	4.1	
Communications equipment	2.9	.5	
Nonferrous metals	1.7	.6	
Rubber	.8	.4	
Transportation and Utilities	12.3	7.3	1.98
Proportional			
Construction	1.8	1.7	1.24
All Other Manufacturing	16.4	16.0	1.21
Food	3.8	5.8	
Apparel and textiles	3.5	2.6	
Paper and printing	1.8	1.5	
Furniture	0.0	1.4	
Other chemicals	2.7	1.3	
Lumber	.8	.9	
Tobacco	.3	.9	
Misc. manufacturing	2.1	.6	
Stone, clay, glass	.3	.6	
Petroleum & coal	.9	.4	
Underrepresented			
Other nonmanufacturing	3.4	11.4	.35
State and Local Government	.3	2.9	.14
Mining	.8	3.8	.02
Trade	0.0	15.4	0.00
Finance, business	0.0	12.1	0.00
TOTAL	100.0	100.0	

[1] Civilian employees in the Navy and War Departments, and workers in emergency executive agencies such as the WMC, OPA, and War Labor Board. Other categories are listed at the end of business code section in Appendix 4.3.

Sources: Analysis of casework data by author, $n = 4,117$; labor force statistics from *FEPC, First Report*, in Foner and Lewis, eds., *The Black Worker*, pp. 265–72.

agencies of the central state produced more than triple the number of complaints, as did "all other manufacturing." Workers outside of war-fighting institutions simply did not produce complaints at levels comparable to those produced by employees and charges of the central state.[96]

When America's central state extended secure, profitable contracts to certain sectors and locales at the same time that it constrained their competitors through quotas and restricted access to materials, it exerted exceptionally direct control over capital flows. But new centers of ship-building and aircraft construction concentrated in northern and in southern California, respectively, obtained not only immense infusions of capital, but also scores of administrators in the bargain. San Francisco and Los Angeles had become, in the apt phrase of Gerald Nash, "federal cities."[97] Where black workers found Uncle Sam looming large as a builder, owner, and manager, the FEPC received higher rates of complaints, for three principle reasons: complaints filed by state officials, state-sponsored installations' hiring policies, and the fortuitous concentration of race advancement organizations in and near federal cities.

Determinants of Employment Complaints: Central State Authority

First, the proximity and density of central state officials promoted complaint reporting most obviously because these officials often filed complaints themselves, particularly those concerning advertisements and refusals to hire. During the most vigorous period of investigative activity, these central state agents, primarily FEPC regional officers and sympathetic USES officials, generated three out of ten complaints nationwide. Here, again, there was significant regional variation. Federal complaints accounted for roughly half of the cases investigated in New York State and in the region covering Michigan, Kentucky, and Ohio (see Table 4.5). The highest rates of state-sponsored complaints, therefore, occurred in the two regions that were thoroughly dominated by one large urban economy; these two offices in effect monitored New York City and Detroit, respectively. This attentiveness also coincided with central state officials' concern for black discontent in the aftermath of serious epi-

---

96. The two lowest scoring sectors, trade and finance/business, included many all-black enterprises serving segregated communities. Workers in the mining industry, under the leadership of United Mine Workers president John L. Lewis, thoroughly alienated themselves from the war administration. Resisting economic controls, the union pursued higher wages so relentlessly through strikes that Congress enacted the War Labor Disputes Act in 1943. Polenberg, *War and Society*, pp. 161–70.
97. Gerald Nash, *The American West Transformed*, pp. 24–6, 66.

Table 4.5. *FEPC Regional Casework Profiles, for Cases Reported Between July 1, 1943 and December 31, 1944, Regions Reporting at Least One Hundred Complaints.*

FEPC Regional Office HQ; States Served	% Complaints Filed by State	Complaint-Disposition Lag in Days	% Complaints Investigated	% Complaints Postponed	Composite Ranking (Rank)
New York City NY	47.9 (2)	101 (2)	76.3 (1)	12.5 (2)	1.75
San Francisco AZ CA CO NV OR WA	37.0 (3)	109 (3)	61.8 (2)	15.2 (3)	2.75
Philadelphia NJ PA DE	32.6 (4)	171 (5)	60.3 (4)	11.6 (1)	3.50
Dallas TX LA	37.0 (3)	97 (1)	51.7 (6)	28.9 (6)	4.00
Chicago WI IL IN	22.7 (7)	156 (4)	60.9 (3)	21.7 (4)	4.50
Detroit KY MI OH	51.6 (1)	178 (6)	44.8 (8)	28.9 (6)	5.25
Washington, D.C. DC MD NC VA WV	16.9 (8)	171 (5)	58.6 (5)	28.4 (5)	5.75
Kansas City KS AK MO OK	28.5 (5)	222 (7)	48.0 (7)	41.3 (7)	6.50
Atlanta GA FL SC TN AL MS	24.5 (6)	239 (8)	24.3 (9)	64.6 (8)	7.75

Note: Regional office rank within each category in parentheses.
Source: Analysis of casework data by author, records of the FEPC, 1941–46.

sodes of violent disorder in each city in the summer of 1943. Conversely, state agents accounted for only 24.5 percent of the casework in the Deep South's regional office in Atlanta (GA, FL, SC, TN, AL, MS) and only 16.9 percent of the casework generated by the upper South states of Region 4 (DC, MD, NC, VA, WV).

Second, the record indicates that state institutions were generally more likely to adhere to federal antidiscriminatory policy than private firms when advertising and hiring. Somewhat paradoxically, as Weaver noted, those installations with relatively liberal hiring policies, such as U.S. Navy Yards, actually cultivated complaints concerning work conditions and upgrading.[98] Those plants with a substantial federal presence contained state officials acting as owners and/or operators seeking uninterrupted and efficient production in part through the enforcement of federal nondiscrimination policy as a matter of institutional policy, particularly in hiring. This contrasted with private owner-operators whose formal policy on the matter tended to be either biased or nonexistent. Thus, the degree to which a plant's management pursued antidiscrimination policies, and the rate of complaint reporting by workers, were, in part, a product of the degree of central state oversight there.[99] A production site was generally one of three types: private ownership and operation, government ownership and private operation, and government ownership and operation. In privately owned and privately operated establishments, central state authority was most distant. The military secretaries informed the FEPC that they were prepared to inform such firms that contractual obligations regarding fair employment must be fulfilled. Such instructions, they advised the committee, "shall not be interpreted as an intrusion upon the contractor's responsibilities in handling personnel," but rather as the clarification of an "obligation" that

98. The committee received complaints from three types of sources: workers, either individually or collectively; organizations such as unions or civil rights organizations; or a government office, including the FEPC itself. Complaints could be aimed at three types of targets: a firm, a government office, or a union.

99. Defense program administrators struggled for some time to solve the problem of facilities expansion. In a familiar pattern, two systems were employed and discarded in turn when they proved excessively inefficient. The National Defense Advisory Council, searching for a method to repay contractors making defense-related capital outlays so as to ensure in advance the full recovery of expansion costs, developed the Emergency Plant Facilities Contract (EPF). The system failed due to the inefficiency of providing funds twice – once by the banks, and again by the War Department – the inadequacy of 50 percent financing for subcontractors and vendors, and inordinate delays. This system was replaced by the Defense Plant Corporation (DPC or Plancors) contract, which was used to construct and equip facilities for such basic industries as aircraft, synthetic rubber, and steel. DPC facilities, most of which were Army Air Force facilities, were simply leased to private firms for production. The twenty-six largest Plancors accounted for a majority of the DPC program; twenty of the twenty-six most costly plants were north of the Ohio and east of the Mississippi Rivers. Chrysler's huge Chicago engine plant and the Las Vegas Basic Magnesium plant together represented one-fifth of the cost of the twenty-six largest DPC facilities. Each was among the five individual plants that generated the greatest number of FEPC complaints over the eighteen months of FEPC casework at midwar. Smith, *The Army and Economic Mobilization*, pp. 476–7, 483–7, 494.

existed by virtue of the nondiscrimination clause in the production contract.[100] The War Department's contract compliance officer in Detroit, for example, was particularly dedicated in his pursuit of obedience to the fair employment executive orders, and arranged for the suspension of several troublemaking workers in June 1943.[101]

In intermediate settings, that is, government-owned, contractor-operated (GOCO) plants, the War Department believed itself party to a "unique relationship" with the private contractors directing production. The factories were wholly devoted to war production and the entire cost of the plant's operation was borne by the government; the property typically was designated a military reservation and was supervised by a commanding officer.[102] By the end of the war, 60 percent of the value of all War Department-owned, -sponsored, and -leased industrial facilities were plants directly funded and constructed by the War Department. These were primarily large plants for the production of munitions, big bomber assembly plants and the related modification centers of the Army Air Forces, and many smaller facilities serving chiefly as ordnance warehouses.[103] As with vast new Army installations, the construction of many of the fifty largest War Department-owned establishments was equivalent to the creation of a sizable new city, complete with streets, railroad lines, power plants, sewage systems, extensive housing projects, and numerous other community facilities.[104]

100. Memorandum, Henry Stimson, Frank Knox, and E. S. Land to Malcolm MacLean, July 2, 1942, in Committee Members file, Office Files of Malcolm Ross, June 1940–June 1948, FEPC Headquarters Records, SDR-COFEP.

101. To be sure, many subordinate officials in the armed forces also obstructed compliance. For a case of naval officers' efforts to quash a FEPC hearing, see Meier and Rudwick, *Black Detroit*, pp. 157–61.

102. Memorandum, Henry Stimson, Frank Knox, and E. S. Land to Malcolm MacLean, July 2, 1942, in Committee Members file, Office Files of Malcolm Ross, June 1940–June 1948, FEPC Headquarters Records, SDR-COFEP.

103. GOCO facilities involved by far the greatest investment of any class of plant expansion. By September 30, 1945, the cost of completed War Department-owned industrial facilities exceeded $4.3 billion, approximately 50 percent more than the $2.9 billion invested in DPC facilities. The War Department built these plants with private construction firms under cost-plus contracts and paid a management fee to contractors for directing production. The layout, machinery, and products of the plants – which made tremendous quantities of high explosives, for example – were thought to be so highly specialized as to be in low demand in peacetime. There was no apparent market alternative to War Department ownership. Smith, *The Army and Economic Mobilization*, pp. 496–500.

104. Of the fifty most costly industrial facilities owned by the War Department, fifteen were located in the South, while twenty-one were located in the factory belt. Smith, *The Army and Economic Mobilization*, p. 501.

Due to his interest in regulating and administering the nation's property and investments, the Undersecretary of War believed that his agency had a particular responsibility to ensure that such plants' policies be consistent with the controlling executive order. In fact, if an FEPC investigation showed a complaint to be sound, and if its efforts to resolve the case had failed, the department asked that it receive the complaint so that it could attempt to bring about compliance itself.[105] Consider the justification of state action in the telegram from Secretary of the Navy Knox to white workers at the Hudson Car Company on June 17, 1942, in response to news that a strike had resulted from the introduction of several black machine tool operators, who were union members:

> This plant is engaged in vital war production, is entirely owned by the government, which bears all operating costs, and has been designated as a military reservation.

Under these circumstances, Knox believed that the refusal to work warranted the conclusion that the strikers were disloyal to the government and thus were subject not only to immediate dismissal, but to a ban from obtaining employment at other war production sites.[106]

Finally, the third category of government-owned and -operated establishments – U.S. Navy Yards and Army arsenals – were governed directly by cabinet officials who simply directed compliance. While bias certainly remained, it tended to occur relatively more frequently at the work rather than at the hiring stage. Although the Navy Department, for example, initially restricted black recruits to the rank of messmen in the service, it imposed no barrier to the employment of black apprentices in its nine Navy Yards.[107] Navy Department regulations differed from the general civil service "1-in-3 system," in which appointing officials were required only to choose from among the three highest test scorers, in effect freeing hiring officials to pass over nonwhites who had excelled in

---

105. This latter policy recommendation was later extended to government-owned and -operated plants. Memorandum, Robert Patterson to Malcolm MacLean, July 2, 1942, Labor Discrimination (Racial Character); memorandum, J. H. Ohly to J. P. Mitchell, August 4, 1942, Labor Discrimination (Racial Character), both in Ohly papers, HSTL.
106. Quoted in Weaver, *Negro Labor*, p. 74.
107. The U.S. Navy Yards were located in Boston; Charleston, SC; Mare Island, CA; Brooklyn; Norfolk, VA; Philadelphia; Portsmouth, NH; Puget Sound, WA; and Washington, DC. "1,051 Negroes Now Employed by Navy Dep't," Atlanta *Daily World*, March 29, 1942; F. G. Fassett, Jr., ed., *The Shipbuilding Business in the United States of America*, Vol. I, New York, The Society of Naval Architects and Marine Engineers, 1948, pp. 161–5.

tests.[108] In the Navy Yards, hiring officers were required to appoint the highest scoring eligible trainee; any black applicant who scored well on the semiannual examinations thus had an exceptional chance of appointment. The unusual policy governed hiring in a sector where overall employment growth was explosive, for the industry was the largest nonagricultural employer in the nation by September 1943.[109] In part due to the hiring regulations, more than five thousand black skilled and semiskilled workers were employed in U.S. Navy Yards as early as 1940.[110] The next year, the proportion of black workers at the Charleston Navy Yard rose from 9.5 percent to 17.7 percent. A similar increase obtained in the Norfolk Navy Yard, although most jobs were at the operative or laborer rating.[111]

The yards' relatively open hiring practices produced massive multiracial workforces, and thus complaints about a variety of matters. Visitors to the Brooklyn Navy Yard were stunned by the size of the crew, which had grown from a peacetime workforce of approximately five thousand to at least sixty thousand, including several thousand black men and women. Complaints of discrimination rarely referred to the yard's hiring policy, since the yard accepted most fit people who applied for work with the necessary experience. Instead, minority workers claimed that race determined a worker's rating, salary, assignment, and shift.[112] This yard produced the highest number of FEPC complaints from any single government facility in the nation.[113] While complaints related to hiring practices comprised nearly half of all committee cases (see Appendix 4.4), they accounted for only 11.9 percent of the casework generated by

108. On this rule and contemporaneous challenges to it, see Desmond King, *Separate and Unequal: Black Americans and the US Federal Government*, New York, Oxford University Press, 1995, pp. 51–7.

109. In 1939 there were thirty-eight shipyards employing 120,000 workers; by 1944, eighty-four shipyards employed 1,700,000 workers. Fassett, Jr., ed., *The Shipbuilding Business*, pp. 161–5. Lester Rubin, et al., *Negro Employment in the Maritime Industries: A Study of Racial Policies in the Shipbuilding, Longshore, and Offshore Maritime Industries*, Vol. VII, Studies of Negro Employment, Industrial Research Unit, University of Pennsylvania, 1974, pp. 31–4.

110. "Dr. Weaver Reveals 5,000 Skilled and Semi-Skilled at Work," Kansas City *Call*, February 28, 1941.

111. Rubin, et al., *Negro Employment in the Maritime Industries*, pp. 31–4.

112. "How Brooklyn Navy Yard Retards Colored Workers," Baltimore *Afro-American*, January 15, 1944.

113. A citizen's committee charged that the workers' "fear of intimidation by superiors" had actually suppressed the number of formal complaints from workers there. "Racial Bias is Scored," Savannah *Tribune*, September 30, 1943; "Bias Against Negroes, Jews Laid to Navy Yard," New York *P.M.*, February 11, 1944; "Navy Will Lift Race Marks from Brooklyn Yard Badges," New York *P.M.*, May 22, 1944.

the Brooklyn Navy Yard, where upgrading, working conditions, work assignments, classifications, and discharges combined to account for 62.7 percent of the casework.

After U.S. Navy Yards first hired blacks and widened the range of occupations available to them, nearby private yards tended to follow suit.[114] The San Francisco area was one of the largest shipbuilding centers in the country, housing the gigantic Richmond, Moore, Western Pipe and Steel, Pacific Bridge, General Engineering, Bethlehem, and Marinship yards, all scattered near the Navy Yard at Mare Island.[115] Again, the industry showed a dramatic increase in nonwhite employment. By the spring of 1944 there were fifteen times more blacks in shipyards than in 1940, and nine yards reported that blacks accounted for more than sixteen percent of all workers employed.[116] By early 1943, the Richmond shipyards of the Kaiser Corporation alone reported sixty-one hundred black employees, even though the AFL International Brotherhood of Boilermakers, which also had locals in the Kaiser Shipyards in Portland and Vancouver, refused to admit black workers.[117] Overall, private yards remained much more resistant to integration than Navy Yards, despite WMC intervention in labor-short areas.[118] In sum, black applications fared best when state sponsorship was most complete. These multiracial workforces subsequently produced high rates of complaints regarding working conditions. One final factor helped shape the production of complaint activity nationwide.

Determinants of Employment Complaints: Organizational Support

The degree of organization of the local workforce translated into higher rates of complaint reporting in two ways: through unionization in fac-

114. Weaver, *Negro Labor*, p. 35.
115. "Union Ban Against Skilled Jobs Lifted," Baltimore *Afro-American*, October 17, 1942.
116. Three reported cohorts of over thirty percent: Sun Shipbuilding in Chester, PA; Alabama Shipbuilding in Mobile, AL; and North Carolina Shipbuilding in Wilmington, NC. FEPC, *First Report*, in Foner and Lewis, eds., *The Black Worker*, pp. 265–72; "Negro Employment 15 Times Greater than 40, OWI Reveals," New York *Daily Worker*, May 10, 1944.
117. The Richmond installation produced the largest number of FEPC complaints of any privately owned facility in the nation. "Progress Report, WMC, March, 1943," in Foner and Lewis, eds., *The Black Worker*, p. 231; "Jimcro Tactics Foment Trouble in Kaiser Yards," New York *People's Voice*, July 31, 1943.
118. Rubin, et al., *Negro Employment in the Maritime Industries*, pp. 31–4.

tories and through membership in race advancement organizations. Due to their representing members in negotiations with firms, labor boards, and federal officials, unions facilitated worker awareness of federal labor standards and policies, as well as grievances stemming from the violation of these policies. In addition, union efforts – particularly those of AFL affiliates – to bar black workers from new factories and occupations directly caused hundreds of complaints to the FEPC.[119] Other unions, most often those affiliated with the CIO, aided minority workers in complaint reporting. A second form of organization, race advancement groups, assisted individuals and groups in reporting complaints, and often filed complaints of their own. Those cities producing the largest shares of complaints, therefore, harbored dense networks of activism and advocacy both favoring and opposing fair employment practices.[120] Employees in areas with low organizational density also often lacked the other factor facilitating complaints – central state presence – and thus encountered an inverted grievance opportunity structure: the lessened salience of nondiscrimination policy, and a lack of access to information and expertise. Blacks in this situation were hence more vulnerable to intimidation and outright exclusion, and were less likely to submit and pursue effective complaints.

In addition to facilitating complaint reporting, organizations also often filed them directly. For example, when the Commandant of the Brooklyn Navy Yard denied charges of discrimination filed by the National Negro Congress, the group joined with the local Urban League chapter, organized labor, and other community organizations to push for the full integration of the yard, in part through a drive to register complaints with the FEPC.[121] NAACP member Katharyne H. Jones personally submitted to the FEPC eleven complaints of racial discrimination

119. Complaints against unions accounted for only 249 complaints, or 5.4 percent of the FEPC casework. The AFL was the target of 62.2 percent of these cases, rail unions accounted for 30.5 percent, and the CIO accounted for 5.6 percent.

120. Detroit exemplified this dynamic. The Metropolitan Detroit Council on Fair Employment Practice, an umbrella federation of seventy civic groups, assisted with the committee's investigations and agitated for public hearings. The United Automobile Workers (UAW) promoted both racial integration and complaint reporting, respectively, through an Interracial Committee and a broad alliance linking its leadership with local black organizations, and at the level of locals, fierce resistance to the placement and upgrading of nonwhites. Meier and Rudwick, *Black Detroit*, pp. 115, 165–73.

121. The Citizens' Anti-Discrimination Committee focused on the yard's Labor Board, due to its control of the employment and assignment of applicants. "Racial Bias is Scored," Savannah *Tribune*, September 30, 1943; "Bias Against Negroes, Jews Laid to Navy Yard," New York *P.M.*, February 11, 1944.

– each citing failure to hire – against Springfield, Massachusetts, firms in the space of two weeks, after her chapter and a local community league decided to work with both the FEPC and the USES to improve black employment opportunities there.[122] Four of Jones's complaints resulted in "satisfactory adjustments," six were dismissed for lack of merit, and one was ruled outside the jurisdiction of the FEPC, since the company in question held no government contracts. Of the five complaints "dismissed on merits" for which Final Disposition Reports (aptly, FDRs) were located, four were based on the finding that the USES had referred no black workers to the firms; plants in Springfield required such referral cards. The fifth dismissal concerned the Smith & Wesson Company, where 34 of the 1,227 workers were black. The manager there reported that blacks were hired when they were referred, and that they enjoyed the same upgrading opportunities as white workers.[123] Each of the FDRs contained a letter from the company that outlined its willingness to hire any person regardless of race, creed, color, or national origin.[124] In sum, the efforts of Jones personified the effect of organizational networks of advocacy – both supportive of and resistant to the fair employment initiative – on the concentration of complaints in northern industrial cities.[125] One measure that can serve as a proxy for sympathetic organizational activity is the presence or absence of a branch of the Urban League, the organization most dedicated to increasing economic opportunities for blacks. A map of the forty-nine offices in July 1943 indicates that the distribution of this organization's re-

122. "DeBerry Lauds USES Directive on Discrimination," Springfield *Union*, June 6, 1944.
123. See case nos. 1-BR-108, American Bosch Corporation; 1-BR-97, Brooks Bank Note Company; and 1-BR-107, Smith & Wesson; Central Files of the FEPC, Final Disposition Reports, Region I, SDR-COFEP.
124. Jones declined job offers from each firm where her complaint was adjusted. In a somewhat similar case in 1943, a committee examiner in Detroit was accused of urging the local civil rights federation to recruit black women to develop complaints by seeking employment at war plants. The examiner denied the report. Likewise, in preparation for an FEPC hearing in New York City, the NAACP instructed its local branches to investigate local defense industries and training classes. If staff suspected a discriminatory employment policy, qualified blacks were told to apply for jobs and, if refused, to enter a complaint and notify the NAACP central office. Finally, according to Earl Dickerson, civil rights groups in Washington, D.C., instructed blacks to apply for streetcar jobs there. Letter, Jonathan Daniels to Monsignor Francis J. Haas, August 24, 1943; letter, Monsignor Francis J. Haas to Jonathan Daniels, September 1, 1943, OF 4245, FDRL; Reed, *Seedtime*, p. 35; Terkel, *"The Good War,"* p. 338.
125. Three offices reported that cases formally filed by organizations accounted for more than 12 percent of their casework: Chicago, Philadelphia, and New York, in descending order.

sources and expertise roughly corresponded to patterns of state investment (compare Maps 1.2 and 4.1).

Patterns of Adjustment: The Committee's Response to Complaints

The FEPC's investigative response to complaints was also uneven. The percentage of cases successfully resolved, or "satisfactorily adjusted," varied from 54.1 percent for the subregional office serving Detroit to 18.9 percent for the office serving Washington, D.C., and its neighboring states.[126] In the factory belt of the Northeast and North-central regions, prompt intervention and the likelihood of a positive response most likely encouraged additional complaint reporting. The southern regional office's casework profile, in sharp contrast, was distinguished by the extraordinarily high percentage of cases left unresolved. Over the eighteen months following July 1, 1943, New York's FEPC officials investigated 76.3 percent of the casework and left only 12.5 percent postponed (see Table 4.5).[127] Of all of those cases docketed in New York, 37.4 percent were adjusted to the satisfaction of the field investigator. The casework profile for the regional office serving the Deep South states was inverted, as FEPC officials investigated 24.3 percent of the cases reported and postponed 64.6 percent; only 11.8 percent were satisfactorily adjusted. Postponed responses likely had little or no deterrent effect on discriminatory behavior and undermined the confidence of workers in the efficacy of the system. Delays in the South thus most likely indirectly suppressed the filing of grievances.

If the foregoing analysis of the central state's orientation toward the FEPC is correct, one would expect the national casework to reflect the war-makers' interest in promoting uninterrupted and efficient production in "federal cities." The casework analysis provides four indices of the efficacy of each regional office's enforcement efforts: the percentage of complaints filed by central state officials; the number of days between the date of the complaint filing and the date of FEPC disposition; the percentage of all complaints filed that were investigated by the regional FEPC office; and the percentage of investigations postponed by the regional FEPC office. A comparison of the regional offices' casework

126. This covers the July 1, 1943 to June 30, 1944 period. In Washington, black workers' proximity to national political debates over fair employment policies may have spurred complaints at the same time that southern congressional opposition to the initiative undermined enforcement efforts. FEPC, *Final Report*, p. 115.

127. This includes cases docketed and delayed either by referral to the field director, or by leaving the case pending.

Map 4.1. Affiliated branch offices of the National Urban League, 1943. Source: Memorandum, National Urban League, July 1, 1943, "Lists," SDR-COFEP. Cities listed in Appendix 4.5.

profiles appears in Table 4.5. Within each index, the ranking of 1 indicates an administrative record that most favored black workers through – in order – high levels of state intervention, prompt dispositions, likely investigations, and low rates of postponement. A region's average for the four scores produces a composite ranking of the relative efficacy of each office's enforcement efforts. The analysis produces the expected polar cases of New York City and Atlanta. The latter is distinguished by an exceptionally high average lag time between a complaint's filing and the FEPC's disposition of the case. Committee examiners in the Deep South, on average, required eight months to close a case; the average case required three months in New York. In each of the four measures of efficacy examined here, the southern region ranked among the least effective offices, producing the lowest score three times. New York City, on the other hand, consistently achieved the first or second rank. The problem was not that the southern regional office was understaffed. In 1944, the Atlanta office employed an average of three examiners, equal to the staff of the Philadelphia office, which administered the committee's work in New Jersey, Pennsylvania, and Delaware. At the time, the average case load per examiner in Atlanta was 47.7, compared with 110 in Philadelphia. Indeed, eight other regional offices had heavier caseloads per examiner; only two had lighter ones.[128]

128. The anomalous rankings of the Dallas office on the first two indices is perhaps best explained by the unusually small caseload carried by each of its four examiners, who

Conclusion

Similar statistics compelled the writers of the committee's 1946 *Final Report* to admit that the rates of cases satisfactorily adjusted was "to a degree related to and determined by the problems inherent or peculiar to each region."[129] Elsewhere, the committee's *Final Report* invoked "cultural patterns" to explain the numerous areas, particularly in the South, "in which there are large proportions of minority workers, but relatively few complaints."[130] Southern racial attitudes and political concerns stemming from them undoubtedly helped shaped this casework. From its inception the Atlanta office struggled to gain the cooperation of other government officials and staff in the South, particularly those attached to local WMC and USES offices.[131]

But when an analysis of complaints pending at the FEPC in mid-1944 showed that "only" about a quarter of them had originated in the South, committee officials explained that organizational and mobilization factors accounted for the discrepancy. Discrimination might be more widespread in underrepresented regions, they acknowledged, but two factors accounted for the high levels of complaint reporting in the North: race organizations, which were "active against discrimination," and the concentration of war industry in the North.[132] The South was less

averaged 22.3 cases in January of 1944. This compared, for example, to 60.3 in San Francisco, which was near the average case load of 58.5 at the time. The Detroit office also may have been hampered by an overwork; its four examiners carried an average load of ninety-four cases. FEPC Division of Budget and Administrative Management, "Salaries and Expenses, Committee on Fair Employment Practice, Fiscal Year, 1946," Documents File, March 31, 1945, FEPC Headquarters Records, SDR-COFEP, p. 27.

129. Some argued that southern blacks were simply accustomed to whites' limiting their employment opportunities to semiskilled or unskilled work. While only a small percentage of USES work advertisements still managed to specify white or "colored," black workers may have continued to view only those ads with the latter specification as intended for them. FEPC, *Final Report*, p. 115, 33; "Regional Wartime Experiences" (draft), West Coast Materials, Office Files of Malcolm Ross, SDR-COFEP, pp. 51-5.

130. FEPC, *Final Report*, p. 33.

131. By November 1944 the committee's director of field operations recommended a hearing to consider the practices by which the southern branches of WMC and USES avoided referring qualified blacks to war plants. All levels of WMC disregarded the WMC-FEPC agreements requiring equal opportunities for referrals; despite the white labor shortage, several firms continued to recruit workers from outside the local employment area. The USES staff underreported discriminatory orders to the FEPC, and in some cases submitted defective forms, apparently intending to delay investigations.

132. "Only 26 Pct. of 'Race' Cases Before FEPC Came from South," Atlanta *Constitution*, August 4, 1944.

thoroughly industrialized than the north-central and northeastern regions and provided fewer defense employment opportunities per capita than did other regions. In addition, state-sponsored war facilities were more than mere physical manifestations of industrial production. They served as instruments of federal manpower policies, for black employment patterns and FEPC complaint reporting varied according to workers' proximity to the core institutions of the mobilization effort and to central state authorities. Where the state itself employed civilians – in Army depots, for example – one finds higher rates of complaints. Contracting agencies directed compliance in these facilities, and blacks faced fewer obstacles to hiring. The Kansas City Urban League, betting that "the position and policy of the federal government as one of the largest employers of workers will influence and determine the policies of private industrialists," focused their attention on the three largest local war enterprises, all government owned and federally supervised: the North American Aircraft Corporation, the Remington Small Arms Plant, and the Quartermaster Depot.[133]

The FEPC, in practice, granted concessions to disadvantaged blacks quite selectively, for the president's labor and manpower advisers designed and altered the committee's operations to allow for some flexibility in forging a quasijudicial relationship with the clients they served. As a result, complainants internal and external to the state drove the FEPC in uneven patterns that mirrored economic and political variables, namely, the design of the mobilization effort, the presence of state installations, and the strength of local organizations. The analysis now turns to consider patterns of grievance-formation and adjustment in the Army.

133. Thomas A. Webster, "Employers, Unions, and Negro Workers," *Opportunity*, October, 1941, pp. 296–7.

5

The Racial Politics of Army Service: Central State Authority and the Control of Black Soldier Resistance

Suppose *you* had to run an army, on which the very lifeblood of our country depended. You couldn't have people running around as they pleased, or you wouldn't have an army. Wars have been fought in this world for thousands of years. From all this fighting, soldiers and generals alike have found that lawless and disorderly mobs can only expect to be chased down and killed. On the other hand, great victories have been won by armies of soldiers who respected the law, obeyed orders, and fought together as a team.

from a suggested lecture, "Educational Program for Colored Troops," Camp Stewart, Georgia, July 29, 1943[1]

The problem for American statesmen was an ageless one: to gather and project national power through the collective organization of material and manpower. The group conflict that resulted from this process also was unexceptional, viewed either in the long-term, or as an episode of twentieth-century American war-fighting. In fact, the race manpower problem of the Army shared several features with the fair employment sphere. As in that case, the frenetic mobilization concentrated black manpower spatially and occupationally, and the grievances that followed from such narrowed opportunities had characteristic causes and qualities. Again, for example, complaints resulted from the service role that was commonly assigned to black soldiers. More fundamentally, attempts by statesmen to stanch militancy were activated by elections and national security concerns. Thus, "success" was as elsewhere in the mobilization conceptualized at different times in efficiency or electoral

---

1. Memorandum, "Subject: Educational Program for Colored Troops," to Brigade, Group, and Battalion Commanders and all Officers of Colored Units, July 29, 1943, RG 107, Civilian Aid to the Secretary of War, Camp Stewart, National Archives, emphasis in original.

terms. Failure was indicated by delays in training, transfer, or utilization – or worse, by the need to deploy substantial federal or party resources to control or defuse dissatisfaction. Here again, the administration appointed blacks to high-profile positions during the 1940 campaign. This attempt to bring northern blacks into the party had mixed results, due to the use of the inherited cabinet technique in a new context of militancy. One appointee – rather than merely fielding grievances – aggressively pursued policy change, much like Earl Dickerson of the FEPC. Once statesmen replaced this "societal" agent, the War Department achieved more satisfactory advisement through an informal White Cabinet set-up. Campaigns signaled the temporary ascendancy of political concerns. Here, the administration offered relatively minor, symbolic concessions to secure votes. But reform remained secondary to the supreme goal of war-making and the day-to-day accommodation of social unrest. Agitation and disturbances, according to Undersecretary of War Robert Patterson, interfered with the War Department's duty "to build promptly and efficiently an Army capable of defending the nation in the existing crisis and organized so that it will fit into the accepted social order of this county."[2] Lacking any coherent general plan for managing disorder, the central state simply coped as best it could.

But troop policies also differed from employment policies in ways that contributed to physical confrontations. First, the Army, largely untouched by the New Deal, began the war with a more retrograde race management policy. Military training also naturally collectivized grievances into potentially powerful micromovements (see Chapter 6), and may have heightened the level of aggression among recruits. As General Davis observed, "military training does not develop a spirit of cheerful acceptance of Jim-Crow laws and customs."[3] The harsh, institutionalized racial bias in effect provoked black soldier resistance, fueling violence that in turn accelerated policy reforms. While the FEPC proved to be a relatively successful means for incorporating black leaders and masses into the industrial mobilization – if the dearth of racially motivated work stoppages and the attempts to retain the agency in 1945 and 1946 are any measure – War Department officials finally managed to "solve" its

2. Ulysses Lee, *The Employment of Negro Troops*, U.S. Army in World War II, Special Studies, Office of the Chief of Military History, U.S. Army, Washington, D.C., 1966, p. 364. The Lee volume is by far the finest single study of this subject, and this chapter depends heavily upon it.
3. Memorandum, Brigadier General B. O. Davis to John J. McCloy, Assistant Secretary of War, November 10, 1943, Morris J. MacGregor and Bernard D. Nalty, eds., *Blacks in the Armed Forces*, Basic Documents, vol. V, Black Soldiers in World War II, Wilmington, DE, Scholarly Resources, Inc., 1977, p. 292.

race friction problem only by transferring black soldiers to theaters of war.

Fair employment policy, while launched in an attempt to control the disorder promised by the March on Washington, thereafter generally tracked the election cycle and, only to a lesser degree, the vagaries of civilian unrest. Race policy in the Army, on the other hand, was founded through two key political appointments in the campaign season of 1940, but subsequent reforms stemmed from unrest and violence involving soldiers. Oddly, while the state's policies in this field assailed unfairness less directly than did the FEPC, the Army produced reforms of more lasting effect. This was due to the fact that, despite the efforts of statesmen insulated from public view and control, black soldier resistance permanently altered – in effect, inverted – the War Department's base logic of racial efficiency. Segregation was at the outset of the war thought necessary to avoid irritating whites who, it was thought, would fight to preserve the privilege of separate units. After the violent summer of 1943, however, only additional ameliorating reforms would end the disruptions that resulted from militant black resistance to mistreatment.

The violence stemmed from a long legacy of harsh segregationist policies in the armed forces. At both operations and planning levels, the initial responses to unrest involved policing and punishment. In addition, because most black training facilities were located in the rural South, racial friction in the Army was more likely to erupt between soldiers and police. Inside Army camps, interracial discipline generally was quite high, since potential rule-breakers were deterred by the prospect of swift punishment. In this sense, the camps resembled the rural southern counties in which they were planted.[4] Wholly insignificant to the white press, insulated to a degree from sympathetic civil authorities and the black press, this conflict was at the outset less likely than urban or factory friction to be publicly reported and debated. This changed rapidly. In these settings, where coercion outweighed capital as an organizing logic, challenges to rules were comparatively infrequent; they were, however, more likely to lead to violence.

For several reasons, then, the military appeared on the eve of war to be the state agency least likely to produce significant reforms. First, the War Department, governing the nation's legitimate centralized armed force, was predisposed toward responding to any unrest with coercion. Second, its policies were well-insulated from public and partisan pressure

---

4. Those expecting to find "an island refuge" from local discrimination were disappointed to find that racial attitudes and rules differed little from those of nearby towns. Lee, *The Employment of Negro Troops*, p. 326.

and the New Deal; its highest-ranking manpower managers were professional soldiers animated by efficiency concerns. Third, the War Department was known as the most discriminatory mainline federal agency, due in large part to its reputed domination by southern personnel. But when the war began, there was some room for optimism, for the four civilian appointees directing military race policies happened to be Republicans.

On the eve of the 1940 GOP convention, the White House announced that Roosevelt had secured the services of two Republicans – former Secretary of State Henry Stimson and newspaper publisher Frank Knox – to serve as Secretary of War and Secretary of the Navy. Stimson, whose presence created the first "coalition" war cabinet since that of George Washington, in turn selected two Republicans to serve him: Robert Patterson, an undersecretary directing procurement, and John J. Mc-Cloy, an assistant secretary. The statesman in Stimson emerged during his testimony to Senate confirmation proceedings; his new assignment he explained "had nothing to do with politics." He was as he put it, "out of politics now."[5] As a member of the opposition, Stimson was in retrospect well-suited to turning aside the demands of what he called the "twin devils" of the race problem, "the man who would 'keep the nigger in his place' and the man who wished to jump at one bound from complex reality to unattainable Utopia . . ."[6] But he was clearly not pursuing a moderating course so as to benefit the Democratic Party per se. Social stability in this case can be more directly attributed to the pursuit of optimally efficient warmaking – as one participant defined it, "to defeat the Axis in the shortest period of time with the least cost, particularly in terms of human lives."[7] The Army case, therefore, pro-

---

5. Stimson considered himself "doing nonpartisan work . . . because it related to international affairs in which I agreed and sympathized with his policies." Henry L. Stimson and McGeorge Bundy, *On Active Service in Peace and War*, New York, Harper & Brothers, 1947, pp. 328, 336.

6. Stimson and Bundy, *On Active Service*, p. 461.

7. Beginning in March 1942, the War Department was organized into three main branches below the General Staff: the Army Ground Forces (AGF), the Army Air Forces (AAF), and the Army Service Forces (ASF). The ASF governed the Army's economic mobilization activities, as well as technical services such as the Ordnance Department, and the nine geographic Service Commands, which administered and supplied AGF camps and stations, but held no control over the soldiers housed there. Most of the policy deliberations considered here involved the secretary's office, the AGF, and the ASF. John D. Millett, "The War Department in World War II," *American Political Science Review*, vol. 40, no. 5, October, 1946, p. 864; John D. Millett, *The Organization and Role of the Army Service Forces*, United States Army in World War II,

vides important comparative leverage to the larger analysis, since policies promulgated by the secretary's office cannot be readily ascribed to partisan considerations.

Army Race Policies and the Spatial and Occupational Concentration of Black Manpower

Recall that armed forces policies played an important role in the 1940 presidential election. Roosevelt charted his course in this manpower sphere with two significant African American appointments during that campaign: New Dealer William Hastie as the Civilian Aide to the Secretary, and Brig. Gen. Benjamin Davis, Sr., to the inspector general's office. The White House viewed the appointments as compatible with the complaint-adjustment system that the War Department inherited from the Great War and the New Deal.

A War Department conference with the black press, slated for December 8, 1941, was held as scheduled in part to publicize this system. A "gravely solemn" General George Marshall opened the event by announcing that the nation's primary concern was now a successful mobilization. While he was not satisfied with the progress the department had made in handling the race problem, he praised both General Davis and Judge Hastie for their work in attempting to solve it.[8] A colonel from the adjutant general's office then took the floor to explain that his office handled "all problems, complaints and such," and suggested that the journalists check reports of unequal treatment with the services before publishing them. General Davis spoke about the Army Morale Division, including the inspector general's office to which he was attached, which inspected personnel, buildings and grounds, housing, food and property. During a recent tour, "every camp showed a proper place for complaints and are carefully heard." Davis promised that the inspector general's office would judge all facts fairly in investigations and administer justice to all parties concerned.[9]

Around this time, three proposals on the future utilization of black soldiers circulated in the War Department, prompted by the Selective

Washington, D.C., USGPO, 1954; Smith, *The Army and Economic Mobilization*, pp. 112–15.

8. Wynn, *The Afro-American and the Second World War*, p. 23; Lee, *The Employment of Negro Troops*, pp. 142–3; "Plans for Negro Division at Fort Huachuca Revealed," Atlanta *Daily World*, December 10, 1941.

9. "Plans for Negro Division at Fort Huachuca Revealed," Atlanta *Daily World*, December 10, 1941; Washburn, *A Question of Sedition*, pp. 57–8.

Service Act of 1942, which required the armed forces to absorb blacks
in proportion to their population in the country. This effort proceeded
very slowly. Delayed construction of segregated facilities, a shortage of
training cadres, illiteracy and poor physical health all disqualified or
slowed the induction of blacks.[10] The proposals included placing small
numbers of the least intelligent among larger numbers of average and
above-average soldiers, regardless of race; the rejection of up to 50
percent of all black draftees; and the assignment of blacks to service
work in the armed forces. None of these policies was fully satisfactory.
Since the Army was segregated, low-scoring black soldiers could not be
scattered among the larger collection of higher-scoring white soldiers.[11]
By midwar, while the armed forces had absorbed nearly one-third of the
white males liable for service, the comparable rate for blacks was
roughly one-fifth.[12]

Three months before Pearl Harbor, Hastie surveyed black troop conditions and morale and found widespread discontent. Not only were
three-quarters of black soldiers stationed in the South, but fully half of
these troops were located in the Deep South's Fourth Corps Area.[13]
Many Army officials, Hastie found, were convinced that the southern
white better "understood" the black psyche and therefore deliberately
selected southern junior reserve officers to command black soldiers.
Blacks were three times more likely than whites to be assigned to Overhead installations, performing unskilled and menial tasks. Most areas
surrounding posts lacked recreational facilities, and poorly trained military policemen freely struck and harassed black servicemen.[14] When

10. Southern whites resented the rates at which blacks were left behind, and the region's
    congressional delegation called for the construction of additional camps and hospitals
    for black inductees. Clarence S. Johnson, *To Stem This Tide: A Survey of Racial
    Tension in the Unites States*, Boston, The Pilgrim Press, 1943, p. 83; memorandum,
    Jonathan Daniels to FDR, June 26, 1943, OF 4245, OPM, Committee on Fair Em-
    ployment Practice, Philadelphia, FDRL.
11. Paula S. Fass, *Outside In: Minorities and the Transformation of American Education*,
    New York, Oxford University Press, 1989, p. 141.
12. Letter, Lewis B. Hershey to Jonathan Daniels, June 25, 1943, OF 4245, Selective
    Service, FDRL.
13. This was not a new pattern for federal camps; throughout the thirties, Dixie's congres-
    sional contingent secured a disproportionate number of youth training facilities for the
    southern states. By 1942, for example, The Civilian Conservation Corps had spread
    sixteen camps throughout eleven northeast states; Georgia alone had received thirty-
    one. *Congressional Record*, 77:2:5604, June 26, 1942.
14. One recruit assigned to MP duty in early 1942 recalled that "the training they gave us
    was just like a new sheriff goin' in and gettin' a new bunch of deputies, trial and error.
    It had nothin' to do with police business." Alvin Bridges, quoted in Studs Terkel, *"The*

equitable treatment on a segregated base became inconvenient, commanders almost invariably deprived blacks of facilities and opportunities. The ensuing separation and isolation, Hastie argued, retarded the effectiveness of black soldiers' training. In his view, the policy of minimizing contacts between white and black soldiers – ostensibly intended to prevent clashes – actually deprived soldiers of opportunities to establish normal relationships of respect and understanding.[15]

Hastie proposed transferring isolated black units to stations that would combine them into larger units and moving toward integration in the armed forces through experiments in certain units and locales. The reform of segregation would serve the war, he promised, by deploying manpower more efficiently and by reinvigorating the fighting spirit of a nation that had grown too passive and cynical.[16] Chief of Staff George Marshall categorically rejected the idea. While finding many of Hastie's proposals worthy, Marshall believed that Army attempts to solve the perplexing social problem of race threatened the "efficiency, discipline, and morale" of the armed forces.[17] As a colonel from the adjutant general's office put it a week later, the Army was not a "sociological laboratory."

Good War": *An Oral History of World War Two*, New York, Ballantine Books, 1984, p. 387.

15. This insight would be confirmed by the findings of *The American Soldier*: Additional interracial contact fostered favorable attitudes toward racial integration. "Survey and Recommendations Concerning the Integration of the Negro Soldier into the Army," submitted to the Secretary of War by the Civilian Aide, September 22, 1941, reprinted in full in MacGregor and Nalty, eds., vol. V, pp. 80–100. S. A. Stouffer et al., *The American Soldier*, vols. I & II, Princeton, Princeton University Press, 1949. For a discussion of his February 1941 report and the Army's reaction to it, see Phillip McGuire, *He, Too, Spoke for Democracy: Judge Hastie, World War II, and the Black Soldier*, New York, Greenwood Press, 1988, pp. 25–7; Gilbert Ware, *William Hastie: Grace Under Pressure*, New York, Oxford University Press, 1984.

16. "Survey and Recommendations," Hastie to Stimson, September 22, 1941, MacGregor and Nalty, eds., vol. V, pp. 100–1; Lee, *The Employment of Negro Troops*, pp. 136–8.

17. "Efficiency" was not automatically or simply a proxy for segregation. The fact that officer candidate schools were not segregated – the first modern experiment in racial integration in the armed forces – resulted from the belief that creating separate schools for a relatively small number of students would be highly inefficient. Memorandum, George C. Marshall, Chief of Staff, to the Secretary of War, December 1, 1941, in MacGregor and Nalty, eds., vol. V, p. 114; Morris J. MacGregor, *Integration of the Armed Forces, 1940–1965*, Washington, D.C., Center for Military History, 1985, p. 51; on inefficiency, duplication, and administrative waste, see Sheron and Schlossman, *Foxholes and Color Lines*, pp. 70–5.

Experiments, to meet the wishes and demands of the champions of every
race and creed for the solution of their problems are a danger to efficiency,
discipline, and morale and would result in ultimate defeat.[18]

Although Marshall rejected Hastie's more ambitious proposals, he requested a survey of the allocation of black units in hopes of placing a
"proper proportion" of black servicemen at stations adjacent to black
communities. The decision was prompted by clashes at Camp Bowie and
Camp Brownwood in Texas, where three black regiments were stationed
in a nearly all-white county.[19] Eventually, the War Department realized
that the movement of black units merely transferred intolerance and
resistance from one locale to another; instead, opposition would simply
be dealt with when and where it arose.[20] In response to the survey, few
post commanders indicated that their military facilities and civilian communities could accommodate additional assignments of black troops. In
addition, commanders of southern camps overwhelmingly preferred
southern to northern blacks. The January 1942 report that grew from
the Marshall survey recommended that northern black inductees be stationed in their home region. While this provision proved unworkable, a
second finding – that the size of the local black population be a "determining factor in selecting stations" for black outfits – became a fundamental principle in the search for suitable locations for training camps.
This finding strengthened the already strong tendency to train these
troop in the South, and by midwar, every major replacement training
center and a majority of camps were located in Dixie. Of the forty-four
installations identified by the Office of the Chief of Military History as
housing significant numbers of black troops, twenty-five were located in
nine southern states, while only five were located in the industrial states
of the northeast.[21]

While difficulties in assignments caused a chain of inefficiencies and
attendant problems, racial violence was perhaps the most important
product of this spatial concentration of black units. Army regulations
generally did not consider community attitudes toward black soldiers in
considerations of discipline. Yet the difficulty with which blacks pur-

---

18. Hastie believed the Army routinely and authoritatively experimented with social
    forces. As quoted in Lee, *The Employment of Negro Troops*, p. 142; Ware, *William
    Hastie*, p. 99.
19. Memorandum, W. B. Smith, Colonel, General Staff, War Department, to Army Chief
    of Staff, November 25, 1941, in MacGregor and Nalty, eds., vol. V, p. 143.
20. Lee, *The Employment of Negro Troops*, p. 366.
21. Ibid., pp. 102–6; McGuire, *He, Too, Spoke for Democracy*, p. 68; for another over-
    view, see Map 1.1.

chased accommodations, tickets, and meals in segregated towns and stations, for example, contributed to curfew violations, scheduling snafus, and arguments in bus and train stations. Violence often stemmed from interracial contact on commuter buses and trains, which were governed by widely varying but typically strict local laws and customs. Soldiers arriving at their destinations found themselves in towns and cities that might be openly hostile to their presence, depending on the size of the local community's black population, and the attitude of local white merchants, police, and townsfolk.

Thus, most black troops were stationed where strict customs and repressive laws governed the races. Over the course of the war, disturbances followed the regional deployment at rates that were roughly proportional to their spatial concentration. Southern states accounted for a steady two-thirds of the disruptions (see Table 5.1).[22] Despite the pull of nearby towns, few of them offered sufficient recreational activities for nonwhites.

In the spring and summer of 1941, violent incidents took place at Fort Jackson, South Carolina; Alexandria, Louisiana; and Fayetteville, North Carolina. In June in Murfreesboro, Tennessee, and in August in Gurdon, Arkansas, black soldiers on maneuvers met with armed resistance from white civilians and state policemen. Other incidents occurred at Camp Livingston and Camp Claiborne, Louisiana, and at Camp Davis, North Carolina, where soldiers brawled with military police. "Through all of

---

22. Data for this analysis, unless otherwise noted, resulted from an analysis of 209 wartime incidents involving black soldiers. The data on these military racial confrontations was gathered from official archives, relevant secondary works, and the press, particularly newspapers published by and for blacks found in the Tuskegee Institute News Clipping File (see Appendix 5.1). Incidents were considered military racial confrontations if they included: (1) the participation of a black soldier or a group of black soldiers and (2) a claim on authorities, resistance to authorities, or repressive racial action. Confrontations that stemmed from criminal activity unrelated to segregation were excluded. For the full codebook of this data set, see Appendix 5.2. This methodology differs from Charles Tilly's and Sidney Tarrow's, in that it gathers cases of the repression and resistance of individuals as well as of groups. Research into social movement activity that discards encounters between individuals and authorities – capturing only collective acts – narrows our view of how individuals learn to reduce risks and amass power by joining groups. Group data produced, for example, by Tilly's research into "contentious gatherings" of at least ten people may give the impression that social movements spring fully grown to oppose their targets, rather than develop slowly as a byproduct of many routine repressive acts. Sidney Tarrow, "Cycles of Collective Action: Between Moments of Madness and the Repertoire of Contention," *Social Science History*, vol. 17, no. 2, Summer, 1993; Charles Tilly, *Popular Contention in Great Britain, 1758–1834*, Cambridge, Harvard University Press, 1995.

Table 5.1. *Percent of Racial Confrontations Involving Black Soldiers and Military and Civilian Authorities, 1942–45, by Region.*

Region	1942 $n = 59$	1943 $n = 68$	1944 $n = 62$	1945 $n = 20$
Deep South	28.8%	41.2%	38.7%	30.0%
Other South	39.0	26.5	29.0	25.0
TOTAL SOUTH	67.8	67.7	67.7	55.0
Northeast	13.6	5.9	1.6	10.0
North Central	3.4	1.5	8.1	10.0
West	8.5	8.8	9.7	10.0
Abroad	6.8	16.2	12.9	15.0
TOTAL	100.0%	100.0%	100.0%	100.0%

Source: Analysis of data by author ($n = 209$).

these ran the common thread of friction between Negro soldiers and both city and military policemen."[23] During the first years of the mobilization, incidents generally took two forms: police officers arresting, beating, or shooting individual blacks – often to be challenged in turn by other black soldiers and civilians – and second, brawls between soldiers from racially segregated units.

General Davis's work for the inspector general's office took him to installations in Louisiana, Missouri, Texas, and Oklahoma in early 1942.[24] A new series of disturbances, sometimes including crowds of defiant or aggressive black soldiers, began about the same time in Alexandria, Louisiana; Tuskegee, Alabama; and Fort Dix, New Jersey. The southern incidents stemmed from resistance to the arrest of a black soldier, while the latter, a gunfight over the use of a telephone, cost the lives of a white MP and two black soldiers.[25] In March 1942, a crowd

23. Lee, *The Employment of Negro Troops*, pp. 349–55; Stanley Sandler, "Homefront Battlefront: Racial Violence in the Zone of the Interior, 1941–1945," np; Wynn, pp. 27–38.
24. Black soldiers reacted to Davis in various ways. When he visited MacDill Field in Tampa, roughly one-third of the eighteen hundred black soldiers stationed there lined up to offer him their complaints. At Fort Dix, New Jersey, a month later, the soldiers were uncooperative. Marvin E. Fletcher, *America's First Black General: Benjamin O. Davis, Sr., 1880–1970*, Lawrence, University Press of Kansas, 1989, pp. 96–7.
25. Alexandria, flooded by servicemen from four nearby Army camps and three airfields, was a troubled town for the duration. Memorandum, Cornelius L. Golightly to John

gathered in Little Rock when a civilian policeman assisting MPs clubbed a black soldier, bloodying his head. When a black sergeant in the crowd reprimanded the MPs, he was arrested after a scuffle. The crowd, growing larger, began to close around the police, but the MPs held them at bay. A civilian policeman tried to pull the captive soldier to a car, but they fell to the ground. While one MP beat the GI, the policeman regained his feet and shot the prone soldier four times, killing him. The crowd, it was reported, then moved back.[26] This and other incidents prompted the adjutant general to instruct the commanding general of the Eighth Corps Area to take steps to ensure that black soldiers were not subject to abuse.[27]

As with such instructions, often issued at the urging of Judge Hastie, innovation at this stage mainly involved the professionalization of policing. The establishment of the Corps of Military Police under the Provost Marshal General in September 1941 aimed to improve the policing system through more careful training, indoctrination, and supervision.[28] Likewise, in 1942 the Intelligence Division recommended that post commanders attend to the selection, training, and supervision of military police, and encouraged the use of black military policemen in camps with significant black troop strength. The latter proposal was particularly controversial, coming at a time when many civil rights organizations were calling for the deployment of black civilian police in black neighborhoods.[29] The Intelligence Division also hoped to "reduce and control the publication of inflammatory and vituperative articles in the colored press." Many post commanders tightly controlled black servicemen's access to ammunition. Ameliorative programs were, however, slower to materialize. Judge Hastie recommended that the adjutant general organize informal interracial discussion groups on tense posts. The Special Service branch suggested that black officers be stationed at camps to facilitate discussions between troops, the press, and civilian groups, while the branch itself planned to provide the press with more

A. Davis, February 10, 1945, "Major Riots in the United States, 1906–1945," Documents File, SDR-COFEP.

26. Maj. Bell I. Wiley, "The Training of Negro Troops," Army Ground Forces Study No. 36, 1946, MacGregor and Nalty, eds., vol. VII, p. 276.

27. Memorandum, The Adjutant General to Commanding General, Eighth Corps Area, February 10, 1942, MacGregor and Nalty, eds., vol. V, pp. 149–50.

28. Lee, *The Employment of Negro Troops*, p. 357.

29. The late thirties produced demands for the integration of southern police forces as "a means, not only of reducing crime, but likewise of preventing racial friction." Recall that the twenty-seven southern cities employing separate units of black civilian policemen in 1941 included none from the Deep South. "Walter Cheevers Says: Atlanta Needs Negro Police," Atlanta *Daily World*, September 21, 1941.

positive news stories. Neither of these modest programs would be implemented for another year.[30]

The Reorientation of Race Manpower Policy

In August 1942, the Army recast its race policy-making apparatus. As in employment matters, white advisors in effect replaced black ones. As a result of wide variation in the enforcement of segregation and training policies on different posts, and as a by-product of Hastie's difficult relationship with the secretary's office, the War Department formed a new review board, the Advisory Committee on Negro Troop Policies, chaired by John J. McCloy, the Assistant Secretary of War.[31] Stimson brought McCloy, a Wendell Willkie supporter, into the administration, because he admired his expertise in investigating and prosecuting foreign subversion.[32] While General Davis was made a founding member, Hastie was neither included in the committee nor informed of its appointment.[33] The members of this committee, like most white participants in the fair employment initiative, set about trying to "defuse the attacks from the black community," as General Davis's biographer put it.[34]

At its second meeting in October, the committee considered a proposal to abolish segregation in Army movie theaters, endorsed by Hastie and the Special Service Division. Although the proposal included a procedure for allowing enforceable exceptions to the rule, and was approved by Undersecretary of War Patterson, McCloy vetoed the proposal. The committee agreed to research the subject and to avoid issuing a public policy on the topic; "it would deal with each situation as it arose." General Davis echoed Hastie in suggesting that the committee recommend dismantling "Jim Crow practices" in the War Department and in Army posts; issue a directive on interracial cooperation and amity; and organize an educational program on the historic contributions of blacks

30. Lee, *The Employment of Negro Troops*, pp. 356–62.
31. Two months before the committee appointment, McCloy notified Hastie that he did not share his belief that waging war against undemocratic practices abroad required questioning such practices at home. Lee, *The Employment of Negro Troops*, pp. 158–60.
32. McCloy worked part-time throughout the 1930s investigating the German sabotage effort that resulted in the massive explosion at the "Black Tom" loading facility in Jersey City harbor in 1916. By 1940, he was widely viewed as the leading expert on foreign states' subversive activities. Kai Bird, *The Chairman: John J. McCloy, the Making of the American Establishment*, New York, Simon & Schuster, 1992, pp. 77–95, 113.
33. Wynn, *The Afro-American and the Second World War*, p. 27.
34. Fletcher, *America's First Black General*, p. 100.

to the evolution and defense of the country. But the committee's work attended more often to symbols than to substance. In addition to increasing assignments of blacks to high-visibility units such as harbor defense and ambulance corps – with concurrent reductions in anti-aircraft and medical sanitary assignments – the McCloy Committee recommended the creation of a black parachute battalion to improve black citizens' morale. Likewise, it supported the assignment of blacks to combat engineer units in order to defeat "what may prove to be a perfectly justifiable charge" of racial discrimination through the assignment of black troops to general service engineer regiments. Excluded from these deliberations, Hastie warned in December that the mounting violence might at any time lead to rioting.[35]

But Hastie's advisement was no longer seriously considered. McCloy thought that resistance to discrimination had become such a dominant theme in the black press that "one demand granted leads only to another." Concessions, he worried, failed to "bury any issue permanently."[36] In late 1942, Stimson wrote that he found Hastie's attitude unrealistic: "I am afraid his usefulness is limited."[37] When Hastie resigned in January 1943, following an extended struggle with the department over the question of separate training facilities for blacks, W. E. B. DuBois, among others, noted the gravity of the loss.[38] Hastie's African American assistant, Truman K. Gibson, Jr., became acting civilian aide on February 5, 1943, and pursued a course much closer to that of the McCloy Committee.[39] He analyzed policy questions in the comprehensive and strategic manner of a statesman concerned with national security, and dealt with complaints "singly," as individual rather than as systemic problems, and in "terms of their probable effect upon the Army, the public (white and Negro), and the developing military situation," as Lee put it.[40] Although he was never a formal member of the group, Gibson began to attend committee meetings in March 1943. Two

35. Lee, *The Employment of Negro Troops*, pp. 158–61; Ware, *William Hastie*, p. 116.
36. Instead of suppressing the press, a route preferred by many officials at the FBI and Post Office, McCloy called for "vigorous counter-propaganda." Quoted in Washburn, *A Question of Sedition*, p. 113.
37. Phillip McGuire, "Judge Hastie, World War II, and Army Racism," *Journal of Negro History*, October, 1977, p. 357.
38. W. E. B. DuBois, "As the Crow Flies," undated, as quoted in Ware, *William Hastie*, p. 131.
39. Using familiar language to describe this work in late 1944, Gibson called it serving "as a 'middle-man,' absorbing gripes and complaints in person by mail and telephone all day and most of the night." Memorandum, Truman K. Gibson, Jr. to John McCloy, September 5, 1944, MacGregor and Nalty, eds., vol. VII, pp. 8–9.
40. Lee, *The Employment of Negro Troops*, pp. 175–6.

months before the executive order transforming the FEPC, Hastie's departure and Gibson's ascendency had shifted the aide's work "from confrontation to accommodation" just as the FEPC was being recast in a broadly similar way.[41]

The Peak of the Unrest, Summer 1943

One ironic result of the early reforms was a new form of intraracial violence pitting black soldiers against black MPs, including a fight on Thanksgiving Day, 1942, in Phoenix, Arizona.[42] The unit at the center of this incident – the 364th Infantry Regiment – was transferred to Camp Van Dorn, Mississippi, where in May 1943 it proclaimed that it would take over the nearby city of Centerville before moving on the state of Mississippi. On the 29th, a large group of soldiers marched through the town in a provocative formation. Police and deputized civilians arrested seventy-five of them and placed them in the custody of military police. The next day, an MP stopped a black private for being improperly dressed, and when the soldier attacked the MP and then threatened a county sheriff who intervened, the sheriff shot him dead. Black troops, enraged, armed themselves and gathered near a station PX where they were fired upon by an MP riot squad. Somehow the regimental commander managed to quiet the crowd and direct them to their hutments. While confined to quarters for several days, the unit assaulted white soldiers passing through their area.[43]

While closer collaboration between Gibson and the advisory committee led to a growing routinization of black troop policy review, disaffection among black soldiers peaked in mid-1943, as Lee has noted (see Figure 5.2). In early summer, blacks and whites fought in Camp Stewart, Georgia; March Field, California; Fort Bliss, Texas; and Camp Breckinridge, Kentucky. The disorders of 1943 seemed to follow a new pattern: As in the Camp Stewart case, they were more likely to occur inside a camp (see Table 5.2), often between identifiable military units, and were as likely to be caused by blacks as by whites. Increasingly, what had

---

41. Mershon and Schlossman, *Foxholes and Color Lines*, p. 101.
42. The fact that these black military police units often were unarmed and worked in smaller units than normal contributed to their inability to control crowds and arrest and transport resisters. In this episode, an initial fight between black MPs and soldiers intensified after other black GIs broke into weapons stores and rushed into the city. A white officer, a white policeman, and a black civilian were shot and killed. Lee, *The Employment of Negro Troops*, pp. 276, 356–62.
43. Ibid., pp. 276–7.

Table 5.2. *Percent of Racial Confrontations Involving Black Soldiers and Military and Civilian Authorities, 1942–45, by site.*

Location	1942	1943	1944	1945
On facility	10.2%	32.4%	43.5%	60.0%
Off facility	89.8	67.6	56.5	40.0
TOTAL	100.0%	100.0%	100.0%	100.0%

Source: Analysis of data by author (*n* = 209).

been routine disciplinary cases became racial incidents, often for vague reasons.[44] The friction, manifest in both large and small incidents, was still concentrated in the South. Of twenty major military racial disturbances during the war, eleven were southern, while only two occurred in the industrial northeast.[45]

Generally, the Army's instructions to commanding officers called for perfecting policing and punishment. Chief of Staff Marshall called the widespread racial disturbances "an immediately serious problem" in a July 1943 memo to the Commanding Generals of the Army Air, Ground, and Service Forces. Noting that each of six recent incidents followed a similar pattern involving the failure of commanders to appreciate and correct dissatisfaction and unrest, Marshall called for close unit supervision and strict handling of disciplinary matters.

> Mutinous conduct will be dealt with as such and violations of the principles of military discipline will not be countenanced in any element of the Army. Prompt and effective disciplinary measures must be taken to punish those guilty of such derelictions. Failure on the part of any commander to concern himself personally and vigorously with this problem will be considered as evidence of lack of capacity and cause for reclassification and removal from assignment.[46]

44. This was another finding of the Stouffer study: "Many complaints common to soldiers of both races acquired a special significance among Negro soldiers by being invested with the quality of racial discrimination." Stouffer, *The American Soldier*, vol. I, p. 502.
45. Stanley Sandler, "Homefront Battlefront: Military Racial Disturbances, Zone of the Interior, 1941–1945," paper presented to the 1991 American Historical Association Conference, Chicago, Illinois, December 27–30, 1991; for a survey of incidents abroad, see Mershon and Schlossman, *Foxholes and Color Lines*, pp. 84–8.
46. Memorandum, Chief of Staff G. C. Marshall to the Commanding Generals, Army Air,

Resistance within the units, however, was not evenly distributed. Surveys conducted by the Special Service Division revealed that southern black recruits with little education were the least likely to question segregation. Such findings reinforced Army officials' impression – and reinforced conventional wisdom in the South – that educated northerners would fail to adjust to military life and would incite racial disturbances.[47] The governor of Arkansas, resigned to the arrival of black troops at Camp Robinson, asked officials to "please send southern negroes and not the northern negroes." These men, he believed, should be directed by white southern officers.[48] Unfortunately, from the point of view of segregationists both inside and outside the War Department, socioeconomic conditions in the region combined with minimum health and education requirements to reduce the rate at which southern blacks qualified for induction.[49] Despite a roughly equivalent number of black civilians liable for service in the military, at midwar the number of black inductees from New York State exceeded the number from South Carolina by more than 50 percent (see Appendix 5.3).[50] Not only were these northern men generally better educated, but the process of forming regiments out of a geographic area's recruits in effect took an already cohesive group, made it more so through shared duress, and moved it en masse to a racially charged setting that devalued the racial dimension of the unit's shared identity. Analysts agreed that the June 1943 Camp Stewart, Georgia, incident, for example – where black soldiers ambushed white MPs, killing one and wounding four – was fueled by the arrival from a northern station of the 100th Coast Artillery Regiment, composed largely of northern blacks who resented their transfer to Georgia. These soldiers and the 369th Regiment of New York, which arrived shortly afterward,

Ground, and Service Forces, July 3, 1943, MacGregor and Nalty, eds., vol. V, pp. 270–1.

47. Lee, *The Employment of Negro Troops*, pp. 303–4.
48. Letter, Homer Adkins to Robert P. Patterson, Under Secretary of War, April 23, 1942, OF 93, Colored Matters, FDRL.
49. More than 75 percent of black inductees who failed the Army General Classification Test came from southern and border states. McGuire, *He, Too, Spoke for Democracy*, p. 7.
50. Roughly forty-two thousand New York State blacks served in the armed forces on June 1, 1943; the comparable number for South Carolina was about twenty-six thousand, despite the fact that the latter state had more black persons liable for service. This pairs one of the highest rates found in the northern states with the lowest rate found in the South. "Distribution of Black Persons Liable for Military Service and Percent of Such Persons in Armed Forces on June 1, 1943." Memorandum, Lewis B. Hershey to Jonathan Daniels, June 25, 1943, OF 4245, Selective Service, FDRL.

"aroused latent resentment" in the minds of the soldiers already at the camp.[51] Such mistreatment affected civilian race relations as well. Following the deadly Harlem disturbance of August 1943, Robert Weaver blamed not only the social ills plaguing the residents there, but other "fundamental causes" of militant black attitudes nationwide. "The primary, fundamental cause," he reported, was resentment toward discrimination in the armed services.[52]

Exacerbating the violent potential of regional patterns of troop placement were the mobilization's distinct effects on the police presence in northern and southern cities and towns. As J. Edgar Hoover repeatedly reminded the attorney general and the head of the Selective Service system, the Army drained personnel from northern industrial areas' civilian police forces at the same time that the expanding war economy drew thousands of white and black migrants into the same areas to struggle with longtime residents in overtaxed transportation networks and over housing and employment. Hoover viewed the Detroit tumult of late June 1943 in particular as growing out of the combined effects of the in-migration of nearly half a million people and a concurrent decrease in police personnel, and he feared that the continued loss of officers to the Army would result in the "breakdown of local agencies." Taken together, the forces of ninety cities polled in 1943 were 11.4 percent below their minimum personnel requirements; only three of the police forces were larger than minimally necessary.[53]

Communities near Army camps, however, provided a sharply different set of opportunities and disincentives for agitators and challengers.[54] Small-to-medium sized southern towns lacking large factories not only failed to attract very large numbers of migrants, and often lost residents due to out-migration. By mid-1943, of all the southern states, only

---

51. This insurrection is analyzed in detail in Chapter 6. Memorandum, Ground Adjutant General for Chief of Staff, U.S. Army, November 28, 1945, "Subject: Participation of Negro Troops in the Postwar Military Establishment," in MacGregor and Nalty, eds., vol. VII, pp. 110–23.

52. Memorandum, Robert C. Weaver to Jonathan Daniels, September 4, 1943, OF 4245, WMC, FDRL, p. 1.

53. Memorandum, John Edgar Hoover to the Attorney General, July 8, 1943, OF 93, FDRL; memorandum, Jonathan Daniels to the President, July 29, 1943, papers of Jonathan Daniels, SHC-UNC.

54. San Diego's police force was 8.9 percent below its minimum personnel requirement, but "the prominent role played by the United States Navy in the municipal affairs of San Diego also contributed to the maintenance of order, particularly of the transient population of servicemen and women." Gerald D. Nash, *The American West Trans-*

Virginia and Florida had experienced a net increase in civilian population.[55] Most important, cities and towns adjacent to southern military installations gained detachments of military police and materiel that supplemented the civilian force on weekends and during furlough periods. An Army tank with a searchlight, for example, patrolled the streets and helped to disperse a crowd following a rather minor racial disturbance in Tampa, Florida, in February 1944. The incident began with the arrest of a black soldier by a white MP and the arrest of a black civilian by a city policeman. Approximately twenty-five hundred blacks gathered until they were faced down by reenforcements from the Tampa Police Department, the county sheriff's office, and thirty-seven military policemen. No one was injured as the MPs fired a few shots into the air and the city police arrested twenty-four blacks. In a similar incident three months later in Augusta, Georgia, an angry crowd refused to disperse until city police, aided by military police, fired tear gas. Although the military police force had agreed to accompany local policemen on patrol, at the time of this disturbance almost all of the MPs were off duty, eating dinner. The resistance was caused by the resentment the black soldiers felt at being confronted by civilian police in the absence of MPs.[56] Whereas early in the war the presence of military and civilian police forces in towns near military facilities often contributed to racial conflict, later in the war better-trained MP detachments, regular collaboration between civilian and military police forces, and a more fully developed intelligence apparatus combined to prevent and deter such unrest.

As we might expect from the data on the shift from off- to on-post unrest, the share of confrontations that occurred during military training also rose, from 5.1 percent in 1942 to 21.0 percent in 1944 (see Table 5.3). After the wave of violence in the summer of 1943, ranging from the grave shoot-out at Camp Stewart to a series of minor clashes at Camp Tyson, Tennessee, there was again a period of relative calm until the following summer. Cooler weather, punishment, ameliorative reforms, and the transfer of units worked to suppress resistance for a time, but it reappeared in other forms within other units.[57] The summer months of June

formed: *The Impact of the Second World War*, Bloomington, Indiana University Press, 1985, p. 62.

55. "Notes on the Effects of the War on the South," undated manuscript, papers of Jonathan Daniels, SHC-UNC, p. 4.

56. Letter, J. Edgar Hoover to Jonathan Daniels, March 16, 1944; letter, J. Edgar Hoover to Jonathan Daniels, May 17, 1944, OF 4245, FBI Materials Concerning Minorities, FDRL.

57. The disturbances seemed to occur in clusters – during the fall of 1941, the early

Table 5.3. *Percent of Racial Confrontations Involving Black Soldiers and Military and Civilian Authorities, 1942–45, by sphere of activity.*

Sphere	1942	1943	1944	1945
Jailing/policing	32.2%	16.2%	19.4%	10.0%
Military training	5.1	13.2	21.0	25.0
Recreation	39.0	44.1	30.6	30.0
Transportation	16.9	13.2	19.4	20.0
Commerce	1.7	2.9	3.2	5.0
Unknown	5.1	8.8	3.2	10.0
Other	0.0	1.5	3.2	0.0
TOTAL	100.0%	100.0%	100.0%	100.0%

Source: Analysis of data by author ($n = 209$).

through September, with recreational and other activities moving outdoors, produced more interracial contact as well as the majority of confrontations (see Figure 5.1).

The War Department continued to investigate conditions inside the camps. In July, General Davis and Truman Gibson visited Forts Huachuca, Arizona; Bliss, Texas; and Clark, Texas, all sources of recent complaints and incidents.[58] At each station, the visitors interviewed as many enlisted men as they could. Gibson reported that they never "mollycoddled" the men; Davis, in fact, repeatedly lectured the men on their responsibilities and reminded them of the proper institutional channels for complaints. After sampling the attitudes of the men, Davis and Gibson met with camp officers to discuss the soldiers' discontent. The litany of complaints at Fort Huachuca was long and familiar: the segregation of black officers at mess, the beating of soldiers, and officer promotion practices that violated Army policy. The investigators showed little concern for conditions at Fort Bliss, since the commanding officers there had not only adjusted the racial situation with sensitivity after a disturbance in El Paso the previous month but also had sponsored the creation of an interracial committee there that had begun to address the difficult

months of 1942, Thanksgiving 1942, and the spring and summer of 1943 – suggesting that knowledge of other incidents contributed to militancy inside the camps.

58. Memorandum, Truman K. Gibson, Jr., Acting Civilian Aide to the Secretary of War, to the Assistant Secretary of War, August 23, 1943, MacGregor and Nalty, eds., vol. V, p. 273.

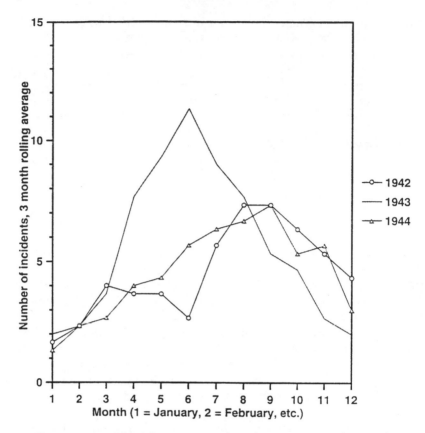

Figure 5.1. Racial confrontations in the military, 1942–44, by month.
Source: Analysis of racial confrontation data by author.

problem of community-camp relations. But the "very humiliating and distasteful" racial system at Fort Clark resembled Huachuca's. The division commander seemed disinclined to take seriously the complaints collected by Davis and Gibson, since the smart and precise execution of orders and movements suggested to him that the unit was in proper condition.[59] In response to the investigators' criticism that black chaplains had not been helpful to unit commanders in "matters of racial

59. Gibson explained in his report that, while the black soldier carried deep resentment, "due to long-suffering and working under conditions highly distasteful to him, he had developed, as a defense mechanism, the ability to present a calm outward appearance." Ibid., p. 277.

adjustment," the preachers claimed that attempts to communicate complaints would lead to their transfer. After this matter was discussed with the commanding general, the division commander called a meeting of the chaplains to discuss their utilization.[60]

Neither Gibson nor Davis was merely an adjuster of complaints. The former's recommendations included the removal of particularly offensive white officers and the desegregation of post messes and theaters for black officers. He also believed that all commanders granting furloughs and passes should withhold them from those GIs who would not conform to local laws and expectations.[61] Davis reported that visits to northern camps in 1943 impressed him with the positive morale of black officers and soldiers stationed in New York, New Jersey, and Michigan. Still, the general found that the War Department had introduced Jim Crow policies, at home and abroad, into areas that had never practiced them. The general proposed a biracial General Staff bureau to plan reforms, as it was "utterly impossible for any white man to appreciate" the difficulties black officers and soldiers faced in maintaining high morale under the circumstances.[62] In the early years of the war, then, Army policy had concentrated black soldiers in the southern states and had fashioned a fairly crude, coercion-intensive system to respond to the racial disturbances that followed from these choices. Over time, however, Army authorities adjusted segregation policies in significant ways.

New Techniques of Race Management

In the spring of 1943, the adjutant general directed all camp authorities to enforce a policy of equal access to recreational facilities, and commanders were instructed to remove signs that restricted use to either race alone, though the policy of requiring the separate use of these facilities remained unchanged.[63] This significant if incremental relaxation of segregation was implemented just as the violence began to peak (see Figure 5.2) Like most black troop policies, the directive was

60. Ibid., p. 276, 277. Part of the problem was that "few, if any, white men can successfully secure considerable amounts of information from Negroes, particularly those from the south." Ibid., p. 278.
61. Ibid., p. 278.
62. Memorandum, Brig. Gen. B. O. Davis to John J. McCloy, Assistant Secretary of War, November 10, 1943, MacGregor and Nalty, eds., vol. V, pp. 291–3.
63. The directive allowed commanders to exercise considerable discretion in enforcing the policy. In many places, it was simply ignored. Lee, *The Employment of Negro Troops*, p. 308.

unevenly enforced.[64] In June, Gibson requested that the War Department insist on equal accommodations for the two races on buses in the South.[65] The McCloy Committee and the adjutant general issued a second directive the following summer, again as violence neared its peak, which broadened and tightened the facilities policy substantially.[66] According to these regulations, post exchanges, motion picture theaters, and buses could not be reserved for the exclusive use of either race. The instructions prohibited restricting personnel to certain sections of transport vehicles, "either on or off a post, camp, or station, regardless of local civilian custom." The regulations also codified the review process – somewhat akin to FEPC procedures – by which inspectors general informed camp commanders that such discrimination was contrary to War Department policy. If a subsequent inspection indicated that remedial measures had not been taken, the commanding general of the service command would take action to ensure compliance.[67] Although these measures were applied unevenly, no serious racial incident occurred on buses serving camps that followed this policy.[68]

64. Memorandum, Truman K. Gibson to the Assistant Secretary of War, June 2, 1943, OF 4245, War Department, 1943, FDRL.
65. The 1940 *Mitchell* case clearly allotted the Interstate Commerce Commission (ICC) responsibility for guaranteeing equal treatment on common carriers, but the War Department still received the bulk of such complaints. Gibson recommended that complaints be directed to the Office of Informal Cases at the Interstate Commerce Commission. The executive secretary of the FEPC recommended that such complaints be routed quietly to the ICC so that it could investigate the problem without stimulating additional complaint submissions. Memorandum, Truman K. Gibson to the Assistant Secretary of War, June 2, 1943, OF 4245, War Department, 1943, FDRL; memorandum, Lawrence W. Cramer, to Marvin W. McIntyre, February 9, 1943, OF 4245, FDRL.
66. The McCloy Committee responded to the unrest of the summer of 1943 by recommending the quick dispatch of black troops to overseas theaters "as the most effective means of reducing tensions among Negro troops." Eleanor Roosevelt, on the other hand, suggested the creation of a "Fair Practice Committee" within the War and Navy Departments at a meeting of race relations advisors in December 1943. Dalfiume, *Desegregation*, p. 93; memorandum, Philleo Nash to Jonathan Daniels, December 18, 1943, OWI Files No. 1, box 29, papers of Philleo Nash, HSTL.
67. Stimson later recalled that his "mistrust of the use of the Army as an agency of social reform dissolved under the impact of the manpower shortage . . ." Memorandum, Major General A. J. Ulio, the Adjutant General, to Commanding Generals, All Service Commands, July 8, 1944, MacGregor and Nalty, eds., vol. V, pp. 340–1; Stimson and Bundy, *Active Service*, p. 463.
68. Lee, *The Employment of Negro Troops*, p. 324. On racially mixed infantry companies in the European theater and experimentation with desegregation in the Navy, see Mershon and Schlossman, *Foxholes and Color Lines*, pp. 124–34.

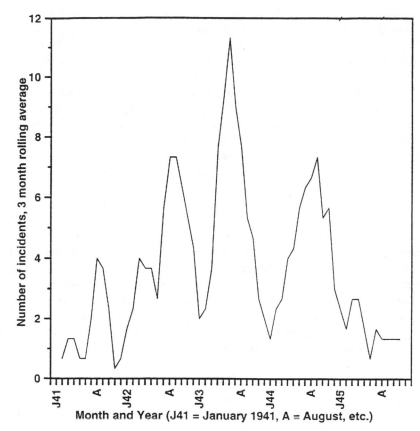

Figure 5.2. Racial confrontations in the military, 1941–45, by month, three
month rolling average.
Source: Analysis of racial confrontation data by author.

In another shift away from inherited manpower policies that was implemented in June 1943, the War Department created a remedial literacy
program for all "salvageable" recruits. Placing half of the twenty-four
training units in the Fourth and Eighth Service Commands, Army planners expected that two-thirds of their clients would be black soldiers,
but they would in fact account for about 45 percent of the 384,000
illiterates schooled. One of the most powerful effects of the program was
to reinforce a new official interpretation of relative measures of black
intelligence. Manpower officials in this program concluded that the
Army General Classification Test, the primary basis for rejection and
assignment on intelligence grounds, was not simply a measure of

"genetic" or "native" intellectual aptitude, but primarily gauged unequal levels of educational opportunity and socioeconomic background.[69] Blacks were thus officially designated teachable and the accomplishments of the students, according to one Army report, helped to refute the theory of "innate Negro inferiority."[70] There were three other, more advanced, Army educational programs that did not favor the black soldier: service schools, which taught skills dictated by unit needs and the Army table of organization; the specialized training program, which trained soldiers in necessary professions such as foreign languages, medicine, and engineering; and the educational branch of the Special Service Division, which helped to arrange for individual off-duty coursework by correspondence or through contract colleges.[71]

The War Department also increased its public relations activities aimed at blacks. In 1942 the Army's Bureau of Public Relations launched a liaison office for black reporters, and by mid-1943 the War Department and the black press had greatly improved their working relationship.[72] This broad morale initiative took several other forms as well: the continued construction of recreational facilities, the production and distribution of two films – *The Negro Soldier* and *Teamwork* – reviewing the critical contributions of black servicemen to America's wars; visits by officials such as General Davis to dedications, graduation exercises, and celebrations; and tours of camps by celebrities such as Joe Louis and Lena Horne.[73] The OWI's 150 prints of "The Negro Soldier" were viewed by approximately 3.1 million Americans during the second half of 1944.[74] The Army's broad reassessment of race also led to the dissemination of a pamphlet, entitled *Command of Negro Troops*, to white

---

69. The largest single remedial literacy unit was located in Georgia's Fort Benning, with 3,809 men. This post was the most frequently cited identifiable home facility in the racial confrontation data set, with eleven incidents between 1942 and 1945. Fass, *Outside In*, pp. 146, 148–51.

70. Army Service Forces Manual, M5, "Leadership and the Negro Soldier," October 1944, U.S. Center of Military History, as quoted in Fass, *Outside In*, p. 151.

71. Memorandum, Philleo Nash to Jonathan Daniels, undated, ca. August 1943, OWI Files No. 1, box 29, papers of Philleo Nash, HSTL.

72. The Office of War Information also created an advisory committee of black reporters in 1943. Mershon and Schlossman, *Foxholes and Color Lines*, pp. 100–1.

73. Philleo Nash of OWI, whose work is reviewed in greater detail in Chapter 7, helped prepare and distribute "The Negro Soldier" and "The Command of Negro Troops." Letter, Philleo Nash to Leo Rosten, July 3, 1944, OWI Correspondence, 1943–44, papers of Philleo Nash, HSTL; Fletcher, *America's First Black General*, pp. 121–49; Lee, *The Employment of Negro Troops*, pp. 330–47.

74. Memorandum, C. R. Reagan to Truman Gibson, Jr., January 4, 1945, OWI Files No. 2, box 29, Papers of Philleo Nash, HSTL.

officers in 1944. The document rejected claims of the inherent intellectual or emotional inferiority of blacks and described those aspects of training and policing most likely to cause racial tensions. It also urged unit leaders to expect impressive performances from all well-trained soldiers. The text took an intermediate position on segregation: it argued that separation was wasteful and inefficient, but defended it as a practical deterrent to "interracial friction."[75]

Despite the reforms, racial disturbances in the Army continued apace, mainly in the South. Of the fourteen "typical incidents" of racial disturbances listed in one study spanning August 1944 and June 1945, twelve occurred in six southern states. Louisiana alone produced four between September 1944 and January 1945. But the quality of the confrontations was changing. Modest policy reforms provided a legal foundation for certain peaceful acts of resistance at the same time that a more efficient repressive apparatus minimized careless overreactions on the part of police and increased the risk of punishment to those considering militant acts of rebellion. Thus, as the professionalization of policing advanced, the share of confrontations caused by jailing or policing declined somewhat (see Table 5.3). Several disturbances began when black soldiers specifically cited the July 8 recreational facilities directive. Three black lieutenants from Camp Gordon Johnston, Florida, for example, referred to the memorandum when they refused to take rear seats on a public bus. At an orientation lecture at an unspecified Army Air Force installation, a black private took from his pocket several copies of the directive and asked a white lieutenant whether the rules were being observed.[76] Nonviolent, organized protest of this sort grew more common over the course of the war. To cite another example, a black company of the 92nd Infantry, stationed at Fort McClellan, Alabama, appointed a committee to meet with the commandant to discuss the reform of camp conditions. Although their initiative was refused, the technique was a familiar one by 1944 and 1945.[77] The share of racial confrontations

75. War Department Pamphlet 20–6, *Command of Negro Troops*, February 29, 1944, in MacGregor and Nalty, eds., vol. V, p. 314. On similar initiatives, see Mershon and Schlossman, *Foxholes and Color Lines*, pp. 114–20.

76. The private, the intelligence report noted, was an active member of the NAACP. "Army Service Forces Study Concerning Participation of Negro Troops in the Postwar Military Establishment," September 19, 1945, MacGregor and Nalty, eds., vol. VII, pp. 41, 45.

77. Camps Patrick Henry and Pickett, VA, and Camp Sutton, NC, as well as the Louisiana camps provided cases of collective protest in the October 7 ASF "Summary." At Henry, black soldiers voiced "extreme race consciousness" at lectures. Johnson, *To Stem This Tide*, pp. 87–8; memorandum for Colonel Roamer, "Subject: Summary of

Table 5.4. *Percent of Racial Confrontations Involving Black Soldiers and Military and Civilian Authorities, 1942–45, by Cause.*

Cause	1942	1943	1944	1945
Fighting	28.8%	20.6%	11.3%	10.0%
Organized protest	3.4	7.4	19.4	20.0
Defying MP orders	11.9	8.8	14.5	5.0
Defying CP orders	15.3	8.8	6.5	15.0
Defy segregation	16.9	14.7	19.4	25.0
Interfere MP/CP	11.9	1.5	9.7	0.0
Crowd action	3.4	14.7	12.9	15.0
Unknown	8.5	13.2	4.8	10.0
Other	0.0	10.3	1.6	0.0
TOTAL	100.0%	100.0%	100.0%	100.0%

Source: Analysis of data by author (*n* = 209).

caused by organized protest by black soldiers rose from 3.4 percent in 1942 to 19.4 percent in 1944 (see Table 5.4). Further evidence of the progressive reorientation of soldier dissatisfaction is found in the decline in the share of confrontations caused by fighting from 1942 to 1944. This trend also followed from the reform and professionalization of policing, which increasingly either channeled resistance into other forms of activity or resolved potential confrontations more quickly and peaceably.

Intelligence and Counterintelligence Initiatives

The new facilities and transport fairness policies, along with the growth of research and analysis, marked a general policy trend toward a two-pronged approach to racial tensions: A more sophisticated intelligence apparatus to gather and analyze information about potential unrest, coupled with preventive, ameliorative reforms aimed at defusing tensions. Open monitoring continued as before; the inspector general's staff conducted yet another "public" survey of camp conditions in many camps during the latter half of 1943.[78] By the fall of 1944, however,

Racial Situation," October 7, 1944, OF 4245, War Dept. Material Concerning Minority, Oct.–Dec. 1944, FDRL.
78. Lee, *The Employment of Negro Troops*, p. 378.

Gibson praised the weekly reports of the Intelligence Division, Army Service Forces, for enabling officials to identify communities and areas where racial tension might produce serious problems.[79]

Established on January 1, 1942, the War Department's Counterintelligence Corps contained a countersubversive network of enlisted and civilian secret agents within military organizations who investigated alleged subversion in the Army and evaluated the loyalty of military personnel and civilian employees of the War Department.[80] The number of persons attached to the Counterintelligence Corps grew from 165 agents in May 1942 to 157 officers and 3,219 enlisted men by the end of the year. At the end of the bloody summer of 1943, agents and officers numbered 4,901.[81] At that time, two-thirds of the personnel were stationed in the United States, as shortages of intelligence personnel plagued operations in the theaters of war.[82] To take one crucial region as an example of the penetration of the camps by intelligence-gatherers, the ASF Fourth Service Command governed 188 Army stations in the southern states, which employed and trained 1.4 million persons in January 1943. The Command's 37,780 countersubversive operatives, scattered throughout the installations, produced 84,271 reports for that month alone.[83] Authorities in Camp Stewart and in the regional Service Command, however, failed to anticipate the disturbance at this post, despite the fact that military intelligence operatives had thoroughly penetrated these black units by the spring of 1943. A single coast artillery regiment in the camp – with a total strength of 2,165 – employed 120 operatives,

---

79. Memorandum, Gibson to McCloy, November 2, 1944, MacGregor and Nalty, eds., vol. V, pp. 480–4.

80 With the attack on Pearl Harbor, many members of the relatively small American intelligence community worried that the American state was unprepared for a global war. Memorandum, Major General Virgil L. Peterson, Inspector General, to the Deputy Chief of Staff, "Subject: Intelligence Activities in Service Commands," November 6, 1943, U.S. Military History Institute, Carlisle Barracks, Carlisle, PA [hereafter SIASC].

81. "History of the Counter Intelligence Corps," in *Covert Warfare: Intelligence, Counterintelligence, and Military Deception During the World War II Era*, vol. 12, "The Counter Intelligence Corps in Action," John Mendelsohn, ed., New York, Garland Publishing, Inc., 1989, p. 25 [hereafter HCIC].

82. HCIC, p. 47; SIASC, p. 3.

83. This averages to one operative per 37.4 persons, and 2.23 reports per operative per month. The eagerness with which operatives filed reports was partially a product of the novelty of the system. "Fourth Service Command Subversive Activities, Report No. 29," December 21, 1942–January 20, 1943, Army Intelligence Division, Project Decimal File, 1941–1945, RG 319, National Records Center, Suitland, Maryland [hereafter NRC-SM].

who produced ninety reports for April alone.[84] But the reports were marred by what Gibson considered to be systematic racial bias on the part of the intelligence-gatherers. The race-related reports were organized as lists of criminal and undisciplined acts by blacks, with no consideration of context or cause. The fact that the incidents were described only after they occurred made it impossible, he wrote, to consider any "preventative action other than harsh, repressive measures to curb unruly and criminal Negroes." He endorsed the further consolidation of intelligence reporting and the centralization at the War Department level of the three major commands' activities in racial matters.[85]

Nationwide, the first seven months of 1943 produced approximately one million reports, which identified six hundred suspicious persons. Although secrecy was essential to the effective operation of the countersubversive system, its existence became widely known. In late 1943, Major General Virgil Peterson, the Inspector General, noted that it had been "adversely 'written up' " in at least one newspaper with a wide black readership. The publicity had two inhibiting effects: It placed potentially subversive individuals on notice to avoid detection, and it appeared to relieve regular military personnel of their responsibility to report suspicious behavior.[86] The system, however, functioned well enough. Despite his criticism of their reporting methods, Truman Gibson believed the weekly reports of the Intelligence Division enabled officials to identify troubled communities and to develop "preventative plans and procedures."[87] By mid-1944, the Director of Intelligence of the Army Service Forces described domestic intelligence coverage as "very complete," citing extensive cooperation and coordination between the FBI, the Office of Naval Intelligence, and intelligence agencies in the Service Commands.[88]

84. "C. S. Control Report" for Camp Stewart, in "Fourth Service Command Subversive Activities, Report No. 32," March 21, 1943–April 20, 1943, Army Intelligence Division, Project Decimal File, 1941–1945, RG 319, NRC-SM.

85. Reviewing various surveillance and intelligence reports, Gibson condemned their apparent "basic underlying assumption" that "conditions have deteriorated because of Negro criminal aggression against Whites . . . the listings of offenses are pessimistic and one-sided. They are reminiscent, and painfully so, of manufactured crime waves." Memorandum, Gibson to McCloy, November 2, 1944, MacGregor and Nalty, eds., vol. V, pp. 480–4.

86. Much of the attention focused on the search for enemy sympathizers or agents. SIASC, pp. 11, 14.

87. Memorandum, Gibson to McCloy, November 2, 1944, MacGregor and Nalty, eds., vol. V, pp. 480–4.

88. Memorandum, J. M. Roamer to the Commanding General, Army Service Forces, "Subject: Racial Situation in the United States," April 17, 1944, RG 319, Army Intelligence Division, Decimal File, 1941–48, NRC-SM.

Morale and Transfer to Theaters of War

Although the military was initially inclined to view problems of dissatisfaction within black units in terms of morale and esprit de corps, the traditional measures of unit cohesiveness, efficiency, and well-being were not necessarily the most appropriate frames for understanding the racial motivations and perceptions that underlay both mistreatment and the resentment. Many educational programs that aimed at improving fighting spirit were therefore perceived to be instruments of further control. Facing very low morale in black units, a typical "recommended corrective program" might include a new unit commander, a training regimen oriented toward military rather than service operations, patriotic plays, complaint periods, lectures discouraging rumors, or the transfer of agitators. Despite these operations, many black soldiers knew that it was unlikely that they would ever be assigned to combat, and their lack of training in weaponry and battle tactics seemed to confirm this fear. Kenneth Clark noted that the nature of black soldier morale had grown more "reality-bound" since World War I when appeals to patriotism and "slogans of a general nature" were effective rallying tactics.[89]

In the second half of the war, then, command and camp officials paid greater attention to convincing black soldiers that their mission – whether combat or quartermaster unit – was essential to the war effort, and that their leaders understood their problems. As American GIs poured into the Pacific Islands and prepared for the invasion of Europe, the War Department arrived at a policy that effectively improved morale, reduced disruptive events, and increased war-fighting strength: the transfer of units toward theaters of operations. When one post commander in 1944 reported that the black troops in his command were "bored, over-trained, domesticated, and subject to any bad influence upon their emotions," an Army Service Forces inspection committee recommended that the troops be moved. "The mere activity of moving would satisfy them for a reasonable length of time," the report continued, "and strange surroundings would quiet their restlessness."[90] The McCloy Committee responded to the unrest of the summer of 1943 by recommending the quick dispatch of black troops "as the most effective means of reducing tensions among Negro troops."[91]

89. To "use those methods now . . . would be a blundering mistake." As quoted in memorandum, Robert C. Weaver to Jonathan Daniels, September 4, 1943, OF 4245, WMC, FDRL, p. 2.
90. Lee, *The Employment of Negro Troops*, p. 343.

General Davis had raised this issue in March 1943, arguing that black soldiers' morale would be best served by service in combat.[92] By mid-1944, the majority of black soldiers had been sent overseas, where most worked in service units.[93] News that the 93rd Infantry Division was slated for assignment overseas, for example, led to an extraordinary improvement in morale.[94]

Like the policy innovations of 1940, the decision to place black soldiers in combat was propelled in part by a presidential election. For most of 1943 and early 1944, the War Department was actually more likely to convert black combat units to service duties.[95] Secretary of War Stimson attributed this to national security concerns. Early planning for continental defense and the need to prepare for transfer and invasion abroad compelled the mobilizers to provide a relatively large number of defensive units, such as anti-aircraft and coast artillery units. While this effort allowed for the relatively equitable distribution of black personnel in all branches, the shift toward an intercontinental system of supply for vast invasion forces, he argued, combined with low educational classifications to require the conversion of many defensive units to service units.[96] Rep. William Dawson (D, IL) called Stimson's claims "a direct insult to every Negro in the country," and Gibson warned that the explanation – which seemed to suggest that blacks would be used principally in service roles – would "have very serious political repercussions" among black activists of both parties.[97]

William Hastie joined the debate, informing Stimson that the seventeen black units fully mobilized early in 1941 produced only five that had been committed to combat overseas, all anti-aircraft artillery regiments. Trained in the myth of black inferiority and "fearing to add a 'racial problem' to other headaches in the theater of war," field commanders and War Department officials resisted assigning black infantry, field artillery, and cavalry units to overseas service; they were used in-

91. Dalfiume, *Desegregation*, p. 93.
92. Fletcher, *America's First Black General*, p. 113; Dalfiume, *Desegregation*, p. 93.
93. Lee, *The Employment of Negro Troops*, pp. 622–30.
94. The 92nd Infantry Division was the other all-black unit that saw combat, in addition to numerous smaller units. Lee, *The Employment of Negro Troops*, pp. 338–40. On the records of these two divisions, see Mershon and Schlossman, *Foxholes and Color Lines*, pp. 57–61.
95. Mershon and Schlossman, *Foxholes and Color Lines*, p. 56.
96. Letter, Secretary Henry L. Stimson to Rep. Hamilton Fish, February 19, 1944, OWI Files No. 2, box 29, papers of Philleo Nash, HSTL.
97. Letter, Rep. William L. Dawson to John J. McCloy, February 28, 1944; memorandum, Truman Gibson, Jr. to the Advisory Committee on Negro Troop Policies, February 29, 1944, OWI Files No. 2, box 29, papers of Philleo Nash, HSTL.

stead as "glorified 'home guards.' " Anti-aircraft units were among the few that could be semipermanently assigned to a racially separated defensive station in theaters of operations, for little contact with other combat forces was necessary. The deployment of anti-aircraft units, Hastie argued, was "the device best calculated to confound the critics" of black troop policy without changing that policy.[98] When it became apparent that the Republicans were poised to use the issue to their advantage in 1944, the Army quickly planned to transfer more black units overseas, calling it a matter of "vital National Policy."[99]

Conclusion

When the Army began evaluating a future black troop policy in 1945, Gibson recommended that the Army incorporate into the planning process what he considered to be several important lessons learned from this war. First, he recommended a critical reappraisal of the founding principles of black troop segregation: that social relations were not the province of the Army, that racial characteristics – including inferior intelligence – prevented blacks from serving effectively in modern combat roles, and that black officers were not suited for command. He noted that the racial problem facing the Army had changed substantially in five years. The political and social attitudes of black draftees had changed and education levels had risen among recruits. Black citizens also were more critical of War Department policies. Instead of assuming that combat failures were due to racial characteristics, Gibson argued that unit histories should consider the possibility that black soldier inefficiency was due to educational, social, and economic disadvantages, or even the possibility that the failures "may be due to defects in Army policy."[100]

Similar findings resulted from the committee's evaluating policy. In October 1945, the War Department charged the Gillem Board with reviewing and reforming black soldier recruitment and promotion policy. The board's nineteen recommendations reflected four principles. First, the Army must develop the full capacities of all soldiers assigned to it. In addition, blacks' "improved capability for participation" in

98. William H. Hastie to the Secretary of War, February 29, 1944, OWI Files No. 2, box 29, papers of Philleo Nash, HSTL.
99. The White House campaign strategy in 1944 is treated in Chapter 7. Lee, *The Employment of Negro Troops*, p. 484–5, 498–9; as quoted in Mershon and Schlossman, *Foxholes and Color Lines*, p. 57.
100. Memorandum, Truman K. Gibson, Jr., to John McCloy, August 8, 1945, MacGregor and Nalty, eds., vol. VII, pp. 16–18.

society, stemming from recent achievements in education, industry, and government, provided a broader base of fully qualified personnel. As bona fide citizens, blacks deserved the opportunity to participate in military service on the same grounds as other citizens. Finally, studies demonstrated that the disadvantages suffered by the black soldier undermined his prospects for success in the war. The report directly contradicted the claim made at the beginning of the war that segregation served military efficiency; the record displayed widespread inefficiencies, in part due to a lack of staff preparation and planning. The report also repeatedly referred to the "progress made" by black citizens, particularly in he wartime period. In a similar spirit, the board recommended the adoption of "progressively flexible" policies aimed at the full utilization of all personnel, "consistent with the democratic ideals upon which the nation and its representative army are based."[101] But while recommending more job opportunities for black soldiers and the grouping of black and white units within larger composite organizations, the board chose not to reject the principle of segregation.[102] What accounts for these results?

Central authorities' responses to wartime racial unrest followed from the same two overarching political factors at the core of employment policy: the sectional nature of the mobilization and the president's partisan and war-fighting goals. In the workplace, voluntarist "adjustments" helped to resolve individual complaints because black workers viewed the mechanism as legitimate, due to its radical roots. When this approach proved unworkable in the Army, officials relied on repression and incremental reform – heavily on the former at first, though in time, reforms lessened the need for brute force. To a greater degree than in capitalized cities and towns, for which state officials created a more flexible, adaptive, and ameliorative racial regime, the Army policed the races. Again, the goals were to maintain optimal warfighting and party strength by insulating war-vital sectors and the Executive from social unrest. Army officials gradually shifted their emphasis from reaction and punishment to proactive surveillance, bargaining, and planning, for stanching the new racial disturbances required new regime "tools" in turn, including small steps toward substantive reform, such as the desegregation of post facilities and transportation enacted and tightened during the unrest of 1943 and 1944.

101. "Report of Board of Officers on Utilization of Negro Manpower in the Post-War Army," February 26, 1946, McGregor and Nalty, eds., vol. VII.
102. David G. Mandelbaum, *Soldier Groups and Negro Soldiers*, Berkeley, University of California Press, 1952, pp. 113–15.

The evidence supports three propositions. First, the central state invented new forms of race conflict as a by-product of the initial "command" stage of the mobilization for World War II. Most black troops – disproportionately northern – trained amid the open race hostility of the white South. The purposeful assignment of blacks to work details, inferior facilities, and overcrowded transport vehicles insulted them. In numerous instances, overzealous and undertrained police were as likely to cause as to control resistance. In the second, "adjustment," stage, the War Department invented new policies by which to prevent or control disruptions, including intelligence gathering, recreation, indoctrination, and the incremental relaxation of segregation. In the field of surveillance in particular innovation was substantial.

Third, the quality of the grievance pattern, measured as military race confrontations, changed significantly during the war.[103] Black soldier action evolved from attempts by individuals to withstand violence, to efforts at group defense as in the Camp Stewart scenario, and finally to collective claims for the enforcement of ameliorative policies. One of the first racial confrontations of the mobilization may have been a lynching – recall that the hanging body of a black private was discovered at Fort Benning, Georgia, in April 1941 – which recalled the white supremacist terror that peaked in the 1890s. One of the last was a disciplined, nonviolent occupation by black Air Force officers of a white officers club at Freeman Field, Indiana, in April 1945, foreshadowing the organized activism of the early sixties' sit-ins. Although this simple juxtaposition exaggerates the brevity and fullness of the transition caused by the war, blacks appeared less often as individual objects and more often as collective subjects of confrontations. Because of this, the War Department's repertoire of responses rapidly diversified, from a reactive and relatively coercive system to a more complex array of measures, including a reformed policing system, an intelligence-gathering network, effort at diversion and indoctrination, and even the incremental relaxation of segregation.[104]

103. If fair employment data had been collected for the entire mobilization period, complaints would have likely displayed a comparable shift in complaint causes, from training, to hiring, to work conditions, and to termination.
104. War mobilization similarly affected popular politics in Great Britain between the 1750s and the 1830s. Locally oriented, violent, and symbolic acts, such as crowd retaliation, declined significantly in that period, while nonviolent, authorized assemblies aimed at national policies and institutions increased. "The crude figures indicate a decisive shift from spur-of-the-moment provocation and violent retribution toward planned gatherings aimed at declaring collective positions with regard to public

Perhaps the clearest indicator of change were the costs that repressive segregation now entailed. Both social justice and military efficiency, black activists and soldiers made clear, were incompatible with inherited methods of race management. After the Camp Stewart uprising, Hastie again condemned the techniques by which the Army defended white supremacy:

> Formal investigation and report, an occasional court martial, the removal of some individual from his command, and the shifting of a troublesome regiment to another station – these are the Army's customary and familiar devices. It sticks to them doggedly. The events of the first week in June [1943] have served bloody notice that such attempts to muddle through cannot succeed. The Administration cannot ease racial tensions by working quietly behind the scenes. The Army cannot check the increasing wave of violence by ponderous investigations of each case as it occurs. The Government must take the issue to the people boldly, giving America a measure of understanding and of leadership which is now lacking.[105]

While there would be no such leadership on this issue – the Roosevelt administration was at best ambivalent about reforming these social relations – the violence did force authorities to reevaluate their positions. The Army Service Forces Manual M5 of October 1944 now recognized that race discrimination was "fatal" to military efficiency.[106] Police and white supremacist repression of blacks, so routine and negligible in the thirties, was suddenly unacceptable for the total war required the utilization if not cooperation of all social groups.

Segregation was once thought necessary to avoid the irritation of whites. In 1941, an Army official in South Carolina explained that the camp used separate theaters: "Down south, we do as the southerners do, no matter . . . takes more theaters, but we run less risk of trouble."[107] Likewise, in 1944 McCloy argued that "segregation makes difficulties, but mixing units would create even more upheaval, and we cannot take

issues." Charles Tilly, *Popular Contention in Great Britain, 1758–1834*, Cambridge, Harvard University Press, 1995, p. 344.

105. William H. Hastie, "Only U.S. Action Can Protect Negroes in Army, Says Leader," New York *P.M.*, June 14, 1943.

106. According to Stimson, "in every theatre there were special considerations which made Negro troops a problem . . ." Efficiency claim quoted in "Prejudice! – Roadblock to Progress," Army Talk Orientation Fact Sheet, no. 70, Washington, D.C., War Department, May 5, 1945, Minorities-Army Talk, papers of John Ohly, HSTL, p. 5; Stimson and Bundy, *On Active Service*, p. 462.

107. "Object to Colored in S.C. Theatre," Norfolk *Journal and Guide*, September 6, 1941.

such risks."[108] Given the widespread violence at the time, which included attacks on blacks by whites in Mobile and Detroit, the expectation of a violent white reaction to integration was not an unreasonable inference to draw from events. But by 1943, "running less risk of trouble" required a clear turn away from segregation and coercion as war planners searched for other techniques to end the disruptions born of black resistance to discrimination. The analysis now turns to examine one such incident in detail.

108. In 1949, McCloy recalled that he and Stimson agreed after much thought that integration would be "unwise" in part because "there were all sorts of terrible prophecies . . . we didn't want to take the risk of a shake in morale that might be involved." Quoted in memorandum, Harry Alpert to Philleo Nash, April 5, 1944, OWI Files No. 3, Papers of Philleo Nash, HSTL; McCloy quoted in Desmond King, *Separate But Unequal: Black Americans and the U.S. Federal Government*, New York, Oxford University Press, 1995, p. 118.

6

June 9, 1943: "Negro Soldier Trouble" at Camp Stewart, Georgia

Mr. Hastie, is it not true that your people are basically agriculturalists?
Secretary of War Henry L. Stimson to William Hastie[1]

On December 16, 1942, George Nesbitt boarded a railroad car in Ft. Custer, Michigan, with 117 other black army recruits from the North. Bored, their destination unknown to them, they passed the time by swapping lies, singing, reading, and viewing the scenery. Above all, they wondered where they were heading. They began their speculation with wishful thinking; since Detroit was the first stop, they hoped they were heading west. "But reason prevailed," Nesbitt wrote a few days later,

> and tracing the direction of the train movement by the relative position of the sun, observing the thickening of the negro populace along the tracks, the increasing redness in the soil – and on the necks of the pink people, et cetera we strongly suspected that we were Georgia bound. We were.[2]

The next day, the men arrived at Camp Stewart, a vast anti-aircraft training installation carved from the pine forests west of Savannah. Nesbitt – only days before, a NAACP member and staffer at the Race Relations Branch of the U.S. Housing Authority – was now, in addition, a private in the U.S. Army's 613th Battalion, Coast Artillery, Anti-Aircraft (Colored).

He would watch as interracial relations in the camp deteriorated over the next six months, culminating in bloodshed on the night of June 6,

1. Gilbert Ware, *William Hastie: Grace Under Pressure*, New York, Oxford University Press, 1984, p. 123.
2. Letter, George Nesbitt to NAACP, December 20, 1942, *Papers of the NAACP*, Part 9, Discrimination in the U.S. Armed Forces, 1918–1955, Series A: General Office Files on Armed Forces' Affairs, 1918–1955, Group II, Box A-643, in microfilm edition, John H. Bracey, Jr., and August Meier, general editors [hereafter NAACP].

1943, when black soldiers ambushed successive convoys of white MPs, killing one and wounding four. "The affair at Camp Stewart, Georgia, in June 1943," according to a 1945 Army study, "provides the profile of a typical outbreak" of racial violence in the World War II armed forces.[3] Nesbitt's lengthy and thoughtful biweekly reports on camp matters sent to his former colleagues, combined with internal NAACP memoranda and Army documents – including the transcripts of investigators' interviews with scores of camp personnel in the immediate aftermath of the rebellion – provide a detailed account of race relations in one troubled World War II Army camp.[4] Echoing general claims made

3. Other contemporary analysts agreed that the incident was representative. "It should be noted that this disturbance followed closely the pattern of previous riots of this nature investigated by officers from my office. In each case the wrath of the colored soldier seems to have been directed toward the military police (white or colored), following the spreading of a rumor to the effect that these men were mistreating colored personnel. In each instance the action has been sudden and without warning, they have moved in a body to their own or adjoining supply rooms, shoved aside the guards, obtained the arms, and at the first opportunity have opened fire on the nearest military police." Memorandum, Ground Adjutant General for Chief of Staff, U.S. Army, November 28, 1945, "Subject: Participation of Negro Troops in the Postwar Military Establishment," *Blacks in the Armed Forces*, vol. VII, *Planning for the Postwar Employment of Black Personnel*, Morris J. MacGregor and Bernard C. Nalty, eds., Wilmington, Delaware, Scholarly Resources, Inc., 1977, pp. 110–23; "Memorandum, Maj. Gen. Virgil L. Peterson, Office of the Inspector General, to Lt. Gen. Joseph T. McNarney, Deputy Chief of Staff, War Department, 19 June 1943, General Correspondence 1939–1947, Camp Stewart, Inspector General, RG 159, (7)A, 33.9, Box 729, National Archives, p. 3 [hereafter IG-CS].

4. There are a number of synthetic treatments of this realm, of which the best are: Neil A. Wynn, *The Afro-American and the Second World War*, New York, Holmes & Meier Publishers, 1975; Gerald Robert Gill, "Afro-American Opposition to the United States' Wars of the Twentieth Century: Dissent, Discontent, and Disinterest," Ph.D. dissertation, Howard University, 1985; Joyce Thomas, "The Double V was for Victory: Black Soldiers, the Black Protest, and World War II," Ph.D. dissertation, The Ohio State University, 1993; James Albert Burran III, "Racial Violence in the South During World War II," Ph.D. dissertation, University of Tennessee, 1977. The only close history of a comparable incident is Robert L. Allen, *The Port Chicago Mutiny*, New York, Warner Books, 1969. The July 17, 1944, cargo loading accident which claimed 320 lives and led to the largest mass mutiny trial in U.S. Naval history, was not, due to its extraordinary cause and scale, representative of racial disturbances in the armed forces. Nelson Peery, *Black Fire: The Making of an American Revolutionary*, New York, the New Press, 1994, includes a first-person account of organized resistance among one black unit in the 93rd Division. See also William B. Simpson, "A Tale Untold? The Alexandria, Louisiana, Lee Street Riot (January 10, 1942)," *Louisiana History* 35, Spring 1994; James A. Burran, "Urban Racial Violence in the South During World War II: A Comparative Overview," Walter J. Fraser, Jr., and Winfred B. Moore, eds., *From the Old South to the New: Essays on the Transitional South*, Westport, Connecticut, Greenwood Press, 1981; Gary R. Mormino, "GI Joe Meets Jim Crow: Racial Violence

in the previous chapter, this reconstruction of one case describes how the war stimulated racial friction and how the Army responded to the unrest in turn.

Four groups struggled for power in and over the camps. First, black soldier militancy, as we have seen, was generally associated with prior residence in northern cities. Their methods ranged from petitioning for the peaceful reform of assignment and promotion policies, to defying the police who sought to enforce segregation and other discriminatory policies. White officers, MPs, and guards were charged with enforcing these policies, often with the help of white civilian police forces. Outside of the fort, the struggle was between the organized surrogates of the black GIs and white officers. During the war, the NAACP, the most important organization in the field of army reform, gained many scores of thousands of new members, and this expanded base offered somewhat greater leverage over federal agencies. Closely aligned with the NAACP was the black press, which was directly involved in networks of advocacy and reform. Finally, there were central state officials pursuing efficient warmaking and reelection. Generally, War Department staff attempted to maintain the Army's traditional insulation from social forces and debates, but as blacks and their allies campaigned to change the Army's training plans, officials responded with reforms sensitive to the political challenge, though still aimed at preserving a segregated fighting force.

Thus, racial friction drove statesmen to innovate as they sought to cope with the resistance of black soldiers. At first, policing and repression were the most common tools, but they were increasingly costly to deploy, for they undermined the already uncertain dedication of many black Americans to the war effort and often stimulated additional dissent both inside and outside the armed forces. Officials therefore augmented punishment with preventive efforts, which included ameliorative, symbolic, equalization, education, transfer, and intelligence policies. Substantive ameliorative reforms were rare in part because so little was known of their potential effect. Such reforms – including the 1943 designation of all Army camp facilities as open to all soldiers – were extended rather furtively and were unevenly enforced, mainly because they were thought to be disruptive of both discipline and order in camps and

and Reform in World War II Florida," *Florida Historical Quarterly* 73, July, 1994. On the soldiers' reception abroad, see Graham Smith, *When Jim Crow Met John Bull: Black American Soldiers in World War II Britain*, New York, St. Martin's Press, 1987; Kay Saunders and Helen Taylor, "The Reception of Black American Servicemen in Australia During World War II: The Resilience of 'White Australia,' " *Journal of Black Studies* 25, January, 1995.

potentially damaging to the president's political coalition. On the other hand, symbolic concessions such as appointments and investigations posed low risks to social order and political concerns. These policy initiatives, aimed primarily at black voters, clustered near campaigns. A third set of ameliorative techniques involved the equalization of facilities and programs, primarily recreational ones, such as the construction of United Service Organizations (USO) facilities, and visits to Southern camps by black entertainers and athletes. These activities promised to divert the soldiers' attention from their political claims and met no resistance from segregationists. The education of black soldiers and civilians in the compatibility of central state and minority interests was the work of civilian aides William Hastie and Truman Gibson, Jr., and Brig. Gen. Benjamin O. Davis of the Inspector General's office. Public explanations of central state policy were augmented by the systematic indoctrination of black soldiers. Officers told northern black GIs, for example, that Georgia – like Sicily or England – was a "foreign land" with local laws that must be obeyed. A final broad set of tactics was appropriate either for a unit or an individual: physical transfer, either in response to unrest or to prevent it. Disciplinary transfers often relied on the reports of countersubversive and intelligence operatives. In the case of entire units, transfer overseas was an especially attractive choice as the war progressed: It removed a primary cause of homefront disturbances, increased war-making strength, and satisfied black demands for full and equal participation, as stories of heroism and sacrifice replaced accounts of mistreatment and unrest in the black press. The Camp Stewart case is thus a good example of the complex but recurrent political process by which activists and opponents within and outside military camps struggled to affect policy change.

The Setting and the Problem: Savannah and the "Georgia HELL HOLE"

By the end of 1941, Dr. Ralph Mark Gilbert, pastor of Savannah's First African Baptist Church, had discussed with the national office of the NAACP the possibility of reviving the city's branch, which had ceased operations some years earlier. At the first branch meeting on February 27, 1942, thirty-eight persons paid the membership fee of $1, and the group applied for a charter from the national office.[5] In its first public

---

5. "Making Plans to Form NAACP Branch in This City," Savannah *Tribune* [hereafter ST], February 19, 1942; see also "To Ask for Reinstatement NAACP Br'ch," ST, March 5, 1942; "To Form Permanent Organization," ST, March 12, 1942.

act, the association protested arrangements for the city's April 6 Army
Day parade, in which whites preceded all of the twenty-five hundred
black marchers, who included Red Cross workers, auxiliary police, air
wardens, and a company of troops from the Savannah Air Base. The
latter were armed only with water containers. Separating the two races
were several service wagons and trucks filled with scrap iron and junk.[6]
The local group, in a formal complaint to William Hastie, conceded that
they expected to march behind the white units. "We know we are 'Below
the Potomac,' " they wrote. The black units, however, expected to be
assigned positions directly behind the respective white units, and black
citizens expected their soldiers to be properly equipped.[7]

For most city residents and the reborn NAACP, local employment and
training opportunities outweighed in importance the treatment of newly
arrived soldiers. Press reports suggested that Dr. Gilbert was organizing
a more militant alternative to the extant leadership – largely derived
from other churches and a local college – which was apparently well
connected to the federal relief and recovery efforts of the New Deal.[8]
Thus, the NAACP called for one delegate from every black organization
in the city to meet publicly to discuss defense training opportunities in
Savannah.[9] Although they were 47 percent of the population of Savannah, blacks received almost no defense training, while two well-
equipped, twenty-four-hour defense training projects had already prepared eighteen hundred whites for jobs. With this focus on jobs, the
association gained more than 1,350 new members in ten months; the
503 members between the ages of sixteen and twenty made up the largest
Youth Council in the country.[10] By March 1943, the Savannah NAACP
boasted 2,323 adult members and over 600 Youth Council members.[11]
The number of NAACP branches in Georgia as a whole grew rapidly

---

6. The two divisions of "colored auxiliary police" had trained with the Office of Civilian
   Defense to respond to air raids or other emergencies. "Assigned Position an Insult,"
   ST, April 9, 1942; "Colored Auxiliary Police Holds Meeting," ST, October 1, 1942.
7. Letter, Savannah Branch NAACP to William Hastie, April 8, 1942, in "Their First
   Protest," ST, April 16, 1942.
8. Maceo Hubbard, an attorney then serving on the Fair Employment Practices Committee (FEPC), spoke at one NAACP meeting, and the branch sent several delegates and
   witnesses to the Birmingham FEPC hearings to present evidence of local employment
   discrimination. This committee reported on its work at a June NAACP meeting, where
   Gilbert announced that a shipbuilding firm had asked him to send them 150 skilled
   workers. "Local Delegates to FEPC See Much Good Coming from the Conference,"
   ST, June 25, 1942.
9. "Organization Heads Asked to Attend NAACP Meeting," ST, June 4, 1942.
10. "NAACP Drive Results in Gain of 1360 Members," ST, December 17, 1942.
11. At the February 28 meeting that closed the membership drive, Walter White addressed

during the war, from fewer than five in 1942 to more than forty in 1946.[12] This explosive growth was not exceptional, for the national NAACP added 160,000 new members in 1942 alone.[13] Despite this organizational vitality within black neighborhoods, the city was ill-prepared for the arrival of legions of soldiers, and in the summer of 1942 officials of the Soldiers' Social Service of Savannah, the WPA, and the Federal Security Administration met with local Army officers to discuss the problem. Since there were "absolutely no recreational facilities for colored troops at this point," according to the Federal Security Agency, the conferees agreed to provide dormitory and educational facilities for troops in Savannah. They also agreed to try to procure a recreational center at the local air base and provide swimming and boating facilities at the nearby beach.[14]

There was apparently little interaction between race advancement organizations in the city and the transplanted GIs, who must have felt quite isolated upon their arrival. In the fall and winter of 1942–43, the black-owned Savannah *Tribune* carried a feature, "Camp Stewart on Parade," which reported on the social activities of the soldiers; nearly all of the bustle occurred at the Camp Service Club and typically featured its extraordinary assemblage of professional musicians, which may have helped draw some locals out for visits.[15] These stories of camp concerts and dances gave no hint of the trouble to come.

Inside the camp, the soldiers seem to have split into potent regional cliques. While Nesbitt complained of discriminatory treatment by whites from the start, he also reported his distaste for the collaborationist attitudes he found among his compatriots from the South. One intelligent black noncommissioned officer, Nesbitt thought, made an "effective Uncle Tom" because his servility was presented in the "language of the educated Negro." The northerners, he wrote, had been placed under "slave-driving, illiterate, uncouth" blacks from a Coast Artillery Training Center at Fort Eustis, Virginia.

"one of the largest crowds to ever greet any speaker" in Savannah. "Nearly 3000 Join NAACP," ST, March 18, 1943.

12. The previous high in number of branches in Georgia occurred during the Great War; all other states analyzed showed comparable wartime peaks. Richard M. Valelly, "Banging at the Doors: The NAACP Voter Registration Campaign, 1944–1954," paper prepared for the 1994 Annual Meeting of the American Political Science Association, New York, New York, September 1–4, 1994, Appendix I.

13. "1942 Was NAACP's Banner Year," ST, December 31, 1942.

14. "More Recreational Facilities for Troops in Savannah Area," ST, July 30, 1942; "90th C.A. Reg. Gives Introductory Dance," ST, June 4, 1942.

15. "Camp Stewart on Parade," September 3, 1942, ST; "Camp Stewart on Parade," September 17, 1942, ST.

They say 'suh' and 'yessuh' to the whites every other breath . . . They are crude and brutally officious with us and patronizing towards the blue-eyed coms. The Detroit and Chicago boys say that they but await the coming of the Chicago and Detroit jitterbugs that will mark the turning of the tide; the Chicagoans and the Detroiters will then take over. I do fear a little civil war among the Blacks . . . [16]

Whether Army officers systematically assigned southern blacks to non-commissioned officer positions – and later to the military police force – cannot be proven here. But others noted the tensions between the northerners and southerners, a product of interregional assignments and travel necessitated by military training. Before arriving at Stewart, thirty-year veteran James Hill was a member of the 100th Coast Artillery Regiment and traveled with it from North Carolina to Michigan in 1941 to receive new recruits from northern states. The move had two consequences, according to Hill. First, some of the southerners were radicalized by the experience:

> some of the southern boys got up there and found out there was no segregation, except to a certain extent. They got what you might call a taste of freedom.

And the new recruits claimed in Illinois and New York "caused us trouble later." There were in each battalion, he claimed, fifteen or twenty men who were troublemakers: either militant, improperly disciplined, or products of jail or reform schools. Attention would focus increasingly on the 100th Regiment, which arrived from Michigan on April 28, 1943. In a procedure that was routine for veteran units, it was disbanded and broken into training cadres.[17] Upon its arrival, camp officials put a guard on the gate, and the soldiers resented being stopped to show their passes, for they had never been asked to do so. A white lieutenant colonel, Albert S. Baron, believed, like Hill, that the 100th fostered unrest. "Since

16. Nesbitt's informal work on behalf of fellow soldiers was nonpartisan. He reported "going from hut to hut looking for negro newspapers; speaking up for all the boys in the battery on the lack of recreational facilities; helping the old men write letters to secure their discharges; telling the jitter-bugs that packing their ranks with coarse petroleum is bad for the scalp, makes their long heads look longer, and indicates their feelings of inferiority; teaching my class of 40 illiterates how to read, 'rite, and figger (and why Judge Hastie resigned, after telling them who he is and what he was . . .)." Letter, George Nesbitt to NAACP, December 20, 1942; letter, George Nesbitt to NAACP, February 7, 1943, NAACP.

17. The 100th served in Michigan between March 13, 1942, and its transfer South. It was then broken into the 100th Anti-Aircraft Artillery Gun Battalion and the 538th Anti-Aircraft Artillery Auto-Weapons Battalion. Shelby L. Stanton, *World War II Order of Battle*, New York, Galahad Books, 1991, pp. 466, 486.

that unit came here there has been an entirely different attitude throughout the post," he reported shortly after the insurrection.[18]

The uneasy early relations between African Americans was quickly
surmounted by confrontations between the races. White officers stalled
the black soldiers' inquiries about gaining officers' candidacies. One told
Nesbitt that the men in his unit could train only for commissions in their
own service, in this case, Coast Artillery, Anti-Aircraft. That evening,
Nesbitt, who knew that this violated War Department policy, organized
several well-educated Chicago-Detroit men into the G Battery "Ticks" –
an acronym for "those interested in commissions." The group's purpose,
Nesbitt wrote, was "staying in the hair and under the skin of these guys
– until they send us to training schools." If their applications were not
accepted, Nesbitt promised to call on his colleagues in the U.S. Housing
Authority to pass their complaints on to Judge Hastie.[19] By the spring,
Nesbitt's prospects had improved considerably. He had been offered
several promotions – including a first sergeantcy, and a warrant officer-
ship – apparently on the condition that he cease attempting to gain entry
to Officer Candidate School.[20]

Disaffection in the camp grew more serious and widespread in 1943.
By April, Nesbitt's letters were filled with reports of rumors, friction, and
resistance to mistreatment. When a white military policeman stationed at
a camp gate failed to salute a black captain from the 100th, remarking "I
don't intend to salute nigger officers," the officer seized the soldier,
"shook him good," asked again for a salute, and received it. Another
story had a black knocking down a white officer; in another, a group
from the 100th commandeered a bus for a brief joyride. On a local bus, it
was said, two black soldiers threatened to kill a local man who objected
to a black woman's taking a seat next to a white soldier. Rumors and
tension spun around the 100th, in particular. Nesbitt's battery commander, in granting his soldiers weekend passes to Savannah, directed

18. Baron later told investigators of differences between northern and southern blacks.
    The educational background of the southerner, he thought, "limits him as an individ-
    ual." They do not resent segregation like northerners and avoid "affairs like that of
    June 9th," knowing that "they are bound to come out on the short end of things."
    Hill, section B-8; Ochs, B-24; Baron, B-6, "Investigation of Negro Soldier Trouble at
    Camp Stewart, Georgia, during the night 9–10 June, 1943," National Archives, Rec-
    ord Group 159, Inspector General, General Correspondence, Box 729, Camp Stewart,
    Georgia, (7)A, 333.9, [hereafter INST].
19. Letter, George Nesbitt to NAACP, December 20, 1942, NAACP.
20. He refused, and his application, seeking an assignment to the Adjutant General's
    Division, the legal branch of the Army, was received. His battery commander ap-
    proved the application with the highest possible rating. Letter, George Nesbitt to
    NAACP, March 4, 1943, NAACP.

them plainly to leave any establishment if men from the unit arrived. The Training Center Commander met with officers of the 100th and demanded that they control the unit. "The place is a powder keg – dry powder," the soldier warned in April.[21]

By the spring, appeals and grievances began to arrive at NAACP headquarters, and many of the writers warned of bloodshed. Walter White received a handwritten letter in April from the 100th Coast Artillery itself. "My Dear Mr. White," it began,

> Please for God Sake help us. These old southern officers over us have us quarantined like slaves come down and see . . . They really hate colored. Please appeal to the war dept about our treatment at once. We are no slaves. [*sic*][22]

Another missive took the form of a mimeographed form letter explaining that "each one of us" was writing to three "people who are of importance" to ask that the recipients appeal to the black press and write to the adjutant general's office to request that the 492nd Battalion be moved out of Georgia, "before a lot of lives are unmercifully sacrificed." This unit was formed at Stewart on February 10 with a cadre from the 369th Anti-Aircraft Artillery (AAA) Regiment, recently returned from Hawaii. The letter claimed that their black officers – all formerly of the 369th – had been physically isolated in dining and living arrangements and attached to another unit because white officers resented their superior experience and knowledge. The writer claimed that sanitary conditions were "unspeakable" and that the camp was not receiving sufficient supplies of food. The letter attributed to a white captain from Mississippi a quote that would be repeated in other appeals: "This is Camp Stewart, the toughest camp in the U.S.; Army regulations do not exist here. We make the laws." A white lieutenant was reported to have recently kicked a black private.

> If action is not taken soon several lives (our boys) will be lost . . . Things are at such a state that we all have to walk around *armed*, even in an Army camp and serious casualties are expected.[23]

A very similar letter appeared in the New York *Amsterdam News* of May 29.[24]

---

21. Letter, George Nesbitt to NAACP, April 22, 1943, NAACP papers.
22. Letter, "Soldiers" to Walter White, April 1943, NAACP.
23. Unsigned letter, S/Sgt., Hq. Btry. 492nd Bn. C.A. (A.A.), Camp Stewart, Georgia, April 29, 1943, NAACP, emphasis in the original.
24. " 'Cold Cuts' for 369th Unit," New York *Amsterdam News*, May 29, 1943.

For a month, at least, black New Yorkers had inquired about the men formerly attached to the 369th, which arrived in Camp Stewart in February. On April 25, a corporal in the 492nd wrote to his aunt to complain that his unit was not properly fed and had not been paid in nearly two months. MPs, he wrote, held them in the guardhouse for as long as a month without a trial. "There has been a little trouble so far," he wrote, "and will be plenty more if things aren't better very soon."[25] Interest in these particular troops stemmed in part from Harlem's pride in the Great War heroics of its parent regiment, the 15th Infantry, New York National Guard. The French government awarded the unit the Croix de Guerre with a silver star for its valor, which included 191 consecutive days in the trenches without relief. It was the only black national guard unit maintained in its entirety in the interwar period, and when FDR promoted Col. Benjamin O. Davis, Sr., to brigadier general in 1940, he commanded the all-black 369th.[26] When the unit quit Fort Ontario, New York, in January 1941, the editor of *Opportunity* used his monthly column to extend to the men his best wishes.[27]

Citing the assignment of substandard housing and equipment, and the replacement of black officers with whites – among other "atrocities" – a Bronx couple wrote to the secretary of war on May 3 to demand the transfer of the 369th to a northern camp. The writers insisted that authorities take steps "other than issuing nicely pictured O.W.I. booklets to bolster the morale of colored troops and civilians."[28] The next day, Cpl. William Lawhorn wrote to the NAACP to ask them to investigate the beating that he and eight other black soldiers had suffered while returning to camp from nearby Glennville. Their bus suddenly stopped, he wrote, and two civilian police officers boarded it. The driver walked to the rear, pushed the back door open and demanded that the soldiers leave; the policemen stood at the front and the rear doors with pistols drawn. As the soldiers exited, the driver hit four of them with a blackjack.

25. The letter included a version of the aforementioned phrase: "You're in Georgia now where regulations mean nothing." Letter, Corporal Wilbur Timpson to Adele Timpson, April 28, 1943; see also letter, Adele Timpson to FDR, May 5, 1943, NAACP.

26. The 369th Infantry, New York National Guard, was converted and inducted into the federal service on January 13, 1941, as the 369th Coast Artillery, Anti-Aircraft. Only a vigorous fight by the governor of New York saved the unit from extinction as a combat unit. Lee, *The Employment of Negro Troops*, pp. 6–8, 29, 66, 79, 121–2; "The 369th Departs," *Opportunity*, February, 1941, p. 35.

27. While no one could guess the ultimate destination of the regiment, he wrote, "this we do know – that with a fair chance it will be a shining example of the loyalty of the American Negro to his country." "The 369th Departs," *Opportunity*, p. 35.

28. Letter, Mr. and Mrs. J. L. Bowman to the secretary of war, May 3, 1943, IG-CS.

A middle-aged black civilian also was beaten.[29] In mid-May, the New York City newspaper *People's Voice* asked its readers "what they were going to do about unspeakable conditions at Camp Stewart down in Georgia, where Jimcrow is riding high, wide and handsome." Parents and friends of men in the 369th immediately pledged support for the paper's campaign to "clean up" the camp. The editors promptly received a telegram from Truman K. Gibson, Jr., informing them that General Davis was investigating the situation. Concerned Brooklyn citizens in turn formed a "Save Our Soldiers" committee, which coordinated its efforts with the local NAACP and other community groups; the coalition sponsored a joint rally on May 30.[30] The tabloid cover of *People's Voice* on May 22 called Camp Stewart the "Georgia HELL-HOLE."[31]

One measure of the black soldiers' isolation was how they spent the $600 allotted to the battalion for "the welfare of enlisted men." Over $400 went to subscriptions: five subscriptions to approximately twenty different magazines and three newspapers. The camp command had provided them with a list of publications available for subscription, but the newspapers included only The New York *Times* and unspecified white papers from Jacksonville and Chicago. No black publication was listed "nor any truly liberal magazine or newspaper," Nesbitt wrote, proof that white officers failed to comprehend their assignment's difficulty. The soldiers subscribed to their favorite newspapers with their own funds, however, and Nesbitt read the Pittsburgh *Courier* at Service Club No. 2, which also received the Chicago *Defender*, the Norfolk *Journal and Guide* and the New York *Amsterdam News*. One morning he left his copy of "PC" on a table and watched a succession of white officers pick it up and immediately drop it "with seeming apprehension." To Nesbitt, the restricted list and the newspaper incident helped to explain the incompetence of the white officers. In early May he was told that the provost marshal had banned the *Courier* from the post.[32]

29. Letter, Cpl. William Lawhorn, 742nd C.A. Bn. (AA), Battery "B", to the NAACP, May 4, 1943, NAACP.
30. "Gen. Davis to Make Investigation; B'klyn Forms Citizens' Committee," *People's Voice*, May 22, 1943.
31. The paper reported that two corporals, AWOL, had surrendered to authorities in New York City. "Special Bulletin," *People's Voice*, May 22, 1943.
32. A week later, an investigator of racial unrest at a Virginia camp recommended against banning the paper, for fear of inciting protest, instead advising officers to dispose of unattended copies quietly. In orders of June 1941 and May 1942, the Adjutant General directed Army libraries to inspect donations of reading material for subversive content, and then permitted commanding officers to destroy materials deemed subversive or obscene. Many vendors of northern newspapers were arrested or harassed, or had their papers confiscated by police or civilians. In late 1943, the War Department

Colonel William Ochs, the camp commander, thought the black press published grossly exaggerated and inflammatory articles about incidents involving soldiers "which would normally be ignored by the white newspapers." One inaccurately reported a lynching. Ochs later told officials investigating the insurrection that he had received a query from the "Africo-American" [*sic*] regarding camp theaters and the policies governing access to them. Ochs replied that while blacks had only two theaters to the whites' four, the former group had more seats per soldier. Later, he complained, a reporter representing the black press visited the camp for a story. After announcing himself satisfied with the conditions, he published a "very derogatory account" that violated his agreement with local and national public relations offices.[33]

For his part, Nesbitt occasionally challenged his white officers. When the 100th marched down the road fronting his battalion office, Nesbitt joined other black enlisted men standing at the windows admiring the parade. This drew the attention of several whites; one asked which outfit they were watching and was told the 100th.

> 'Oh,' said the disappointed lieutenant, 'that's a dog-ass outfit.' I had to speak. 'Sir, that's a damn good outfit in the hands of someone who knows enough to know how to handle them.'

Nesbitt believed that these men, like the Civilian Conservation Corps men from the North that he knew from a previous assignment, were actually excellent officer material.[34] A pervasive mood of militancy is suggested by cases of soldiers who challenged rules with considerably less diplomacy than Nesbitt. On April 28, for example, when a civilian employee found three black soldiers drinking from a "Whites Only" water fountain, he upbraided them. When a soldier from the 100th replied that "such shit as that did not mean anything" to him, the civilian asked his name and was informed that "his name was very precious, and that he was very particular to whom he gave it to." A

---

ordered that no publications be banned without approval, but the directive was difficult to enforce. Letters, George Nesbitt to NAACP, May 9, 1943, and May 11, 1943, NAACP; Washburn, *A Question of Sedition*, pp. 112, 153–5, 191.

33. Shortly after the disturbance, the *Afro-American* published a statement by Brig. Gen. S. L. McCroskey, which, the paper claimed, was provided one week before the disturbance. McCroskey said that adverse reports of the camp were exaggerations of a few isolated malcontents. He predicted that the black soldier would "give a splendid account of himself" when tested. Col. William Ochs, p. 75, INST; "General McCroskey Said All's Well at Stewart, Then Came the Riot," Baltimore *Afro-American*, June 26, 1943; "Editorial," Baltimore *Afro-American*, June 26, 1943.

34. They were "full of militancy and fairly well-educated . . . able-bodied and afraid of nothing." Letter, George Nesbitt to NAACP, May 11, 1943, NAACP.

major arrived to question the soldier, who informed him that at home –
in New York City – "he drank at any public drinking fountain he cared
to." The officer ordered him to obey all post regulations but the soldier
interrupted with questions and challenging statements. A black sergeant
broke in to ask why the detail had to be "treated like dogs." Notified of
the incident, Colonel Ochs recommended that the GI be court-martialed,
and the sergeant reduced in grade to private.[35]

Nesbitt visited Chicago on leave in late April, and attended a predraft
party for Elmer Henderson of the FEPC and scholar J. G. St. Clair
Drake. Nesbitt's brief remarks at the event provided, he wrote, "living
proof" of the men's anxiety at joining the army. He declined to detail
his own experiences, which, he told the gathering, merely reflected what
was well documented by the black press. He warned that, while there
had not yet been serious trouble at Stewart, a "major incident can come
at any moment . . ."[36] By this time, the wave of complaints from Camp
Stewart had caught the attention of Roy Wilkins, NAACP assistant
secretary, who reminded Walter White that they had not yet contacted
the war department on behalf of these soldiers. "The men seem to be
desperate," he noted, repeating the complaint, gleaned from the form
letter, that a group of enlisted men was broken up and assigned to
different units. "One result of this, of course, is to disperse their complaints and weaken any united protest." Wilkins wondered if they
should delay a formal protest until White had returned from a visit to
the camp planned for later that month.[37] The next day, Prentice Thomas,
NAACP assistant special counsel, reminded White that Judge Hastie also
had suggested that he visit the camp, and summarized for White the
complaints that he found in the twenty-three letters received from soldiers there: physical isolation, "unspeakable" sanitary conditions, white
officers kicking black soldiers, lack of medical care for venereal diseases.
The memo also relayed claims that "at least 3 men die every month as a
result of race riots . . . [and] at least 2 men die every month as a result
of over-exertion."[38]

Two days before General Davis visited the camp, Roy Wilkins pressed

35. Memorandum, Colonel William V. Ochs to Commanding General, AATC, April 30,
    1943, INST, Exhibit D, pp. 1, 2, 5.
36. The men belonged to Chicago's antidraft organization, "Conscientious Objectors
    Against Jim Crow," which attempted to establish an exemption based on the inequal-
    ity of segregation in the armed forces. Despite black columnists' attempts to build the
    movement, the organization collapsed. Letter, George Nesbitt to NAACP, May 5,
    1943, NAACP; Wynn, *The Afro-American and the Second World War*, pp. 25–6.
37. Memorandum, Roy Wilkins to Walter White, May 13, 1943, NAACP.
38. Memorandum, Prentice Thomas to Walter White, May 14, 1943, NAACP.

Civilian Aide Truman Gibson to investigate the complaints. Wilkins quoted a Harlem man recently discharged from Stewart, who described it as a "concentration camp." From the tone of the letters he had seen, "some tragedy may result unless steps are taken."[39] Gibson responded promptly, citing the assurances of a surprising source.

> George Nesbitt . . . gave a much different picture of life at Camp Stewart. It, of course, is not nearly perfect but it is a long way from the exceedingly dismal picture painted by the individual from Harlem.

Gibson explained that the inspector general had already sent a team of investigators, including Davis, to hear testimony of the men firsthand; Davis was, in fact, at the camp that very day. Gibson's reading of the letters indicated that the cause of the difficulties was the transfer to Georgia of a New York unit – the 369th – which had been serving in Hawaii, where there was relatively little prejudice.[40]

The Army and the NAACP Attend to Camp Stewart

Gen. Davis and Lt. Col. Davis G. Arnold of the inspector general's office visited Camp Stewart on May 17–21. Their conferences with higher officials of the post resulted in agreements to improve the management of black troops on pass, including, for example, attempting to secure additional recreational facilities off post; staggering pass privileges to prevent the overcrowding of buses and entertainment facilities; and deploying additional black military police at entrucking points.[41] The latter required negotiations with local civilian police officers, and Davis – the Army's highest ranking black officer – met with the police staffs of nearby Glennville, Reidsville, and Lyons. During these sessions, Arnold, a white, "took testimony" of the policemen. Davis discussed recent events with the chief of police of Lyons, where, on two separate occasions on May 15, civilian police had jailed a black soldier for public drunkenness. In each case, shortly after the arrests, a truckload of black soldiers arrived at the jail and asked for the release of the soldier. One of the men in the truck had a Thompson submachine gun strapped across his back. While no threats were made and the gun remained on the GI's back, the soldiers were released, each on the promise that the

39. Wilkins's litany of complaints drew heavily from the April 29 form letter, citing among other things, untreated cases of venereal disease and men housed in a garage. Letter, Roy Wilkins to Truman K. Gibson, Jr., May 14, 1943, NAACP.
40. Letter, Truman K. Gibson, Jr., to Roy Wilkins, May 18, 1943, NAACP.
41. "Gov't Official Discusses Violence Toward Negro Soldiers," ST, July 1, 1943.

men would take him out of town.[42] During the conference with Davis, it was suggested that black MPs would be placed in the town, but the Lyons chief of police refused: "We ain't going to have any nigger police." Davis replied that if they "couldn't work with him," the Army would keep its soldiers out of the town altogether. "Upon my explanation," Davis wrote in his diary, "he decided he would take them."[43] Davis spent the 19th and the 20th interviewing men. "Complaints," he noted tersely in his diary.[44] In a later, informal exchange with Gibson, Davis described the situation as "very tense and likely at any time to precipitate a riot of serious proportions."[45]

From the point of view of many soldiers, the Davis inspection was a failure. Sgt. Edward Molette's complaint to the NAACP, for example, is similar to those that preceded the Davis trip, with an important difference that reflected ongoing policing reforms. During the Davis visit, Molette and his friends listened to an address in which the general promised, among other things, to eliminate military police brutality. Afterwards, the soldier walked to a service club, where an MP asked Molette for his ticket, which he claimed he produced. According to the soldier, the MP then said "get the hell on in," and threw a punch; three or four MPs then jumped on Molette and beat him about the head and face, while other MPs stood by with drawn guns. They forced him to enter a truck with three MPs. At gunpoint, a policeman gave him

> one of the most brutal and unmerciful beatings ever witnessed by a human being. While clubbing me he said 'you son of a bitch I'm going to kill you, and no one will know the difference.' If the M.P. sitting in the rear had not stopped him by saying 'For God sakes stop before you kill him' . . . he would have carried out his threat, which is the usual procedure carried out by these arrogant and belligerent Military Police.

"Incidentally," Molette noted in his letter, "the Military Police are colored." Molette also claimed that one black GI had already died because

---

42. Summary of Information, Richard J. Wallace, Jr., Assistant Post Intelligence Officer, May 21, 1943, INST, Exhibit F.

43. Ochs used the same threat with the mayor of nearby Hinesville when asking that a policeman be suspended for bludgeoning a black soldier in a bus station. Letter, Col. William Ochs, Commanding, Camp Stewart, to Dr. T. W. Welborn, Mayor of Hinesville, May 7, 1943; Letter, T. W. Welborn to William Ochs, May 11, 1943, INST, Exhibit E, pp. 1–2.

44. Davis also noted that the white troops from New York complained about their treatment by southerners. Benjamin O. Davis, Sr., Diary, 1939–1943, Archives of the U.S. Army Military History Institute, Carlisle Barracks, PA.

45. Memorandum, Truman Gibson, Jr., to the Assistant Secretary of War, June 2, 1943, attached to letter, Gibson to Daniels, September 15, 1943, OF 4245-G, OPM, COFEP, "War Dept., 1943," FDRL.

of the Army's unwillingness to transport the injured man to a hospital, an apparent reference to a black soldier killed in an automobile accident on May 18. "Only God knows how many more bodies will follow if we are kept in Southern Camps."[46] A white lieutenant investigated the Molette incident for the camp command and reported two versions of the case, "in virtually complete disagreement with each other."[47]

During Nesbitt's interview with the general, he courteously complained to Davis about the lack of recreation in nearby cities. The general not only insisted that the Army bore no responsibility for the welfare of the men away from camp, but angrily waved his hand in the soldier's face. The men in Nesbitt's battalion who witnessed this exchange lost their faith in the officer, and for several days they used the phrase "General Davis" to mean "Uncle Tom."[48] According to Davis's report, the soldiers spoke so carelessly in presenting their complaints that he felt compelled to remind them of the demeanor expected of disciplined soldiers.[49] *People's Voice* reported that, upon learning of Davis's impending visit, Camp Stewart officials ordered black soldiers out of a garage in which they had been sleeping, but the men had refused. "With all due credit to Brigadier General Davis" and his investigation of the camp, the paper wrote, "the air has far from cleared."[50]

Prior to this incident, Nesbitt asked Walter White for a personal interview during the director's upcoming visit. White asked the GI to bring his journal to a meeting at the home of Reverend Gilbert, and suggested that the soldier inform only those "who have *exact* information" of his visit, since several letters from the camp had contained exaggerated claims: the complaint that two or three black soldiers died every month in race riots at Stewart, for example, was simply untrue. The purpose of the trip, he said, was "to get facts as accurately as it is possible for me to get them." In the event, White could not secure a train ticket to Savannah, and he and Nesbitt did not meet.[51]

---

46. Molette, from New York City, also referred to himself as "colored." Letter, Edward Molette, 846 AAA Bn., Btry. D, to NAACP, May 21, 1943, NAACP.
47. Depending on whom you believed, Molette either struck out freely at the MPs during the fight, or stood among the group of policemen protecting his head with his arms and hands. According to one MP who accompanied the soldier in the station wagon to the stockade, Molette "kept raving and cursing and threatening what he was going to do to the M.P.'s, and said he was going to get even . . ." "Report of Investigating Officer," Charles A. Woods, Jr., June 7, 1943; INST, Exhibit G.
48. Letter, George Nesbitt to Walter White, July 17, 1943, NAACP.
49. Lee, *The Employment of Negro Troops*, p. 371.
50. " 'Investigation' of 369th Camp Slows; Who's Kidding Who?," New York *People's Voice*, May 29, 1943.
51. Hastie and Gibson now believed that there was little need for White to visit the camp, since the Army had taken steps to correct problems there. The bus system, community

In place of his investigation, Walter White asked Reverend Gilbert for his views of the situation, and the minister in turn submitted a thorough report based on numerous conversations with black officers and enlisted men. He shared White's concern about exaggerations. Sanitary and medical conditions were generally excellent, and a complaint about cold sandwiches for supper was "hardly a point." The PXs for black troops were indeed inferior, however, and there were three guest houses for white officers, but none for blacks. In two cases, a white lieutenant had kicked a black soldier. In one, the soldier had refused to identify the lieutenant; in the other, the lieutenant was being transferred. While it was true that "tactless" white officers had driven the men to "a state of morale bordering onto mutiny," the camp's atmosphere had apparently improved with the arrival of an unnamed lieutenant colonel. Most black officers, Gilbert reported, thought the term "concentration camp" was merely "one man's opinion," though a reasonable young enlisted man reported feeling "as though he were in a prison camp." Gilbert's informants felt that Col. William Ochs, the camp commander, and Col. Felix Gross, the executive officer of the training center, "both Germans," should be removed from command, while Brig. Gen. O. L. Spiller, the Commanding General of the training center, was described as "definitely in sympathy with the whole policy of discrimination."

Reverend Gilbert confirmed the need for more recreational facilities in town, for Savannah's prewar population of ninety-five thousand strained to accommodate the new arrivals. Two area shipyards alone employed approximately fifteen thousand workers, while three times as many men camped at Stewart. Each weekend the post launched a convoy of as many as one hundred trucks toward the city, bearing up to fifteen thousand soldiers; often, three-quarters of them were black. The Savannah Army Air Base held an additional nine thousand troops, and Navy and Coast Guard personnel also crowded into the downtown area on weekends.[52] Six service centers and a "tent city" provided overnight accommodation for white soldiers in Savannah but there were only two such centers for blacks, who slept in trucks, or sat on the curbs, or roamed the streets all night long. Gilbert's report noted an imbalance of six white buses to one black bus, while 40 percent of the

attitudes, and recreation and housing away from camp simply required additional reforms, they thought. Letter, George Nesbitt to NAACP, May 15, 1943, letter; Walter White to George Nesbitt, May 22, 1943; letter, Walter White to Dr. Ralph Gilbert, May 27, 1943; letter, Walter White to George Nesbitt, May 26, 1943, NAACP, emphasis in original.

52. Lee, *The Employment of Negro Troops*, pp. 370–1.

camp was black. Taxicabs in nearby Hinesville refused to carry black soldiers at all. Finally, while some blacks had been assigned to MP duty, they lacked any real authority. Indeed, all the MPs assigned to Savannah were white, which was very much resented in the black neighborhoods.[53]

Throughout the spring, the camp received a great deal of attention from the Army as well as from the NAACP. In late May, Maj. Gen. Joseph Green of the Anti-Aircraft Command at Richmond visited to confer with the training center commander, O. L. Spiller, and other officers of the post. They reviewed General Davis's conclusions and Green directed the camp command to take "all possible steps" to end the discriminatory conditions causing dissatisfaction among black troops. Green, after visiting the inspector general's office in Washington on June 1 to share findings and plan reforms, invited Spiller to Richmond where he was told frankly that the situation was grave and "loaded with dynamite."[54] Green ordered his director of training to visit the camp in early June; the officer spent three or four days at the camp just before the outbreak, but reported seeing no serious troubles. The inspector general from Green's headquarters also spent the first week of June at Stewart and also reported no signs of an impending mutiny. Given the across-the-board failure of these officials to foresee the disturbance, the Army's inspector general would later describe Green's preventive actions as "reasonably prompt and appropriate" and would conclude that both criticism and disciplinary action were unwarranted.[55]

Following his conference with Green, Spiller discussed the situation with his staff. He instructed them "to watch carefully for, and to suppress immediately" any rebellious conduct, to watch for any discriminatory treatment of black soldiers, and to recommend new recreational facilities outside the camp. He urged close supervision for the 100th and the 538th Battalions and for those battalions with cadres from the

---

53. "Report of Investigation at Camp Stewart, Ga.," Dr. Ralph Mark Gilbert, June 4, 1943, NAACP.
54. They discussed moving some troops to bivouac areas outside of the camp; careful supervision of the 100th AA Battalion; correcting discriminations in the bus transport system; posting adequate guards; using additional MPs in Savannah on weekends; using a special complaint officer; conferring with city officials in connection with recreational facilities for black troops; and staggering passes in order to conserve bus space. Green considered giving Spiller specific orders to "prevent or suppress riotous conduct," but since he was so far removed from the camp, and since he admired Spiller's experience and record, Green decided that he could not justify assuming command of the training center. Memorandum, Maj. Gen. Peterson to Lt. Gen. McNarney, p. 4, IG-CS.
55. Ibid., p. 4.

369th. He tightened MP supervision and assigned a motorized patrol to the camp's east gate – where black soldiers entered and left – between 9:00 and 11:00 each night. In the days leading up to and on the day of the outbreak, Spiller spent many hours with the units mentioned in Peterson's June 4 memorandum and was impressed with their "general easy attitude and morale."[56] Segregation and separation had apparently obscured Army officials' view of the temper of the camp. Unknown to them, a vicious rumor circulated among the black units that combined with their bitter resentment at mistreatment to spark the insurrection.

The Rumor and the Insurrection

When the inspector general's office later investigated Camp Stewart's deadly rumor – of the rape and murder of a black woman and the murder of her soldier husband by white soldiers or MPs – it turned out to be a melange of truth and fiction. Its credibility surely profited from the suspicious and harsh tone of race relations in the camp. For example, white soldiers routinely harassed black soldiers and their wives and girlfriends, especially near the camp's black-white frontier.[57] Black units had recently been removed from the area now occupied by the white 566th, 794th, and the 791st battalions, in the common practice of shifting nonwhite units outward from the center as the camp's population grew (see Map 6.1). Since then, the soldiers claimed that when they passed through that area, they were always bothered in some way by whites.[58] A black corporal and his wife had met trouble there on a springtime Saturday night. As they passed a group of white soldiers on

56. Ibid., pp. 4–5.
57. This hostility mirrored that found in Savannah, where, it was reported, police were conducting a "vice drive," stopping black soldiers and their female companions and asking the women to display a health card attesting that she was not infected with venereal disease. Lacking it, she was arrested and examined for venereal disease; if she was found to be infected, she was sent to a farm on the outskirts of town for further examination and treatment. "Guns and Clubs Used to Enforce Mass Jim Crow," Baltimore *Afro-American*, June 12, 1943.
58. Following the insurrection, Joseph T. McNarney, the deputy chief of staff, instructed the inspector general to send an officer to investigate. Lt. Col. Clarence Murray, assistant service command inspector general, and Lt. Joseph Brorby conducted the investigation on June 11–13 pursuant to a June 10 directive from the commanding general, 4th Service Command. The bulk of the account to follow draws on their interviews of forty-one soldiers, officers, and civilians. Memorandum, Maj. Gen. Peterson to Lt. Gen. McNarney, IG-CS; testimony of Lt. Joseph Taylor, INST; Index, INST, p. 5.

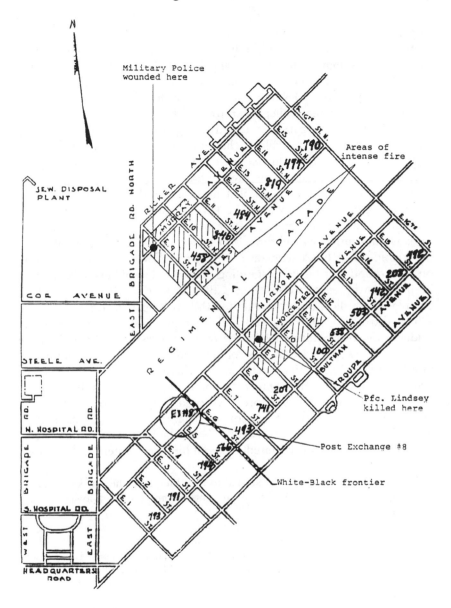

Map 6.1. Map of east wing training area, Camp Stewart, Georgia, June 1943, showing battalion areas; notations and graphics related to racial frontier and June 9 incident added. Source: INST.

Bultman Avenue, one bumped into the woman and nearly knocked her into a ditch.[59]

As for the source of the incendiary rumor, one chaplain identified a Pvt. Clyde Heyman of the 741st, who had told him of being assaulted when he went to the aid of a soldier and his wife, who had themselves been brutally beaten. Heyman told investigators of having been beaten on May 31st by white soldiers near 4th and Bultman, after an encounter with MPs at a nearby gate, but denied seeing any black woman. The day before the insurrection, a black chaplain of the 207th learned that a woman and two black soldiers had been beaten by white soldiers and that she had died the night before. Unlike Heyman, the source of this story gave investigators a detailed account of the woman's murder. Completing his guard duty at 10:00 P.M. on June 1, Pvt. Calvin Brown said, he heard of a beating in the area of the 741st. At 8th Street he saw three white lieutenants and three MPs trying to disarm a crowd of angry black soldiers. A black woman in a torn red flowered dress was laying on the ground, her husband standing nearby. The soldiers said she had been beaten by white troops.[60] Lt. Col. DeMaurice Moses – the black commanding officer of the lone unit with "all Negro" officers, the 207th – had also heard this story and had interviewed Brown. Lacking any evidence or corroborating testimony from sentries, MPs, or ambulance drivers, Moses argued that the soldier had experienced "a hallucination," based on a similar incident elsewhere. As for the practice of believing stories they had simply "thought up," Moses testified that he had "heard of such things before in colored people."[61] Another version of the rumor concerned a black soldier from the 503rd who came with the cadre from the Hawaiian Islands. When he tried to visit his wife at her job on post, whites supposedly barred him from entering the office:

> they started quarreling and she started to help him, then she was killed. . . . A couple days after, the MP's came and got him and took him away. Then he was killed.[62]

59. Testimony of Cpl. Thurman Utterback, INST, p. 47.
60. The *Tribune* reported the woman was "in delicate condition." Testimony of Lt. Joseph Taylor, p. 41; Pvt. Clyde Heyman, p. 45; Cpt. Jesse Moses, p. 43; Pvt. Calvin Brown, pp. 69–70, INST; "Alleged Attack on Negro Woman Causes Clash at Camp Stewart," ST, June 17, 1943.
61. In a similar vein, Nesbitt referred to men from the region as "the southern 'cullud' boys." Moses's black 1st lieutenant preferred the term "Negro" since "colored might put them in a class with the yellow and brown people." Lt. Col. DeMaurice Moses, INST, p. 72; Letter, George Nesbitt to NAACP, December 20, 1942, NAACP; Lt. William Taylor, p. 40, INST.
62. Cpl. Claudin Gillespie, INST, p. 100.

The investigators interviewed hospital and ambulance corps personnel, who said they had neither transported nor treated any such persons. A white officer stated that one of his unit's black sergeants was killed in an automobile accident on May 18; he was unmarried but had arrived in a cadre from the Hawaiian Islands. The camp's intelligence office reported that the rumored assault had in fact occurred at Fort Benning, Georgia.[63] In retrospect, it appears that the frequent mistreatment of soldiers' wives provided a fertile context for the rumor, the automobile accident contributed an account of a corpse, and the Fort Benning incident provided the narrative for the Camp Stewart version of the event.

In any case, the story had poisoned the atmosphere of the camp by June 9, which was an unexceptional day; nothing was noted by staff to indicate that serious trouble was imminent.[64] The flashpoint for the disturbance, Post Exchange No. 8, had been a black troop exchange until about three weeks before the incident, when black units were moved outward. Well before the changeover, black troops had repeatedly threatened and cursed the white civilian who managed the PX. They said "they would get me if they ever caught me on the outside," he later told investigators.[65] The white guard at the front door that Wednesday night thought he understood his orders: to let no black enlisted men into the exchange and to "see that everybody's buttons are buttoned when they come in." Black officers, he knew, were allowed to use the exchange, but the private mistakenly believed that noncommissioned officers were allowed access as well. At about 9:30 P.M., he let two black sergeants enter the shop. A black civilian female was dipping ice cream for a group of white soldiers, and the two soldiers asked to be served. She did not have time to respond before the white guard posted at the back door began "running the two colored soldiers out of the exchange." That guard told investigators that when he "told them in a nice way to get out," they did so without arguing. Neither of the guards were MPs.[66]

A few minutes later, Lieutenant Colonel Moses of the "all Negro" 207th stood on Worcester Avenue around 8th Street and encountered a column of about one hundred black men "in seemingly military formation" calling out for others to join them. Perhaps six carried rifles and

---

63. Lt. Col. Lawrence H. Calloway, pp. 104–5; Maj. Enis Scott, p. 60, INST.
64. Memorandum, Maj. Gen. Peterson to Lt. Gen. McNarney, IG-CS.
65. Indeed, a month earlier, Nesbitt had heard the aprochryphal story that the exchange manager had been beaten to death. Lt. Joseph D. Taylor, p. 41; Andrew Taylor, p. 4, INST; letter, George Nesbitt to NAACP, May 5, 1943, NAACP.
66. Pvt. Perry Bean, p. 15; Carolyn Gooden, p. 5; Sgt. Robert Dingerson, pp. 29–30, INST.

others wielded bayonets and clubs. He went to the head of the group and tried to stop them. "We're going to get him," some said, using obscene language; another yelled that they were "going to get the military police." Moses was pushed out of the way and they continued to march.[67] He ordered his executive officer to assemble his unit and organize enough men to intercept this group. One of his lieutenants, thinking the men unorganized, "just milling around and talking loudly," went to the head of the crowd but failed to disperse them. Most of the soldiers headed toward the regimental parade ground. When the lieutenant walked southeast to the PX and found the white 566th "standing to" with rifles and fixed bayonets, he asked its officers to disperse their unit.[68]

After telephoning the provost marshal to tell him that an armed "mob" was "out of control" and heading toward white troops on 6th Street, Moses returned to his battalion. The crowd was growing, and shouting soldiers streamed past his unit. Moses wanted them out of his area; he stationed officers on the street corners to make the soldiers move double-time past his hutments. The camp's intelligence officer drove to the exchange and learned of the crowd of black soldiers clamoring that "the whites are killing our women." As he tried to gather more information, a white captain rushed up to ask whether ammunition could be issued to his men. "The fireworks," another white exclaimed, "were about to open up right then."[69]

When Lieutenant Colonel Moses called at 9:45, Major Enis Scott, who as provost marshal headed the camp's MP detachment, assembled a riot squad of about twelve men and proceeded to the area of trouble. Two were on motorcycles, four – including Scott – in a jeep, and the others were in a station wagon. At Worcester Avenue between 8th and 9th streets, he found Moses and several of his officers among a crowd of some fifty black soldiers. Under the conditions, disarming the crowd seemed impossible. As more troops moved down Worcester to 9th Street, guards of the 207th tried to run them back, and officers continued to try to disperse the crowd across the drill field. A detachment of black military police arrived at this time. Scott asked Lieutenant Colonel Moses to leave his next senior officer in command and accompany him northeast on Worcester Avenue. They stopped in each battalion area

---

67. Lt. Col. DeMaurice Moses, INST, p. 64–65; Maj. Gen. to Lt. Gen. McNarney, p. 1, IG-CS.
68. Replacing white MPs with black MPs had helped defuse disturbances in the past. Lt. Col. DeMaurice Moses, p. 65; Lt. William Taylor, p. 39, INST.
69. Lt. Col. DeMaurice Moses, p. 65; "Summary of Information" from Lt. Withers, exhibit A-2, pp. 1–2; memorandum, Clarence F. Murray to Commanding General, 4th Service Command, INST.

and ordered officers to drive all soldiers from the streets and direct them to their hutments.[70] Moses later recalled that there were very few white officers present at the time; those available seemed to be afraid to reenter the battery area. Some men broke and ran to an open area between 9th and 10th streets, and the MPs arrested three or four of them. Scott's assistant, Cpt. William Black, started to the stockade with these prisoners in a staff car, and the motorcycle police returned to their patrol. Moses, Scott, and the remaining MPs continued toward 12th Street.[71]

Pvt. Travis Perkins of the black 458th believed that the military police started the gunfire. Having just heard the rumor, he recalled watching the "noise and trouble" at PX No. 8 with five others when they heard a single shot fired. The crowd had grown to fifty or sixty unarmed soldiers, he said, when an MP truck stopped and asked for directions. As a black "noncom" walked to the back of the truck to speak with the MPs, one of them fired a shot. Perkins and his comrades ran back to their battery area, took the keys to the rifle racks from the noncoms, and armed themselves with ammunition gained by breaking into the battalion supply office.[72] In at least one battalion, the key to the ammunition room hung on the wall of the battery. Many of the rifles fired by the soldiers were routinely left in their care as part of their training.[73]

Shortly before 10:00 the mob dispersed, and for perhaps thirty minutes the area was quiet. Moses' officers had secured the racial frontier separating black and white units, and no one was left on the street around 9th and Worcester. By 10:30, however, another crowd had gathered at the corner of 12th and Worcester; one group crossed the firebreak between 9th and 10th on the southwest side of the avenue. Again, in what may have been a signal or a provocative act, one of them fired a rifle into the air, then ran through the barracks area.[74] Scott, circling the area in his jeep, also remembered hearing shots from the vicinity of

---

70. Major Scott, a peacetime employee of the Agriculture Department, was not a graduate of the Provost Marshal General School and had no previous police experience. Maj. Enis Scott, p. 55–6; Lt. William Taylor, pp. 39–40, INST.

71. Capt. William Black, p. 62; Lt. Col. DeMaurice Moses, p. 65, INST.

72. Witnesses associated soldiers with the distinctive reports of rifles, officers with pistols, and MPs with pistols or submachine guns. See, for example, Pvt. Travis Perkins, p. 90, INST.

73. As one officer put it, the best way to instruct men in the use of rifles "is to practically have them live with the gun . . . in this way they get over their fear of firearms." Pvt. Travis Perkins, pp. 89–90; Cpl. Ashield Watt, p. 96; Lt. Col. Albert Baron, p. 44, INST.

74. Lt. Daniel Hager, pp. 11–12; Lt. William Taylor, p. 40; Capt. Frederick Quist, pp. 34–5, INST.

the 100th or 538th at the time. He was first fired on at 12th and Worcester; sheets of tracer bullets then rose from the parade ground, and general firing began.[75]

Another version of the arrival of Scott's unit and the start of the fight came from one of Moses' officers, who saw motorcycle police arrive at 8th and Worcester, and then heard pistol shots in rapid succession. From a ditch he had entered for safety, he saw a jeep, apparently Scott's, arrive and fire a .45 caliber machine gun at his position.[76] At about this time, Scott sent Moses back to his unit in the station wagon and ordered a white lieutenant with three men to walk to the 207th and meet the vehicle there. Someone yelled from the adjoining barracks area: "They are military policemen – let 'em have it." The men tried to crawl to safety, but Pvt. Ronnie Lindsey was shot in the neck.[77]

Capt. Frederick Quist of the 100th heard this gunfire and believed that it was returned by military police near the corner of 9th and Worcester.[78] Moses also heard these shots, and drove the loaned MP station wagon south to the 207th, where he found his battalion under control. When several white military policemen told him that one of their men was wounded in the field across from his area, Moses and his men made their way into the firebreak just inside the corner of 9th and Worcester. As hidden soldiers opened fire on them, Moses identified himself and told the insurgents that he intended to retrieve the wounded man. The group then carried the bleeding MP to their own dispensary, where they laid him on a table. The MP was dead within minutes. Since ambulances were unable to retrieve the soldier, Moses and his men carried the body to the camp hospital.[79]

Capt. William Black and his prisoners were in a staff car traveling across 9th Street when he saw an MP "carry-all" that had turned over in a ditch, with three or four military policemen huddled nearby. Gunfire erupted again, and Black ordered the prisoners into the ditch, where the group spent two hours under fire, trapped halfway across the parade ground. Unarmed, according to Black, they formed a semicircle to "keep from being shot at from both directions."[80] Part of the firefight across

75. Maj. Enis Scott, pp. 56–7, INST.
76. Lt. William H. Taylor, p. 40, INST.
77. Scott escorted a full civilian bus out of the area to a gate and remained there until the disturbance ended. Maj. Enis Scott, pp. 56–7; Maj. Gen. Peterson to Lt. Gen. Mc-Narney, p. 2, IG-CS.
78. Capt. Frederick Quist, p. 55, INST.
79. Lt. Col. DeMaurice Moses, p. 66, INST.
80. Capt. William Black, p. 63, INST. This may have been the group that had lost Pvt.

the darkened parade ground appears to have been between black units mistakenly convinced that they were under attack by military police or soldiers, for some troops had fled into the surrounding woods in fear, some had armed themselves with the purpose of seeking revenge, while others had formed firing positions to defend their area. A number of witnesses, including a captain of the 100th, reported that around midnight there was sustained fire from just east of the area occupied by the 846th and 484th; as tracers tore across the parade ground toward him, soldiers at 9th and Worcester returned fire.[81]

The camp was engulfed by the tumult of battle. The pounding of night firing on a nearby practice range continued uninterrupted during the incident, and gas alarms rang out in many battalion areas as well. Encamped to the north, on the other side of the parade ground, Lt. Col. Albert Baron, commanding officer of the 458th AAA Battalion, awoke to the sound of shots shortly after 10:00 and moved toward a group of men under trees across Murray Avenue until someone shouted for him to halt. One yelled, "Don't let the Colonel make a fool out of you. He'll take your rifles and then call back the military police." Other voices urged the soldiers to hold their fire, and the men finally allowed Baron to approach. He asked them what was wrong.

> They told me that if my people were being treated like theirs were I would understand better, that I wouldn't like to get shot up by miliary police either and that I would want to protect myself too.

The soldiers asked whether the story of the murdered soldier and wife was true, and Baron immediately called the provost marshal's office and was assured that it was not. When he returned to the area, the men were on the floor of their hutments, "clutching their rifles as a defense feature." They claimed that MPs – firing into their area from Nile Avenue – had forced them to arm themselves. Baron then watched a torrent of shots from both sides of the street fall upon a military police detail driving down Murray Avenue.[82]

This detail was led by Sgt. Charles Almand, who entered the northern section of the camp in a station wagon with eight men; he trailed two

---

Lindsey, and then had retrieved the station wagon from Moses at the 207th. None of these men were interviewed by investigators.

81. Investigators learned that many blacks feared "an actual attack on the colored camp by Military Police." Memorandum, Col. C. H. Day to Commanding General, ASF, August 11, 1943, INST, p. 1; Lee, *The Employment of Negro Troops*, pp. 370–3; Capt. Frederick Quist, p. 34, INST.
82. Lt. Col. Albert Baron, pp. 19–21, INST.

motorcycle riders from the previous detail. Proceeding southwest, the convoy traveled five or six blocks in a storm of tracer bullets. Suddenly, at the south end of Murray Avenue, "there was a terrific barrage of fire" directly aimed at the convoy. Almand cut off his lights and accelerated; he knew that if he had stopped they would have been killed. The convoy sped for the station hospital, where doctors found that Almand and three others had been shot.[83] All of the injured men were in this detail.[84] None of them had any machine or submachine guns, Almand said, and only one had fired a single shot at the troops. Two members of the 458th, however, reported seeing shots fired from these cars. Capt. Philip Dreissigacker called the ambush of the MP convoy around 10:35 "the biggest volley of shots" he heard, but saw the MPs return fire. A private also saw shots fired from the cars.[85]

After that barrage, firing was sporadic. Around 1:00 A.M., General Spiller sent two white anti-aircraft battalions with half-tracks armed with .50 caliber guns down Harmon Avenue to disperse the black troops from the drill field. After first patrolling the roads, the armor went through the fields and flushed a few men who ran toward the area of the 100th Battalion. After these vehicles arrived, the shooting ceased and the camp was pacified.[86]

One investigator reported that between five and six thousand rounds of .30 caliber ball and tracer ammunition were fired, while another estimated that six hundred to eight hundred rounds were fired. Although much of the gunfire was in the air, numerous vehicles were damaged, including one civilian bus whose driver was slightly injured.[87] Witnesses disagreed about whether the MPs were firing their guns. Baron testified that three of his white officers witnessed MPs shooting from their vehicles on Murray Avenue. He thought the police started the exchange by firing into the air. Scott, on the other hand, assured investigators that only three rounds were fired by MPs during the entire incident; his men, he reported, had checked out and checked in their ammunition. One

83. Sgt. Charles Almand, pp. 79–80, INST.
84. Isolated later press reports listed two MP deaths. The discrepancy possibly concerned Sgt. John McEachern, who was in serious condition for several days. "MP Killed When Negro Troops Riot At Camp Stewart," Columbia, S.C. *State*, June 11, 1943; "Charge Soldiers Overworked at Camp Stewart," August 18, 1943, Atlanta *Daily World*.
85. Sgt. Charles Almand, p. 80; Capt. Philip Dreissigacker, p. 82; Pfc. Melvin Peterson, p. 87, INST.
86. Lt. Daniel Hager, p. 12; Lt. Col. DeMaurice Moses, p. 56, INST.
87. Memorandum, Maj. Gen. Peterson to Lt. Gen. McNarney, p. 2, IG-CS; "Report of Investigation," June 20, 1943, INST, p. 2; Lee, *The Employment of Negro Troops*, pp. 370–3.

Army report concluded that indeed three rounds of ammunition had been fired by the military police. In at least one battalion, "some sly comments" greeted the official announcement that the military police had fired only one shot.[88]

The Investigations

Investigators quickly learned that the outbreak was the culmination of a series of troubling incidents of disobedience. One officer, asked about disparaging remarks by white soldiers about black troops, replied that such comments would have been due

> to the fact that the negroes had done something to have them uttered. Some had ganged up on guards at the post exchange and on other men at various times. The men fear to walk the streets at night.[89]

A major in the same unit revealed that his battalion's intelligence officer quickly ordered his men to arm themselves on June 9; since there had been previous trouble, he had permission to do so. Longtime veteran James Hill referred to a confrontation at the gate involving members of the 100th – which required a machine gun as a solution.[90]

He was apparently referring to an incident on April 14, when, around 10:30 P.M., some black soldiers from the 100th refused to line up at Gate No. 3 to have their passes inspected. They began pushing and shoving the guard, who fired his gun into the air to halt four soldiers who ignored his orders to return to the gate. As the soldiers continued to jostle the guard, he was joined by four more MPs brandishing clubs and guns, who lined the soldiers against a fence before taking several to the stockade. Minutes later, black officers arrived to curse the guard and accuse him of shooting at their men. The officers warned that "the soldiers would treat the MPs the way the Georgians treat their men sometimes."[91] After the incident, as Hill told it, the black officers instructed their men that MPs

> would beat hell out of any colored soldier when caught by himself and they took their lives in their own hands when they left the post and that the civil police would back up the military police.

"That naturally started some agitation," as Hill put it.[92]

88. Lt. Col. Albert Baron, pp. 21–4, 26; Maj. Enis Scott, p. 60; "Report of Investigation," June 20, 1943, INST, p. 2.
89. Lt. Seymour Silber, p. 63, INST.
90. Maj. Calvin P. Sandifer, p. 54; Pvt. James Hill, p. 32, INST.
91. Memorandum, Pfc. Bernard C. Goleyzynski, April 15, 1943, Exhibit C, INST, pp. 5–6.
92. Pvt. James Hill, p. 32, INST.

Attempting to defuse this tension, the camp command and individual guards relaxed white oversight somewhat. In late April, a Caucasian military policeman at Gate No. 4 saluted officers as usual when several batteries of troops came through, but when he heard a soldier say "there is another Dog damn mother fucking M.P. [*sic*]" he ignored the remark and returned to his booth. Minutes later, another soldier from the 100th taunted him: "come out of there, Mickey Mouse." He did not salute any more officers of the unit and, when the troops returned en masse about forty-five minutes later, he remained in the booth so as to avoid further trouble.[93]

More disturbing still were two attempts to incite crowds. On the night of April 22, a large crowd of black soldiers gathered around Service Club No. 2, mistakenly believing that tickets to a separate dance entitled them to attend this event. While three black MPs attempted to secure the area, soldiers began removing screens from the building's windows and climbing into the club. MPs forced one solider into a station wagon, but no blows were struck. An hour later, a soldier ran through the area of the 100th, yelling for the unit to turn out to avenge the beating of one of their men at the service club. Although two lieutenants addressed the men and told them to return to their areas, a group of soldiers stood in the road cursing and taunting the MPs, one of whom was struck by a thrown bottle. The arrival of five additional white MPs worsened matters, for the crowd refused to move and began throwing rocks and cement. A white lieutenant ordered the military police to retire and instructed six black officers to direct the men back to their area. The MPs' commanding officer concluded that withdrawing whites from the situation was a sensible response given the skills and goals of the radicals.

> It is apparent that any action on the part of the military police in any situation is passed on to the 100th CA (AA) Regiments. The 100th CA (AA) seems to have agitators that urge the other soldiers to action.

The MP commander suggested that black units furnish a guard force for such occasions sufficient to prevent unauthorized soldiers from gathering.[94]

---

93. Memorandum, Pfc. James Fleming, April 28, 1943, Exhibit C, INST, p. 3.
94. According to the Army's review, the camp's MP detachment was neither better nor worse than similar units at other stations in its "handling of colored soldiers." The board noted that a "special resentment" toward the MPs was common, since, "to the Negro soldiers, the Military Police represents the restraining authority with which he has direct contact and against which resentment can be directed." Memorandum, T. M. Ackley, Captain, Commanding Officer, M. P. Detachment, Camp Stewart, April

Less than a week before the insurrection, a near-riot occurred at PX No. 8 so similar to the actual outbreak that it may have been a rehearsal for a later mission. At about 8:30 P.M. on May 21, MPs received a call that there was a riot at the exchange, where an "alert squad" of police found a large crowd of both black and white soldiers. A number of blacks had tried to force themselves into the PX, despite being barred by the white guard. Just before the attack, two black officers asked the guard who the officer of the day was and whether he had live ammunition in his rifle. He pulled the bolt of his rifle back to show that the chamber was empty. Soldiers immediately seized him and tried to take his rifle and bayonet. The black officers already on the scene calmed the men "and seemed quite friendly with them," departing in the company of the three GIs. Twenty-five or thirty soldiers also were standing just north of the PX. Three were armed with rifles, and, as a white officer approached, they ran. The camp's director of intelligence made extensive but unsuccessful efforts to identify these men.[95]

A board of officers headed by Gen. Samuel McCroskey immediately convened to investigate the June 9 incident. Lieutenant Colonel Moses, who had acquitted himself with such distinction during the uprising and had rescued the mortally wounded MP, was the lone nonwhite member of the board of inquiry. The board acknowledged that the violence grew in part from long-standing frustration and resentment within the black regiments. The surrounding communities mistreated the soldiers, and Camp Stewart largely reflected and institutionalized that harsh discriminatory treatment. Despite these findings, the board's recommendations were limited to reforming enforcement and disciplinary systems. Because the "average negro soldier's meager education, superstition, imagination, and excitability" made him prone to a "mass state of mind," the Army's coercive system required reform. In addition to bringing charges against individuals suspected of criminal activity, the board recommended that the Army supply better machinery for ridding itself of agitators; that the camp plan "additional special training in the handling of colored soldiers" for the military police; and that the 458th Battalion be disbanded.[96] This last recommendation seems especially at odds with the

23, 1943; INST, Exhibit C, pp. 1–2; memorandum, Col. C. H. Day, AGD, to Commanding General, Army Service Forces, August 11, 1943, INST, p. 2.

95. The black officers claimed not to have thought of asking the soldiers' names. Summary of Information, Lt. G. M. Hill, Jr., Director of Intelligence Division, C-2, June 3, 1943, Exhibit H, INST.

96. The Anti-Aircraft Command and Army Ground Forces rejected the recommendation that the 458th be disbanded. Lee, *The Employment of Negro Troops*, pp. 370–3; memorandum, Col. C. H. Day to Commanding General, ASF, August 11, 1943, INST.

account of the unit given by its commanding officer, who described the fear animating the "defensive posture" of the soldiers. But the inspector general's report found that this unit was the "most seriously involved" organization. Worse still, noncommissioned officers proved "worthless" in helping to bring the men under control. Apparently, the 100th Regiment and the units to which the cadre of the 369th were attached were no more seriously involved than many others. While practically all the black organizations – except Moses' 207th Battalion – contributed personnel to the incident, it was nearly impossible to identify actual shooters.[97]

The case of Cpl. Israel Reed reveals some of these difficulties. Reed was one of at least fourteen soldiers arrested and charged with crimes under the Articles of War. His older brother Robert, a member of the Washington, D.C., police force, arrived to aid his brother's defense, appealing to the NAACP for help in finding an attorney, preferably a southern white.[98] The charges, however, were limited to willful disobedience of a superior officer and being unlawfully armed. According to the charges, a white lieutenant and a black private ordered a fleeing black soldier to halt, then chased and caught the soldier bearing a loaded rifle. This occurred in a dark area, but the arresting officer claimed that he saw the soldier's face – and noticed his corporal's chevrons – when they passed a lighted area during the chase. Reed, who was not arrested at the time and who was not identified until nine days later, responded under oath that he had remained in barracks from the beginning of the incident until 6:00 A.M. the next day, and three fellow soldiers confirmed this account. Although Dr. Gilbert had recommended a white attorney "as straight on the Negro question" as a Georgian could be, NAACP involvement in the case would not be necessary. On August 4, Reed was charged; the next day, after reading letters concerning his background, the court-martial found him not guilty and released him. The soldier thought he had received a fair trial.[99]

97. As had been the case elsewhere, noncoms and sentries either could not or would not identify culprits. Memorandum, Maj. Gen. Peterson to Lt. Gen. McNarney, IG-CS, pp. 2–3.
98. Letter, Robert Jerome Reed to Leslie S. Perry, July 11, 1943, NAACP.
99. Memorandum, Leslie Perry to Walter White, Judge Hastie, and Thurgood Marshall, July 31, 1943, NAACP. Col. Gross spoke bitterly to the elder Reed about the incident: "We could have gone over there into their area and shot every one of them to hell (pause) but that is unthinkable. Do you know that one white man was killed and four injured while not a single Negro got a scratch on him?" Letter, Thurgood Marshall to Frank Reeves, August 6, 1943, NAACP; letter, Robert J. Reed to Thurgood Marshall, August 10, 1943, NAACP.

Specific punishments would be less useful than general directives, however, and discussions of the proper policy response to the June 9 action diverged according to the interpretation of the event itself. The critical question was whether the insurrection was organized. Whites generally believed that it was; blacks did not. Black GI Hill, for example, called the incident a surprise: "it must have just sprung up." Lieutenant Colonel Moses agreed, since most of the men did not even know what caused the incident; "they all sort of groped their way around. . . ."[100] Ochs, on the other hand, when asked if there was an organized effort to "excite" the black soldiers at the camp, replied, "Yes sir, definitely." Three months earlier, with the arrival of the 100th and the 369th,

> all of a sudden there seemed to be dissatisfaction and discontent among the colored troops, particularly those who had served in northern posts and camps. That looked, in my opinion, as if there was a concerted effort at this time on the part of some organization to demand equal rights in the State of Georgia.[101]

Capt. Philip Dreissigacker of the 458th reported that "some of the boys say it's been a build-up of incidents apparently pushed by some leaders. They admitted it was not a spontaneous affair." Baron also thought the insurrection was planned. The unrest "hasn't just sprung up," he said; it accompanied the arrival of the 100th CA. His unit included a few men drawn from that outfit. "This is the result of subversive activities. I don't have any doubt about it."[102]

These varying appraisals of the problem corresponded to different solutions. Moses's black assistant, Lieutenant Taylor, for example, thought the situation could be improved by throwing open the entire camp to both races without restriction. According to Colonel Ochs, on the other hand, equal rights had already been extended to blacks "so far as could be done considering the safety of all concerned." Given their location, any further relaxation of segregation would have caused "continuous riots and disturbances." Separate latrines and post stockades were necessary, he believed, because of the number of white soldiers from the South. Again, "constant irritation and disorder" would result if they were combined. Asked if he thought the military police should be "doubled up" so that a white and a black soldier patrolled as a unit, Ochs replied that it would be unsuccessful. Taylor was asked the same question and replied affirmatively; "the negro would then feel that he is represented."[103] Asked if the

100. Pvt. James Hill, p. 33; Lt. Col. DeMaurice Moses, p. 68, INST.
101. Col. William Ochs, p. 74, INST.
102. Capt. Philip Dreissigacker, p. 82; Lt. Col. Albert Baron, p. 22, INST.
103. Col. William Ochs, p. 77, 75; Lt. William Taylor, p. 40, INST.

Army should consider reforming the military police force at Stewart, Ochs said no. The problem was that the camp held "about ten times" too many black troops.

> I don't believe that any human being can solve the problem until they are sent out, or at least until a portion of them are sent out.[104]

Other whites, like Baron, preferred the same solution:

> We are packed, have orders from the Port, and we should carry them out. I think that would take care of all the malcontents I may have in my outfit.[105]

On June 22, the Fourth Service Command in Atlanta transmitted to Camp Stewart officials a copy of the inspector general (IG)'s report. Their attention was directed to its recommendations regarding the collection and evaluation of rumors, the careful selection of officers commanding black troops of black NCOs, and other security measures, such as rumor suppression and weapons control.[106] Shortly thereafter, Col. Felix Gross, executive officer of the training center, reported the inauguration of a new intelligence system acting at the unit level to relay all relevant information to commanders and to "collect, evaluate, disseminate and if necessary to suppress rumors."[107] The IG found that General Spiller had tried to improve basic conditions while monitoring certain units. Since this had proved ineffective, officials considered whether Spiller ought not to have taken more drastic actions, such as storing and guarding unassigned weapons and ammunition and keeping armored forces prepared for prompt action. While such action probably would have prevented the incident, the IG concluded, it would have indicated that the commanding general had lost confidence in these units and would have seriously damaged morale and subjected the camp "to severe criticism by organizations interested in the welfare and development of colored troops." Spiller therefore was spared from criticism and disciplinary action.[108]

At the end of July, officers of Anti-Aircraft Command Headquarters in Richmond completed an investigation and inspection of current conditions at the camp. They found that Spiller was personally supervising

104. Col. William Ochs, p. 77, INST.
105. Lt. Col. Albert Baron, p. 28, INST.
106. Memorandum, Major General William Bryden, Commanding, Headquarters Fourth Service Command, to Commanding General, AATC, Camp Stewart, June 22, 1943, IG-CS.
107. Memorandum, Col. Felix Gross, C.A.C., to Commanding Officer, Service Command, ASF, Camp Stewart, June 29, 1943, ibid.
108. Memorandum, Maj. Gen. Peterson to Lt. Gen. McNarney, IG-CS, pp. 5–6.

all black battalions and had held frequent conferences with brigade, group, and battalion commanders, during which he stressed the special responsibilities implied by their assignments. Several officers who failed to demonstrate the character necessary for service with black troops also had been transferred. In addition, "the required furniture" in the living rooms of the two black guest houses had been furnished and a comprehensive athletic program was in place. Attention had been paid to the activities of the black hostess and to the grounds and maintenance of a service club. Latrines, buildings, and recreational facilities – while still segregated – were no longer reserved for the exclusive use of either race.

The Service Command also increased the number of black Military Police from eleven enlisted men to one officer and thirty enlisted men. The inspectors also reported "close coordination" between intelligence sections of the Service Command and the camp, in part due to the assignment by the command of two black Military Intelligence Division enlisted men to Camp Stewart. These "operators" were to report to training center headquarters all information they obtained regarding individuals whose proclivities tended to incite unrest. The agents had already produced valuable information, including reports that had led to the transfer of "suspected" personnel to other outfits at the camp and elsewhere. There were now clear indications that "discipline, morale, and efficiency" had all improved since the incident.[109]

The Educational Program

Indoctrination programs supplemented the policing, intelligence, and facilities initiatives. In July, Nesbitt forwarded to Walter White copies of the camp's plans for a black troop "educational program."[110] At a July conference, E. A. Stockton, Jr., the new commanding general of the camp, met with brigade, group, and battalion commanders, and instructed the latter to conduct a series of educational conferences with officers and NCOs of black units. In turn, battery commanders would meet with and instruct black enlisted personnel. The goal of the program was to teach the soldiers to understand and respect the Articles of War, to avoid rumor mongering and a "chip on the shoulder attitude," and

109. Memorandum, Brigadier General C. V. R. Schuyler, Headquarters Anti-Aircraft Command, to Commanding General, Army Ground Forces, Army War College, "Subject: Investigation and Inspection Conducted at Camp Stewart," July 23, 1943, ibid., pp. 1–3.

110. Letter, George Nesbitt to Walter White, undated, NAACP. Nesbitt apparently feared that his correspondence might be intercepted, for he asked White to write to him using handwritten envelopes bearing no return address.

to stop "babying himself with the belief that every little inconvenience he suffers is racial discrimination." The conferences would repeat every eight weeks and greet any new arrival of African American troops.

The plan included an outline of material suggested for use by white officers of black units. "This is a war of production," it began. "We must develop realistic ways of preventing manpower waste in our Army."[111] While Hitler and Goebbels believed that the United States could be defeated through adroit propaganda and by encouraging brutalities that set one group of Americans against another, since it was "perennially on the brink of revolution," the best defense against this strategy was simply to examine one's mind for unreasonable prejudices.

> A man who can wear the uniform of our Army is not a "wop," not a "spic," not a "hunky," not a "kike," not a "mick," not a "Chink," not a "nigger." He is a soldier, an element of fighting manpower, an important cog in our war machine. . . .

The instructions repeatedly challenged the "good officer" to anticipate and prevent race troubles. Toward this end, he must accept his troops' limitations. Since test scores revealed that black soldiers "have had less opportunity for education and are consequently less able to assimilate knowledge rapidly and accurately," the effective officer must be extremely patient, as "some Negroes are more like children than adults, in their degree of emotional development." He should firmly discourage any inflammatory talk and point out that *"winning the war is all that matters now."* Since "mob violence" develops and spreads very quickly, "a good officer *smells trouble before it happens, doesn't get excited about it, and uses plain, everyday common sense to prevent it.*" The emphasis on prevention rather than reaction was compatible with innovations in the use of intelligence techniques, since now "you must know what your men are doing and thinking all the time." The document suggested constant observation on the part of the officer, vigilance with respect to arms and ammunition, as well as the use of the S-2, or intelligence, section to organize a countersubversive system by selecting patriotic men in the unit and secretly instructing them to report on developments in their units. In addition to stopping rumors before they spread, the instructions recommended developing a standard operating procedure in case of unrest. The officers should explain offenses under military law in a simple but thorough way. Once such instructions were

111. "Suggested Material for Inclusion in Talks to Officers of Negro Organizations," NAACP, emphasis always in original.

clear to the men, "let punishment for deliberate offenders be swift, certain, and adequate."[112]

The education memo also outlined two talks on military and civilian law. While American laws and policemen "keep everything pretty quiet and peaceful" at home, protecting individuals from those who would otherwise "go ahead and do what they please . . . walking all over someone else's rights," only war is able to "make criminal *nations* behave."[113] If Hitler should win the war, the text explained, blacks would be plunged into a new form of slavery far worse than that found in antebellum times. "So the Negro really has something to fight for." Before fighting together, however, to "bring law and order and justice back to the world, we must first learn to obey the laws ourselves." Some soldiers might argue that certain familiar rights were now denied to them.

> But think for a moment . . . Wars have been fought in this world for thousands of years. From all this fighting, soldiers and generals alike have found that lawless and disorderly mobs can only expect to be chased down and killed.

The instructions then considered several violations of military law and their corresponding punishment, including desertion and absence without leave, for which a soldier would face prison or "may even be shot or hanged." They also would be severely punished for saying disrespectful things "to shake people's faith in" President Roosevelt, the vice-president, a member of Congress, the governor of a state, or a state legislator. A similar fate awaited one who was disrespectful toward a superior officer. In discussing sedition, the document again ascribed disruptions in mines, factories, and army camps to rumors spread by "enemy spies and agents."[114] The soldier who fights his comrades-in-arms was a traitor, and "richly deserves the hang-man's rope he is sure to get." The instructions also discussed other "war offenses," such as murder, rape, mayhem, and arson. If a soldier is a good American, he

---

112. Such arguments were utilized before the release of these formal instructions. On the day after the insurrection, Lt. Col. Baron assembled his battalion in the recreation hall, where he explained the 67th and 68th Articles of War and told the men that the rumor was a hoax, "done probably by German or Jap money." Lt. Col. Albert Baron, p. 22, INST.

113. "Suggested Material for Inclusion in Talk on Military and Civil Law to Soldiers of Negro Organizations," NAACP.

114. Repeated assertions of Axis involvement contradicted the facts of the Stewart case as well as the findings of the War Department's Intelligence Division, which concluded as early as June 1942 that no evidence existed of activity by such agents in the armed forces. Lee, *The Employment of Negro Troops*, p. 362.

will respect and obey the law; otherwise, "you can look forward to long, hard, and dreary punishment."

The second suggested talk notified the soldiers that the commanding general at Camp Stewart and his staff guaranteed that there would be no discrimination there.[115] Still,

> a good soldier doesn't have time to fool with his home town politics, or to go around telling other soldiers how the country ought to be run. Any question about white people and Black people will never be settled by barracks talk. *Let's forget these things for the time being, buckle down to real soldiering, and win this war.*

The lecture also instructed the men to cooperate with the camp military police. Noting that American GIs in England, Sicily, and Africa are lectured on how to adapt to foreign people and their different habits and customs, the lecture reminded the black soldier that while he was in Georgia, he must obey the state laws.[116] Advice was offered on comportment:

> Be polite and respectful in any talk you may have with white people. Don't try to start conversations with white strangers. Stay out of white places, and sit where you are supposed to sit on trains and buses. Above all, don't say or do anything that somebody might take as an insult to any white or colored woman. In short, remember your manners.[117]

Many of these same themes appeared in the Army Service Forces Manual M 5, issued in October 1944, particularly the emphasis on the enemy's skill at exploiting racial divisions in Europe and Asia. The Nazis, according to the manual, believed that the American mobilization would be crippled by group conflict. These same arguments against race prejudice were reprinted yet again in an Army orientation fact sheet in May 1945.[118]

---

115. "Suggested Material for Inclusion in Talk on Military and Civil Law to Soldiers of Negro Organizations, No. 2," NAACP, emphasis always in original.

116. This advice is very similar to instructions distributed to a nonwhite British colonial regiment in 1944, which read in part: "The U.S.A. is divided roughly into two zones, North and South separated by a line known as the Mason Dixon line. We are going to NORTH VIRGINIA which is South of this line." Memorandum, 2nd Service Command, ASF, Subject: British Indian Troops," June 16, 1944, OF 4245-G, OPM, COFEP, War Dept., 1944–5, FDRL.

117. This directive was obtained and excerpted by *People's Voice*, which condemned the document. " 'Education for Negro Troops' Pamphlet Issued at Camp Stewart Is Contradictory," *People's Voice*, August 28, 1943.

118. "Prejudice! – Roadblock to Progress," Army Orientation Fact Sheet number 70, Washington, D.C., War Department, May 5, 1945, p. 1, Minorities-Army Talk, John Ohly papers, HSTL.

In addition to the lectures, resources were also dedicated to black soldier recreation. A new USO building opened in Savannah on October 10, and, perhaps in an attempt to recapture the spirit of "Camp Stewart on Parade," the No. 3 band from the base played several numbers at the ceremony.[119] Three weeks later, the staff of the older black USO joined with the service club director to present the great contralto, Marian Anderson, at a post theater. Her appearance on October 31, according to the *Tribune*, "definitely boosted the morale of the soldiers very high."[120] Soldiers also cheered Sgt. Joe Louis, heavyweight champion of the world, and Cpl. Sugar Ray Robinson when they visited the base on December 12 for a one-day boxing exhibition.[121] It was the thirteenth of nineteen visits scheduled for Army camps in the southern states covered by the Fourth Service Command.[122] Finally, in January 1944, the Army dedicated a new federal recreation building, operated by the USO for black troops, in nearby Hinesville, Georgia.[123] But such improvements did not reach the camp's most troublesome unit; the 100th departed from San Francisco on November 18, 1943, to serve without incident in Australia and New Guinea.[124]

---

119. "Capacity Crowd Attends Opening W. Broad St. USO," ST, October 14, 1943.
120. "Marian Anderson Thrills Crowd at Auditorium," ST, November 4, 1943.
121. The previous May, when the camp's black and white light heavyweight boxing champs were introduced to a cheering, segregated crowd at the camp's sports arena, someone yelled, "How in the hell you gonna have two champions?" When the crowd roared in approval – "Let 'em fight!" – the confused announcer rushed to ringside to consult camp officials, who flatly rejected the idea. Letter, George Nesbitt to NAACP, May 9, 1943, NAACP.
122. It is unclear whether Louis was allowed to box white soldiers at Stewart, as he sometimes did elsewhere. Louis was the archetypical "race hero," who was permitted to "beat the white man at his own game," as he did in 1938 with the German Max Schmeling in a fight with clear racial and ideological overtones. He appeared on the front page of the Chicago *Defender* no less than eighty times between 1933 and 1938; a distant second in such media prominence was Haile Selassie, with twenty-four appearances. "To Be at Camp Stewart January 12," ST, December 30, 1943; Lee, *The Employment of Negro Troops*, p. 307; J. G. St. Clair Drake and Horace R. Cayton, *Black Metropolis: A Study of Negro Life in a Northern City*, Vol. II, New York, Harper & Row, 1962 (1945), pp. 391, 403; Harvard Sitkoff, *A New Deal for Blacks: The Emergence of Civil Rights as a National Issue*, New York, Oxford, 1978, p. 299.
123. "New Federal Recreation Building at Hinesville," ST, January 6, 1944.
124. Other battalions listed as potentially disruptive – the 492nd and the 503rd – departed for overseas theatres in early 1944. The 458th did not see action overseas. Stanton, *World War II Order of Battle*, pp. 466, 486, 500–2.

Conclusion

The Camp Stewart incident was representative of a new pattern in military racial violence: the battle occurred inside a camp, between identifiable military units, and was launched by black soldiers. According to a 1945 memorandum by the adjutant general on "typical disruptions," the incident stemmed from the arrival of the 100th Coast Artillery Regiment, composed of many northern blacks who resented their transfer to Georgia, and the 369th Regiment of New York, which arrived shortly afterwards. The report listed the movement of black troops as one of the five primary causes of such disturbances, since a "wide gulf existed . . . in the treatment of the Negro in the several sections of the United States."[125] Since this was as close as any Army analyst would come to ascribing the troubles to segregation and discrimination, substantive reform would not be the primary policy response. Increasingly, however, Army officials associated Jim Crow and coercion with two types of costs. First, the black press was quick to publicize such violent incidents, and the subsequent uproar weakened the fragile alliance between the administration and racial advancement organizations. Second, the camp command understood that the use of force by military police was often a prime irritant in tense encounters. The expansion of the black military police force can thus be viewed as an effort to improve the efficiency of policing systems. This reform also was an example of substantive amelioration, since it opened relatively high-status assignments to blacks, and it was also highly symbolic. Thus, not only were policies more complex and sophisticated than they had been in 1941, but the Army was often able to satisfy several goals at once with these later responses to friction.

The incident also demonstrates why this democratic war did not simply promote egalitarian reforms as Myrdal expected. Militant blacks did not automatically pursue formal or peaceful methods of reform. Commenting on the soldiers' motives, a columnist for the Chicago *Defender* wrote on June 19:

> Mainly, their bitterness adds up to – "I would just as soon die fightin' for democracy right here in Georgia . . . Kill a cracker in Mississippi or Germany, what's the difference!"[126]

125. The other four were: policing methods, lack of discipline, lack of recreational facilities, and the black press. Memorandum, Ground Adjutant General for Chief of Staff, U.S. Army, November 28, 1945, MacGregor and Nalty, eds., *Blacks in the Armed Forces*, vol. VII, pp. 110–11, 113.
126. This passage led J. Edgar Hoover to request that the Justice Department prosecute the paper for violating the Espionage Act; Assistant Attorney General Tom Clark replied that the column was legal. Washburn, *A Question of Sedition*, p. 187.

Such radical reactions to exclusion and discrimination actually called forth new forms of policing and monitoring, in addition to somewhat fairer policies and practices.

The Camp Stewart incident occurred at the midpoint of the war, in what Ulysses Lee called the "harvest of disorder" of the summer of 1943, after the effects of discrimination were well known, but before the Army had crafted a suitable set of responses. Black GIs resented the Army's equivocation precisely because they had directly felt its raw power.

> . . . of all the arms of government subject to condemnation for discrimination and segregation, the Army is least to be forgiven. It is without excuse because it is so powerful and assertive.[127]

In the first half of the war, Army policy had concentrated black soldiers in the southern states and had fashioned a fairly crude, coercion-intensive system to respond to the racial disturbances that inevitably followed. While tensions appeared to be widespread – between factions of blacks and between black soldiers and white civilians – violence occurred mainly at the physical frontiers of black-white relations, between black soldiers and white MPs. Army authorities gradually developed a varied set of responses to the violence, but refused to dismantle federal segregation. In the spring of 1943, for example, the War Department, through the adjutant general, directed camp authorities to implement a policy of equal access to base recreational facilities. By the end of the summer of 1943, however, planners had happened upon an especially attractive policy option: shipping black troops overseas. The central state successfully suppressed further rebellions in the Army mainly by sending the irritants abroad until the surrender of Japan in the summer of 1945 occasioned the rapid demobilization of the armed forces and lessened pressures for reform.

127. Letter, George Nesbitt to NAACP, May 9, 1943.

7

The Racial Politics of Urban
and Rural Unrest: Monitoring
Farms and Surveilling Cities

> Our plans for handling possible racial disturbances have two aspects: the
> administrative handling of tense situations before they reach the breaking
> point; and the assurance that prompt police action will put an end to actual
> disturbances as quickly as possible.
> Philleo Nash, Office of War Information, April 18, 1944[1]

The countryside and city streets are essential comparative touchstones
for an analysis of the relationship between manpower policies and race
tension, because these two settings employed the largest share of black
workers, and produced the most serious race violence during the war,
respectively. The accelerated development of a centralized system for
analyzing widespread urban violence is analyzed in the latter half of this
chapter. Constitutionally excluded from local police work and eager to
dedicate military manpower to other uses, central statesmen instead
patched together a network of surveillance and monitoring initiatives,
consolidating similar projects in the FBI and in various branches of the
armed forces, in hopes of targeting trouble spots for ameliorative and
police action. As in the Army, the mobilization caused a permanent
increase in surveillance capacity.[2] An analysis of this sphere of advisement between 1943 and 1944 demonstrates the policy effects of disorder
and a presidential campaign in turn.

The rural South, on the other hand, produced very little collective
violence despite accounting for three-quarters of the black labor force in

1. Memorandum, Philleo Nash to Jonathan Daniels, April 18, 1944, OWI Files No. 7,
   Box 29, papers of Philleo Nash, HSTL.
2. This is only appropriate for the president whose mastery at gathering, guarding, and
   using information prompted Neustadt to describe him as "instinctively an intelligence
   operative." Richard E. Neustadt, *Presidential Power and the Modern Presidents: The
   Politics of Leadership from Roosevelt to Reagan*, New York, The Free Press, 1990,
   p. 145.

1940, including large numbers of majority black counties.[3] Farming employed a quarter of all black workers in 1944, the largest share of the nation's African American labor force. The uneasy and uneven social peace can be attributed in part to the extreme race hierarchy ruling the South's black belt counties, where white oligarchs and voters elected and retained the most reactionary and often disproportionately powerful congressional Democrats. Beyond the option of leaving the area, these geographically dispersed and politically powerless workers lacked any direct means with which to influence campaigns or threaten the mobilization. For the same reasons, socioeconomic advance seemed most unlikely in this sector. Wages, working conditions, and worker autonomy improved so rapidly, however, that it was the white farm owners who petitioned central authorities for relief in this case. The substantial material benefits – and additional power over local labor markets – that white landowners reaped from the war mobilization helped ease this race friction.

As in the other manpower spheres, serious race tension concerned central state officials. But in this case, it was the departure rather than the arrival of black workers that disturbed whites.[4] The availability of new jobs created a more competitive local labor market that freed many farmers from age-old sharecropping obligations. Surveying this newly energized black labor force moving out to exploit labor shortages nationwide or gleaning the local benefits of this migration, white landowners decried what they called a loss of field hand "efficiency." The central state's response to this friction was restrained, but by favoring whites, it followed the norm in a region where elites had "managed to subordinate the entire South to the service of their peculiar local needs," as Key put it.[5] Statesmen responded in two ways: they ceded the power to regulate rural manpower to local authorities and expanded the field staff of the Agricultural Extension Service (AES). The first step aimed to anchor local labor more firmly in the farms, while the second promised to maximize the product of those workers, relieve race tensions, and promote a moderate black leadership at the same time.

---

3. U.S. Bureau of the Census, *Sixteenth Census of the United States: 1940, Population*, Vol. III, "The Labor Forces," part 1: United States Summary, Washington, D.C., USGPO, p. 18.
4. The same effect obtained in the domestic service sector, the other labor market in which blacks were overrepresented prior to the war (see Appendix 1.3).
5. V. O. Key, *Southern Politics in State and Nation*, New York, Alfred A. Knopf, 1950, p. 666.

The Roots of Racial Manpower Policy in Agriculture

Despite eighty years of formal freedom, and despite the immediate effects of the mobilization, African American workers were still most likely to be farmers in 1944. Much more so than in the Army and industry, wartime trends boosted the value of the labor of these poorest of African American workers. In part because of this, the region's black leadership – rooted in the agricultural and technical programs of historically black colleges – never attempted to exploit the war emergency as fully as the militant "New York Negroes," to use the statesman's term. As in other manpower spheres, the president's staff began the war relying on black cabineteers to interpret and promote administration policies. Significantly, these men alone among the black leaders examined in this study survived the war, assisting local and central authorities through their work with the Department of Agriculture and the AES, a cooperative agency linking the department to state land-grant colleges. The central-local partnership of the Extension Service, of which local whites approved because it drew federal funds and expertise into the region without disturbing social relations, succeeded in its formal mission to increase agricultural production by instructing small farmers, "the nation's largest untapped source of manpower," in year-round productive work such as canning, curing, and gardening.[6] But the Extension Service also provided an institutional vehicle through which one White House official attempted to promote the conservative southern black leadership as an alternative to "unrealistic" northerners. Extension Service agents also played valuable moderating roles in isolated rural areas by paying particular attention to the attitudes of white farm owners struggling to replace labor lost to migration, and by lessening the impact of the migration by boosting the efficiency of those workers who remained.

The beginning of World War II marked the approximate halfway point of what historians now call the Great Migration of African Americans out of cotton tenancy in the rural South and into wage work in towns and cities. While 55 percent of the black population was working in agriculture in 1910, the share had fallen to less than one-third by 1940.[7] Below the ongoing social and demographic transformation of the South lay an agricultural system shifting away from cotton production. Demand for cotton had fallen dramatically by the end of the First World

6. L. Herbert Henegan, "The Small Farmer Goes to War," *The Crisis*, January 1943, p. 10.
7. Oliver C. Cox, "Population and Population Characteristics," Tuskegee Institute, *Negro Year Book*, 1947, pp. 6–7.

War, and prices continued on a jagged downward course until 1930, when a bale of cotton drew one-seventh of its 1919 price.[8] Cotton acreage had over the same period increased dramatically, and the resulting glut was partly responsible for dramatically lower Depression-era returns.[9] By the mid-thirties, slowly rising cotton prices made wages paid in shares relatively more expensive than those paid in cash, giving landowners further reason to replace tenant families with wage laborers, whose share of crop subsidy payments could also be appropriated by employers. These factors combined with the acreage reduction programs of the Agricultural Adjustment Administration to deny land to King Cotton and to release workers from the confines of tenant-based staple crop production.[10] In addition, northern industrial and commercial interests sought throughout the thirties to integrate southern labor markets and their low wages into the national economy. The labor codes of the 1933 National Industrial Recovery Act attempted to arrest the flight of northern capital seeking the comparative advantage of the southern wage. The Fair Labor Standards Act of 1938, which set a minimum wage and a maximum work week, together with the wage and hiring policies of the National Recovery Administration and the Works Progress Administration, brought southern manufacturing wages still closer to northern standards.[11] These policies' real effect on farm wages were very modest, however, and abundant cheap labor and generous federal subsidies and guarantees combined to make the South a "planter's heaven" in the late 1930s.

The ongoing transformation did push many thousands of blacks away from their plots to test their luck in nearby towns and cities.[12] Even though the war quickly caused sharecropper and laborer incomes to rise, it was difficult to retain experienced workers, and planters rarely relinquished such labor voluntarily. One symptom of the rural labor shortage was the wave of peonage complaints arising during the preparedness and

8. Doug McAdam, *Political Process and the Development of Black Insurgency, 1930–1970*, Chicago, University of Chicago Press, 1982, p. 77.

9. In 1931 southern farmers collectively received 62 percent less cash for their cotton than they had two years earlier, while offering a crop two million bales larger. John Samuel Ezell, *The South Since 1865*, Norman, Oklahoma, University of Oklahoma Press, 1975, pp. 428–9; Gavin Wright, *Old South, New South: Revolution in the Southern Economy Since the Civil War*, New York, Basic Books, 1986, p. 236.

10. Jeannie M. Whayne, *A New Plantation South: Land, Labor, and Federal Favor in Twentieth-Century Arkansas*, Charlottesville, University Press of Virginia, 1996, p. 216.

11. Phillip J. Wood, *Southern Capitalism: The Political Economy of North Carolina, 1880–1980*, Durham, Duke University Press, p. 138.

12. Gavin Wright, *Old South, New South*, p. 236.

mobilization periods.[13] Despite planter resistance, the net wartime out-migration of blacks from rural farm areas was more than seven times that of the 1930s.[14]

White landowners feared that this new migration and the prosperity it promised to those remaining would permanently change the relative strength of the races in the countryside. The loudest complaints often came from white farmers of medium-sized family holdings who normally hired a seasonal laborer or two. Struggling to afford higher wages, these families often shifted out of row crops – which required more labor – to grain and livestock. As farmers adjusted their ventures with labor-saving strategies and devices, the Agriculture Department predicted great changes for southern agriculture after the war, since most landless workers would be unwilling to return to the seasonal employment and low living standards that characterized cropping arrangements. Southern farms would now simply sustain fewer people.[15]

The migration also reenforced a significant change in the balance of power among federal institutions sharing responsibility for agriculture and farm labor. The "progressive" farming arrangements of the New Deal were promoted from within the Department of Agriculture by social scientists in the Bureau of Agricultural Economics (BAE) advocating egalitarian federal intervention into farms and the social relations surrounding them. Over time, the BAE had assumed primary importance in planning and directing the work of other agricultural agencies.[16] The American Farm Bureau Federation (AFBF), on the other hand, in concert with the Extension Service, largely controlled policy implementation and

---

13. The contract-labor laws of Georgia and Florida were ruled unconstitutional by the U.S. Supreme Court in 1942 and 1943, respectively. These were two of the last state laws that punished sharecroppers for breaking contracts if they were unable to repay an advance. Pete Daniel, *The Shadow of Slavery: Peonage in the South, 1901–1969*, Urbana, University of Illinois Press, pp. 174–5.
14. Cox, "Population" pp. 6–7; James C. Cobb, "Making Sense of Southern Economic History," *The Georgia Historical Quarterly*, vol. 71, no. 1, Spring 1987.
15. Cox, "Population," pp. 5–6.
16. BAE planners' efforts to refashion the cotton economy later in the war – including allowing prices to fall to world market levels and facilitating the movement of poor farmers out of production – struck many conservatives in the Farm Bureau and in Congress as "a deliberate attempt by leftists to disrupt race relations and social stability." Gregory Hooks, "World War II and the Retreat from New Deal Era Corporatism," in *Organizing Business for War*, Providence, Rhode Island, Berg Publishers, 1991; Richard Kirkendall, *Social Scientists and Farm Politics in the Age of Roosevelt*, Columbia, University of Missouri Press, 1966, p. 236; Pete Daniel, "Going Among Strangers: Southern Reactions to World War II," *Journal of American History*, vol. 77, no. 3, December 1990.

generally succeeded in shaping major legislation according to the preferences of large landowners and commercial farmers. Cotton interests, for example, received generous, locally controlled subsidies. The Extension Service, in conjunction with the AFBF, also helped to pack Agricultural Adjustment Administration (AAA) county committees with representatives of larger and wealthier landowners. By the end of the thirties, the BAE had created Land Use Planning Committees in an attempt to promote "economic democracy" and recapture local implementation from Extension Service/AFBF networks. In July 1941, the new Secretary of Agriculture, Claude Wickard, created a set of county and state defense boards to administer the wartime farm program, in effect promoting the AAA and ending the corporatist experiments of the BAE and the planning committees.

Statesmen thus provided substantial relief to whites by ceding control of the farm labor program to local farm agents and draft boards, who were more sympathetic to landowners' manpower needs, as well as by allowing a rapid rise in farm prices. White employers also were pleased that the induction of rural black men into the armed forces had been slowed by rejections due to health and education requirements. Finally, while the federal government guaranteed a minimum price for agricultural commodities, farm produce was excepted from the Office of Production Management price freeze. Farm prices doubled between 1940 and 1944, and net farm income rose by 300 percent. [17]

Local authorities pursued their own policies to try to prevent the adjustment of local labor markets to the ongoing economic expansion.[18] In one exemplary case, Governor Eugene Talmadge of Georgia responded to the announcement that the Bell Aircraft Corporation planned to build a huge bomber plant just outside Atlanta by urging the state legislature to grant counties jurisdiction over all black wages and salaries.[19] Alabama Governor J. M. Broughton proclaimed a "work or jail" policy that directed every male between eighteen and fifty-five not employed for more than thirty-five hours a week to take a full-time job in essential industry or agriculture.[20] In another manifestation of "work or

---

17. Hooks, "World War II," p. 91.
18. By allowing race preferences to affect the redistribution of labor, local authorities played roles similar to those of southern USES staffs dealing with industry.
19. Blacks in the South were paid low wages, he explained, because of their low standard of living and their "low average of intelligence." "Governor Opposes Equality in Plant," Pittsburgh *Courier*, March 21, 1942.
20. Broughton also refused a war contract for cloth offered to a state prison mill because it contained antidiscrimination clauses. The mayor of Shreveport refused a grant to

jail" sentiment, the Sandersville, Georgia, police chief required local blacks to carry identification badges listing the name of their employer and their work schedule; any black over sixteen without the badge was subject to arrest and prosecution. In addition, all blacks employed in town were required to report every Wednesday morning during the harvesting season for a day's work on the farms.[21] In Valdosta, Georgia, the State Guard displayed their new Browning machine guns in a downtown business window, and the exhibit seemed to have a "wholesome effect" on both races.[22] By late 1942, war manpower officials bridled at these local practices' effects on the free movement of labor. WMC staff members were "frankly annoyed" with the attitude of the governor of South Carolina, who at one point ordered the arrest of all "labor agents," including federal employees.[23]

The planters' traditional goal of a labor-rich, low-wage, and high-price cotton economy contradicted production officials' efforts to achieve price stabilization and secure manpower for the Army and industry. To mobilization officials, small farmers' low production rates, particularly in the rural South, meant that their "manpower, land power and productive power" were severely underutilized. Planters and the Department of Agriculture officials believed that the solution was to give these farmers "enough productive work" – through the Extension Service – to keep them busy for the entire year. To central state manpower officials, on the other hand, it meant moving labor out of the fields.[24] County extension service agents were responsible for recruiting and placing labor on farms in 1942, when the War Manpower Commission directed the USES to identify labor-short and labor-rich areas. The reform-minded Farm Security Administration (FSA), in turn, helped to house and transport surplus workers en route to areas of labor scarcity. When the WMC began to find labor surpluses in Mississippi Delta and hill counties – meaning that there were workers there available for redistribution – planters demanded the transfer of responsibility for farm

build a public health center because the contract required the use of black labor. "Work or Jail," Pittsburgh *Courier*, August 7, 1943; Montgomery *Advertiser*, July 24, 1942.

21. The Army also sent 150 soldiers to assist the county's farmers. "Latest 'Work-Or-Jail' Order Forces Negroes to Wear Badges," Pittsburgh *Courier*, August 28, 1943.

22. S-2 Report to Commanding Officer, Georgia State Guard, June 7, 1944, State Guard, Intelligence Reports, Georgia DOD, 22, Adjutant General, RG 22, Georgia Department of Archives and History, Atlanta, GA.

23. "Southern Politicians Make 'White Supremacy' Issue in Campaigns," Florence, S.C. *Morning News*, August 30, 1942.

24. L. Herbert Henegan, "The Small Farmer Goes to War," *The Crisis*, January 1943, p. 10.

labor from the WMC to the U.S. Department of Agriculture. Toward this end, in 1943 Public Law 45 created the Emergency Farm Labor Supply Program and prohibited the spending of federal funds on the transportation of workers lacking a release signed by the county farm agent.[25] The task of designating labor surplus areas now fell to committees of county agents and local representatives of the AAA, and they typically exaggerated their labor needs. White landowners had raised sufficient alarm against New Deal labor provisions and the FSA that Congress had responded by shifting primary responsibility for farm labor from the WMC and the FSA to the Extension Service and local authorities.[26]

Landowners sitting on local draft boards tended to defer those laborers who would work on farms and to draft known clients of the FSA. Planters often offered to petition for a worker's draft deferment if he promised to work a plot for five years, prompting one cropper to complain that he "would rather the U.S. draft board draft me, and not the planters."[27] Under Public Law 45, as applied in South Carolina, a worker could not quit one "essential job" for another without a three-month period of unemployment; farming – often for less than $25 a month – qualified as "essential" work. Black migration was thus restrained, since workers could gain releases from the USES or their employers only by sacrificing three months' wages or in some cases a month of free labor.[28] By 1941, in some parts of the South where black migration threatened the labor supply, blacks were unable to purchase railroad tickets. To conceal their actual destination, migrants bought tickets to the next station on the road – then left the train and repeated the process until they had escaped the state.[29]

With the additional authority over manpower came new responsibilities for adjusting the daily lives of this workforce. The war prompted the Delta Council, a planters' forum for discussions of regional economic and political developments, to recognize and respond to substantial,

25. Nan Elizabeth Woodruff, "Pick or Fight: The Emergency Farm Labor Program in the Arkansas and Mississippi Deltas during World War II," *Agricultural History* 64, Spring 1990, p. 78; Whayne, *A New Plantation South*, p. 221.
26. Longmore, "Desha County, Arkansas," p. 6; Gerald D. Nash, *The American West Transformed: The Impact of the Second World War*, Bloomington, Indiana University Press, 1985, pp. 47–9.
27. Whayne, *A New Plantation South*, p. 216; Woodruff, "Pick or Fight," p. 81; Daniel, "Going Among Strangers," p. 891.
28. "Migration and the Army Have Stripped Dixie," Baltimore *Afro-American*, November 27, 1943.
29. "Thousands From South Flocking to New York," Chicago *Defender*, October 2, 1944.

permanent changes to the region's political economy as well as a new "race consciousness" among black workers.[30] Importing foreign manpower was yet another policy tool used to regulate farm labor markets. Local and central state officials augmented the supply of labor by recruiting a half-million Mexican and West Indian laborers to work primarily in the South in 1944.[31] As daily wages in the Mississippi Delta rose to $3 in 1944, planters often hired Hispanic migrant labor at lower rates.[32] Despite union protests against the use of POW-workers, the WMC also increased the number of such workers in Arkansas and elsewhere in 1944.[33]

War Mobilization and Racial Friction in Southern Agriculture

Despite all of these efforts, long-standing arrangements and farm wages, if not the attitudes that accompanied them, had begun to change to the disadvantage of white landowners. Many whites were disturbed by the growing independence of black women receiving dependency checks from family members in the armed services, or shares of wages earned by relatives in factories. These women – one report called them "the mud-sill of the South's social structure" – were understandably losing interest in field work. Even a small increase in black female independence threatened the full labor supply traditionally available during peak harvesting seasons.[34] By midwar, White House Assistant Jonathan Daniels learned from the BAE that southern landowners were not "comfortable" with the changes.

---

30. Recognizing that a union's appeal stemmed in large part from the workers' harsh and unhealthy lives, the planters launched a campaign of "general social education" including instruction in sanitation, farming, and "leadership." Anticipating increased federal attention at war's end, the council also funded a comprehensive study of the land tenure system in the Delta and promoted reforms of plantations and black schools, both to stave off postwar federal intervention and to retain laborers on the land. Nan Elizabeth Woodruff, "Mississippi Delta Planters and Debates over Mechanization, Labor, and Civil Rights in the 1940s," *The Journal of Southern History*, vol. LX, no. 2, May 1994, pp. 270–7.
31. "Dixie Ties Colored, Helps Poor Whites Come North," Baltimore *Afro-American*, March 11, 1944.
32. In 1945 planters secured a federal wage ceiling that capped wages well below the popular demand of $3.50 per day. Woodruff, "Mississippi Delta Planters," p. 266 fn.
33. Whayne, *A New Plantation South*, pp. 223–4.
34. "Race Tensions and Farm Wages in the Rural South," September 22, 1943, pp. 1–2, attached to Letter, Arthur Raper to Jonathan Daniels, September 25, 1943, 4245-G, OPM, Committee on Fair Employment Practices, Agriculture Department, Franklin D. Roosevelt Library, pp. 2–3.

They fear that out of the situation may come violence. They are accustomed to having the labor they want, and at the price they decide among themselves to pay for it.[35]

Arthur Raper, senior analyst in the BAE's Farm Population and Rural Welfare Division, reported that employers of farm labor were complaining that blacks were becoming too independent "and that to hold them concessions are being made not in harmony with traditional race relations." Employers had attempted a number of adjustments: shifting farm laborers to sharecropper or tenant status, making improvements on houses, competing among themselves for local labor, overlooking tardiness and poor work, and paying higher wages. Still, the general labor shortage and the resulting competition among planters had yielded enormous bargaining leverage to workers. Daily wages for a set of twelve southern counties under study, for example, rose from an average of about $1.60 to about $2.35 in the course of a year.[36]

Wages rose across a wide range of farm production, including cotton, tobacco, and fruit, as landowners competed for sharecroppers as well as day labor. The farm owners and employers in tobacco-growing Pittsylvania County, Virginia, worried about finding sufficient labor for the 1943 harvest. Ever since a mass of workers fled the county the previous summer, locals found that "you can't hardly hire a hired man" – that is, there were very few experienced men to hire by the month or for the saving season. Most wage-hands could choose where and how they would work.[37] While $2 per day for tobacco-saving hands was considered high the previous year, when it represented a two-bit or four-bit raise, by the summer of 1943 that rate was merely the average for adults.

The Extension Service set up a county Farm Labor Committee, and by June 1943 a Farm Labor Assistant began directing the emergency farm labor program, attempting to recruit for work some of the ten thousand men in the area classified as 4-F. Adult, male, and experienced workers were, of course, preferred over green hands, but they also were

35. "Race Tensions and Farm Wages"; Hooks, "The U.S.A.: The Second World War," p. 92.
36. Most employers hoped that seasonal agreements would enforce a stable community wage level. "Race Tensions and Farm Wages," pp. 1–2; see also Daniels, "Going Among Strangers," pp. 892–3.
37. Bureau of Agricultural Economics, "Rural Life Trends Report No. 5, Pittsylvania County, Virginia," September 22, 1943, OF 4245, Agriculture Department, FDRL, pp. 8–9. Written by the staff of the department's Bureau of Agricultural Economics, these reports review five fields of interest: community and institutional life, production, consumption, war participation, and manpower. Note that the reports cited here were located among the official files of the White House.

the scarcest workers to come by. The assistant also met with the black preachers in the county and requested that they encourage all their members to seek full-time employment.[38] Farmers hired children more often, for they received as little as fifty cents a day.[39] At the same time, Extension Service agents tried to help these farm families grow more productive and efficient. Most black families lacked experience in storing crops as well as a place to protect canned goods from freezing. Thus, Pittsylvania County's "Negro" Home Demonstration Agent devoted most of her time in July to teaching five hundred farm wives how to keep their root crops and beans for the winter.[40]

The area had not seen much race trouble in recent years.[41] But the county's "sorry" temper at the time was due in part to rationing and in part to "rumor and talk" about worsening race relations. The most often heard white complaints concerned the increasing number of blacks employed in traditionally white mill jobs in Danville and the paychecks that soldiers sent to the poorer families. Many black field hands, it appeared, had "no real incentive to seek full-time employment" and were quitting work. Townsfolk spoke critically of a somewhat forward black minister, and suspected that a private school headmaster was the "leader of an 'underground movement' among the Negroes." While the talk of a violent outbreak had lessened lately,

> with the shifting conception of the "Negro's place" brought by the war, many people feel that racial tension is not easing up, that the danger of a riot even is not wholly over.[42]

Residents still talked about the case of Odell Waller, a local sharecropper condemned to death for murdering his landlord in a squabble over payments. A similar incident had occurred in Pittsylvania County during the previous winter, and white folk feared that it might attract as much

---

38. Ibid., p. 14. The agent obtained a list of the men's names from the draft board and sent a letter to each asking about his work status. He also sought boys between the ages of twelve and sixteen, largely from mill families, and a few convicts for work in the large hayfields. He publicized the program through newspaper articles, radio addresses, and personal visits.

39. Ibid., p. 12.

40. Ibid., p. 3.

41. One white planter reported that "we never had any trouble with the 'Nigras.' We treat them well, give them good jobs and never have any trouble with them." But further discussions with the tobacco workers led an *Afro-American* reporter to wonder whether " 'good race relations' are not somehow tied up with low salaries and inhuman working conditions." "Tobacco Plant Official Calls Winston-Salem a Powder Keg," Baltimore *Afro-American*, November 13, 1943.

42. "Rural Life Trends Report No. 5," pp. 18–19.

outside attention as the Waller case. In a cryptic allusion to a lynching, one researcher heard that "the Negro 'died' before he was brought to trial."[43] There was enough local violence for it to be explicitly characterized as "concentrated largely among the county political group, and the most suppressed group of poorer Negroes and whites."[44] As a rule, substantial portions of these BAE reports concerned racial instability and white complaints.

The project's research methodology also is notable. For its study of Pittsylvania County, Virginia, the BAE drew upon a broad and diverse network of federal employees and clients. Of the "informants" listed in the report, eleven of the twenty-three officials consulted were either Extension Service staff or supervisors from the AAA and FSA. Of the hundred or so "farm people" interviewed, forty-one were farmers' wives who belonged to a local Extension Service Home Demonstration Club, and ten more were couples who were FSA rural rehabilitation borrowers.[45] The Agricultural Extension Service thus served a variety of administration interests concurrently. It seeded the South with additional federal agents who would indirectly contribute to interracial stability in rural counties during a period of rapid social change. The agents helped explain the new times to white planters. As one extension service agent put it:

I know that the Negroes have been exploited here in the past, and for our own good we are going to have to educate them, pay them better, and give them better housing. The farmers used to drive them and they have got to get that out of their minds. I tell them that. I tell them that they are living

43. Waller shot landowner Oscar Davis on July 15, 1940, after the latter evicted the cropper's family and denied them their share of a wheat and tobacco crop. The Workers' Defense League and a young writer, Murray Kempton, appealed the subsequent murder conviction but were unable to prevent Waller's electrocution in 1943. Ibid., pp. 20–1; Gilbert Ware, *William Hastie: Grace Under Pressure*, New York, Oxford University Press, 1984, pp. 160–2.

44. At the same time, other county residents lived very stable, neighborly lives, as proved by a strong tradition of work-swapping among the better-off tenants and the family farm owners. The war emergency and the labor shortage actually reinforced this traditional community interdependence at planting, gathering, and canning time. "Rural Life Trends Report No. 5," p. 21.

45. In 1934 the Federal Emergency Relief Administration designed a rural rehabilitation program to aid the rural poor. State relief administrators located unused land – typically foreclosed or "rented" to the AAA – for destitute farmers, and furnished them with tools, credit, and surplus livestock, feed, and seed. Ibid., pp. 22–3; Paul E. Mertz, *New Deal Policy and Southern Rural Poverty*, Baton Rouge, LSU Press, 1978, pp. 68–80.

in new times . . . Things are changing, and they are going to have to change their minds about labor. Things are never going to be like they once were. But when I tell them this they always say that I am with the Government (the Administration).[46]

These agents also composed a broad network of federal "informants" in a time of social dislocation and racial friction, performing the first-order race management role of tension monitor.[47]

The problems in Desha County, Arkansas, reflected concerns peculiar to cotton production. Across the board, locals complained less about the labor situation and national politics than in tobacco country; there were no signs of the "emotionality bordering on frenzy" that had characterized the community the previous year.[48] Only 10 percent of the farms in this county hired laborers, and many were using more children in the field. In addition, draft boards had deferred significant numbers of farm workers and had rejected nearly all the black draftees.[49] Even so, white planters claimed that they had lost nearly half their workforce, and appeals for federal assistance were largely granted.

In Poinsett County, Arkansas, labor difficulties intensified as the cotton-picking season approached in the summer of 1943. The demand for labor was well above normal and the supply had nearly been halved.[50] Throughout rural Arkansas, white planters were finding it difficult to

46. U.S. Department of Agriculture, Bureau of Agricultural Economics, Division of Program Surveys, "Plans and Attitudes of Winter Vegetable Growers in Palm Beach and Broward Counties, Florida," July 21, 1943, 4245, Agriculture Department, FDRL, p. 5; parenthetical note in original.

47. The FBI apparently did not draw on these personnel as confidential informants for its *Survey of Racial Conditions* of 1943. The analysis therein that related to rural areas relied primarily on information provided by local police and sheriffs, as well as military authorities. See *The FBI's RACON: Racial Conditions in the United States During World War II*, compiled and edited by Robert A. Hill, Boston, Northeastern University Press, 1995.

48. Daily wages seemed to have stabilized at the $2 level. T. Wilson Longmore, "Rural Life Trends Report No. 5, Desha County, Arkansas," Bureau of Agricultural Economics, July 1943, 4245-G, OPM, COFEP, "Agricultural Department," FDRL, p. 12.

49. Three-fourths of the county's deferments were granted to blacks; most of these were plantation workers on whose behalf a planter had applied to the board. At the same time, the USES operated an office in McGhee to recruit agricultural labor for manufacturing and industrial work. Before farm workers could accept new jobs, however, the USES required the worker to obtain a signed release from their former employers, usually for a specified period of time. Longmore, "Desha County, Arkansas," pp. 9–12.

50. The county managed the record-breaking 1943 harvest with the smallest number of workers on record. During the next two seasons, thousands of German prisoners of war helped ease the labor shortage. Whayne, *A New Plantation South*, p. 221.

find and hire black workers and the increasingly favorable conditions that accompanied the competition for labor had begun to exhaust the "generosity" of whites. Planters in Desha County had adapted somewhat to labor scarcity by granting "more leniency toward infractions of previously well-defined norms," allowing workers' some choice of work, raising wages, and reducing work loads. There was some evidence that the accommodation could not go further "without some overt effort to enforce more 'desirable' relationships." Again, observers were particularly impressed with the new independence of black women.[51] Toward the end of the war, one Mississippi newspaper estimated that in three years, at least fifty thousand farm laborers had quit working the Delta's fields, most of them women.[52]

In the "black belt" town of Bremen, Georgia, State Guard reports indicated that the racial friction there was "brought on and is being fostered very largely by white people, if not entirely so."[53] The winter vegetable farms in Palm Beach and Broward counties in Florida generated similar forms of race friction. Even though the tomato, bean, and pepper crops of the preceding year were the largest in history, as were profits, the farmers believed their laborers – 75 percent black – were "inefficient." The concern resulted in part from the nature of the farming itself; each of Florida's two seasonal crops required relatively large amounts of hand labor. But the primary cause for concern appeared to be poorer work records and higher wages, ranging from $7 to $15 per day.

> We are not getting 50 percent efficiency from these Negroes . . . The problem is that the Negroes are getting from five to ten times as much money as they used to for farm work here and it has ruined them; they will work for two or three days a week – just long enough to get the money that they want to spend and then they quit.[54]

Or as another farm owner put it: "Negroes have got to be bossed, and you can't boss them when they make that kind of money and when they can get another job anywhere they want." As elsewhere, planters

51. Longmore, "Desha County, Arkansas," pp. 2, 5–6, 12.
52. *Clarksdale Delta Farm Press*, January 11, 1945, as quoted in Woodruff, "Mississippi Delta Planters," p. 266.
53. Memorandum, Gelon Wasdin to B. W. Whorton, Ga. State Guard, Intelligence Reports, Georgia DOD, RG 22, Adjutant General, September 1, 1944, p. 2, Georgia Department of Archives and History, Atlanta, GA.
54. U.S. Department of Agriculture, Bureau of Agricultural Economics, Division of Program Surveys, "Plans and Attitudes of Winter Vegetable Growers in Palm Beach and Broward Counties, Florida," July 21, 1943, 4245-G, OPM, COFEP, Agriculture Department, FDRL, pp. 2–3.

attempted to control the effects of the previous season's labor shortage by a preseason wage agreement, but wage bidding and labor pirating undermined the pact. Authorities eased the situation somewhat by importing Bahamian labor and by arresting idle workers on vagrancy charges and forcing them to work.[55] The mayor of Belle Glade reported that the town had arrested some 450 farm laborers and had collected $20,000 in fines from landowners willing to pay for a worker's release from custody in return for his labor.[56] Many farmers suggested that the federal government enforce a weekly pay cap of $25. A white farm agent in Palm Beach County thought that the northern black press was exaggerating the extent of the racial violence elsewhere in the nation. Such propaganda

> is getting these Negroes stirred up here . . . I've been looking for a riot; out around the 'Glades I've got a bunch of farmers who are rugged individualists and one time last winter we had 12,000 Negroes out there – it's a wonder we didn't have trouble.[57]

Despite the deteriorating racial climate on southern farms, overt unrest in cities was of such concern to one White House official that he sought additional black farm agents as a means to undercut the militant northern black leadership.

Farm Manpower Policy Innovation in the Agricultural Extension Service

It was in the context of this racial animosity that Agriculture Department officials called for the expansion of "Emergency Negro Extension Work" in all counties with a large black population, that is, five hundred or more farm families. By midwar, the southern states accounted for 1,167, or 54.2 percent, of all farm and home demonstration agents and assistants, and the placement of black agents was even more heavily concentrated; the twelve states hosted all but 10 of these 530 agents. Secretary Wickard hoped that the Extension Service would help farmers increase production of food despite fertilizer and machinery shortages and help farmers understand price controls and other wartime farm policies. In

---

55. In Mississippi's cotton belt, the auxiliary workforce was composed of eight to ten thousand Mexican braceros and many POWs. Woodruff, "Pick or Fight," p. 82.

56. By 1945, a civil rights organization investigated complaints of such practices against Broward County's sheriff and unsuccessfully called for the intervention of Florida and federal authorities. U.S. Department of Agriculture, "Palm Beach and Broward Counties, Florida," p. 7; Daniel, *The Shadow of Slavery*, pp. 184–5.

57. U.S. Department of Agriculture, "Palm Beach and Broward Counties, Florida," p. 4.

addition, agents were charged with training and aiding volunteer local leaders, farm women, and farm youth, primarily in food production and conservation.[58] Their responsibilities expanded with war to include activities related to Selective Service, farm transportation, machinery rationing and repair, conserving, salvage, building permits, and the slaughter of animals for meat. Overburdened with these new tasks, the county agents needed assistance. Even the decision to train approximately 650,000 volunteer neighborhood leaders to help alert rural Americans to wartime information had not solved the workload problem.[59]

The Department of Agriculture thus requested additional funding for emergency county agents and assistants, again to promote efficient crop production and to explain wartime programs to rural homemakers and girls. The initiative aimed to double the 280 black assistant county agents already in place and increase the number of female assistant home demonstration agents from 249 to 569.[60] At the time, officials in the White House were reexamining the proper development and use of the Black Cabinet beyond their largely symbolic deployment at election time. An explicit goal of the initiative was the neutralization of black radicals associated with Randolph and White. Again, as in other fields of manpower policy, race reforms gained momentum from elections and from a concern for social order.

Five months into the war, at the beginning of the 1942 campaign, an assistant to the attorney general advised FDR that the "uniformly poor" quality of black leadership in the New Deal resulted from the fact that the Democratic National Committee "simply doesn't have vigor enough to organize a good Negro group which could be played off against the Walter White group." If it were done properly, he argued, the development of this alternative leadership could "give the Democratic party the same sort of permanent control over the Negro vote" that the Republicans held from the Civil War until the early thirties.[61] Administration

58. Letter, I.O. Schaub to Jonathan Daniels, November 4, 1943, 4245, "Agricultural Department," FDRL; "Race Extension Agents Have Job in War Effort," Atlanta *Daily World*, March 3, 1942; for an overview of the issue, see "Negro Farmers in Wartime Food Production," Washington, D.C., U.S. Department of Agriculture, 1943.

59. The extension educational program was "fundamental to an understanding by rural people of each war program individually and all programs as a unified whole." Attachment to letter, F. D. Patterson to Jonathan Daniels, September 11, 1943, 4245, Aug.–Sept., 1943, p. 10, FDRL.

60. Letter, F. D. Patterson to Jonathan Daniels, September 11, 1943, OF 4245, Aug.–Sept. 1943, FDRL.

61. Memorandum, James Rowe, Jr., Assistant to the Attorney General, to FDR, April 15, 1942, OF 93, Colored Matters, FDRL.

officials reflected popular discourse in routinely distinguishing black organizations and leaders into northern radical and southern conservative
camps.[62] Mark Ethridge, the first chairman of the FEPC, thought the
dichotomy corresponded to a fundamental disagreement over the goals
of abstract ideals or economic gain.

> The main line of cleavage is that one [northern] crowd thinks that if they
> can secure the abstractions, even if they are written in federal law, they have
> made a great advance; whereas the others think if they improve the eco-
> nomic condition of the negro, they have solved a great many of the other
> problems they have. The difference is between reality and unreality inter-
> ested in abstractions.[63]

Others noted the regional divide in critiques of the Black Cabinet. A
black newspaper claimed that southerners needed a new class of unsel-
fish leaders to replace the ineffective educators who currently served in
such roles. While their names "bounce back and forth in the headlines
. . . they do hardly more than pay lip-service to Negro struggles for
citizenship."[64] The African American president of Alabama's Tuskegee
Institute, F. D. Patterson, argued, on the other hand, that the NAACP
should abandon its attempts to direct the broad strategy of black protest
and instead restrict its efforts to challenging discriminatory law in the
courts, where it had been successful. "Its militant and uncompromising
procedure had failed to effect the "practical adjustment of Negroes in
American life," he wrote.

> The extent to which White has been able to get the official ear in Washing-
> ton in terms of appointment to key positions has been practically nil
> through the appointment of ineffectuals who have been able to do little
> except protest any proffered adjustment short of what they deemed was
> complete democratic integration. Very laudable indeed but we get nothing.[65]

Patterson personified the Tuskegee theory of race advancement, which
counseled hard work, self-reliance, and a degree of patience. The best
way to erase de jure segregation, most southern leaders argued, was to

62. For another example of state officials' attentiveness to "New York Negroes," see
    "Negroes in a Democracy at War," Bureau of Intelligence, quoted in Desmond King,
    Separate and Unequal: Black Americans and the U.S. Federal Government, New York,
    Oxford University Press, 1995, p. 118.
63. Mark Ethridge, "The Race Problem in the War," address to Harvard War Institute,
    undated, papers of Mark Ethridge, SHC-UNC, p. 15.
64. " 'Young Man, Go South,' " Memphis *World*, June 6, 1944.
65. F. D. Patterson, "Walter White's Ego Undermining NAACP," Pittsburgh *Courier*,
    March 21, 1942; see also "Black, White Keys Needed to Play National Anthem,"
    Norfolk *Pilot*, April 22, 1944.

insist on its full and equal application, so as to make it prohibitively expensive.[66] The fit between this class of educators and the southern farm manpower problem was a close one. T. M. Campbell and J. B. Pierce of Tuskegee and Hampton Institutes, respectively, served as black field agents in the Federal Extension Service and worked closely with black farm and home agents throughout the South.[67]

Because the national leadership of organizations such as the NAACP pushed for the immediate elimination of discrimination and the rapid modification of segregation, the White House considered Patterson and the southern group valuable allies in an attempt to shift policy debates toward more modest goals. The notion that a larger field staff could help serve this purpose dates from January 1943, when Jonathan Daniels first suggested that the president meet with three southern black university and association presidents who had designed a plan to provide additional agricultural extension services to black farmers. Patterson of Tuskegee Institute, Claude Barnet of the Associated Negro Press, and John W. Davis of the Association of Negro Land Grant Colleges, had worked out a reasonable plan, Daniels argued, and the president had not met a representative of black America since the war started. Noting that "most of the Negroes are in the South and most of them in agriculture," Daniels strongly supported the committee's initiative, which would provide tangible assistance to farm families and offend very few "sensible" white people. Furthermore, the plan offered a chance to nurture a relationship between the White House and "some other Negro group besides that largely radical group in the North." Daniels also relayed the opinion of the WMC's Will Alexander – like

66. The divide between the northern and southern wings revealed itself in the controversy surrounding the firing of the NAACP director of branches, "Dean" William Pickens, on February 9, 1942, at the urging of Walter White. Pickens, an archetypal Black Cabinet member, had worked for the Treasury Department for almost a year promoting defense bond sales. The firing followed a press release in which he allegedly approved of Army racial segregation after a visit to Tuskegee Airfield, though executive director Walter White had apparently believed for some time that Pickens was unsuited to a more militant association policy. Patterson called White's charges "trumped-up." "Executives Quail as White is Given Dictatorial Power," Pittsburgh *Courier*, February 27, 1942. This relatively conservative faction also included newspaper editors Eddie W. Reevers, of the *Messenger*, and Charles M. Thomas, of the Washington *Tribune*. McGuire, *He, Too, Spoke for Democracy*, p. 15.

67. These two farm agents began dispensing information to black farmers via mule team in 1906. By the end of World War I, all southern extension service programs included black agents. Pete Daniel, *Breaking the Land: The Transformation of Cotton, Tobacco, and Rice Cultures since 1880*, Urbana, University of Illinois Press, 1985, pp. 9–10; "Race Extension Agents Have Job in War Effort," Atlanta *Daily World*, March 3, 1942.

Daniels, a moderate to liberal southern white – that the only "pressure" to which the administration had responded was from the northern group. This southern leadership was as widely respected and as devoted to reform as "the New York leaders," but willing to proceed "much more realistically." Daniels endorsed Alexander's recommendation to welcome and respond to the pressure for additional agricultural assistance, for "any expression of confidence in them from the White House would strengthen them within their own race."[68] The initiative languished until late that summer.[69]

In September, at the end of the summer season of racial unrest, Patterson forwarded to Daniels the section of the 1943 appropriation measure containing these items and indicated that the need for additional agents was more serious than it appeared to be in the supporting materials.[70] Daniels repeated his plea to the president twice in the space of two weeks, noting that the primary supporters of the plan, Patterson and Barnett, had been working for two years as special advisors to the secretary of agriculture. Secretary Wickard, who had committed himself to the project the previous year, feared that the black sponsors were beginning to feel that they were "receiving a run-around." Daniels repeated his recommendation that the president support "this plan to give real assistance to the Negroes and demonstrate the influence with the administration of the conservative Negro leaders."[71] Daniels notified Roosevelt again when the Bureau of the Budget rejected the proposal because it was combined with others from the Extension Service that officials deemed too costly; he now recommended an independent submission. The program would indicate the "influence with the administra-

68. Memorandum, Jonathan Daniels to Marvin McIntyre, January 2, 1943, OF 93, FDRL.
69. Howard Odum, a University of North Carolina sociologist and scholar of race relations, also reminded Daniels in August that "irresponsibles have taken charge of the 'northern' group." Letter, Howard W. Odum to Jonathan Daniels, August 18, 1943, OF 4245, "Odum," FDRL.
70. These materials do not explicitly mention race relations. Letter and attachment, F. D. Patterson to Jonathan Daniels, September 11, 1943, OF 4245, Aug.–Sept. 1943, FDRL.
71. This general Extension Service initiative appears to have disproportionately favored southern states at the expense of optimal agricultural production. The director of the Extension Service "heartily" approved of the proposal, but noted that the Corn Belt and cities were by comparison understaffed. Daniels arguably had a broader view of the mobilization's needs. Letter, with handwritten marginal note, F. D. Patterson to Jonathan Daniels, September 11, 1943; memorandum, Jonathan Daniels to Franklin Roosevelt, September 14, 1943, OF 4245, Aug.–Sept., 1943; letter, I. O. Schaub to Jonathan Daniels, November 4, 1943, 4245, "Agricultural Department," FDRL.

tion of such moderate Negro leaders" who provide the only alternative to "the more violent leadership" of Walter White and Philip Randolph.[72]

Daniels later bemoaned the fact that the White House could do so little in response to violent explosions of racial unrest such as those of the summer of 1943. In addition to monitoring high-tension areas, evaluating FBI and Military Intelligence reports, and attempting to commission additional black officers in the armed services, he recalled, "we tried to get Agriculture to provide more black farm agents."[73] Although the funding was not arranged at this time, this initiative was part of a larger attempt to promote and reward southern leaders. At the Tuskegee Farmers' Conference on December 15, 1943, Secretary Wickard ascribed the department's improved ability to serve black farmers to a policy of "using colored leadership more extensively." He praised his special assistants, Patterson and Barnett, for keeping black farmers informed of department activities and for "shaping the department's programs to the needs of the colored farmer." He also claimed that the department had increased the number of black employees by 200 percent in the previous two years, including a tripling of personnel in clerical, administrative, and professional grades in the Washington, D.C., central office.[74]

Summary

In the case of farm labor, the primary dislocation caused by the mobilization resulted from the out-migration of black workers. The resulting friction took the form of white planters' concern over the "inefficiency" and higher wages that resulted from the labor shortage. This friction appears not to have interfered with farm production. The more serious problem was the general underutilization of manpower and land in the region; this predated the war. Federal authorities responded with three

72. Memorandum, Jonathan Daniels to Franklin Roosevelt, September 24, 1943, OF 4245, Aug.– Sept., 1943, FDRL.
73. Agriculture Department officials recognized during the First World War that extension work was a method of combating "poverty, dissatisfaction, and unrest prevailing among negro farmers, and of thus checking the migration from the rural sections." Jonathan Daniels, *White House Witness, 1942–1945*, New York, Doubleday and Co., 1975, p. 205; Department of Agriculture bulletin of 1923, quoted in Daniel, *Breaking the Land*, p. 12.
74. He gave a total figure of 1,701, which did not include 583 farm and home demonstration agents and approximately two hundred "committeemen and collaborators." "Operators of Farms Colored," Baltimore *Afro-American*, January 1, 1944.

initiatives intended to boost production for the mobilization and buttress local social order, while maintaining the party coalition. First, in a bow to the power of southern Democrats representing planter interests, federal manpower officials ceded authority over labor markets to local elites and imported foreign labor, relieving the upward pressure on wages somewhat. Equally important, the central state in effect purchased southern white acquiescence to the rapid social change by allowing significant rises in farm produce. The third policy thrust involved black farm agents, which White House officials viewed as serving several goals concurrently: improved economic efficiency and additional war-fighting strength through increased agricultural output; better nutrition and returns for black farm families and the prospective workers and soldiers they raised; improved prospects for social order external to the region through the promotion of the "realist" southern leadership and the weakening of the northern militants; and a heightened ability to monitor and pacify racial tensions within the sharecropping system, which threatened to undermine wartime production as well as the president's coalition.

In sum, several factors account for the peculiar shape of race manpower policies in agriculture. First, the essential precondition for a measure of black political power was absent. State laws by and large barred blacks from voting. Second, the farm working population was widely dispersed; rather than additional spatial concentration, the war lessened black population density in the rural South. In general, a lack of resources and opportunities limited black farm worker leverage; thus, the indigenous race leadership was more conservative than in northern cities. Whites were, in this case, the privileged Democratic faction demanding race "adjustments" from the White House. For all of these reasons, central state policies favored white planter interests, primarily because of their overriding influence in the national Democratic Party. The pattern appears not so peculiar after all: leaders of a "race advancement organization" threatened to disrupt the coalition, while common folk predicted race violence if the central state did not offset the effects of the war mobilization. Predictably, the administration responded so as to guard the party and social order.

The White Cabinet and the Peak of the Urban Unrest, 1943

While the analysis has touched on several interventions by Jonathan Daniels, a more thorough examination of his policy advisement during 1943 and 1944 demonstrates that the White House had grown more capable of responding to unstable race relations over the course of a single presidential term. Formally designated a White House administrative assistant on March 25, 1943, Daniels offered the president evaluations of race debates and policies far more sophisticated than the relatively careless reactions of White House staffers McIntyre, Coy, and Early.[75] The president – whose energies by 1943 were almost entirely consumed by the war – allowed Daniels to pursue an informal consolidation of the central state's race monitoring and surveillance efforts. His rise as race relations coordinator, and his attempt to consolidate preventative measures, were propelled in a substantial way by the violence of 1943.[76] The chapter will then turn from these social order concerns to examine White House race advisement in the 1944 campaign, thus completing the analysis of an entire presidential term from reelection to reelection.

Several of the war's most serious racial clashes occurred between May 25 and June 22, 1943, including crowd violence in shipyards in Mobile and Port Chester, Pennsylvania; running street battles in Centerville, Mississippi, Los Angeles, and Newark; and bloodshed in the training grounds of Camp Stewart, Georgia, and Camp Shelby, Mississippi. Unrest in Detroit claimed thirty-four lives and wounded more than seven hundred in the last week of June. The staggering scale and scope of the violence turned the attention of both central state and civic actors to the search for preventive policies. From within the administration, Robert Weaver decried what appeared to be case-by-case responses, for the wave of conflict appeared to endanger the war effort. Anticipating the work of Daniels in his broad outline if not the specifics, he recommended a "national program of prevention" that would "ameliorate" friction through substantial reforms by the Justice, War, and Navy Departments, as well as the National Housing Agency and the Office of War Information.[77] By mid-July, NAACP branches in nineteen "fever spots" had organized to prevent new outbreaks of race violence, mainly through the creation of interracial committees and the cooperation of daily

---

75. Like other administrative assistants, Daniels was expected to pursue his multifaceted work in anonymity. His other wartime responsibilities included rural electrification, baseball, the TVA, and selective service. Charles W. Eagles, *Jonathan Daniels and Race Relations: The Evolution of a Southern Liberal*, Knoxville, University of Tennessee Press, 1982, p. 99.

76. At the time, the staff of the attorney general, for example, proposed that "consideration be given to limiting, and in some instances putting an end to" black migration into overcrowded communities such as Detroit. Other advisers proposed a high profile, cabinet-level bureau to demonstrate the administration's dedication to racial equality. Secretary Ickes, for example, suggested a National Committee on Race Relations. Letter, Francis Biddle to FDR, July 15, 1943, OF 93, FDRL.

77. Memorandum, Robert C. Weaver to Jonathan Daniels, undated, ca. June 27, 1943, OF 4245, FDRL.

newspapers in suppressing rumors. The Baltimore and Chester, Pennsylvania, branches, among others, reported that they had helped form local citizens' committees to prevent and control riots and increase race harmony.[78]

In a June 29 memo to FDR that echoed Weaver's points, Daniels noted that, while the racial situation was growing more dangerous, responsibility for various pieces of the problem was parceled out to the Army, the Department of Justice, the OWI, and FEPC, among others. In a recommendation that differentiated white from black cabinet members, Daniels merely proposed collecting information on the incidents and the responses of the agencies involved, rather than making substantive policy changes.[79] On July 23, following additional incidents in Mississippi and Pennsylvania, he reassured the president that the proposed clearinghouse on race policy would be "entirely informal." A formally appointed committee would likely be no more effective, while becoming "another pressure point for the numerous agitators in the field."[80] Instead of administrative expansion, Daniels sought to insulate the executive from social disruption. Roosevelt quickly confirmed Daniels's informal appointment as presidential "fact-finder." The initiative became publicly known by midsummer, when the black press began mocking the so-called White Cabinet of Biddle, McCloy, Daniels, Haas, and Alexander.[81] There would be little direct intervention by the president. But, as in the struggles surrounding the FEPC, staff members deferred to FDR's innate conservatism regarding race.

Within a week of his assignment, Daniels sent letters to all wartime administrators asking for their cooperation in gathering and sharing information on racial matters. Noting that the recent disturbances in Detroit and Los Angeles had revealed that federal responsibility for such incidents was dangerously fragmented, he asked each bureau head to designate an official in charge of race matters who would work with him to create "a coherent and inclusive picture" of the evolving situation.[82]

78. "NAACP Units on Guard Against Race Outbreaks," Atlanta *Daily World*, July 14, 1943.
79. Biddle also preferred an interdepartmental system of information exchange, with Daniels at its head. Memorandum, Jonathan Daniels to the president, June 29, 1943, papers of Jonathan Daniels, SHC-UNC; Eagles, *Jonathan Daniels*, pp. 104–5.
80. Memorandum, Jonathan Daniels to Franklin Roosevelt, July 23, 1943, OF 93, FDRL.
81. They were in order the attorney general, assistant secretary of war, assistant to the president, chairman of the FEPC, and war manpower commission official. Reed, *Seedtime*, p. 123.
82. Letter, Jonathan Daniels to William H. Davis (Chairman, NWLB), July 29, 1943, OF 4245, NWLB, FDRL.

Researchers throughout the executive weighed in, and Daniels moved to consolidate the information-gathering system, assisted by Philleo Nash, an applied anthropologist serving at the Office of War Information who believed that a careful reading of newspapers and other sources would reveal patterns of racial conflict and allow officials to identify potential outbreaks.[83]

An exchange of memoranda in August 1943 suggests the extent of Nash's influence on Daniels's advice to the president. On the 2nd, following deadly unrest in New York City, Daniels sent FDR a short memo that made two well-worn points. Citing the previous night's street battles in Harlem – in which six individuals were killed and 1,450 stores damaged or destroyed – and other deadly incidents nationwide, Daniels recommended that the president make a "direct and disciplinary" radio statement to the nation on the subject of racial violence, but should not appoint a committee to study the unrest, since their report "would only serve as a new ground for controversy." Roosevelt asked Harry Hopkins for advice on the matter and was told that Biddle should be the first source of any such statement.[84] A few days later, Nash summarized the key aspects of the "Nash-Daniels Project" for his collaborator. He first outlined the program's guiding principles, namely that total war's demand for manpower led to rising wages and new opportunities for blacks, which strained prewar patterns of race relations and segregation. Black militancy and white defensiveness sometimes sparked riots, to which the government should respond with prompt but equally applied force, followed by "action programs" and educational campaigns. A coordinated program to deal with interracial friction, Nash claimed, involved three components: the centralized collection and analysis of information about areas where tensions were highest; the use of action agencies to adjust these situations; and the use of information to temper white hostility and decrease black militancy. Daniels would spearhead the first function, while Nash's affiliation with the OWI made him particularly well-suited to the third. Potential sources of public information initiatives included presidential statements, action agencies' publicity offices, and national and local citizens' committees. OWI's minority information program was, at that time, no different from programs serving other specialized groups with particular interests. Nash recommended

---

83. Eagles, *Jonathan Daniels and Race Relations*, p. 103.
84. Daniels advised against emphasizing the theme of "ultimate justice for all"; rather, the president should clearly state his "determination that no violence at home, regardless of cause, shall be tolerated." Memorandum, Jonathan Daniels to FDR, August 2, 1943; letter, Harry Hopkins to FDR, August 10, 1943, OF 4245, FDRL.

changing it to "increase the flow" of news reports, both to encourage favorable attitudes toward minorities and to educate minorities about war issues. Two sets of recommendations followed, broadly oriented toward repression and amelioration, each accompanied by a publicity initiative. The proposals for "control of civil disturbances" included clarifying the procedures by which mayors and governors could request federal troops, deploying black troops for riot control, and training police in the handling of "minority situations." The second category, "softening the grievance pattern," included improving bus systems for black troops, deploying black troops to combat, securing recreation facilities for and thoroughly protecting black soldiers in camp communities, and distributing materials on the successful incorporation of black workers in factories.[85]

On August 10, Daniels submitted to the president a new, more complex set of recommendations than he had presented a week earlier. While reiterating his call for a presidential statement condemning violence, Daniels also suggested that federal officials pursue six initiatives: collaborating more closely with state and local officials to control violence; creating local committees to consider causes of and remedies for racial tension; enhancing depleted local police forces; attending to the disciplinary problems caused by black soldiers within and outside training camps; refraining from new promises as a result of violence but fulfilling those already made; and enlisting black leaders in the planning for "postwar human security" in the United States.[86] The last proposal was the only one that offered even a modest political benefit.

Nash argued against the use of public statements as tools of law and order, since they supplied no means for controlling behavior. He drew on administration experience gained earlier in the war.

> Now I am thinking of the difficulties the first FEPC got into when it tried to handle an enforcement job by the technique of public disclosure. Hearings have a function but they should be used judiciously, in conjunction with negotiations and not as the sole enforcement procedure unbacked by coercive measures . . . it would be a mistake to handle the law and order problem through pronouncements or public statements.

If done so, every breach of order would become a symbol of the ineffectiveness of the whole program. Instead, the program should be based on a positive theme such as unity. Governors and police chiefs should

85. Memorandum, Philleo Nash to Jonathan Daniels, August 7, 1943, OWI Files No. 1, Box 29, papers of Philleo Nash, HSTL.
86. Memorandum, Jonathan Daniels to the President, August 10, 1943, Daniels papers, SHC-UNC.

receive advisory memoranda on the control of racial tensions and disturbances and citizens groups' formation should be encouraged. Again
Nash urged Daniels to call for an interdepartmental meeting to target
the most dangerous cities for preventive action, since they had not had
"much luck putting out individual fires this summer, and I feel we ought
to look toward large-scale conflagrations next summer."[87] At this stage,
free from electoral concerns, planners focused exclusively on establishing
and enforcing social order.

Race Policy Innovation in Anticipation of the Summer of 1944

In the two years since Pearl Harbor, the state had developed a substantial
intelligence network, and large segments of it now turned to seek the
causes and symptoms of the friction. Fed by FEPC researchers and by
the FBI and Navy and Army intelligence services, analyses and lists of
potential trouble spots proliferated rapidly. In December 1943, an ASF
official sent Daniels a confidential report that summarized available information on fifty-seven cities, including the number and nature of local
complaints before the FEPC, in hopes of helping to "remove the causes
of racial tension and prevent interference with war production." The
analysis classified each city into one of four classes ranging from cases
of "critical racial tension" to areas where "minor conflicts . . . may interfere with war production." Daniels thought it an "excellent brief statement" and requested additional reports on the cities over the near-
term.[88]

A few months later, Daniels charged the FEPC with listing particularly
tense cities so as to target them for ameliorative action. Although prediction was an uncertain enterprise, he thought that officials should monitor
"those cities which experience tells us require special attention."[89]

---

87. Nash believed that racial animus alone was insufficient to cause disruptions; what was
truly dangerous was "the ease with which racial feelings can be manipulated for
political or other purposes." Objective conditions such as inadequate recreation facilities combined with in-migration might breed racist sentiments, but a flashpoint was
most likely to occur when "agitational" groups used the race issue for their own
purposes. Memorandum, Philleo Nash to Jonathan Daniels, August 31, 1943, OWI
Files No. 1, box 29; memorandum, Philleo Nash to Jonathan Daniels, November 25,
1943, OWI Files No. 1, box 29, Nash papers, HSTL.
88. Letter, James P. Mitchell to Jonathan Daniels, December 3, 1943; letter, Jonathan
Daniels to James P. Mitchell, December 12, 1943; "Racial Tensions in War Production
Areas," OF 4245, War Dept. 1943, FDRL.
89. Letter, Jonathan Daniels to Malcolm Ross, April 22, 1944, OF 4245, FDRL.

Daniels's most productive and eager ally, however, was J. Edgar Hoover. FBI surveillance reports poured across Daniels's desk daily. Hoover's reports to Daniels ranged from the investigation of so-called pushing clubs, allegedly organized by blacks to jostle whites in shopping areas or at bus stops, to a set of short summaries of the racial climate in ten cities "where racial outbreaks could conceivably occur at any time."[90] FBI analysts delivered to Hoover the bureau's most comprehensive study, the 730-page *Survey of Racial Conditions in the United States*, in September 1943. Only six copies of the report, classified as "secret," were distributed; at least one arrived at the White House.[91] While such information helped target trouble spots, Nash felt that distributing the facts about blacks' opportunities and accomplishments would help resolve tensions, for the "management of race relations is largely a public relations problem." Whites did not believe that minorities were contributing to the war effort, while blacks were increasingly militant. But the integration of black Americans into all aspects of American life, Nash believed, had increased substantially in only two years, and this story needed to be told.[92]

With the arrival of another spring in 1944, many officials warned of violence. In April the director of intelligence of the ASF reported evidence that "widespread" disturbances were likely to develop during the summer, especially in cities depending disproportionately on a single Army-supported industry, since production cutbacks would create new charges of official discrimination.[93] Hoover responded to another Dan-

90. The June 1943 meeting of the March on Washington Movement reveals the public's appreciation of the bureau's reach. In his opening address, the chairman of the Chicago unit offered a special welcome to undercover FBI agents in attendance. Letter, J. Edgar Hoover to Jonathan Daniels, October 21, 1943, OF 4245, FBI Material Concerning Minorities, FDRL. On the "pushing clubs," see letter, J. Edgar Hoover to Jonathan Daniels, March 15, 1944; and letter, J. Edgar Hoover to Jonathan Daniels, March 31, 1944, OF 4245, FBI Materials Concerning Minorities, FDRL; "What They Said and Did at March-on-Washington Confab," Baltimore *Afro-American*, June 10, 1943.

91. The complete survey upon which the summary volume was based consisted of approximately seventy-seven thousand pages, much of it concerning the possibility of "foreign-inspired agitation" among blacks. The project essentially launched the FBI's surveillance of black organizations that continued through the fifties and sixties. See the note on sources and the introduction to *The FBI's RACON*, compiled and edited by Robert A. Hill, pp. xvii, 29.

92. Memorandum, Philleo Nash to Jonathan Daniels, December 18, 1943, OWI Files No. 1, box 29, Nash papers, HSTL.

93. This report listed fourteen cities as "high racial tension areas." Memorandum for the Commanding General, Army Service Forces, Subject: Racial Situation in the United States, April 17, 1944, OF 4245, War Department Material Concerning Minority, March–April, 1944, FDRL.

iels request, also in April, for "cities which require special watching" with a list of thirty-five, warning of the return of warm weather and the concomitant increase in outdoor gatherings and contact.[94] These were not randomly selected; of the fourteen cities that the Military Intelligence Division [ASF] submitted the same month, only one did not also appear on the FBI list.[95]

The Office of the Chief of Naval Operations suggested that unrest was particularly noticeable in areas where black servicemen came into contact with large numbers of black workers.[96] At the beginning of the summer season, then, Nash and Daniels planned to have all federal agencies with field offices report to them on minority group matters. Then they hoped to consolidate the agencies' work and prepare a list of the "hottest hot spots," with lists of probable causes and suggested responses.[97]

Many other reports found their way to Daniels. Warning of an impending rise in "civilian racial disturbances unfavorable to the war," the ASF chief of staff ordered his director of intelligence to prepare and implement a program of measures to prevent overt racial disturbances.[98] In reply, the adjutant general noted that the Army had "a secondary and essential interest and responsibility" in the maintenance of social peace, both because of the potential delays to military production and the potential use of federal troops in peacekeeping efforts.[99]

94. At this point Hoover promised to forward to Daniels all information relating to race issues. Letter, Jonathan Daniels to J. Edgar Hoover, April 22, 1944; J. Edgar Hoover to Jonathan Daniels, April 26, 1944, FBI Material Concerning Minorities, OF 4245, FDRL.
95. Memorandum, Philleo Nash to Jonathan Daniels, May 10, 1944, OWI Files No. 1, Box 29, Nash papers, HSTL.
96. Letter, Wallace S. Wharton, Captain, U.S.N.R., to Jonathan Daniels, April 19, 1944, OF 4245, FDRL.
97. The surveillance had grown so extensive that by September, the Army's adjutant general issued directives to *curtail* the submission of excessive numbers of "Immediate Spot Reports." Henceforth they were to be limited to racial incidents involving substantial numbers of military personnel or the operation of a War Department installation, disturbances involving mutiny or disaffection of substantial numbers of military personnel, or activities involving evidence of espionage. "Action Steps Following OWI Conference," undated and unattributed memorandum, ca. June 1944, OWI Files No. 1, Box 29, Nash papers, HSTL; memorandum, Maj. Gen. J. A. Ulio to Commanding Generals of Service Commands, September 26, 1944, OF 4245, War Dept. Material Concerning Minority, July–August, 1944, FDRL.
98. Memorandum to staff, Major General W. D. Styer, Chief of Staff, General Staff Corps, June 8, 1944, OF 4245, War Department Material Concerning Minority, May–June, 1944, FDRL.
99. The director of intelligence, GSC, defined the phrase "high racial tension areas" so as to reflect this interest in an optimally efficient mobilization. "It is common usage for intelligence agents to employ the term 'tension' where a situation exists in which an

He identified the immediate causes of tension as agitation, warmer weather, and cutbacks in war production. The AG suggested that commanding generals should instruct local authorities to work with local organizations to publicize black soldier accomplishments and build better relations with black journalists and leaders. He also suggested using black officers with legal training or black civilian attorneys in trials before general courts martial, black officers as trouble shooters and press liaisons, and "negro undercover agents" to gather and update intelligence.[100]

Nash believed that the proper management of racial disturbances entailed research, prevention and, failing that, police control. Given that the War Department's plan dealt mainly with the third prong of his plan, the "police problem," he focused his work on the first two mechanisms: data collection and analysis, and ameliorating policies by action agencies such as the FEPC, the War Relocation Authority, and the National Labor Relations Board.[101] In May, Nash was particularly concerned about several cities in the Fifth and Sixth Service Commands – including Louisville, Cincinnati, and Gary – where fourteen incidents had been reported the previous month, including a street battle between one hundred black soldiers and several policemen, the beating of a white policeman by a crowd of blacks in Cincinnati, and eight race-related work stoppages. These cities, he concluded, were the "real hot spots requiring special attention," which already included a conference on race matters between officials of the security and intelligence divisions of the service commands at risk, attended by Army and Navy intelligence and FBI representatives. The conference estimated that race violence was probable during the summer months and would require federal troops to restore order, and Nash recommended that the War Department prepare itself to launch the Army police plan for these commands. Someone from the provost marshall general's office also should "visit the hot cities one by one, quietly, for interviews with the police chiefs," during which copies of a California state manual on policing and race conflict would be distributed. Finally, news media and ministers in the area

inflammatory incident would be the point of crisis which would necessitate the use of an organized militant body somewhat larger than the local police force." Memorandum, Maj. Gen. J. A. Ulio to Commanding Generals, June 14, 1944, OF 4245, FDRL; letter, Colonel J. M. Roamer, G.S.C., Director of Intelligence, to Jonathan Daniels, May 26, 1944, OF 4245, FDRL.

100. Memorandum, Maj. Gen. J. A. Ulio to Commanding Generals, June 14, 1944, OF 4245, FDRL.
101. Memorandum, Philleo Nash to Jonathan Daniels, April 18, 1944, OWI Files No. 1, Box 29, Nash papers, HSTL.

should be encouraged to stress the gravity of the imminent European invasion and the concurrent need for unity.[102]

Throughout the season, Nash and Daniels met daily to review their data, target trouble spots, and "to remove by negotiation and arbitration" obstacles to peaceful black-white relations. Frequently they alerted local officials to a potential problem, advised contending parties of White House interests, and facilitated communications among parties to disputes and the federal bureaucracy. In May 1944, for example, Daniels contacted the Federal Security Agency and the mayor's office in an effort to prevent a major racial incident predicted for Chicago by the ASF.[103] But the violence of the summer of 1944 arose primarily in Army camps rather than industrial areas. Three Louisiana camps generated incidents in the spring and summer of that year. Cleveland, on the other hand, identified as the most likely source of summer unrest, survived unscathed.[104]

Ironically, in asking agency heads to designate a race specialist to contribute to interdepartmental deliberations, Daniels mirrored the design of the original Black Cabinet advisory system founded by Harold Ickes in 1934. The White House now utilized a broad and relatively professional surveillance and monitoring system that was unavailable only three years earlier. Fortunately for the administration's political prospects, these efforts to prevent further violence had consolidated by the beginning of FDR's final reelection campaign.

White House and War Department Planning for the 1944 Presidential Election

As the 1944 presidential elections neared, and as the threat to order receded, policy-makers' attention shifted again to consider the president's electoral prospects. Daniels now had the "delicate task" of trying to prevent "explosions injurious to the President's chances" from either

102. The California report, commissioned in August 1943, was one of several such studies written during the war. Memorandum, Philleo Nash to Jonathan Daniels, May 10, 1944, Box 29, OWI Files No. 1, Nash papers, HSTL; *Interim Report of Peace Officers Committee on Civil Disturbances*, Sacramento, California State Printing Office, 1944; J. E. Weckler and Theo E. Hall, *The Police and Minority Groups: A Program to Prevent Disorder and to Improve Relations Between Different Racial, Religious, and National Groups*, Chicago, The International City Managers' Association, 1944.

103. For a review of this effort, see Eagles, *Jonathan Daniels and Race Relations*, p. 113.

104. Memorandum for Col. Roemer, Army Service Forces, October 7, 1944, RG 4245, War Dept. Material Concerning Minority, October–December, 1944, FDRL.

proponents or opponents of race reform.[105] The FEPC's Malcolm Ross, for example, was "too ready to rock the boat" for his taste.[106] Generally, as we might expect, this season's initiatives included a number of largely symbolic concessions from the president. The postponement of House hearings on a bill making the FEPC permanent had been a mistake, Daniels argued, for it had offended black leaders, and the Republican Party was preparing to exploit the issue. He advised the president to repeat his support of the idea as a means to reinvigorate the enthusiasm of blacks in crucial swing states.[107] His judgment was confirmed by a letter from Walter White and others later that month, which identified four areas of "immediate" concern to American blacks: the passage of S.2048, making the FEPC permanent; and of S.1227, providing for the punishment of violent acts against soldiers; the reform of inequality and segregation in the armed forces; and the end of American compliance in the return of captured territories to imperial control.[108] FDR met with this delegation briefly in October and told them of his support for a permanent FEPC.[109]

Nash recommended a number of initiatives aimed at rebuilding the " 'Ten Percent' that holds the balance of power," as he called the black vote, including additional midlevel government appointments, the release of "affirmative" racial news through the party committee, and additional liaison efforts with the black press, churches, and civic associations.[110] The civilian aide to the secretary of war, Truman Gibson,

---

105. Daniels had recommended that the attorney general postpone the prosecution of the state of Alabama for its all-white primary, because it might cause a "revolt at the polls." He also successfully sought the appointment of Judge Walter Stacy of North Carolina to a committee investigating rail sector discrimination, because he understood the need to postpone action against the southern railroads until after the election. Memorandum, Jonathan Daniels to FDR, September 28, 1944, OF 93, FDRL; Eagles, *Jonathan Daniels and Race Relations*, pp. 105–17.

106. Jonathan Daniels, *White House Witness*, pp. 246–7.

107. A FEPC staffer likewise thought it important to communicate with media that reached "the articulate, opinion-shaping" liberals who needed information as "ammunition" with which to articulate their support for the committee. Memorandum, Max Berking to Malcolm Ross, May 4, 1944, Office Memoranda, October 1942–January 1945, "B," Office Files of Malcolm Ross, June 1940–June 1948. FEPC Headquarters Records; see also memorandum, Theodore A. Jones to Malcolm Ross, September 5, 1944, Documents File, both in SDR-COFEP; memorandum, Jonathan Daniels to Maj. Gen. Edwin M. Watson, September 6, 1944, papers of Jonathan Daniels, SHC-UNC; Reed, *Seedtime*, p. 162.

108. Letter, Mary McLeod Bethune et al. to Franklin Roosevelt, September 28, 1944, Daniels papers, SHC-UNC.

109. Reed, *Seedtime*, p. 164.

110. Memorandum to National Democratic Committee, unsigned, undated, Negro Vote, box 62, Nash papers, HSTL.

Jr., recommended transforming the Army's race policy from a reactive to a planning and political orientation.

> Whenever undue and strong pressures are applied and action results, nobody is satisfied. It would be much the wiser policy for the Army, in my opinion, to recognize and anticipate the political situation and take immediate steps to prevent the necessity for drastic action next summer.[111]

Gibson noted that the last campaign had produced enormous pressure for reforms of Army practices and resulted in a presidential statement on black participation in the Army Air Force as well as the appointment of Judge Hastie. Currently, the treatment of blacks by the armed forces was the most important issue in the "general effort to capture the Negro vote." While much of the violence involving black soldiers occurred outside the jurisdiction of the federal government, many people still believed that the administration was ultimately responsible for the safety of these men. Coalition peacekeepers had apparently succeeded in holding the "solid" Democratic South, Gibson reasoned, so several initiatives might safely mobilize critically important black majorities in north-central and northeastern industrial states. These included committing black units to combat, requesting immediate Senate action on the bill providing punishment for the killing or assaulting of federal officers, moving black troops out of the South, and distributing pamphlets and movies concerning the role of these soldiers in the war.[112]

Gibson's strategy was a product of the last election. Of the five Deep South states stretching from South Carolina to Louisiana, Roosevelt's 1940 share of the popular vote was lowest in Georgia, at 84.8 percent, and ranged as high as 95.6 percent in South Carolina. As one moved away from this core, electoral safety lessened slightly; the five states bordering the black belt states produced Democratic majorities ranging from 67.3 percent in Tennessee to 80.9 percent in Texas. The 113 electoral college votes produced by these ten extraordinarily safe but moderately populated states, however, exceeded the combined share of New York, Pennsylvania, and Illinois by only one. Unfortunately for the president, the contest in the latter three states was very competitive. In neither the 1940 nor the 1944 election did the president's share of the

---

111. On the advantages of preventive measures, see also Robert C. Weaver, "The Problem of Race Relations in Public Administration," *Opportunity*, July 1943, p. 110.

112. The South, he wrote, "will have little choice but to vote for the President, so that a number of actions now considered impolitic might not seem so in the midst of a campaign to secure the control of eight or nine states and particularly states like New York, Pennsylvania, Michigan and Illinois." Memorandum, Truman K. Gibson, Jr., to the Assistant Secretary of War, November 3, 1943, MacGregor and Nalty, eds., *Blacks in the Armed Forces*, vol. V, pp. 288–90.

popular vote exceed 53.2 percent in any of the three; this was Pennsylvania in 1940, which turned in the largest percentage for Roosevelt in either election from any of the eight industrial states linking Illinois to Massachusetts.[113] Most of the approximately three million potential black voters were concentrated in cities in eight states: Indiana, Michigan, New Jersey, Missouri, Ohio, Illinois, Pennsylvania, and New York. Each state's African American vote derived its importance from the fact that it was larger than the local vote differential between the two presidential candidates in 1940. According to polls, the state most favorable to FDR was New York, where he held about 65 percent of the black vote.[114]

As the 1944 election neared, Gibson recommended other visible concessions, since black resentment toward the treatment of soldiers had made the Army "sort of a whipping boy for both parties." The Army had learned over the past four years that "Negro opinion in this country cannot be disregarded and particularly at election time." Again citing four military concessions offered in 1940, including the announcement of the acceptance of blacks into the Army Air Force – although planning for the project began a full year later and actual training started two years after that – Gibson urged the secretary of war to make a public statement announcing "a study for the purpose of developing plans" for the postwar use of black troops. At the same time, Gibson counseled the inherently difficult task of avoiding any move that would "smack of politics." Gibson's concern was that the War Department embrace "a decent and fair overall policy" that would avoid the errors of the recent past.[115] Black attitudes had changed significantly since the previous election campaign, and votes could no longer be purchased by distributing money "to and through party hacks" or by distributing jobs "to a few individual Negroes," one editorial warned.[116] Given the caution inherent to this campaign, however, the most significant federal race policy of the year was the Supreme Court's ruling in *Smith* v. *Alright*, that white primaries violated the 15th Amendment and were therefore unconstitutional. The campaign season was also marked by the close attention of African American organizations to FDR's choice of Harry Truman as

113. Congressional Quarterly, *Presidential Elections Since 1789*, Washington, D.C., Congressional Quarterly, Inc., 1979, pp. 52–3, 94.
114. "Evaluation of the Negro Vote," unattributed and undated memorandum, ca. August 1943, OWI Files No. 1, Box 29, Nash papers, HSTL.
115. The administration should initiate constructive steps itself or expect to be "forced again by pressures from outside sources." Memorandum, Truman K. Gibson, Jr., to John McCloy, September 5, 1944, MacGregor and Nalty, eds., *Blacks in the Armed Forces*, vol. VII, pp. 8–9.
116. "A Declaration by Negro Votes," Charlotte *Star of Zion*, January 13, 1944.

his running mate at the party convention, the struggle in Congress for an additional year's appropriation for the FEPC, and the passage of the GI Bill.

Summary

Americans reelected their president in 1944, although his margins were the smallest of any of his four victories. As Gibson had foreseen, the Democratic vote fell, affordably, from 3 to 8 percent in southern states. Close races, however, marked the eight industrial core states. Roosevelt managed to carry seven, although six returned Democratic margins smaller than 1940, and his strongest showing in any one of them was the 52.8 percent he tallied in Massachusetts. Michigan, won by Republican Wendell Wilkie in 1940 by roughly seven thousand of two million votes cast, turned Democratic; in 1944, Roosevelt beat Thomas Dewey by over twenty-two thousand. Had blacks throughout the nation voted in 1944 for Dewey in the same proportion as they in fact did for Roosevelt, the Republican would have won.[117]

Roosevelt began planning his campaign as soon as he returned from the Tehran Conference in December of 1943, for he had concluded that he required another term to finish his work abroad. But the American public was more concerned with the postwar domestic economy, and remained generally uninformed about foreign affairs and foreign policy, polls showed. His comments in late 1943 that there was now no need for the New Deal proved misleading, since he spent the following campaign year "polishing" his reform credentials, starting with the unusually liberal State of the Union address of 1944, in which he called for a "second Bill of Rights" to establish economic security for all Americans "regardless of station or race or creed." Throughout the year, FDR managed foreign policy in part to prevent disruptions to his election prospects.[118]

One measure of the transformation in federal race policy is the change in the White House response to two challenges to race stability in the capital over two years. In the spring of 1941, the administration quickly exhausted its short supply of relatively meager concessions before settling on the executive order founding the FEPC. In June of 1943, rumors

---

117. For a discussion of what C. Vann Woodward called "the strategic location of the Negro minority in the North," see Doug McAdam, *Political Process and Development of Black Insurgency, 1930–1970*, Chicago, University of Chicago Press, 1982, pp. 81–2; C. Vann Woodward, *The Strange Career of Jim Crow*, New York, Oxford University Press, 1966, p. 129.

118. Dallek, *FDR and American Foreign Policy*, p. 481.

again raced through Washington, D.C., propelled by the rallies and pickets surrounding the FEPC's ongoing investigation of the city's public transportation system, which refused to hire black platform workers and motormen in part because its AFL union refused to cooperate. In this case, skillful police work, and a declaration of the rally site as out-of-bounds to servicemen, prevented any violence from interfering with the case.[119] Daniels brought his intelligence assets to bear, contacting Hoover's office to ask for information on the attitude of white workers toward the prospect of the integration of the operators; the majority of workers objected to the plan, he was told, and would mount a paralyzing wildcat strike if it were attempted.[120] Within a week, Daniels, having learned of FDR's belief that there should be no hearing on Capital Transit for the duration of the war, characteristically offered to postpone the hearings himself in order to "take the heat off" both FDR and the FEPC.[121] The January 1945 hearing, held well after the elections as planned, proved to be ineffective in changing the firm's hiring policy.[122]

119. Memorandum, Philleo Nash to Jonathan Daniels, June 21, 1943, OWI Files No. 1, box 29, Nash papers, HSTL.

120. Letter, J. Edgar Hoover to Jonathan Daniels, December 9, 1944, FBI Material Concerning Minorities, 4245, FDRL.

121. Memorandum, Jonathan Daniels to FDR, December 15, 1944, General Files, Daniels papers, SHC-UNC.

122. A confidential source in government advised the FBI that the committee would be pursuing compliance to the nondiscriminatory policy in the near future; through Hoover, Daniels learned from this informant that January 1945 would be "crucial." "Racial Conditions in the District of Columbia," December 7, 1944, attached to letter, Hoover to Daniels, December 9, 1944, FBI Material Concerning Minorities, OF 4245, FDRL; Reed, *Seedtime*, p. 332.

8

"America Again at the Crossroads": War and Race in the Twentieth-Century United States

All this organizing of death-dealing energy and technique is not a natural but very sophisticated process. Particularly in modern nations, but also all through the course of modern European history, it could never exist without the State. For it follows the desires of no religious, industrial, political group.

Randolph S. Bourne[1]

Modern war is a conflict between societies organized by states. No polity can escape this law, least of all when a war is as encompassing as World War II. Its unprecedented destructive force and its enduring effects re-shaped global politics as did no other event in history: it dealt colonialism a mortal blow, defeated fascism outright, "solved" the most severe global economic depression, and vaulted the United States and the Soviet Union to superpower status. So far as this century is concerned, what preceded it was prologue and what followed it, epilogue. But despite causing extensive innovation in race management techniques, and bringing new economic opportunities to all Americans, the war contained rather than facilitated movements for black liberation.

This chapter's title is identical to that of Myrdal's concluding chapter, because this book reconsiders a core problem of that great work and of American political development more generally: What are the political effects of war? The inquiry began with a distinction between a political and institutional explanation of this episode and Myrdal's ideational theory of interracial change, which predicted reform as the by-product of a cognitive dilemma caused by the contradiction between racist practices and foundational democratic ideals. Given the inconsistency between America's war aims and her biased conduct in daily life, Myrdal

1. Randolph S. Bourne, "The State," in Carl Resek, ed., *War and the Intellectuals: Collected Essays, 1915–1919*, New York, Harper & Row, 1964, p. 81.

243

claimed that the war would both enable black organizations to better press their claims and open white psyches to the just pursuit of core principles via inclusive and egalitarian reforms. In a representative passage, Myrdal noted that blacks understood that the war's democratic aims were not initially intended for them.

> But there was more reason and more opportunity for protest. The democratic ideology stimulated by the war . . . outweighed the emphasis upon "wartime unity and harmony," and gave the Negro protest an ear among the whites, at least in the North. These same things made the Negro want to protest more.[2]

In every manpower sphere examined here, however, statesmen interrupted the tendency of this ideological war to promote collective, ideological claim-making. While incremental reforms of the postwar period may have been influenced by this ideational process, the frontal attack on statutory segregation fell short of victory for an additional twenty-three years after Pearl Harbor launched this democratic war. Even if white attitudes did shift substantially to support freedom, fairness, and the franchise, other factors blocked reform. One predominant constraint over the ensuing two decades was the southern segregationist contingent in Congress. But so far as explanations of wartime policies are concerned, a less appreciated variable is the American Executive.

In this case, democratic ideals clearly failed to decisively affect White House decision-makers, who explicitly rejected such ideals as a basis for its policy preferences. From the midwar vantage point of Mark Ethridge, the first chairman of the FEPC, the northern black leadership's interest in "abstractions" placed them decidedly behind the times. Claiming that it was the *previous* war that concerned "abstracts" such as extending self-determination and democracy, Ethridge argued that blacks' interest in such ideals placed them "about fifty years behind us in their interpretation of liberalism." In this regard, the FEPC official articulated what was a consistent orientation of American statesmen, including the chief of state.[3] Shortly after FDR returned from the Tehran Conference in December 1943, for example, a press conference shifted to consider the

2. Gunnar Myrdal, *An American Dilemma: The Negro Problem and Modern Democracy*, with the assistance of Richard Sterner and Arnold Rose, New York, Harper & Brothers Publishers, 1944, pp. x–xvii, p. 755.

3. As Francis Biddle later described FDR's wartime mindset: "He was never theoretical about things. What must be done to defend the country must be done." Mark Ethridge, "The Race Problem in the War," address to Harvard War Institute, undated, ca. 1943, papers of Mark Ethridge, SHC-UNC, p. 15.

president's personal impressions of Marshal Josef Stalin. "What type would you call him?" a reporter asked. "I would call him something like me," Roosevelt said, ". . . a realist."[4]

Sectional Political Economies and the Mobilization of the Races

On the war's eve, American statesmen surveyed a political patchwork of sectionally organized economic and racial groups. Because the federal government as a whole was thoroughly penetrated by these social forces and had established, buttressed, or tolerated widely varying local regimes of race policy, the geographic location of subsequent agency activity helped to determine policy outcomes in this period.[5] The power of sectional interests stemmed from the concurrence of several factors: the regional bifurcation of the ruling party into powerful southern conservative and non-southern liberal factions; the related regional bifurcation of predominate industrial interests in the North and agricultural interests in the South; and the emergency mobilization itself, which initially exaggerated these regional differences, particularly as they related to black-white relations. Sectional patterns of friction quickly emerged as the byproduct of variance in the political and economic opportunities available to African Americans nationwide.

Of the three manpower fields examined here, the South contained the sphere most closely supervised by federal authorities, the Army, as well as the least "federalized" farm labor market. A tradition of southern white control, and the exaggerated importance local elites attached to race supremacy, combined to stock Army facilities with racist rather than statist attitudes. Although officials expected rigid segregation to deter racial conflict, inherited policies inadvertently caused, collected, and bottled up resentment among black soldiers because officials reacted against even superficially deviant behavior and because many soldiers believed that formal grievance-handling mechanisms were illegitimate. The absence of a Black Cabinet office in the thirties had left the War Department ill-prepared for its new tasks. When challenges finally

---

4. Quoted in Robert Dallek, *Franklin D. Roosevelt and American Foreign Policy*, New York, Oxford University Press, 1989, p. 439.

5. While the central state helped sustain segregation through the first half of the twentieth century, it began to turn away from it in the thirties; various agencies shifted their positions on race with various degrees of commitment and through various means. For an analysis of twentieth-century race policies in a range of federal agencies, including prisons and the civil service, see Desmond King, *Separate But Unequal: Black Americans and the US Federal Government*, New York, Oxford University Press, 1995.

emerged, they were explosive and violent. The overriding concern in the Army, therefore, was to restore efficiency by checking unrest through a wide range of regime tools: symbolic concessions, appointments, incremental but substantial reforms, as well as monitoring, surveillance, and punishment.

For capitalized cities and towns, particularly production capitals in the northern factory belt and on the west coast where blacks could vote, a more flexible and ameliorative racial regime provided for the administrative adjustment of relatively minor disputes. Recourse to the investigative process and access to race advancement organizations encouraged groups and individuals to quickly challenge discriminatory practices, generally as individuals. While the FEPC goal of adjusting individual disputes differed little from that of the work of Gen. Davis in the Army, the legitimacy of the former was enriched by its birth as a product of threatened direct action; the utility of the latter suffered from the official's supposed moderation. Dense networks of state facilities and official oversight produced more FEPC complaints, and in turn the most prompt and effective rates of enforcement. Thus, the utilization of black factory labor progressed much further in the North and in the "federal cities" of the far West, where acute labor shortage areas and state authorities and installations also were concentrated. Because different sections of the United States experienced different mobilizations of the races, and because the ruling party in different sections was variously an agent of repression or liberation, the mobilization established a number of diverse battlegrounds within the broad campaign for racial advantage and fairness.

Whether these race initiatives were effective uses of the discretionary power of the president depended on whom was asked. In January 1944, rumor had it that New Deal stalwart Robert Weaver would resign from the administration after eight years of work. Friends reported that he had recognized the "hopelessness of the Federal approach." This threat to resign was his third of the war, but in a clear indication of the decline of black leverage that coincided with the advance of Allied forces abroad, the first to be accepted by War Manpower Commission officials.[6] Indeed, the period during which political and economic currents

6. Early in the mobilization, when William Knudsen, Office of Production Management chairman, balked at a memo to contractors pressing for the full utilization of black labor, Weaver offered his resignation and Knudsen relented. He also wanted to resign when the FEPC was reorganized the previous June, but McNutt prevailed upon him to stay, where he assisted in drafting the agreement linking WMC to FEPC and establishing field offices for the minorities group section with liaison to FEPC offices. "Bob Weaver, Fed Up With New Deal, Ready to Quit," Baltimore *Afro-American*, January 8, 1944.

favored race organizations was as short-lived as the total war economy. As early as December 1943, only eighteen months after African Americans first found widespread employment, industry experienced a net loss of workers and despite the exhortations of the president, the public began focusing on postwar plans. Noting that cutbacks had already caused plants to discharge black workers, the San Antonio *Register* urged that "the Race prepare itself, for the goose that has been laying the golden egg is on her way out." Organizations such as the National Urban League had likewise turned its attention to retaining job gains made during the war.[7] Other Black Cabinet members abandoned their work with the executive, instructing their followers to develop other ways of affecting policy. Alfred E. Smith, former race relations officer of the Works Progress Administration, noted that the heyday of the Black Cabinet had ended. Addressing a 1944 NAACP membership meeting, Smith noted that the cabinet included less than a dozen high-level executives, and fewer officials were listening to their advice. The cabinet, he announced, "can no longer reach the President."[8]

At the same time, FDR's "White Cabinet" exulted in its accomplishments. In September 1944, one month before Roosevelt's fourth election victory, Jonathan Daniels proudly reminded his chief that the nation's cities had been more calm that summer. "This did not just happen," he wrote. "This whole matter has been carefully and steadily watched for you in order that issues could be met as they arose."[9] Philleo Nash also believed that the administration had triumphed in the cities, according to rules of thumb in federal agencies: "Success in this field means that tensions have been reduced, violence averted, and law enforcement left in the hands of local authorities."[10] The War Department's John McCloy later "marveled" at the fact that, given the concentration of troops and the escalation of tensions, "we escaped some ugly difficulties."[11] These insulating war administrators, who rose to prominence after Black

7. "The Goose That Lays the Golden Egg is Leaving," San Antonio *Register*, March 19, 1944; "Nationwide Campaign to Retain Jobs in Post-War Period Planned," Atlanta *Daily World*, February 3, 1944.

8. "Black Cabinet is Blacked Out, Smith Tells Audience," Baltimore *Afro-American*, January 29, 1944.

9. Memorandum, Jonathan Daniels to FDR, September 28, 1944, OF 4245, OPM, Committee on Fair Employment Practice, FDRL.

10. Memorandum, Philleo Nash to David Niles, undated, ca. June 1945, "Admin. Files, Civil Rts., 1937–1944," Papers of David Niles, HSTL.

11. Testimony of John McCloy, Minutes, President's Committee on Equality of Treatment, March 17, 1949, HSTL, as quoted in Desmond King, " 'The Longest Road to Equality:' The Politics of Institutional Desegregation Under Truman," *Journal of Historical Sociology*, vol. 6, no. 2, June, 1993, p. 143.

Cabinet advisement proved unsatisfactory, unanimously believed in the rightness of their cause. These men were not racial chauvinists; their satisfaction stemmed not from obstructing race advancement per se but from contributing to the restoration of social order in the critical war years of 1943 and 1944.

The Timing of Challenges and the Quality of Responses

The initial assumption of this work was that war causes statesmen to refashion governing relationships with social groups so as to secure services or resources for national defense. In the United States, the formal constitutional powers of the president evolved over the course of the 19th and early 20th centuries into an expansive power to pursue both national security and political party imperatives. These two overriding goals suggest two distinct and characteristic policymaking patterns. The case histories sustain the expectation that the system's two executives – the chief of state and the more recently developed public head of party – pursue social peace as an essential precondition of success in each arena. Electoral considerations asserted themselves most forcefully in the six months prior to a presidential election. A competitive race made the party head even more vulnerable to opponents' attempts to poach independent or swing voters, as were African Americans at the time. Thus, several of the most ameliorative and symbolic presidential acts of this episode can be attributed to campaign seasons. In 1940, FDR appointed well-known African Americans to prominent positions in war agencies. In 1942, the elections empowered "radical" northerners who caused the consolidation of the FEPC's position in the mobilization hierarchy. In 1944, FDR rededicated himself to liberal economic policies generally, and, among other things, officials directed the Army to speed the deployment of black soldiers overseas.

National security concerns on the other hand are unpredictable by definition: The most effective attacks and the most unsettling disruptions gain their strength from surprise. Three episodes of insecurity forced statesmen to alter race policies in 1941, 1942, and 1943. Until December 1941 the likelihood of war was growing at an incremental but also indeterminate rate. Randolph's novel March threat was difficult to assess, but in conjunction with international uncertainty, and serious instability in cities, he momentarily invented leverage enough to force the president to act. The FEPC concession in turn launched a sustained period of conflict between statesmen and committee members. After the American war began, and the second, more grave episode of national insecurity commenced, the mobilization-instability-adjustment sequence functioned as outlined in Chapter 1. The foreign threat to national security was severe and relatively stable through 1942 and early 1943, and officials struggled to speed production at home. The mobilization indirectly caused new forms of contention, and statesmen seeking efficiency invented new ways to ease the friction. This period is characterized by fairly crude efforts at repression in the armed forces, coupled with the rejection of the advisement and enforcement efforts of the radical Hastie, and in industrial manpower, by the neutralization of militants in FEPC operations. In each case, officials attempted to insulate the president from disruptive protest and agitation by promoting "realistic" elites of both races. Significantly, FDR removed himself from the midterm campaign of 1942, in effect suspending presidential party politics to focus on his responsibilities as chief of state.

The third and final period of national insecurity was the widespread race violence of May–August, 1943, which threatened to disrupt the mobilization in all three spheres. In agriculture, officials moved to neutralize militant whites by allowing them additional control over farm labor; Congress passed Public Law 45, creating the Emergency Farm Labor Supply Program, to better anchor black farm labor in rural areas. As an indirect means of undermining northern militancy, Jonathan Daniels attempted to promote the conservative southern leadership through federal support of agricultural education. In the Army, officials promulgated an equal access policy that eliminated one form of segregation for facilities and transportation. In addition, there was substantial innovation in the fields of surveillance, recreation, indoctrination, and public relations. In the employment field, FDR recast the FEPC in the spring of 1943 to weaken extremists of both races and to improve the utilization of black manpower in factories. By late 1943, challenges to national security declined in intensity in both foreign and domestic settings. The elections of 1940 and 1944 thus served as bookends to three unexpected national security threats that emerged in the interim.

In addition to a shared trajectory of policy making, each of the three manpower spheres generated plans that in broadly similar ways attempted to reduce the inefficiencies caused by race discrimination and exclusion as they related to manpower placement.[12] All plans ideally sought three essential goals: the optimally efficient distribution of the

12. A concern for domestic social order and mobilization efficiency are in general best served by reforms directed at the masses, while vote-seeking concessions in a party machine context are more likely to reward and promote influential elites. The 1944 campaign, which prompted broad revisions in black troop policy but no important appointments, thus signals a shift away from the Black Cabinet techniques with which FDR began the war.

factors of production and warmaking, including manpower; uninterrupted production, supply, and deployment; and the consolidation of mobilization-centered advising. In factory employment, the first goal required the channeling of unemployed and underemployed labor to essential industries and attaching factory labor to appropriate occupations. Weaver's work explicitly pursued this goal, while the fieldwork of the second FEPC in particular also served this purpose. In the Army, segregation obstructed the optimal assignment of personnel. The problem resisted indirect solutions such as remedial education programs, while the attempt to maximize efficiency within segregation, through the use of black battalions in service roles for example, caused collateral problems such as low morale, duplication, and waste. In farming, mobilization officials preferred to allow farm labor to leave the countryside, but white planter demands forced them to concede a measure of labor control to local elites. Under these conditions, inefficiency simply meant less intense work routines, resulting from higher black family incomes occasioned by the war economy. In addition to these sector-specific conceptualizations of efficiency, all of these cases clearly bred race friction and a search for social peace. Finally, each manpower sphere eventually produced statesmen, largely white, who viewed warfighting and party building as their primary duties. In the FEPC and in the War Department, such officials replaced black appointees who, it was believed, too closely tracked their group's particular agendas. The replacement of personnel was one symptom of the ongoing attempt to reassess the initial design of manpower policy advisement and policymaking to better insulate the executive branch from disruptive social forces and to reorient practices toward transcendent party and security imperatives.

Although the war intensified militancy, the protest never consolidated into a broad unified movement of black liberation because statesmen acted to increase production, defuse tensions, and restore moderation to policy debates. Officials helped right the American ship of state by wielding old tools and by developing new ones. In the field of surveillance in particular, innovation was substantial. In sum, whereas the central state began World War II with a reactive orientation and a rather narrow range of party machine and policing techniques, it finished the conflict with a more complex repertoire of measures to prevent and defuse new forms of unrest. The administration's responses were almost always expedient ones. But it is to black organizations' credit that the concessions evolved in a direction favorable to them, from symbolic, individual appointments to the reform of substantive policies affecting the masses.

War and Black Militancy

The longer historical record of race advocacy during war is consistent with one of Myrdal's central predictions and appears to contradict a second. As he observed and predicted, black organizations developed during twentieth-century wars. Major wars helped propel unusually large, successful, and radical all-black liberation movements: Marcus Garvey's Universal Negro Improvement Association, Randolph's March on Washington Movement, and the Black Power movement of Stokley Carmichael's Student Non-Violent Coordinating Committee and the Black Panthers. But each case exemplifies both the sense of opportunity and the mechanisms of constraint that characterize wartime state-society relations. Garvey, for example, denounced almost the entire black leadership for seeking cultural assimilation and white support during and on the heels of the Great War. Driven by a pessimism about the possibility for the races to live together, he opposed black participation in World War I, rejected pacifism, and planned a mass repatriation in Africa, building the largest and broadest mass movement in African American history up to that time.[13] By 1925, Garvey was in Atlanta's federal penitentiary and his movement was doomed.

But it is very difficult to confirm the claim that wars have revealed the American Dilemma to white psyches. The three peaks of racial crowd violence – around 1920, 1943, and 1968 – also occurred during and just after major wars.[14] Most of the violent crowd actions of the First World War were white-on-black events, with the exception of the portentous Houston incident of 1917. Most black citizens either subscribed to Garvey's nationalistic project or DuBois's well-known appeal to "close ranks" for the duration of the war. Instead of greater civil rights and fairer treatment, however, the Armistice produced a rash of lynchings

13. "The first dying that is to be done by the black man in the future will be done to make himself free." Garvey's military pageantry and aristocratic courtliness were analogues of the martial political culture of World War I. By the end of 1919, he claimed two million members for the UNIA, but this is more realistically a rough estimate of the number of his followers. Lawrence W. Levine, "Marcus Garvey and the Politics of Revitalization," in John Hope Franklin and August Meier, eds., *Black Leaders of the Twentieth Century*, Urbana, University of Illinois Press, 1982, pp. 112, 116–17.

14. Allen D. Grimshaw, ed., *Racial Violence in the United States*, Chicago, Aldine Publishing Company, 1969; Morris Janowitz, "Patterns of Collective Racial Violence," in *Violence in America: Historical and Comparative Perspectives*, Hugh Davis Graham and Ted Robert Gurr, eds., New York, Signet Books, 1969; Harvard Sitkoff, "Racial Militancy and Interracial Violence in the Second World War," *Journal of American History*, vol. 58, December, 1971.

and deadly invasions of black neighborhoods by whites. By 1941, the failure of this prior strategy was clear, and DuBois renounced the advice he once gave. The Great War "proved a disillusioning experience for the Negro," wrote Horace Cayton at the time. The editor of the Louisville *Courier-Journal* warned a 1941 NAACP conference of the lessons of history.

> . . . the promises made to the Negro after the first world war by politicians and leaders and leaders were not kept. It was all a lot of eyewash but they think of the Negro when the crisis comes.

Black soldier morale, observers noted, had grown more realistic since the earlier war, when appeals to patriotism were generally effective.[15] Black organizations demanded reforms from federal authorities much more forcefully than they had previously, through tactics ranging from the militant and provocative March on Washington Movement, to systemic soldier resistance, to defiant resignations of black administrators. The government's practices during the Second World War did not alter white attitudes as Myrdal claimed they would. It seems clear, however, that black attitudes toward the Second World War were powerfully shaped by experiences in the First World War.

Thus wartime militancy had an important historical dimension. With the nascent Cold War as a backdrop to his testimony on a conscription bill before the Senate Armed Services Committee in 1948, A. Philip Randolph now openly advocated resistance to the draft, basing his call in part on the disappointing record of the federal government in World War II. This second campaign of noncompliance was again parried by an executive order, No. 9981 of July 1948, in which Harry Truman directed not integration but "equality of treatment and opportunity" for all races in the armed services. Like the executive order launching the FEPC, this one created a Committee on Equality of Treatment and Opportunity to study the question of Army integration. Full integration actually arrived via war. The Korean conflict began with segregated Army forces, but by the Armistice, 90 percent of black soldiers served in integrated units, as "the realization that desegregation could help to solve urgent military operational problems" finally defeated the institution's mistrust of sociological experimentation.[16]

15. Horace Cayton, "Negro Morale," *Opportunity*, December, 1941, p. 371; "Stress Seven Acts Against Democracy," Chicago *Bee*, July 6, 1941; as quoted in memorandum, Robert C. Weaver to Jonathan Daniels, September 4, 1943, OF 4245, OPM, COFEP, WMC, p. 2. See also Pearl S. Buck, "Too Much Unity is a Danger," *Opportunity*, April, 1941, pp. 110–11.
16. Benjamin Quarles, "A. Philip Randolph: Labor Leader at Large," in Franklin and Meier, eds., *Black Leaders*, p. 159; Martin Binkin et al., *Blacks in the Military*,

Finally, the radical turn in part of the civil rights movement in the 1960s toward a black nationalist agenda overlapped with the intensification of a war that – even at its outset – very few believed would liberate black Americans. If the first three wars of the century were plausibly animated by a resistance to tyranny abroad, the Vietnam War bore less resemblance to the nation's founding ideals in this regard. By the summer of 1965, SNCC's James Forman and Robert Moses had both openly criticized the nation's involvement in the conflict, and as they aligned their organization with international movements against white imperialism and capitalism, congressional and FBI hostility toward them increased in turn. As it rolled on, more African Americans viewed the war as an effort to restore a regime rooted in western colonialism and now saw the Defense Department's generous deployment of minorities as a reflection of the bias of statesmen. The racial separatism of the sixties was once again a by-product of a war fought by statesmen unwilling to intervene to protect its own citizens' rights at home. White opinion actually began to turn away from principled integrationism during this war. Measures of the salience of the civil rights issue began to decline in 1966, after the passage of the Civil Rights and Voting Rights Acts, and as black nationalism gained more followers.

To African Americans, each generation's war was not unlike an election: a recurrent, federally sanctioned collective enterprise with an important and systematic exclusionary aspect. America's wars failed to fulfill the nation's promise first in their utilization of black manpower. By the time the nation had corrected the means of war, the president pursued a conflict that failed the nation in its ends. In every case, the failure focused attention on the fraud of the American Creed – but in the minds of African Americans rather than of European Americans, for large segments of the white population has repeatedly rejected race egalitarianism during and after wars. The bitter racial divide of the late sixties was in part a culmination and in part a reprise of a long-running sideshow to America's wars, as once again central authorities engaged a rising wave of militancy while, in the background, many whites quietly sought out ways to reestablish race prerogatives.

Democratic Presidents If Not Democratic Wars

These recurrent themes are in part a product of the fact that the president's partisan orientation has shown a remarkable if accidental degree

Washington, the Brookings Institution, 1982, pp. 26–30; Sherie Merson and Steven Schlossman, *Foxholes & Color Lines: Desegregating the U.S. Armed Forces*, Baltimore, Johns Hopkins University Press, 1998, p. 219.

of similarity over the last four wars. In each case, the war was launched by a Democrat committed to maintaining the party's heterogeneous collection of class, racial, and regional factions: Woodrow Wilson, Franklin Roosevelt, Harry Truman, and Lyndon Johnson. Thus, one reason why this century's war-induced black militancy failed to propel the cause of black liberation until the breakthrough of the 1960s was that party coalitional imperatives reenforced the wartime executive's instinctive conservatism regarding social reform (see Figure 8.1).

Perhaps more importantly, the first three presidents had also more or less exhausted the nation's appetite for reform; the fourth did so concurrently with his war mobilization. Wilson set this "curious pattern," as Robert Divine has called it, winning the 1912 election on a New Freedom platform that essentially ignored foreign concerns.[17] He helped bring the Progressive movement to fruition in his first term through the Clayton Anti-Trust Act, the Federal Reserve Act, and the regulation of fair trade through the Federal Trade Commission. Wilson combined this progressivism with an embrace of southern racial conservatism, segregating federal agencies and reducing the number of black federal appointees. The outbreak of World War I in 1914 turned his energies toward international issues, culminating in the American entry into the conflict in April 1917. While American forces tipped the balance in the war in the trenches, Wilson's attempts to reorder international politics at the Paris Peace Conference and later through his prized League of Nations left him a broken man and left the nation suspicious of active presidents. This sequence of domestic reform and international war also obtained in the case of FDR, whose domestic reform initiatives were even more ambitious. He sought nothing less than the revitalization of the nation's competitive spirit and economic potential through two full terms of experimental regulatory, relief, and recovery measures that included the enactment of the Wagner Act, the Social Security Act, and a progressive taxation plan. Voters responded to his leadership in 1936 with a lopsided reelection victory. The second term, however, entailed the defeat of his plan to pack the Supreme Court, which split his supporters, and his half-baked attempt to purge conservative Democrats in the 1938 primaries. His claim to have mastered the Depression was undermined by the recession of the same year, and intraparty conflict over race and labor policy began to rise. With the effort to arm England against the Nazis, and with the beginning of the Pacific War in late 1941, the founding phase of the New Deal had ended.

17. Robert A. Divine, *Roosevelt and World War II*, New York, Penguin Books, 1969, p. 1.

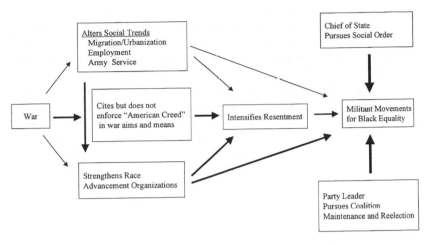

Figure 8.1. War and social change in the twentieth-century United States: state
and party imperatives in the African American case.

When Harry Truman became president in 1945, he was determined
to fulfill the promise of his predecessor, and after his surprising election
victory in 1948, he pursued his own Fair Deal. But a bipartisan conservative coalition in Congress resisted his plans, and the invasion of South
Korea in 1950 eliminated whatever chance he had for a successful domestic record. The American people grew tired of the bloody stalemate
and turned to a Republican who promised to end both the conflict and
domestic policy experimentation. Lyndon Johnson likewise arrived at
the White House determined to fulfill the reform potential of his predecessor, and he quickly achieved major legislation in the spheres of civil
rights and social insurance. Under the banner of the Great Society, he
declared a war on poverty that gained him the votes of liberals in the
1964 campaign. The summer after the election Johnson began the grim
escalation of the conflict in Vietnam, leading to the sustained bombard-
ment of the north, and the deployment of over a half-million American
soldiers to combat in the south. Most of his experiments in social policy,
including new programs for the environment, education, and the arts,
were crippled by budgetary constraints caused by the war, and the early
years of a bitter national war debate drove him from the White
House.

The American polity has never completed a twentieth-century war
except as a postscript to a wave of progressive Democratic reforms and
the concurrent reorganization of central state capacity. The Roosevelt

case thus exemplifies two intraparty factors that influenced race policy during wars. First, each president discarded or altered his domestic social agenda to fight his war, and in doing so reduced the executive's dependence on and attentiveness to those movement organizations, policymaking networks, and executive branch advisors seeking egalitarian reform. Second, each of these war presidents struggled to retain the support of the southern party faction. Over time, racial politics became nationalized as African Americans voted in greater numbers, and Democratic presidents increasingly defied the Dixiecrats' preferences. But the president's dependence on this faction was a constraining influence on liberal reform in each instance. Thus, for both general national security and contextual partisan reasons, this century's war presidents were predisposed toward containing rather than enabling recurrent African American insurgencies.

The Legacies and Lessons of World War II Race Struggles

In sum, did World War II energize or undermine the nascent race advancement movement? Both, and in that order. The period resulted in real gains for the campaign for the liberation of African Americans, particularly in the form of a striking decline in black poverty and striking increases in organization membership. But in each case examined here, favorable policy outcomes were a by-product of the central state's pursuit of primary goals. This dynamic limited the direct influence of these innovations on peacetime developments. For example, the war strengthened the prospects of fair employment policy by promoting the idea of using federal funds as a tool by which to alter the practices of citizens, firms, and local governments, even though the contract-cancellation mechanism was never used during the war for race-related ends. In addition, many local states subsequently created their own fair employment bureaucracies after the war. But these efforts, as well as those of the Equal Employment Opportunity Commission, a component of the 1964 Civil Rights Act, exploited the legacy of the FEPC primarily by eliminating those characteristics that had debilitated the pioneering agency: a vague charter, a lack of enforcement power, and a high degree of dependence on and deference to local authorities and norms. In agriculture, the primary effect of this war was to reenforce an ongoing migration by moving several million blacks and whites out of rural areas. Black women in particular seized new opportunities in contributing twice as many new workers to the war economy as did black men. Even if their work as field laborers was finally ending, however, the migration of blacks from farms during the war gained only the qualified and temporary approval of statesmen in the most labor-short areas. Finally, the Army, despite a fundamentally new appreciation of the race problem, retained its segregation policies for an additional five years. Here, however, World War II launched a slow adjustment process at the core of the central state where coercive command as well as the martial ethos could be used to bring about white compliance with integration. The military also continued to offer black youth education and training opportunities superior to those generally found in private labor markets, as well as one of the nation's first integrated professional career ladders. The Cold War ensured that the number of such opportunities would grow. But, again, the record of this organizational shift toward integration during World War II was the result of efficiency concerns as much as of the core ideals of the Republic.

There were costs to the FEPC initiative in particular. A broad social movement requires stable and appropriate sets of routines – joining movement institutions to authorities and administrators – to pursue its goals in an efficient, focused, and sustained way.[18] While the war invented several new avenues for the pursuit of egalitarian race reform, the FEPC in retrospect appears to have been a detour from the main lines of the development of race politics. In creating, neutralizing, empowering, and then allowing the abolishment of the FEPC, statesmen essentially feigned interest in establishing a permanent federal employment apparatus. Race policy holdovers in the Truman administration, such as Jonathan Daniels, acquiesced to congressional elimination of the committee in 1946 just as the agency had learned to reduce tensions stemming from the relocation and growth of the black factory labor force, and more importantly just as civil rights organizations had become adept at targeting and utilizing this bureaucracy. After the familiar federal host had vanished, ten years passed as various wings of the movement redeployed its expertise and resources toward Congress, subordinate levels of government, and the judiciary. Robert Weaver's decision to become the director of the mayor's Race Relations Committee in Chicago personified this broad transformation of political opportunities. When he resigned, he advised blacks to turn away from their reliance on federal authorities and participate more fully in local and state government. The upcoming congressional elections, he announced, were more

18. In Tilly's terminology, the FEPC temporarily encouraged a new repertoire of collective action, by which he meant a small, "limited set of routines that are learned, shared, and acted out through a relatively deliberate process of choice." Charles Tilly, "Contentious Repertoires in Great Britain, 1758–1834," *Social Science History*, vol. 17, no. 2, 1993, p. 264; Charles Tilly, *Popular Contention in Great Britain 1758–1834*, Cambridge, Harvard University Press, 1995, pp. 41–8.

important to them than the presidential race.[19] For several years, Thurgood Marshall's relatively narrow pursuit of legal rights in the courts replaced Philip Randolph's mass agitation as the most promising path to federal intervention. Twenty years would pass before race activists, including those seeking a permanent FEPC, were able to overcome the resistance of segregationists in Congress through the combination of legal appeals, institutional lobbying, and, most important, through the mobilization of the masses for direct action against local authorities. In sum, it is difficult to directly connect race policymaking during the war with what we know now to be the primary agent of black liberation, African American institutions and civic organizations, particularly those in the South.

Conclusion

Because of an uncertain mix of opportunity and instability, statesmen and fully vested citizens should expect movements of disadvantaged groups to pursue all of their advantages during wars. Members of groups that are not fully incorporated into the polity can reasonably conclude that they are under no obligation, as are full citizens, to subordinate their particular claims to the collective interests of the nation. Thus it is not surprising that the major policy reforms of the wartime period – the original fair employment executive order and the post facilities desegregation order, for example – resulted from social order concerns rather than from party campaigns. These case studies suggest that disadvantaged groups at such moments of opportunity can help arrange the terms by which they are incorporated into mass war mobilizations. Militants may, for example, choose to eschew their symbolic incorporation into governing regimes through elite appointees for more substantive and permanent policy gains. Gaining major party acquiescence to or acceptance of core claims is preferable to if more elusive than temporary executive acts in any case. Pursuing this logic, retrograde policies, such as Army manpower policies in 1940, can be used to reveal the most dramatic forms of injustice, assuming insurgents are willing to suffer the consequences of challenging the policies and are able to communicate these strategies and tactics to a wider public. To the extent that an insurgency begins to challenge policies in this way, effective statesmen will attempt to prevent disturbances and limit challengers' access to a wider public. An insurgent movement also brings additional leverage to

19. "WMC Adviser on Race Quits," New York *P.M.*, January 17, 1944; "Dr. Weaver's Admonition," Atlanta *Daily World*, February 5, 1944.

bear through the collectivization of its grievances; the central state may thus be expected to resist such collectivization in every case. Finally, since insurgents' power is most likely only temporarily inflated, it is imperative that challengers conceptualize group interests within a post-war context, and attempt to make these longer-term interests and goals compatible with the executive's short-term party and national security concerns. But these tasks will not be easily accomplished. The already superior strategic position of statesmen is exaggerated during wartime due to their privileged access to information and to the availability of new and old policy tools, above all the legitimate use of force. In addi-tion, given minimally dire circumstances, the executive's decision to forego reforms and their disruptive effects is both a reasonable and risk-adverse position. As for restraints on the state, a nation's tolerance for repressive acts also increases with war, for the executive's efficiency and national security claims gain presumptive validity in a context of limited information. The overarching implication of this study is to lessen our expectations of war presidents as fonts of reform, for while their capac-ities are expanded, their social policies are expedient and their strategic position is fortified.

In 1941 Nobel Prize–winning novelist Pearl Buck warned that gaining the loyalty of black America would require substantive rather than illu-sory reform:

> If we want unity, at this time of national defense, let it not be thought that our people can be cajoled into that unity by promises or sentimentalized into it by emotionalism or threatened into it by force.[20]

The racial manpower policies of the Roosevelt administration clearly failed to unify the nation. But this was not the primary aim of American warmakers, who sought more realistic goals as administrators of a divided arsenal. In doing so, they joined the ranks of the victors of history's great wars.

---

20. Pearl S. Buck, "Too Much Unity is a Danger," *Opportunity*, April, 1941, pp. 110–11.

Appendix 1.1

Army Camps Housing Sizable Numbers of Black Troops, 1941–5.

Alabama	**Maryland**	**Oklahoma**
Fort McClellan	Aberdeen Proving Ground	Fort Sill
Tuskegee Air Field	Edgewood Arsenal	**South Carolina**
Arizona	Fort Meade	Camp Croft
Fort Huachuca	**Massachusetts**	Fort Jackson
Arkansas	Camp Edwards	**Tennessee**
Camp Robinson	Fort Devins	Camp Forest
California	**Michigan**	**Texas**
Camp Hahn	Fort Custer	Camp Bowie
Fort Ord	**Missouri**	Camp Hulen
Georgia	Camp Crowder	Camp Swift
Camp Stewart	Fort Leonard Wood	Camp Wallace
Camp Gordon	**Mississippi**	Camp Wolters
Camp Wheeler	Camp McCain	Fort Bliss
Fort Benning	Camp Shelby	Fort Clark
Kansas	Camp Van Dorn	Fort S. Houston
Fort Riley	**New York**	**Virginia**
Kentucky	Fort Ontario	Camp Lee
Camp Breckinridge	**New Jersey**	Fort Belvoir
Fort Knox	Fort Dix	Fort Eustis
Louisiana	Raritan Arsenal	**Washington**
Camp Livingston	**North Carolina**	Fort Lewis
Camp Polk	Camp Davis	Vancouver Bar.
Camp Beauregard	Fort Bragg	
Camp Claiborne		

Source: Ulysses Lee, U.S. Army in World War II, Special Studies: The Employment of Negro Troops, Washington, D.C., USGPO, 1966; "Stations, Camps, Posts Where Colored Troops Are Located," Pittsburgh *Courier*, June 14, 1941.

Appendix 1.2

Urban Areas Receiving in Excess of $700 Million in War
Supply Contracts, 1940–5, in Descending Order of Value of
Contracts Received.

Over $10 Billion	$1–$2 Billion	$700 Million–$1 Billion
New York	Kansas City	Evansville
Detroit	South Bend	Beaumont
$2–$10 Billion	Milwaukee	Racine
Los Angeles	Flint	Allentown
Chicago	Bridgeport	Norfolk
Philadelphia	Akron	Louisville
Boston	Portland, OR	Dallas
Buffalo	Minneapolis	Syracuse
Cleveland	New Haven	Trenton
Baltimore	Houston	New Orleans
San Francisco	Wichita	Columbus, OH
Hartford	Providence	Springfield, MA
Cincinnati	Rochester	Worcester
St. Louis	Lansing	Tulsa
Indianapolis	Toledo	
Seattle	Ft. Wayne	
Pittsburgh	Ft. Worth	
Albany	Dayton	
San Diego		

Source: U.S. Bureau of the Census, *County Data Book,* Washington, D.C., USGPO, 1947, pp. 13–55.

Appendix 1.3

Nonwhite Share of Labor Market, Selected Sectors, Percentage by Sector, November 1944 [in thousands of workers].

	Total Labor Force	Nonwhite Labor Force	Percent Nonwhite
TOTAL LABOR FORCE	64,110	7,280	11.4
Black overrepresentation			
Unemployed	680	151	22.2
Agriculture	8,140	1,783	21.9
Domestic service	1,730	950	54.9
Proportional			
Federal War Agencies	1,611	193	12.0
Other Federal Government	838	97	11.6
Black underrepresentation			
Armed Forces	11,900	910	7.6
Manufacturing	16,020	1,282	8.0

Source: FEPC, *First Report,* in Foner and Lewis, eds., *The Black Worker,* vol. VII, p. 269.

Appendix 4.1

**Most Often Cited Occupations, FEPC Casework, by
Percentage of All Cases Identifying Occupation, Excluding
"Any," "All," or "Trainee."**

Laborer, Warehouse, Packer, Porter	10.5
Clerical, Typist, C-T, T-C	6.3
Kitchen, Cleaning, Service	3.7
"Helper," to various trades	3.5
Fireman	3.3
Driver, Truck, Semi	3.0
Welder	2.3
Assembler	1.8
Machine Operator	1.8
"Factory Work"	1.7
TOTAL, TEN HIGHEST RANKING	37.9

Source: Analysis of casework data by author, records of the FEPC, 1941–6 ($n = 2,822$).

Appendix 4.2

Nonwhite Labor Force and Access to FEPC, by Percentage, November 1944.

	Nonwhite Labor Force	Percent of Nonwhite Labor Force
TOTAL LABOR FORCE	7,280	100.0
Labor Force Segments Without Access to FEPC		
Unemployed	151	2.1
Agriculture	1,783	24.5
Domestic Service	950	13.0
Armed Forces	910	12.5
TOTAL PERCENTAGE WITHOUT ACCESS		52.1
PERCENTAGE WITH ACCESS		47.8

Source: FEPC, *First Report*, in Foner and Lewis, eds., *The Black Worker*, pp. 265–72.

Appendix 4.3

FEPC Coding Manual

1. Introduction. The data set is the card index to the FEPC casework on complaints concerning only "Negro" workers filed between July 1, 1943 and December 31, 1944. The pin-sortable card index of this casework is reproduced on microfilm roll 1 IND, "Index to Regional Cases and to Cases Referred to the Director of Field Operations," December 1941–April 1946. See Bruce I. Friend, *Guide to the Microfilm Record of Selected Documents of Records of the Committee on Fair Employment Practice, 1941–1946*, Glen Rock, NJ, Microfilming Corporation of America, 1970, pp. 29–30.

2. Selection. All cases with a date of filing between July 1, 1943 and December 31, 1944 were selected. The case was discarded if it lacked an address, a source, or a date of filing, or if the dates were impossible, i.e., a date of disposition that is earlier than a date of filing. If the case includes incomprehensible disposition information ("VVI by CMM"), delete entry.

3. General Coding Instructions

   A. *City charged* = location of entity charged with complaint. Headquarters or "division" city, if office is identified with division or HQ in parentheses. Ex: Louisville (Birmingham Div) is entered as Birmingham. If a main office outside of the local region is the only city given, and aggrieved party lives in local region, record home city of aggrieved party. If both aggrieved and charged are outside of region, enter as given.

   B. *Plant* = The source of the complaint is coded as either
   S state
   I individual
   O organization

C. *Business codes*: (not identical to the 1940 census industry codes)
1. Seeds, bulbs
2. Tobacco
3. n/a
4. Petroleum products, oil, asphalt, fuels
5. Mines
6. Contract construction, engineering
7. Ordnance, tnt, fuses, powder, munitions
8. Food
9. Canvas, lamp shades, textiles, blinds, awnings
10. Apparel
11. Lumber
12. Bags, paper, boxes, cartons, barrels
13. Printing
14. Chemicals, paint, cosmetics, oxygen, labs, heat treatment, pharmaceutical, biological, medicine, drugs, plastic molding, surgical, decal, paste, mosquito bombs, dental mfg., enamel, tile, pneumatic co.
15. n/a
16. Rubber
17. Leather
18. Glass, porcelain, asbestos
19. Iron, steel, armor plate, cable
20. Aluminum, magnesium, non-ferrous metals, bronze, copper, brass, coal, carbon
21. Tools, machinery, locks, diesel engines, gears, valves, razors, boilers, condensers, tanks, guns, tractors, engines, earth moving equipment, zippers, pulleys, pipes
22. Electrical machinery, x-ray equipment, spark plugs, dry cell batteries, electrical motors, vacuum cleaners, transformers
23. RR equipment
24. Aircraft
25. Ships, submarine products
26. Motor vehicles, service stations, gas tanks
27. RR
28. Motor transport, bus lines, local RR
29. Airlines
30. Water freight, steamship, water transport
31. Rail and motor freight, warehousing, trucking, packing, shipping, motor freight transport, express baggage, mail order co., railway mail service, private ordnance depot
32. Communications, telephone, radio, radar, precision instru-

ments, optics, photographic, signal equipment, luminous
panel, motor pictures, panel switchboards

33. Electricity, light, power
34. Schools, training, universities, university scientific research labs
35. Miscellaneous, service industries, bank, hotel, hospital, hospital diagnostic research, concessionaires
36. Department of Agriculture
37. Department of Commerce, Bureau of Standards, Patent Office
38. Immigration & Naturalization, Secret Service
39. Department of Labor, SSA
40. Navy
41. Post office
42. n/a
43. Treasury
44. Army, U.S. School of Aeronautics
45. USES
46. Maritime Commission, Merchant Marine
47. State and local
48. Veterans Administration
49. Civil Service Commission
50. General Accounting Office, Government Printing Office, Library of Congress
51. U.S. Reconstruction Finance Corp., T.V.A., Home Owners Loan Corp.
52. Executive Office, WMC, War Shipping Administration, War Labor Board, War Food Administration, U.S. Smaller War Plants Corporation, Office of Defense Transportation, Office of Price Administration.
53. U.S. Railroad Retirement Board, National Labor Relations Board, Department of the Interior, Federal Public Housing Authority, Civil Aeronautic Authority
54. AFL
55. CIO
56. Rail union
66. Unknown

Labor force sectors listed in Table 4.4.
    Federal War Agencies: categories 40, 44, 52.
    Other Federal Government: 36–9, 41–3, 46, 48–51, 53.
    Munitions: 7, 16, 19–21, 24–5, 32.
    Transportation and Utilities: 27–31, 33.
    Construction: 6.

All Other Manufacturing 1–2, 8–14, 17, 23, 26.
Other Non-manufacturing: 34–35.
Mining: 5.
State and Local Government: 47.
Trade: none.
Finance, business: none.

D. *Source of complaint.* If two sources are listed, record the first given. If complainant is listed as arriving "via" organization, list organization.
CV = complainant visit, form filed, telephone, statement, CS field.
CL = complainant letter, form, telegram, compl affidavit.
White House = White House, Mrs. Roosevelt.
RD = regional director, newspaper advertisement.
U = USES 510

E. *Sex*
M, F, U = unspecified, B = both

F. *Reason for complaint* (code only those cases listed N for "Negro")

G. *Type of party discriminated against.* If party is not named, and if complaint concerns upgrading or work assignment or other forms of employee treatment, record as G not C since specific group is at issue.
I = individual
C = community (specific indiv. or group not named)
G = group

H. *Regional Disposition.* Record disposition and date of disposition. Do not record the entry "reopened" when it stands alone. Record reopening as if it follows a prior disposition. E.g., satisfactory adj, 10/3/44 = 5, reopened, 7/17/45 = 2nd regdisp = 8 (open); if 2RDisp = 5, but then reopened, put 2RDisp = 8 (pending).
1 = dismissed, no jurisdiction
2 = dismissed, insufficient evidence
3 = dismissed on merits
4 = withdrawn by complainant
5 = satisfactory adjustment
6 = referred to field director
7 = other
8 = pending (no date of disposition)

I. *Field Director Disposition.* FDDisp. not considered closed, enter 8; Complaint Issued = CI, Committee Hearing = CH + date.
1 = Retained
2 = Returned to Region
3 = Referred to Contracting Agency
4 = Satisfactory Adjustment
5 = Dismissed
6 = Referred to Committee
7 = Other
8 = pending (no date of disposition)

J. *Date of discrimination.* If date of discrimination given as "continuing" or "current," record date of complaint filing. If date of discrimination given as a month, record 15th day of that month; if the date of the filing in this case is before the 15th, then record the date precisely between the beginning of month and date of the filing. If the date given is "last 6 months," record the date of the filing. If the date given is: an entire year; cites a date prior to 1935, i.e., "since 1929"; or any date prior to 12/7/41; leave the cell blank. If the date given is "prior to 7/18/44," record 7/17/44. If the date given is "March & June 1943," record 3/15/43 (first date of discrimination). If the date given is "3/8/43 and since," record 3/8/43.

K. *Type of Discrimination*
AP = Application
Ad or A = Advertisement
C = Classification /register /merit rating /certification /efficiency rating /refusal to issue certif. of avail. /refusal to release
D = Discharge /release /lay-off /forced to resign /suspension
DM = Demotion
H = Hire /rehire /refusal of employment
O = Other
P = Placement
R = Referral
RC = Recruiting
S = Submit 510s (failure) /refusal to submit data
SN = Seniority
T = Training /"hire-technical trainee"
TR = Transfer
U = Union Membership

UO = Union Other
UR = Union Referral
UW = Union Work permit /union hiring /union clearance
UP = Upgrading
W = Wages /training wages
WA = Work Assignment
WC = Work Conditions, seating

Appendix 4.4

Reason for Complaint of Discrimination, FEPC Casework, by Percentage.

Entry	
Hiring	47.3%
Advertisement, Application	6.5
Referral	4.4
Training	2.6
Placement	1.8
Classification	1.5
Union Membership	.9
Fail to report discrim. hiring	.1
TOTAL ENTRY	65.1
Treatment	
Upgrading	9.8
Work Conditions	4.2
Wages	2.8
Transfer	1.2
Work Assignment	1.0
Demotion	.8
Seniority	.3
TOTAL TREATMENT	20.1
Exit	
Discharge	11.1
TOTAL EXIT	11.1

Other

Multiple reasons listed	2.6
Union other	.6
Other	.5
TOTAL OTHER	3.7

Source: Analysis of casework data by author, records of the FEPC, 1941–6.

Appendix 4.5

Affiliated Branches of the National Urban League, 1943.

Arkansas
  Little Rock
California
  Los Angeles
Connecticut
  Waterbury
Florida
  Tampa
Georgia
  Atlanta
Illinois
  Chicago
  Springfield
Indiana
  Anderson
  Fort Wayne
  Marion
Kentucky
  Louisville
Louisiana
  New Orleans
Maryland
  Baltimore
Massachusetts
  Boston
  Springfield

Michigan
  Detroit
  Flint
Minnesota
  Minneapolis
  St. Paul
Missouri
  Kansas City
  St. Louis
Nebraska
  Lincoln
  Omaha
New Jersey
  Asbury Park
  Englewood
  Newark
New York
  Albany
  Brooklyn
  Buffalo
  New York City
  White Plains

Ohio
  Akron
  Hamilton
  Canton
  Cincinnati
  Cleveland
  Columbus
  Massillon
  Toledo
  Warren
Pennsylvania
  Philadelphia
  Pittsburgh
Rhode Island
  Providence
South Carolina
  Greenville
Tennessee
  Memphis
Virginia
  Richmond
Washington
  Seattle
Washington, D.C.
Wisconsin
  Milwaukee

Source: Memorandum, National Urban League, July 1, 1943, "Lists," SDR-COFEP.

Appendix 5.1

**Tuskegee Institute News Clippings File. Division of
Behavioral Science Research, Carver Research Foundation,
Tuskegee Institute, Alabama.**

This is a collection of newspaper clippings compiled from black and
white newspapers, 1899–1965, held on 29 microfilm reels. Sanford, NC,
Microfilming Corp. of America, 1976; Guide to the microfilm edition
filmed at the beginning of reel 1. John W. Kitchens, Guide to the microfilm edition of the Tuskegee Institute news clippings file, Tuskegee Institute, Alabama, 1978.

Appendix 5.2

Armed Forces Race Confrontation Coding Manual

1. Introduction. This project seeks to code incidents of racial confrontation involving black soldiers/officers and white police, military police and soldiers/officers.

2. Selection. All incidents which occurred between January 1, 1941 and December 31, 1945 were selected. (See also footnote 22 on page 141.)

3. General Coding Instructions

    A. Date of Incident: (Year/Month/Day) 41/01/01 to 45/12/31 inclusive. If incident did not conclude on single day, record the initial date; note additional days in the comments section. A question mark (?) denotes an approximate date. If "recently" is used in an article instead of a date, the date of the incident is recorded as the article date with a question mark.

    B. Location: four parts concerning location of event.
      a) Region: Region of the country in which the incident occurred, as defined by the U.S. Bureau of the Census.
        1 Deep South: AL, GA, LA, MS, SC
        2 Other South: AR, FL, KY, NC, OK, TN, TX, VA, WV
        3 Northeast: CT, DE, DC, ME, MD, MA, NH, NJ, NY, PA, RI, VT
        4 North Central: IL, IN, IA, KS, MI, MN, MO, NE, ND, OH, SD, WI
        5 West: AZ, CA, CO, ID, MT, NV, NM, OR, UT, WA, WY
        6 Abroad: ET (European Theater), PT (Pacific Theater), UK (England), WI (West Indies/Caribbean), OA (Other Abroad)

    b) Locale: Name of city in or facility on which the incident occurred.

    c) State: State or area in which the incident occurred.

    d) On Facility: Was the incident on a military facility? (Y/N)

C. Facility Attached: Name of facility to which the black soldiers involved were attached.

D. Unit: Name of unit to which the black soldiers involved were attached.

E. Sphere of Activity: Class of activity proceeding at the time of incident.

C Commerce: shopping at PX, use of civilian restaurants during stopovers.

J Jail and Police patrol (civilian or military): transfer of prisoners, inspection of papers, arresting AWOL soldiers, executions, and incidents which arise from an arrest or arrests.

P Transportation: public and post transportation, transporting of soldiers, travel of officers to off-base quarters.

R Recreation: any soldier "on furlough" or "on leave", use of post facilities such as telephones, restaurant, theater, soldiers in barracks.

T Training: any activity on camp involving supervision of superiors, such as the mess hall, drill, loading ammunition, or being in a military induction center.

U Unknown: any soldier in town for an unspecified reason.

O Other: all other.

F. Cause or Precipitating Incident: Reason or action(s) that caused the incident to occur.

A Arrest of one or more soldiers.

C Crowd Action: any violent, spontaneous, and/or confrontational act by soldiers, e.g. a "riot."

D Disobedience: soldier(s) disobeying direct orders of civilian police, e.g. resisting arrest.

F Fighting or intense arguing tending toward a fight; response of individual soldier to racial epithet.

I Interference with civilian police or MP's in their actions toward other soldiers/officers; in the case of a crowd, applies crowd gathering after police arrived.

R Refusal: soldier(s) refusing to follow orders or demands of military personnel, e.g. resisting arrest, fleeing from inspection of papers, resisting orders of higher ranking officers, and spontaneous group resistance.

S Segregation: soldier(s) disobeying "Jim Crow" laws of area, e.g. disobeying the orders of a bus driver or train official, or law enforcement official.

Z Organized Protest: creation, planning of and/or membership in peaceful black or biracial organizations; presentation of grievances, e.g. "soldier strike", group of soldiers objecting to racial epithet.

U Unknown.

O Other: all other, including legal activities by soldiers.

G. Participants: Seven measures of various types of participants; record number. A "U" in any of these columns means an unknown number of participants of this class, possibly none.
Black civilians
Black soldiers (excluding black MPs)
Black MPs
White civilians
White soldiers (excluding white MPs)
White MPs
White civilian police

H. Result: Actions resulting from the incident, number of people affected; code letters below.
   1. Result of the incident for the blacks involved in it; multiple results are recorded in probable temporal order.
      A Arrested – Black soldiers arrested by civilians, civilian police, or military personnel
      B Beaten
      C Confined to quarters or to military facility or hospital
      D Death sentence
      E Executed
      J Jailed
      M Court-martial, detention pending trial for same
      MJ Successful prosecution (jailed)
      MD Successful prosecution and death sentence
      R Transferred
      S Shot
      T Tear gas
      O Other
      U Unknown

2. Number of people affected. A "U" in any of these columns means an unknown number of participants of this class, possibly none. A "S" in any of these columns means an unspecified number of people in that category.
   Blacks arrested and/or jailed
   Blacks wounded, beaten, etc.
   Blacks killed
   Whites arrested and/or jailed
   Whites wounded, beaten, etc.
   Whites killed

I. Citation: Newspaper article from which the information was obtained.
   1. Paper:
      AC Atlanta – Constitution
      AD Atlanta – Daily World
      AJ Atlanta – Journal
      AN Amsterdam – News
      AS Amsterdam – Star-News
      BA Baltimore – Afro-American
      BN Birmingham – News
      BP Birmingham – Post
      BW Birmingham – Weekly Review
      CB Chicago – Bee
      CD Chicago – Defender
      CS Columbia – State
      CT Chicago – Tribune
      DB Des Moines – Bystander
      DC Denver – The Colorado Statesman
      DF Detroit – Free Press
      HI Houston – The Informer
      HN Houston – Negro Labor News
      KC Kansas City – Call
      KO Kingston, Jamaica – Public Opinion
      KP Kansas City – Plaindealer
      LC Louisville – Courier-Journal
      LJ Louisville – The Country Journal
      LW Louisiana – Weekly
      LT Los Angeles – Tribune
      MA Montgomery – Advertiser
      MC Memphis – Commercial Appeal
      MJ McComb – Journal

MP Miami – Whip
MW Memphis – World
NA New York – Age
ND New York – Daily Worker
NG Nashville – Globe & Independent
NJ Norfolk – Journal And Guide
NM New York – PM
NP New York – Post
NT New York – Times
NV New York – People's Voice
NW New Orleans – Weekly
NY New York – Yank
OB Oklahoma City – Black Dispatch
PC Pittsburgh – Courier
PT Philadelphia – Tribune
RW Little Rock – The Worker
SA St. Louis – Argus
SH Seattle – Northwest Herald
SN Seattle – The Northwest Enterprise
WP Washington, D.C. – Post
WT Washington, D.C. – Tribune
YP New York – Point of View
YW New York – World-Telegram

    2. Date: Year/Month/Day that the article was published

J. Comments: Details about the incident that were not captured in the coding, making use of the abbreviations used in the participant section, with three additions: WBD = white bus driver, WACO = white alcohol control officer, and BVET = black veteran.

Appendix 5.3

Distribution of Black Persons Liable for Military Service, and Percentage of Persons in Armed Forces on June 1, 1943, Northern and Southern States with Largest Liable Populations.

State	Total Black Persons Liable	Percent in Armed Forces	Black Persons in Armed Forces
Northern			
MA	11,606	28.4	3,298
NY	160,240	26.2	41,983
IL	113,529	25.1	28,535
IN	31,532	24.7	7,773
PA	124,044	24.3	30,166
NJ	62,501	24.1	15,084
OH	88,048	23.9	21,068
MI	64,277	19.8	12,749
Southern			
TX	226,556	22.8	51,718
LA	196,399	22.0	43,159
MS	223,487	21.9	49,045
FL	140,732	19.8	27,859
VA	162,102	18.2	29,561
GA	237,750	18.0	42,828
NC	222,667	17.8	39,615
SC	172,658	15.1	26,071

Source: "Distribution of Black Persons Liable for Military Service and Percent of Such Persons in Armed Forces on June 1, 1943." Memorandum, Lewis B. Hershey to Jonathan Daniels, June 25, 1943, OF 4245, Selective Service, FDRL.

Index